Deviance
& SOCIAL CONTROL
2ND EDITION

LINDA B. DEUTSCHMANN
University College of the Cariboo

 I(T)P Nelson

an International Thomson Publishing company

Toronto • Albany • Bonn • Boston • Cincinnati • Detroit • London • Madrid • Melbourne
Mexico City • New York • Pacific Grove • Paris • San Francisco • Singapore • Tokyo • Washington

I(T)P® **International Thomson Publishing**

The ITP logo is a trademark under licence
www.thomson.com

Published in 1998 by

I(T)P® **Nelson**

A division of Thomson Canada Limited
1120 Birchmount Road
Scarborough, Ontario M1K 5G4
www.nelson.com

Canadian Cataloguing in Publication Data

Deutschmann, Linda Bell, 1943–
    Deviance & social control

2nd ed.
Includes bibliographical references and index.
ISBN 0-17-607279-9

1. Deviant behavior. 2. Social control. I. Title. II Title: Deviance and social control.

IIM291.D47 1997	302.5'42	C97-932109-3

Publisher and Team Leader	Michael Young
Executive Editor	Charlotte Forbes
Project Editor	Evan Turner
Production Editor	Tracy Bordian
Production Coordinator	Brad Horning
Art Director	Angela Cluer
Cover and Interior Design	Marc Henderson
Senior Composition Analyst	Alicja Jamorski

Printed and bound in Canada

1 2 3 4 (WC) 01 00 99 98

CONTENTS

PREFACE

Unlike most other deviance textbooks, this one is organized to introduce the topic of deviance in a sequence that does not force students to grapple with concepts, names, and explanations that have not been introduced, that are explained a chapter or two later, or that are called different names without any explanation for the variation.

Three possible approaches can be used in the organization of a deviance text. The one chosen here has theory as its central theme and uses specific forms of behaviour as examples to illustrate these theories. It focuses on explanations and principles of analysis, and the way in which traditional approaches persist despite the arrival of newer orthodoxies. Unlike many other texts, each theory is presented in a serious and respectful way. This presentation allows the instructor to update the material quickly and adapt it to his or her interests simply by providing more examples or detail.

An alternative approach is to present each form of deviance in a separate chapter and attempt to include all relevant theories as applied to each form, and all the most contemporary data on its incidence and prevalence. Such a book might have a chapter on drug addiction and others on homosexuality and prostitution. This alternative is cumbersome, repetitive, likely to become outdated, and may offend some students who do not agree that a particular behaviour should be labelled deviant. It also allows the instructor little flexibility.

Another alternative is to present most theories as inadequate, while touting the universal applicability of the author's approach. This means that students are repeatedly asked to learn about a theory, only to be told that what they have just digested is useless or pernicious. The favoured theory gets uncritical attention. Thus, students are not given the evidence they need to make up their own minds about the validity and utility of each theory. When they go on to higher studies, they may find that what they have learned needs to be revised.

DEFINING DEVIANCE

This book takes a broad view of the nature of deviance, seeing it as both constructed reality and as a phenomenon in society that has real causes and real consequences, and that often involves real behaviour. The connections between deviance and freedom, fun, and chaos are emphasized as much as its connection to social disapproval. This approach avoids both the extreme assumption that deviance is real and wrongful behaviour, and the more fashionable but also untenable idea that deviance is nothing but a label put on people by others.

METHODOLOGY

A grounding in "how we know what we know" underlies the material in all chapters of this book, not just Chapter 2, which deals specifically with methods. This approach permits students to be self-educating. Whenever possible, the book attempts to demonstrate how theoretically guided research enables us to see connections that were not obvious before. Students take away an enhanced understanding of how ideas about the nature of deviance and social control are related to the social circumstances in which they developed, and why there are so many competing voices in the field.

PRESCIENTIFIC THEORIES

Most texts spend little or no time on the perspectives of deviance that preceded the Renaissance. Nonetheless, these perspectives are still part of modern life and are important to a full understanding of the phenomena associated with deviance. The witchcraft craze, in particular, provides a veritable paradigm for the analysis of what is real and what is constructed about deviance.

NONSOCIOLOGICAL THEORIES

Unlike most sociologically oriented texts, this one carefully considers alternative approaches—in particular, biological and psychological ones. Students are exposed to these ideas daily in the news and in literature. They have a right to know how these explanations "stack up" against sociological ones, and how they might fit in with them.

SOCIOLOGICAL APPROACHES

Sociological approaches are presented in roughly the order in which they achieved popularity in the field, without ignoring the fact that most of them have roots in the late 1800s or earlier. In each case, the theories are presented in the context that made them popular, and with concern for the way in which their ideas continue to influence the field. The structure of the text allows instructors to increase or modify the coverage of these theories (particularly the later ones, where controversy still reigns) without confusing students.

WOMEN AND DEVIANCE

Most textbooks on deviance have assumed, without explicitly saying so, that women's deviance is not a separate issue from men's, or is not interesting enough, except with respect to prostitution, to discuss. This text attempts to "bring women back in" in a real sense, noting when and how theorists have distorted the images of women, and when and how these lacunae are being met in modern approaches such as power-control, conflict, and feminist theories.

READABILITY AND INTEREST

Every effort has been made to make this text into the kind of book that can be read without a great deal of instructional assistance, but also without "writing down" to the reader. Wherever possible, theorists have been presented as real people, whose personalities and social contexts matter. Throughout, examples have been chosen that typically represent the central interests of the relevant theorists, and that also have interest for today's students and instructors.

ACKNOWLEDGMENTS

I owe a debt of gratitude to my family, and to a number of friends and colleagues. I would particularly like to thank Doug Campbell and Marion Blute at the University of Toronto, and Nan McBlane, Dawn Farough, John Cleveland, and David MacLennan at the University College of the Cariboo, for their constant encouragement. I also wish to thank all those who have helped transform this work from its untidy proposal, to overlong manuscript, all the way to finished book. Dave Ward saw the potential of the proposal and had faith that I would finally get down to it. Reviewers helped to make an unwieldy manuscript clearer and more accurate. I would particularly like to thank the following reviewers: Susan A. Reid-MacNevin, University of Guelph; Byrad Yyelland, University of Saskatchewan; and Dorothy Pawluch, McMaster University.

Thanks also to the following reviewers of the first edition: Judith Blackwell, Brock University; Helene Cummins, University of Western Ontario, Brescia College; Lesley Hulcoop, Trent University; Ivan McFarlane, Centennial College; Linda Mahood, Lethbridge University; Doug Skoog, University of Winnipeg; and Anthony Thomson, Acadia University.

And thanks to all at ITP Nelson. Charlotte Forbes provided inspiration and helpful suggestions. Evan Turner assisted in the mountainous task of permissions and in keeping the manuscript on track in its final phases. Erika Krolman provided somewhat painful but necessary cutting and reorganization during the editing. Tracy Bordian coped with a much gone-over manuscript with many last-minute requests and helped create a readable text. All of this effort resulted in a better book.

Linda Deutschmann
University College of the Cariboo

ISSUES
IN THE STUDY OF
DEVIANCE

This book is about murder, rape, robbery, prostitution, homosexuality, suicide, drug trafficking, mental disorder, alcoholism, organized crime, white-collar crime, government corruption, mental aberration, treason, terrorism, nudism, punk styles, obesity, being rude, and anorexia. It is also about social control, which is an inseparable part of all these things.

Deviant activities are largely hidden or misrepresented, and thus cry out for careful investigation. They are troublesome, forbidden, exotic, threatening, or just misunderstood. Some of them are risky, exciting, and well rewarded. Cocaine trafficking, for example, sometimes requires the trafficker to transport large quantities of drugs, risking aircraft failure on makeshift jungle runways, police intervention, and violence at the hands of the local and international underworld. The traffickers may either enjoy or fear the "war games" aspect of the high-tech, high-risk enterprise of avoiding (or neutralizing) detection by authorities (Eddy 1988; Sabbag 1990; Bowden 1987; Rice 1989).

As for rewards, high-level traffickers frequently display a flamboyant lifestyle that involves them with famous and infamous celebrities, aristocrats, and political leaders. Lower-level traffickers often have flashy cars and expensive clothes, making them powerful role models for youths (Boyd 1991; Malarek 1989).

Some deviant activities are openly ugly, weird, unusual, and even "freakish," while still others are subterranean, frightening, and conspiratorial, threatening the fundamental beliefs, values, and rules of a society. But deviance is not just a subject for fascinated voyeurs who seek stimulation and entertainment. Deviance and its control are central aspects of social life. Together they underlie some of society's most serious moral and political problems.

Deviance may harm the social order either directly or indirectly. Terrorists threaten us directly when they blow up a plane, and indirectly when their activities lead to airports becoming so regulated that they are almost impassable. White-collar criminals steal our money or make us work in unsafe conditions. They also indirectly undermine our trust in the social order. The policing of deviance results in rising social costs and increasing restrictions on freedom. For example, shoppers are affected by the fact that stores must protect their goods against robbers, shoplifters, and "internal shrinkage" at the hands of employees. This not only increases the cost of goods, but also gives rise to the need for security personnel and hidden cameras, which may invade consumers' privacy. Pedophiles who use their teacher or "coach" status to prey on vulnerable boys or (less often) girls, harm these people, and those who care about them, directly, while indirectly causing the classroom and sportsfield to become places where the rest of us can no longer freely give "supportive hugs" or pats on the back. Similarly, fear of terrorism, drug trafficking, and organized crime (both real and imagined) has bestowed wide-ranging powers on police, armies, and government agencies. These fears can result in authorities routinely wiretapping, opening mail, and otherwise intruding on the private lives of citizens. In some countries, such as Brazil, police have been involved in the torture and murder of homeless "street" children, in the name of public order (America's Watch 1993; Chevigny 1996; Knox 1996). When those entrusted with the control of deviance are themselves corrupted, society loses twice.

WHY STUDY DEVIANCE?

VICARIOUS EXPERIENCE

Psychiatrists tell us that fascination with deviance can be a way of dealing with disowned parts of ourselves—an indirect way of coping with the forbidden urges that most of us learn to suppress as we grow up. It is also a habit reinforced by our culture, which treats deviant behaviour as exciting. Reading about the lives of wrongdoers permits us to experience their world safely, at a distance, while giving us a sense of the exotic and adventurous lives they lead. Researching them may give us legitimate access to a lifestyle that is unconventional and challenging. There exist, even for the most conforming of us, certain "moral and sensual attractions of evil" (Katz 1988). These entice some people into deviance and inspire others to study it. This motivation, when unrecognized and unchecked, can distort deviance research. Despite their rarity, the Bluebeards and Jack the Rippers of the world are disproportionately represented in the work of deviance specialists and journalists. The result is a tendency toward superficial descriptive studies and a concentration on violent and sexual forms of deviance (Liazos 1972).

REFORMING IMPULSE

Annoyance, anger, fear, or repulsion may motivate research. Child abuse, racist intimidation, vandalism, political corruption, and pornographic exploitation are interesting to people who want to know what creates "moral monsters" and what can contain them. Sometimes this interest is personal. Living in a district plagued by open street prostitution and drug use can produce daily annoyance and sharpen a person's interest in understanding deviance and its control. Similarly, personal knowledge of the devastation of drug dependence, rape, murder, or drunk driving may provoke in someone a desire to know more about their causes and cures.

Sometimes the interest is more abstract and professional, but still oriented toward changing something. Some of us study deviance because we recognize that there is value in knowing how (and whether) to do something about deviance. Being the expert who knows how to make hyperactive children happy in a classroom, or how to set up the most effective parole system is very satisfying. Historically, deviance studies emerged out of social problems courses and attracted people who wanted to become social workers, planners, or teachers.

Deviance research can also be useful to those involved in social movements that aim to change the status of certain types of behaviour. Family violence was tolerated as a private matter until research into its extent and consequences thrust it into the public realm and changed its status to "deviant" (DeKeseredy and Hinch 1991; Ellis 1987). In the 1950s, no name existed for date rape. When it occurred, it was often automatically assumed to be the woman's fault. Now, such assumptions are under attack. Many campuses have witnessed No-Means-No campaigns, open resistance to which has resulted in students being suspended or expelled.

Conversely, many forms of behaviour formerly labelled deviant have come to be increasingly tolerated, even accepted, by society. Homosexuality used to mean virtual exclusion from respectable society. Over time, though, homosexuals have found greater acceptance (if not always equal rights) in such areas as jobs, housing, medical benefits, and the adoption of children. Similarly, people with disabilities who earlier might have been sent to institutions are now gradually being integrated into, and accepted by, mainstream society.

Theoretical interpretations are heavily influenced by their political implications and by the philosophical positions dominant at the time of the research. This reality has sometimes distorted the research process in unexpected ways. For example, early efforts to communicate with street youth through the provision of outreach social workers in fact helped increase delinquency by strengthening the cohesion of local youth gangs (Short, Jr. 1975; Empey 1982). Two experimental treatment programs in the late 1960s had similarly unanticipated consequences. One of these programs involved criminal psychopaths at Ontario's Penetanguishene Mental Health Centre; the other was aimed at convicted drug addicts at Matsqui in British Columbia. Graduates of both programs had increased their social skills and appeared to have viable plans for noncriminal careers. Upon release, however, these "treated" offenders had higher offence rates, and for more serious offenses, than offenders who had not been treated. Apparently, they used their new or improved social skills to become better criminals, not to establish new careers in the noncriminal world (Murphy 1972:29–31; Weisman 1993).

The reform impulse also ignores the fact that many kinds of deviance are not as harmful as they are made out to be. In our efforts to justify reforms, and to raise money for reform programs, we are likely to paint a strongly negative view of the deviance involved and a strongly positive view of our solutions. Also, if we feel that the deviance being studied is truly evil, we may attempt to impose value judgments on our conclusions. For example, we may seek to show how deviance leads people into moral and physical sickness or other negative outcomes. If we believe that homosexuals inevitably become pedophiles, or that users of marijuana invariably become users of hard drugs, we will neither look for nor be satisfied by information that contradicts such positions. Our disdain, our discomfort, and our anger at deviance may keep us from being able to understand it. For example, criminal profilers have learned to set their feelings aside and "to think like the predator"; even if this is very unsettling for the investigators involved, their catch rate has increased (Douglas 1995:110; Ressler, Burgess, and Douglas 1988). Failure to overcome revulsion against deviance can mean failure to understand how it comes about, what maintains it, and what can be done about it.

SELF-PROTECTION AND SOPHISTICATION

There is something inherently appealing about knowing what goes on behind the facades of social life. Familiarity with the tactics of cult recruiters, drug pushers, muggers, terrorists, and con artists can make us feel safer. (Though researching these tactics can be dangerous and difficult.) Being able to see through the "fronts" and "covers" assumed by deviants is useful and satisfying. Equally valuable, though, is the ability to recognize that some deviants are not as harmful as their demonized reputations imply.

It is useful to recognize our own changes in thought when we are confronted by deviance. Generally, when we look at the deviance of outsiders, we focus our attention on the "when, why, and how" of their behaviour. Why do some people use crack cocaine or practise nudism? What form does the behaviour take? Who does it? What are their characteristics? What do they think about what they do?

When we sympathize with the deviant, however, our perspective changes. We are likely to focus on society's reaction to the behaviour. Who makes the rules? When and how consistently are these rules enforced? Might this be different? Under what conditions are some activities, appearances, and characteristics subjected to devaluation, punishment, and disapproval? How do they become categorized as deviant?

UNDERSTANDING ONESELF AND OTHERS

Deviance studies show us how we can influence the way in which others see and respond to us. We can cultivate respectable images or seek notoriety instead. Many people enjoy having a deviant image, even if they can indulge in it only on Saturday night. Others tend to seek more permanent identification with deviant lifestyles and images. They cultivate a style that wins them respect in unconventional milieus. Tattoos, hairstyles, dress, and flamboyant body language all symbolize their "otherness." A different cultivation of deviant identity is seen in popular and fringe artists and performers. Some choose names associated with evil and chaos, and carry this theme through to their album covers, stage performances, and lyrics. Many adopt lifestyles that cross the normal bounds of polite society, and in the process attract media (if not police) attention.

INTELLECTUAL CURIOSITY

A very important reason for studying deviance is pure, disinterested curiosity. Thus, an investigation of the role of the pimp in prostitution may be conducted either with an *interest* in controlling pimps or with a *disinterested* agenda of simply finding out who pimps are, how they become pimps, what they do, and how they leave the role, if they do.

Wanting to know how things work, without worrying about the consequences, has a fairly respectable history in the "hard" sciences such as chemistry and physics (despite their connection to pollutants and bombs). It has had a more troubled history in the social sciences, where the demand for immediate practical results has usually been more pressing, less easily evaded, and more clearly political. Those who study deviance are often pressured to take a stand on it and to provide solutions for controlling it. While disinterested research may ultimately have policy implications, this is not its primary purpose.

Many kinds of deviance are either totally hidden or presented to us only in distorted images. When authorities want to seem effective, they may hide evidence of deviance, but when they want to justify new or greater controls, they may maximize or even invent it. Deviants often develop camouflages to avoid detection and punishment, to make others afraid of them, or to create social space in which they can operate undisturbed. Such hidden activity becomes fertile ground for illusions and misunderstandings, which are not easily corrected without extensive, controlled, and repeated research. The final truth is always a bit out of reach. But good research is rigorous and honest in its approach to deviance, and seeks to discover what lies behind the facades maintained by deviants and authorities alike.

PERSPECTIVES ON DEVIANCE

People do not always agree either about which behaviours are deviant, or about how deviant each is. This is particularly true when people have different backgrounds or standpoints with respect to the behaviour. The standpoint of popular singer Madonna, for example, has little in common with that of advice columnist Miss Manners. There is a range of tolerance for behaviour in any area of social action. For example, acceptable behaviour in the classroom will likely show much less variation than acceptable "normal" behaviour at a sports event. But within the same context, this range of tolerance varies by the social class, gender, ethnic and cultural background, and political power of the actors involved, and it changes over time.

STUDENT VIEWS ON DEVIANCE

In a classroom exercise carried out in the 1980s, Erich Goode asked 230 undergraduates to write down examples of what they regarded as deviant behaviour (1990). The most commonly mentioned forms were murder (50 percent) and rape (37 percent). Among the 80 examples unique to individual students were "pretending you are a bird" or "wearing shorts when it snows." Homosexuality and robbery were cited with equal frequency (23 percent) (Goode 1990:2). Does this mean, then, that they are seen as equally serious forms of deviance? On the whole, no: the evidence indicates that violent deviance is taken more seriously than nonviolent deviance. However, sexual perversion, especially if it involves children, is seen as extremely serious, even if no physical violence has occurred.

A less formal 1991 classroom survey of nearly 300 Canadian university students uncovered the following nominations for deviant status: murderers, rapists, child molesters, flashers, delinquents, junkies, drug sellers who don't use drugs themselves, people with severe mental disturbances, prostitutes, pimps, the "morbidly" obese, idiots, freaks, nymphomaniacs, pyromaniacs (and other maniacs), drag queens, nerds, cheats, clowns, boors, lawyers, politicians, and a wide variety of people judged to be nasty, sneaky, vile, evil, corrupt, sick, twisted, violent, dangerous, decadent, perverted, bizarre, eccentric, outlandish, or simply annoying (Deutschmann 1991).

Campus-residence living produced some special categories of deviance that might not have been mentioned as often outside a university setting. These included freeloading, snoring, smoking in bed, keeping watermelons in the refrigerator, using all the hot water, entertaining all night with loud music, and being a "gross slob." Among the nominations were people "too good" to be normal, including browners, drudges, teacher's pets, (obvious) virgins, tattletales, and religious or political do-gooders.

The greatest consensus appeared in those categories of deviance that are clearly illegal. Robbers, murderers, and sex offenders were listed more than twice as often as any others on the list. The listing of noncriminal and nonviolent people, however, showed much less uniformity. While some students wrote that only violent or dishonest people were deviant, others listed as many as 60 different kinds of eccentrics and suggested they could list more if given the time. For another assignment, the same students were asked to distinguish between people they thought were deviant and those they thought most other students would consider deviant. Lists for the first category were generally much shorter than those for the second, particularly with respect to lifestyle areas such as sexual behaviour and drug use. When asked anonymously, most of these students saw themselves as more tolerant than their fellow students. Only further investigation could show whether this finding can be generalized.

PUBLIC OPINIONS ABOUT DEVIANCE

In the 1960s, J.L. Simmons reported that a sample of 180 persons, varying in age, sex, education, religion, race, and locale, cited 252 distinct acts and persons as deviant (Simmons 1969:3). Most subjects reported criminal behaviour and sexual variants as deviant. Less common nominations included suburbanites, "straights," executives, "smart-alec" students, and "know-it-all" professors.

One way of measuring the seriousness attributed to deviance is to ask respondents to rate the seriousness of a behaviour as it is presented in a vignette or story

(Byers 1993). Repeatedly, and across various nationalities, studies show that people (1) tend to agree about which stories involve acts that are criminal; (2) are likely to rate illegal acts as more serious than immoral or "disgusting" acts; and (3) believe murder and robbery to be much more serious than such infractions as illegal drug use or driving without a licence.

Little work has been done at a general level to isolate the situations or contexts in which various kinds of deviance will be taken seriously. But we can, without resorting to studies, observe wide variations in people's responses to real-life situations. For instance, if an average citizen were to throw a television set out of a hotel window, he or she would probably be arrested or committed for psychiatric observation. When rock stars have done the same, their behaviour has been tolerated (if not totally accepted) by authorities and celebrated by fans (Davis 1985).

ACADEMIC VIEWS ON DEVIANCE

Before the 1960s, academics who studied underclass deviants dominated the field. The texts they produced focused on the behaviour of less powerful "outsiders"— addicts, pornographers, strippers, prostitutes, and con artists—and treated them as exotic specimens in the "deviance zoo." Very few attempts (apart from the work of Edwin Sutherland in the 1930s) were made to address the behaviour of corporate robber barons and other powerful and "respectable" white-collar criminals and cheats, or to reveal the role of powerholders in the deviance process. Only with the rise in popularity of conflict theories in the 1960s was the impression that deviance was a lower-class characteristic seriously challenged.

Conflict theories, and some control theories, guided researchers to data that demonstrated that the crimes and eccentricities of the powerful were common, important, and properly described as deviant. The conflict approach to deviance not only humanized the deviant by looking at lifestyle and circumstances, but also admitted that deviance was partly a label imposed by powerholders in society rather than a characteristic intrinsic to individuals.

DEFINING DEVIANCE

Many attempts have been made to establish an objective criterion of deviance. Such a criterion would distinguish deviance in a consistent way and allow us to clearly delimit the sociology of deviance. Some theorists have forcefully argued that such a criterion is not possible. However, by taking a closer look at the issue we can gain a much clearer understanding of the strengths, weaknesses, and contradictions of the definitions that, valid or not, guide everyday decisions and the process of sociological interpretations.

It is often said that a definition is neither right nor wrong, only more or less useful. (That it may be rightly or wrongly *applied* is a different matter.) Practical experience has shown that the most useful definitions are those that contain no unnecessary assumptions, and that are objective, noncircular, and distinctive.

OBJECTIVE CHARACTERISTICS

An objective definition of deviance can be used in the same way by various researchers, regardless of how they view the moral status or desirability of the behaviour. This is because an objective definition points to empirical features of the subject, to what is physically present, and can be seen and heard. It does not involve moralistic or emotional evaluations of what is seen or heard. The achievement of such "value neutrality" is neither easy nor always possible. Values slip into our choice of subject matter, our division of fields of study, our very language. Social science must frequently work with (or find ways around) concepts like "slum," "pervert," or "bastard," which are negative evaluations more than factual designations. "Slum," for example, really means "a bad place to live," and different observers may well disagree about which areas are slums, or what it is that makes them undesirable.

One way around this problem is to translate value-laden statements into statements that have empirical referents. Thus, value statements such as "These boys are bad" might be translated into statements such as "These boys take things that do not belong to them," or "These boys read pornographic literature," which can be shown to be correct or incorrect by observing the boys' behaviour. Such translation increases the chance that different researchers will classify "these boys" similarly, and thus have a meaningful discussion about the causes of their behaviour and the possibility (or desirability) of change.

A difficult problem with objective approaches to deviance is that, while the researcher may maintain a position of value neutrality (looking only at the empirical evidence), the actual assignment of deviance labels by society does not. Deviance carries a negative moral evaluation as an intrinsic part of its popular meaning, and the label of deviant is sometimes applied to people on the basis of very flimsy evidence. The fact that someone or something is called deviant means that other persons or groups with the power to decide have labelled this behaviour or person as unacceptable. For example, there is no acceptable form of incest in any society. Calling an act incestuous means that there is something wrong with it. The rules about incest have been made, historically, by the religious and political authorities of each society. However, what one society considers incestuous may be normal or even preferred in another. The same is true of almost every kind of behaviour labelled deviant. The actions or topics that are discussed as deviant in this, and other textbooks, generally reflect the objective observation that a large number of influential people think the action is deviant. The researcher can accept this as valid information, without necessarily personally (subjectively) believing that the deviant label is appropriate.

ELIMINATING UNNECESSARY ASSUMPTIONS

The most useful definitions are those that point to the phenomena we want to study without making any unnecessary assumptions about them. Some definitions of deviance include the assumption that deviance is in fact sickness or perhaps a form of political protest (e.g., the robber is working out psychological problems or protesting the institution of private property). Such assumptions (and the assumptions built into other definitions) are premature. Is shoplifting a form of moral weakness, sickness, or politics? A useful rule: don't assume what you may want to investigate.

NONCIRCULAR DISTINCTIVENESS

Useful definitions are noncircular. An example of circularity would be defining a violation of rules as something you can be arrested for and then defining something you can be arrested for as a violation of rules. When a definition goes in circles like this, it is essentially meaningless. The challenge in deviance studies is to find ways of identifying deviance without falling into the trap of circularity.

The useful, noncircular definition isolates some distinctive feature that distinguishes this subject matter from all others around it (Gibbs 1981:x). In the sections that follow, we address five properties or characteristics that are commonly assumed to distinguish deviant from nondeviant acts, namely: statistical rarity, social harmfulness, normative violation, social response, and stigmatizing label. As we shall see, none of these characteristics can be used as a definition without risking circularity, and some of them (such as statistical rarity) can lead to a misleading sense of objectivity.

Statistical Rarity

Many researchers have attempted to establish statistical definitions of deviance. The idea of deviance is equated with the idea of atypicality or deviation from a common centre. Most of us have a sense that "deviance" involves exceptional behaviour, such as failing to bathe, being radically irresponsible, or challenging rules that have always been applied to people in your category. When blacks in the southern United States began rejecting their assignment to "the back of the bus," they were treated as deviants. In Canada, the women who first asked for political rights were also treated as deviants. Throughout history people with exceptional appearance or abilities have been seen as "freaks" and treated as deviants. Deviance may also seem to exist in intentional physical differences, as with punk styles and heavy tattooing.

The main difficulties with the statistical definition of deviance are (1) that not all common behaviours are accepted as normal and (2) that not all rare behaviours or appearances are treated as deviant by those who observe or experience them.

The bell curve, or normal distribution, locates deviance as a major departure from a central standard (see Figure 1.1). Behaviour that is or appears to be most common is deemed to be normal, while behaviour that is measurably far away from the statistical norm is held to be deviant. Intelligence, for example, is often measured by standardized IQ tests devised so that the most common score is 100. Scores that fall near this central score indicate average performance, while those much higher and much lower suggest genius and incompetence, respectively. Data on many kinds of behaviour, from drinking alcohol (abstainer, average drinker, alcoholic) to morality in general (degenerate scum, slightly imperfect, saint) fit this pattern. For example, observed speeds of 16.4 million cars on rural highways in Illinois show an almost perfect normal distribution of speeds, with the mean (average) speed at the posted limit of 65 mph. (Clarke1996:169). While it is likely that the extremely slow

Figure 1.1   The Normal Curve and Alcohol Use

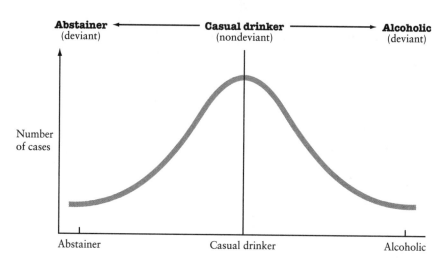

11

and extremely fast drivers will be "deviant" in both the statistical and the social senses of the word, this connection is not always so close. Extremes are sometimes valued rather than rejected.

Not all curves in nature or society are "normal" curves. For example, a deviance class may consist of two groups of students: those who are taking the course because it sounded more interesting than anything else that could fit their timetable, and those who are acquiring a credit that will help them gain access to a competitive program, such as law. In such a case, the grades curve may very well be bimodal (see Figure 1.2). Another very common curve is the J-curve (see Figure 1.3). An example of this curve is the J-curve of institutional conformity. This curve is usually found with respect to activities such as arriving early, on time, or late for events such as church services, the work day, or returning to a parked car before, at, or after the paid parking meter time expires (Allport 1934:167; Katz and Schanck 1938). The J-curve results from the fact that most people will arrive between the "early" and the "on-time" periods, and fewer and fewer will appear after the event has started. You can check this out by recording your fellow students' arrivals at the start of a class.

The assumption that curves are, or should be, normal or J-shaped has occasionally led to distorted conclusions about the degree to which a particular behaviour differs from the norm.

The statistical approach holds out the possibility of precise measurement. By using records, interviews, self-reports, and participant observation, we can obtain numerical values for various actions, beliefs, and fantasies. We can ask people how often they engage in particular activities, as well as how often they think others do so. Sometimes we find startlingly wide discrepancies between what is believed to be

Figure 1.2   A Bi-Modal Distribution: The Age–Crime Curve

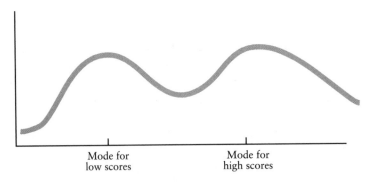

Mode for
low scores

Mode for
high scores

Figure 1.3   The J-Curve of Institutional Conformity

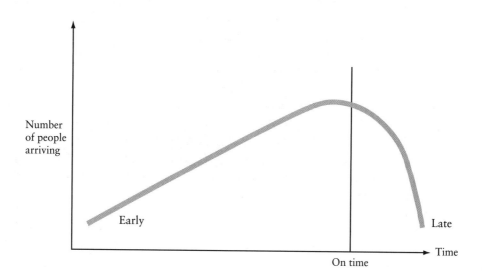

normal in society and what is actually going on. Many kinds of disreputable behaviour are hidden rather than rare. A generation ago left-handed people were strongly (even violently) encouraged to hide this characteristic and develop "normal" right-handedness. Today, reactions to left-handedness have become less repressive, and, as a result, we are far more aware of how many "lefties" there are among us. Similarly, behaviour that is regarded as bad and even criminal (e.g., the use of illegal drugs or the abuse of legal ones) may be statistically normal, or at least quite common.

The work of Alfred C. Kinsey illustrates both the hidden nature and pervasiveness of deviance. During the 1940s and 1950s, Kinsey and his associates interviewed more than 17,000 Americans and produced two major studies on sexual behaviour (Kinsey, Pomeroy, and Martin 1948; 1953). Their studies shocked Americans because of the revelations they contained about the frequency and variety of sexual behaviours and outlets indulged in by a wide cross-section of Americans. For example, Kinsey found that extramarital relationships were far more prevalent than was commonly believed, and, also contrary to popular wisdom, that 4 percent of men were exclusively homosexual and that two males out of every five had "at least some overt homosexual experience to the point of orgasm" (Kinsey, Pomeroy, and Martin 1948:650; Geddes 1954; Boorstin 1975[1962]). At a time when homosexuality was regarded as extremely deviant (as well as being an illegal act in many jurisdictions), this information had considerable impact.

Recent telephone surveys report the male homosexuality rate to be considerably below the Kinsey finding, somewhere around 2 percent (Barringer 1993). These studies have been used to discredit Kinsey's findings. Using a research design superior to that adopted in the Kinsey studies, Janus and Janus (1993) undertook a nine-year, cross-sectional national study of sexuality in the United States. This study found that 9 percent of men and 5 percent of women may be considered predominantly homosexual in orientation. These findings, like those of Kinsey, show that something society considers uncommon may actually (as with left-handedness) be very common. In part, the relationship between statistical frequency and normality is an artifact of social influence. When a large number of people want to engage in a particular behaviour, their numbers can become "votes" for its acceptance as normal. This is particularly true if such people exert political or economic influence in their society.

A final limitation of the statistical perspective is that most of the characteristics and behaviours it singles out as being relatively rare are not treated as deviant. Being trilingual or genuinely platinum blonde, or having R-negative blood may be statistically unusual, but none of these characteristics corresponds in any fixed way to social definitions of the deviant. Similarly, the scientific genius and the innovative artist depart from the average without necessarily being deviant.

Social Harmfulness

It is commonly asserted that deviance is harmful behaviour and should be prevented or controlled for that reason. The main problem with this view is that many forms of behaviour that are labelled deviant are less physically or emotionally harmful than others that are not so labelled. For example, exposing children to depictions of sexuality on TV is considered deviant by most people, yet letting them watch hours of violence is not. Similarly, being mentally ill is seen as deviant, whereas being sane yet contributing to other people's suffering is not. As Pfohl (1985) notes,

> The executive who manipulates prices, who builds unsafe vehicles, and refuses to allow his wife to have interests of her own may do more harm than the thief, the embezzler or the rapist. Witch hunts have done more harm than the doubts of heretics.

Along with considerable and undeniable harm, benefits too may stem from deviance. This might be called the "silver-lining" effect. Organized crime, for instance, causes a great deal of physical, social, and economic harm, but it also provides some ghetto dwellers with a ladder of employment, so that they or their children can eventually "make it" in respectable society if they decide to do so (Bell

1961; Beare 1996). At the very least, the punishment of deviants impresses upon the rest of society the value of conformity. Outrage against rapists and child abusers can contribute to social cohesion by provoking a common effort against them. When baseball player Roberto Alomar spit on an umpire (against the written rules and in violation of customary norms) the incident increased awareness of tensions in major league baseball and forced those in charge to re-examine their leadership.

The three main versions of the argument that deviance is harmful are the physical argument, the functional argument, and the "social reality" argument. Each of these approaches is useful in some ways, but assuming that harmfulness is the reason for calling something deviant is too simplistic. Arguments about harmfulness are often made "after the fact" to justify the treatment of people or situations already seen as deviant.

The Physical Argument

According to this approach, deviance causes physical damage to the deviant, to other people (e.g., crime victims), or to objects. Alcoholism is called deviant because of its associations with medical complications, drunk-driving offences, and the compromised physical safety of those who depend on the alcoholic. Similarly, smoking marijuana is associated with lung cancer and is said to have a negative effect on memory and motivation.

Very often, however, the evidence that deviance is physically harmful is "constructed" (i.e., made up or exaggerated) by those who, for other reasons, want to control it. While heroin, marijuana, and cocaine undoubtedly present real dangers, all of these drugs have been subject to grossly inflated claims concerning the speed, totality, and inevitability of their destructive effects. Marijuana, for example, was once blamed for sudden attacks of violent insanity, for provoking the murder of families, and even for contributing to mental retardation and interracial sex (Murphy 1973 [1922]). These lurid assertions were made by government agencies and by respected people such as judges, even though they were not supported by research. They helped fuel public demand for restrictive legislation that justified police action against a variety of "outsiders" such as jazz musicians, sailors, Mexicans, and Canada's Chinese. In contrast, the destructive effects of *legal* drugs have received very little attention (Boyd 1991; Blackwell and Erickson 1988).

The Functional Argument

In the functional view, deviance undermines the values and relationships that make the different parts of the social system work harmoniously. Thus, sexual deviancy is harmful because it threatens the "proper" setting for sexuality, however that may be defined in a particular society. Deviance weakens the society, or parts of it, so that it cannot make the most of its physical environment or its relations with other societies. If plagued with too much deviance, a social system will not survive.

Normally, each system favours certain people and punishes those who do not help the existing system function effectively. Consider the case of a man who buys products in one city and sells them at a higher price in another. Is he deviant? Not in a capitalist country, where he is simply fulfilling the expected role of the entrepreneur and at the same time helping the system to run at maximum efficiency. In a country with a government-controlled economic system, however, he might well be disturbing the central plan for the distribution of goods, thereby challenging the collective values that maintain the system, and earning himself a prison term.

The functional criterion of harmfulness has several problems. First, so-called deviants do not always have an unambiguously negative effect on the system. That bending the rules can be functional will be clear to anyone who has worked in a bureaucratic organization, where rules must at times be bent or ignored if appropriate action is to take place.

Second, some behaviour that is arguably very harmful to the system is not publicly treated as deviant. Only recently, for example, has the role of "respectable" people in the destruction of the environment and propagation of wars begun to be recognized as deviant. Even so, these offenders are subjected to much less censure than are traditional deviants and criminals.

Third, behaviour that is considered harmful to the existing system may, in fact, represent movement toward a better system, or just a different one. Early scientists like Copernicus and Galileo were censored as deviants and punished by the Inquisition because their work undermined the religious and social certainties of the times. Later they were celebrated for helping us move toward new prosperity and new values. Thus, people who challenge the system often play a role in keeping it strong, flexible, and adapted to the world around it.

The Social Reality Argument

The third kind of harm deviance causes is the least easily defined and measured. According to this view, deviance is harmful because it is "world-destroying." It shakes up the assumptions that make life orderly, understandable, and meaningful. Socialization into our own culture makes us participants in the creation and maintenance of our social world. Buses come because we expect them to come (otherwise we would not wait), and we wait because they come (otherwise the company would collect no fares). This socially constructed reality works as long as most of us believe in it—or at least as long as we act as though we do. Consider how you behave during

Box 1.1   Rules vs. Common Sense

A man lies motionless on the ground just a few metres from an entrance to Fleury Hospital in Montreal. No one brings him inside. A hospital directive prevents this. It says the staff must call an ambulance "for all emergency situations occurring outside the main building." So that is what they do.

A conscientious orderly ventures in to the –20° weather, but he is not authorized to perform cardiopulmonary resuscitation (CPR) without medical supervision. He fetches a doctor who decides the man is brain-dead and makes no attempt to revive him. The persistent orderly then finds a nurse; they begin mouth-to-mouth resuscitation. But it is too late. After the ambulance crew arrives and brings the man inside, the doctors tend to him, but Michele Rainone, 74, is pronounced dead. The cause was a heart attack.

One would think that the failure to rush Rainone inside might have resulted in some disciplinary action. But no. Hospital brass actually approved of their employees' behaviour. Chief Administrator Lucien Hervieux acknowledged that ten minutes had elapsed between the time the man was discovered and his arrival in the emergency room. Yet he said, "Even if tomorrow morning another individual should be found in the same state, we'd do exactly the same thing."

To his credit the head of the emergency room, Dr. Pierre Charbonneau, has said that the right medical attitude in such circumstances should be "directives be damned," that "using one's head" should prevail over timid respect for a piece of paper.

Yet that is quite different from the no-regrets message Hervieux is offering. It is about time that Fleury Hospital got its priorities straight. It may have been –20° on the pavement, but this institution's heart seems colder still.

Source: Jeff Heinrich, "Dead man's family asks if hospital did the right thing: 74-year-old found outside Henry's door. Michele Rainone Case." *Montreal Gazette.* Jan. 5, 1996. A1–A2. Reprinted with permission.

your classes or at religious services. If you sometimes find yourself pretending to appreciate the value of what is going on, you are supporting the constructed reality of the class or the service. People who do not help to maintain the expectations that make the system work threaten us with a frightening sense of chaos. This harms our sense of security, rather than causing actual pain or danger.

We defend ourselves and our world against those who are unable or unwilling to support our collective social-world-making activity. One way of doing this is to call them deviant and to control their interactions with us. Those who cannot support our world-making are defined as mentally ill or possessed by evil, and are locked up, drugged, or subjected to exorcisms. Those who can support the normal vision of reality, but choose not to do so, are branded as heretics or traitors. If relatively small in number, they may be imprisoned or blacklisted. With sufficient numbers and resources, however, they may force us to accept a new social reality. Over time, these processes of reinforcement and change give shape to the dimensions of acceptable and favoured behaviour in a society.

We cannot legitimately define all deviance in terms of harm to social reality, because we are not always threatened by new ideas, interpretations, and off-the-wall people. Thus, with respect to all three kinds of harmfulness, we fall short of finding a distinctive characteristic that would define deviance in a unique and objective way, though we have highlighted some of the elements that are part of such a definition.

Normative Violation

If harmfulness does not "work" consistently as a criterion of deviance, what might be a more reliable defining characteristic? Current definitions of deviance tend to agree with Merton (1961), who says that deviant behaviour

> refers to conduct that departs significantly from the norms set for people in their social statuses ... Deviant behaviour cannot be described in the abstract but must be related to the norms that are socially defined as appropriate and morally binding for people occupying various statuses. (723–724)

Human social life is largely organized by social norms. Humans have few, if any, inborn instincts to control their actions. Unlike insects and "lower" mammals, our species is not hardwired with respect to behavioural patterns. We can do anything that our strength, size, intelligence, and coordination permit. Nonetheless most of our behaviour occurs within a far more limited range than that potentially allowed by our physical nature. Consider, for example, how human clothing varies, from the enveloping black or white robes favoured in the desert to nude or nearly nude beach resort fashions. The sand and temperature may be the same, but the adaptation to it is not. The overall style is not left to the individual in either place, but is enforced through norms that are expressed in rules and customs.

Such limitations on the range of human behaviour are largely the result of socialization, specifically, conforming to the expectations of others. We learn the values of our society and the rules that follow from them. We see how people in our culture do things, and learn to expect that things should be done in this way. We learn that some actions earn praise and a "good reputation," whereas others do not (Cancian 1975). There are many motivations for conformity. We conform because we want respect, because we respect those who teach us, because we fear to do otherwise, or because we cannot imagine doing things differently. The rules that inform this behaviour may or may not be recognized as external ones. Often they seem like the only right way to do things, or simply "the way things are done," without any accompanying rationale. Even if we break the rules, we are likely to do so in ways suggested by them, following the distinctive patterns typical of our society (Sagarin 1977:431; Cancian 1975).

One way of looking at the normative definition of deviance is to look for the normative standard that governs the behaviour. For each form of deviance at least one standard is being violated. For example, in terms of gender roles, the normative standards invoked in Box 1.2 establish heterosexual males as the standard and those who differ from them as deviants. Similarly, the normative dominance of capitalist forms of enterprise over alternative forms has often meant that people who prefer to involve themselves in noncompetitive, nonprofit, environmentally conscious types of enterprise have, at least until recently, been subjected to deviance labels.

Box 1.2   Normative Standards and Definitions of Deviance

Deviant Category	*Normative Standard*
Heretic	Religious orthodoxy, violated beliefs
Sinner	Religious regulation, acts
Traitor	Loyalty
Homosexual	Gender roles, opposite-gender cathexis
Transvestite	Gender-role signification
"Promiscuous" woman	Gender-specific regulations
Dangerous driver	Highway Traffic Act
Robber	Criminal Code
Alcoholic	Self-control, reliability
Welfare recipient	Work ethic

Normative violation would appear, at first glance, to be a good way of defining deviance (certainly it is more defensible than the arguments of harmfulness). There are, however, several problems with it. First, while all deviance violates standards, not all violations of standards are treated as deviance, even when a rule is unambiguously identified. For example, smuggling goods across borders is usually illegal, but in many communities it is a subject of humour and pride, not censure. In many sports, the actual norms of the participants differ significantly from the written rules of the game. James Naismith, who founded the game of basketball in 1891, for example, was dismayed by the transformation of basketball he saw in this century. His rules excluded body contact between players, yet players, coaches, and officials over time collectively determined that "shoving, elbowing, holding and clawing" are part of the game. An attempt to enforce Naismith's rules "would bring the game to a standstill" (Jimerson 1996:359).

While some people who violate the rules may be called deviant, others may be ignored, tolerated, or even admired. Baseball players sometimes brag about getting an edge by cheating (Gutman 1990). The deviant may even be identified by an overly rigid and robotic adherence to regulations. In addition, behaviour that violates rules is not deviant if the individual is not subject to these particular rules. Police may carry weapons or use violence in ways forbidden to civilians; psychiatrists may ask highly personal questions that would not be permitted in a job interview; soldiers in combat situations may obtain equipment through means that would be called theft or fraud in any other context. Similarly, behaviour that violates rules may not be deviant if the situation has been set apart from the usual rules. European wine festivals held in the fall, New Year's celebrations, and the masked carnival of Mardi Gras are events during which behaviour that is normally treated as deviant is encouraged.

A second problem with the normative violation definition is that being deviant does not mean one escapes from all demands concerning one's behaviour. In fact, the moderately conforming citizen probably has more freedom than does the deviant or criminal, who must deal not only with the forces of law and order, but also with the often brutal social controls of the subculture or underworld. In prisons, for example, serial murderers, sex offenders, and police informants often need special protection from the general prison population, which is dominated by the inmate code enforced by the armed robbers and drug kingpins. The "protected" prisoners are deviants within a deviant community, doubly isolated and despised.

A third problem is that objectively visible regulations are not always the most powerful codes of behaviour operative in a particular situation. Some norms are "high etiquette ideals" known only to the elite, such as the rule against applause between the movements of a symphony. Some norms enjoy widespread, active cultural support, while others are regularly ignored. Norms and rules routinely contradict each other. Students, for example, typically juggle the contrary demands of family and friends, school and work, and religious and secular values. Norms may be encoded in law and reinforced by our respect for law, or they may violate the law. The written rules, religious precepts, and even the laws of the land do not

---

Box 1.3   Which Norms Really Count? Hamilton vs. Burr

Most countries have laws against duelling as a private settling of accounts between citizens, and the practice has become quite rare. But duelling persisted long after the passing of legislation against it. The contradiction between custom and criminal law is exemplified by the 1804 duel between Alexander Hamilton and Aaron Burr. Hamilton, a founding father of the United States, was known and respected as a statesman of greater than average intelligence, courage, and moral integrity. He died as a result of a duel in which he had resolved not to fire at his challenger on the first round (and possibly even the second).

About a week before the duel, Hamilton wrote a letter to his wife in which he explained why he felt compelled to participate in this "interview" with Burr. The first part of the letter outlines his arguments *against* taking up Burr's challenge.

1. Hamilton's religious and moral principles were strongly opposed to the practice of duelling.
2. Duelling was illegal in his home state, New York, a law he himself had helped to create.
3. He understood his importance to his wife and seven children.
4. He was concerned about his creditors, to whom he had obligations.
5. He felt (or claimed) no personal ill will toward Burr, but only political opposition.

In Hamilton's calculations, the norms that required a man to defend his honour, or else lose respect and influence, were more powerful than the combined weight of criminal law, religious and moral principles, and his responsibilities as a father, husband, and public figure. Without this respect, Hamilton thought it would be impossible to influence others to do good or to prevent harm (Mitchell 1957:159).

always represent the effective "common values" of society. Many studies have shown that educated, powerful, male owners of property and businesses have had a disproportionately high degree of influence on the development of formal rules, and particularly on law and the way in which law is used. In North America, legal proscriptions and sanctions come from the dominant upper-middle-class value system (Sellin and Wolfgang 1964:249). These regulations do not reflect the day-to-day normative codes of this society's other classes and occupational groups.

Laws may also be "ahead" of the culture in that they are enacted to enforce desirable change. For example, laws have been used to fight pernicious customs such as duelling, blood feuds, ethnic and racial discrimination, and family violence. In Egypt, new laws prohibit the practice of female genital mutilation. These laws, however, have so far proven to be unenforceable in the face of cultural resistance. Often the law lags behind changing customs. For example "blue laws" (named for the colour of early law books) are usually aimed at people's sexual behaviour or at the availability of intoxicants. These maintain normative standards that no longer reflect the will of all citizens. In addition, many laws on the books (e.g., public nuisance laws) are not enforced unless there is a need to arrest someone for other, less easily proven reasons. In the case of organized crime, laws against tax evasion have been used to prosecute individuals when it is clear that the real reason for their trial was what they did to get the money, not their failure to pay tax on it.

Social Response

Deviance is sometimes defined in terms of the social response it evokes. For example, if being cross-eyed consistently produces negative reactions from others, we could define this condition as deviant. We can look at the issue of response under four headings: negative response, tolerant response, denial, and romanticization.

Negative Response

If a particular behaviour normally elicits criticism or punishment, it is deviant in the eyes of those who respond this way, and people regularly associated with it will be similarly labelled. Deviants can be identified by the ridicule, scorn, exclusion, punishment, discrimination, fear, disgust, anger, hate, gossip, arrest, fines, confinement, or other negative reactions that they experience as a result of being labelled deviant.

According to the negative response view, any person who is called deviant, whether a Clifford Olson (serial killer) or a Copernicus (scientific pioneer), will be subject to rejection, treatment, or punishment. When the sanctioning power of a society or social group is customarily used against a particular behaviour, that behaviour becomes deviance. This definition of deviance is probabilistic: it holds that an act or characteristic is deviant if the probability of punishment upon discovery is high, but recognizes that punishment may not be found in each and every case (Goode 1978:24).

Tolerant Response

Not only may society define some deviancy as acceptable, it may also congratulate itself for its tolerance in doing so. Canadians, for example, pride themselves on showing greater tolerance in many areas than they believe is shown by the people of other nations. When Kim Campbell and Jean Charest, as candidates for the leadership of the Progressive Conservative party in early 1993, admitted they had tried marijuana, they were compared favourably with U.S. President Bill Clinton, for example, who had admitted to marijuana use but denied having inhaled. While Clinton's was an extremely rare admission for an American politician, Canadians prided themselves on being able to "handle" a politician who had smoked marijuana and on having such honest and forthright political candidates.

Many rules are "honoured in the breach," and breaking them simply establishes one's claim to a normal level of mischief or flexibility. Thus, children often shun a playmate who follows adult rules too well. Many adults are quite pleased with themselves for successful income tax "avoidance," or driving a little over the speed limit. Just how much one can get away with before tolerance ends varies. Most of us occasionally test limits, only to find that the deviance label is not automatically conferred on us. A great deal depends on the circumstances surrounding the offence and its discovery. Behaviour that touches on the highest values of a culture is more likely to be labelled deviant than is behaviour that is less central. In a society in which bank buildings are higher than the spires and towers of religious buildings, economic heresy will get you into more trouble than will religious heresy.

Denial

Another element that comes between an individual's behaviour and society's response to it is denial. When we do not want others to be deviant (e.g., we may like or depend on them), and especially when acknowledging the abnormality of their behaviour frightens us, we may attempt to reinterpret their behaviour. We may deny the reality of their deviance until alternative explanations are exhausted. Thus, in one study, wives of mentally ill men preferred to "normalize" their husbands' abnormal behaviour by interpreting it as tiredness, strain, or eccentricity. They accepted the diagnosis of mental illness only slowly and unwillingly (Yarrow et al.

1987). In contrast, if a person or group is already unpopular, the connection between odd behaviour and punitive response may be made more quickly.

Romanticization

In the absence of hard evidence, the deviant may become an imagined moral monster (Dracula), a romantic hero (Robin Hood), or a combination of both (Black Beard the Pirate). In Milton's *Paradise Lost*, the demonic character of Satan is presented as something magnificent and positive. When the deviant is one who challenges the status quo, fights back against the ever-present regulation of life, or demonstrates a better way of doing things, many people may come to admire his or her courage and audacity. Although an outlaw in the eyes of the Sheriff of Nottingham, the mythical Robin Hood was a respected insider among his "merry men" and local supporters. (Actual highwaymen were not nearly so well liked.) The Robin Hood myth colours society's response to many deviants, especially those who can lay claim to being skilful, daring, cunning, and tough.

The myth is particularly well supported if the heroic deviant appears to harm only anonymous, unpopular institutions or oppressive, conniving individuals. In the film *Butch Cassidy and the Sundance Kid,* the audience cheers for the bank robbers, not the wooden, vicious, or simpleminded bank and railroad representatives. A Canadian equivalent, profiled in Greg Weston's *The Stopwatch Gang,* concerns "three affable Canadians who stormed America's banks and drove the FBI crazy" (Weston 1992). Canadian criminal heroes have also included a large number of smugglers (Hunt 1988). "Supercrooks" often develop a status not unlike that of movie stars or popular athletes. Similarly, the jailed environmental protester is a deviant in the eyes of the logging company or developer, but a hero to groups that are committed to environmental and humanistic values.

The outsider-hero paradox reflects our ambivalence toward the demands of conformity that "make society work," but that also force us to give up many forms of gratification and self-expression.

> Even as we put down the deviant, he sparks our desires to be free and wild, to chafe at our moral restraints. The world seems to love its outlaws even while it hangs them. For example the Spaniards have traditionally alternated between purging the gypsies and singing romantic ballads about them. (Simmons 1969:22)

Teen rebellion is usually portrayed as deviant, while teens themselves often regard standing up to their parents as normal or even as a badge of belonging. The film *Ferris Bueller's Day Off* is the story of one such teen, who is depicted as a hero.

The humour in this film works only if you accept the rights of the teenaged hero to get back at venal school officials and imbecilic parents for subjecting him to classroom boredom and excluding him from the moneyed world of good restaurants and fancy cars. Even in the teen groups, however, some kinds of rebellion go too far and are not accepted.

An interesting variation on the phenomenon of deviant as celebrity occurs when people who have been convicted of atrocities are pursued by admirers. For example, men convicted of serious offences against women have often attracted a following of men/women who visit them in prison and are even willing to marry them. Ted Bundy, a serial killer of women, was able to marry and father a child while awaiting execution. Rarely if ever does this minority approval cause either the justice system or the public to reverse its "verdict" on the deviant status of these offenders.

Stigmatizing Labels

Another way of addressing the problem of identifying and defining deviance is to focus on the process of "naming" or labelling deviance. Deviants are those people identified by names or images that mark (stigmatize) them as being less worthy than other people. These labels designate characteristics that the deviant is presumed to have, just as a label on a can supposedly tells us what is inside. Although labels of deviance are wide ranging, all of them identify someone who is a likely subject of correction or avoidance, at least by decent people.

Defining deviance as a matter of label or category allows us to see that deviance is not a simple matter of actual behaviour. Deviance is sometimes attributed to people who are not responsible for their behaviour or appearance, and even to people who have not actually done anything but are accused anyway. In our society, stigma inheres as much (or more) in the schizophrenic as in the calculating thief even though diagnosis of schizophrenia is notoriously loose. Moreover, false accusations of wrongdoing are frequently implicit in deviant labels. In Canada during both world wars, many Japanese, Germans, Italians, Ukrainians, Slavs, Jews, radicals, trade union leaders, and pacifists were labelled as "enemy aliens," which meant that they could be interned in camps and have their property confiscated (Koch 1980). In the Cold War period, many other Canadians were blacklisted as suspected "Communist subversives" (Scher 1992). In all cases, there was little or no hard evidence to justify their exclusion, confinement, or loss of employment. Apologies or compensation for their mistreatment have been very slow in coming. Even when a deviant label contains some truth, it usually stereotypes and exaggerates the negative aspects of the person being labelled.

PULLING IT ALL TOGETHER: COMMON GROUND

We have demonstrated how difficult it is to define deviance according to the standards of objectivity, noncircularity, and distinctiveness, while avoiding unnecessary assumptions. How can we forge a path through all the definitional pitfalls and arrive at some useful general definition of deviance? The approach outlined in the following pages takes a great deal from theories that define deviance as a socially constructed category of behaviour or being. From this perspective, a behaviour, act, or condition is deviant if enough important people say it is.

In the most general formulation, deviance is a descriptive name or label used to exclude people who—in the view of others—should not be allowed as regular members in a particular social setting or group context. It is a form of moral exclusion (see Box 1.4). Use of this definition compels us to focus as much on the people who are *definers* of deviance as on the deviants themselves and on the *role of social control* in the process. Social control may work to channel behaviour in nondeviant ways, or, paradoxically, it may give shape to deviance that might not otherwise have occurred. In other words, it takes two, the observer and the observed, to make deviance. It also takes standards and an application of those standards. In the case of a serial rapist, for example, for a definition of deviance (e.g., sexual pervert) to be arrived at, there must be:

1. *observers* who believe that the acts have taken place, whether or not they have personally observed them;
2. *cultural standards* that define this form of interaction between strangers as immoral, disturbing, or illegal; and
3. *application* of *evidence* that shows that the acts and the personal characteristics of the serial rapist fit this person.

The "deviant" may attempt to reject the label by presenting a different image or interpretation of that image ("I'm not an alcoholic. I'm a sociologist doing participant observation of bar culture."). Sometimes the alleged deviant responds by attacking the character of the would-be definers. Prigs, prudes, authoritarians, and hypocrites (if called these names) are would-be labellers who get labelled themselves.

We tend to be more aware of policing when it is official and obvious. We are much less aware of the subtle ways in which other controls guide us. Where do the standards and definitions of deviance come from? They reflect prior battles over "correctness" that are rooted in our cultural inheritance; and they emerge directly from such sources as the media (especially in advertising), schools and churches, interest group organizations, and even government. Agencies set up for the benefit

---

Box 1.4   Responding to "Deviance": Moral Exclusion

The characteristic negative response that identifies deviance is moral exclusion, which places individuals or groups outside the boundaries in which moral values, rules, and considerations of fairness and decency apply (Opotow 1990:1). Gay bashers, for example, claim that their victims are not worthy of respect and "deserve" to be mistreated. Thus, certain categories of people are regarded as moral outcasts for whom civil protection can be righteously denied.

The relationship between the actions of deviants and their moral exclusion is not a simple one. Even in a relatively uncomplicated system such as a small group, responses to specific behaviours do not always occur in an accountable, predictable, accurate, orderly, or fair manner. For example, although recreational use of illegal drugs can be classified as deviant because it often results in moral exclusion, not all such drug use evokes this response; moreover, reactions to the particular drugs being used have varied considerably over time.

---

of particular kinds of "outcasts" (such as "homes," hospitals, and asylums) also play a role in defining who these people are and how they should be treated (Scott 1969).

Deviant designations are part of the control response evoked when the regulators of society—its religious leaders, judges, educators, psychiatrists, social workers, school principals, and newspaper editors—are alarmed by particular people or activities. Even the underworld has regulators who take action against those who violate rules or just get in the way. Some individuals act as "moral entrepreneurs" in the area of rule making and rule enforcement. First, they gain access to the rule-making processes, whether in the legislature, the company standards committee, the board of directors, or the media. In this capacity, they help to create definitions of deviance and then gain profit or prestige from being "experts" at applying them to others.

Thus far in our discussion, we have accepted the premise that the person called deviant actually behaves in some discernibly different way that attracts either negative or romanticizing attention. Once we begin looking at the process by which deviant labels are acquired, however, it becomes clear that deviants usually do not possess all of the characteristics imputed to them. Throughout history, we find that whatever the form of deviance, the labels have been used to describe (1) *presumed behaviour* that (2) *defies social expectations* that (3) are made and *enforced by people with influence* and (4) have been applied to *particular people or groups in particular situations.*

Witches, for example, were presumed to be consorting with the devil and bringing death and disaster to their communities. The rules they were supposedly breaking were made by church authorities, supported by religious beliefs and a variety of superstitions, enforced through a combination of sacred and secular authorities, and applied to particular kinds of people (mainly women) in particular circumstances such as drought, war, or plague.

From this perspective, the actual characteristics of the deviant hardly matter. Scapegoats are chosen because they lack the power to protect their own image and can be made to "represent" any problem. It is much easier to blame witches, Communists, or drug traffickers than it is to grasp the real causes of natural disasters, economic recessions, wars, and civil disorder.

Whatever the form of deviance, it is important to look at the characteristics of the labellers as well as the characteristics of those labelled. Deviants represent the losing side of a moral argument. They include members of "cults," extremists at the far right or far left of the political spectrum, and people who support a country that is at war with their own country. The categories of the morally excluded change over time. Tobacco smokers, wearers of fur coats, and people who make sexist comments are, for example, increasingly finding themselves on the receiving end of deviant designations.

CHARACTERISTICS OF DEVIANCE

As part of almost every introduction to the study of deviance, the reality of deviance is proven by its *universality,* and then qualified out of existence by its *relativity* and *situationality.* In the following sections, we examine these three important dimensions of deviance.

DEVIANCE AS A UNIVERSAL PHENOMENON

In the sense that every social grouping generates deviant designations and rules for their application, deviance is universal. As noted by Durkheim, even a community of saints will include members who fail to live up to the expected standards of saintliness (1965:68–69). In communal groups that maintain highly restrictive standards of conduct, deviant status may result from using the wrong kind of buttons on clothes (Hutterites) or from showing greater interest in one's own children than in the group's offspring as a whole (early Israeli kibbutzim). In some groups, having private property is deviant, whereas in others such "communism" would be considered deviant. In Japan, a high-school student who dyed his hair blond would be suspended until it was re-dyed a conforming black. Deviant communities such as outlaw biker gangs include their own deviants, who may be expelled if their behaviour is insufficiently in tune with what the group requires.

DEVIANCE AS A RELATIVE PHENOMENON

If a visitor from another era, civilization, or galaxy were to ask why users of illicit drugs face possible expulsion from positions of responsibility, the response might be that the behaviour is wrong, immoral, unnatural, and intolerable—in short, deviant. The same sort of answer might have been given several generations ago to someone who questioned the lack of human rights for slaves, or two generations ago to someone asking why women were not allowed to vote. What was once obviously deviant is no longer seen that way. On the other hand, things once seen as quite acceptable, even heroic, are now considered deviant.

In earlier studies on deviance, the fact that something was deviant was often accepted as an absolute attribute or condition. The role of culture and observers in "making" deviance was ignored. This absolute view is rarely expressed in modern academic writing. (It has, in fact, become a deviant perspective on deviance.) Are you a "rate buster" (a worker who ignores group norms and works too hard) or a "slacker" (lazy student)? The degree of your deviation from the norm of student life depends on who is doing the evaluation, and on what standards they believe apply to you. Your friends, fellow students, instructors, and parents may not agree about whether you belong in one of these deviant categories. Your placement will thus be *relative to their standards* rather than absolutely inherent in the amount of work you do.

The observer's point of view is usually *culturally defined*. What the observer feels is right or wrong and acceptable or unacceptable is strongly influenced by the dictates of the surrounding culture. In this sense, deviance is said to be "culturally relative." In a heterogeneous society, deviance has multiple sources of definition. A deviant or outsider in one context may enjoy insider status in another. Indeed, most people who are called deviants are excluded only from some groups, not all. To be seen as deviant by the mainstream may even be a subcultural goal. ("If the teacher hates me, then I'm part of the gang.")

The passage of time can result in re-evaluations of the "deviance" of long-dead men and women. Executed as a traitor in 1885, Métis leader Louis Riel has since become a powerful symbol of French-Canadian and aboriginal aspirations. His passage from "traitor" to "Father of Confederation" shows the potential for designations to change over time (Winsor 1989). Examples of this kind of elevation from deviant status are numerous and include Jesus (crucified) and Socrates (forced to take poison) (Proietto and Porter 1996). Sometimes the change comes within the lifetime of the deviant: the Irgun "terrorists" in Palestine became the new government of Israel; and South African President Nelson Mandela was still listed by the U.S. State Department as "an international terrorist" when he travelled to the United States following his release from prison. Beverly Allen (1996) has observed how *The New York Times*, in the space of about a week (in 1988), transformed the Tamil Tigers of Sri Lanka "from 'terrorists,' to 'guerrillas,' to 'freedom fighters' as the priorities of U.S. foreign policy shifted" (Allen 1996:8). The Tigers did not change, but their position as deviants did.

Within the past few decades, activities once considered socially acceptable have started to take on deviant designations. Cigarette smoking, for example, is gradually assuming deviant status through a drawn-out process of medical lobbying, public pressure, legislation, and changing expectations (Troyer and Markle 1983; Corelli 1997). In a reversal of this process, divorce and common-law relationships have lost their former stigma in much of Western society. Similarly, nudism, certain forms of sexual expression, and a wide range of clothing alternatives, all of which would once have produced outrage, have gained wide social acceptance.

DEVIANCE AS A SITUATIONAL PHENOMENON

Definitions of deviance are more than just a reflection of broad cultural standards. They also emerge from our individual experiences and from our understanding of the situations in which the behaviour occurs.

Deviance is always relative to the situation, to the leadership that prevails there, and to the beliefs and expectations of the observer. Imagine that you have just started watching a film already in progress. One character is gunning down other characters: blood is everywhere. Are you supposed to be cheering for the gunman, or is he a villain? You are suddenly aware of the relativity of the situation. You missed the setup that enables the audience to judge whether this is Rambo-like heroism or an act of depravity. If you watch long enough, however, the situational clues allow you to figure it out.

The observer's judgment concerning the degree of deviance in a situation will depend on context, knowledge of the biography and positions of those involved, and assumptions about their motives. If a person on a city street is behaving eccentrically, it may be because he has just experienced some traumatic event such as a mugging or a bad reaction to medication. Just how deviant the observer judges the behaviour to be will depend on the observer's assessment of these situational factors, as well as on the actual, observed behaviour.

APPLYING CHARACTERISTICS OF DEVIANCE TO SPECIFIC BEHAVIOURS

Almost every action now called deviant has been tolerated or even required in another place or time. The idea that deviance is relative to a cultural or situational perspective rather than absolutely inherent in the act or appearance is not always easy to accept. While we understand clothing, food, and music choices may be culturally relative, and usually legitimately left up to the individual, we have diffi-culty thinking the same of other practices. With human sacrifice or cannibalism, for example, deviance *seems* to be an intrinsic quality, just as real or objective as the weight or height of objects.

Cannibalism

Eating human flesh violates a strong taboo in our time and society. It results in immediate deviant status for those accused of it. It has been used by writers and filmmakers to create moral monsters, like Hannibal Lector in *The Silence of the Lambs,* who jolt us into shivers of horror. Even under extreme conditions (e.g., survivors facing starvation following an airplane crash in a wilderness area opting to save themselves by eating the flesh of the crash's victims), cannibalism is only very reluctantly tolerated in modern Western society (Askenasy 1994). The perpetrators are likely to face criminal charges of murder or of committing an indignity to a human body. Even if acquitted on the grounds of necessity, "cannibals" may be seen as somehow polluted by their experience (Visser 1991; Simpson 1984, Harris 1978).

Despite its current taboo status, the apparent "objective deviance" of cannibal-ism is an illusion. In different times and places, the cannibalization of defeated enemies, even of recently deceased relatives, has been accepted either as the norm (*New Encyclopedia Britannica* 1984:512) or as an unpleasant necessity (Simpson 1984). Anthropologists have established that some cannibalistic cultures even had rules covering the niceties of the practice: who (and what parts) could be eaten, by whom, and when (Visser 1991). Thus, while we may feel that certain activities, espe-cially those with a powerful taboo attached to them, are intrinsically and objectively bad, wrong, and deviant, it is important to recognize that we are judging them on the basis of rules that exist merely in one particular society at one particular time.

Murder

Murder is the *wrongful* taking of human life, not *all* taking of human life. While murder is always and universally condemned, different societies—and even different subcultures within a society—may disagree as to what kinds of killing qualify as murder. Some situations, such as combat, legitimize killing. Indeed, soldiers can be court-martialled (treated as deviant) for failing to kill. Those who kill often resort to such slang or jargon as "wasted" and "acted with extreme prejudice" to avoid calling the action murder. Similarly, police may kill in the line of duty, and, as long as proper procedures have been followed, not be charged with murder.

In some countries, the killing of adulterous wives and their lovers is either considered acceptable or treated as a minor indiscretion. In Canada, women who kill their abusive husbands are less likely now to be charged with murder than they were a decade ago (Johnson 1996:191–92) and, since May 1991, have been able to use, under very limited circumstances, battery as a reason for killing an abusive spouse.

In ancient Greece and Rome, human sacrifice was not treated as murder, but rather as an annual ritual the purpose of which was to unload the burden of sins and omissions that had accumulated over the previous year. Human sacrifice has also been part of rituals undertaken to ward off drought, plague, famine, and other misfortunes, or, as practised by the Aztecs, to satisfy bloodthirsty gods. Around the same time as such activities as cannibalism and collecting human heads as trophies were taking place in Africa, witches, heretics, and dissenters were being burned at the stake in Europe. Each culture would likely have regarded the other's behaviour as barbaric.

Indirect killing has rarely been treated as murder. When the hunting and fishing economies of indigenous North American populations were destroyed by economic exploitation and land pressure, (the restriction of land use through reservations, game laws, and population increases within the restricted areas), death rates in Indian and Inuit communities increased. Homicide, suicide, and infant mortality rates also rose (Shkilnyk 1985). These deaths were not considered murders, at least not by the legal system. Similarly, many foreseeable and preventable deaths in industry are called accidents, not murder. The production of cars, medicines, and other consumer goods that are unsafe costs lives, as does pollution. Is this murder or just "business as usual"? Avoidable but noncriminal deaths and injuries far exceed those that are crime related (Snider 1992:317–319; Simon and Eitzen 1993; Brown 1986:34–42).

Sometimes the line between killing or murder is so unclear the courts must decide the issue. Can a storekeeper shoot a would-be burglar? Can parents who rely on herbal remedies or faith healers be held accountable if their children die? (Molony 1991)

Suicide

Taking one's own life is generally regarded as deviant in Western society. At one time, suicide, whether attempted or successful, drew penalties in both ecclesiastical and criminal courts. Typical punishment involved the confiscation of the suicide's property, burial in unsanctified ground, and mutilation of the corpse. While suicide is no longer a criminal offence, some social stigma still attaches to it.

In contrast, ritual suicide in Japan has historically been an accepted, sometimes required, response to many situations in which "face" has been lost or one's social position has been hopelessly compromised. Japanese children still learn the story of the 47 *ronin* (samurai warriors), which allegedly took place in Tokyo in the early 1700s. By killing an unjust overlord, the master of the 47 left his followers in a situation in which their only honourable choice was to commit ritual suicide. This drama has been the subject of many popular Japanese plays and books. However, the acceptance of ritual suicide is no longer as strong as it once was. In 1970, the three-time Nobel-Prize-nominated Japanese writer Yukio Mishima ended his life in a dramatic ritual *(seppuku)* as a protest against Japanese society's loss of its spiritual way. The mildly critical Japanese media response to this showed that this form of maintaining face is no longer a major force within Japanese culture (Pinguet 1993; Mishima 1970, 1988).

Most societies honour those who lay down their lives for others, for a worthy cause, or for their country. During World War II, selected Japanese bombers *(kamikaze)* deliberately flew their planes into Allied ships. Suicide by students and by Buddhist monks has been a recurrent form of political protest in the Far East. Suicide by working too hard, "working oneself to death" (called *karoshi* in Japan), however, is regarded as pathological in Western society and a social problem in the East (Makihara 1991:41).

Starving oneself to death is usually seen as pathological and given medical labels such as anorexia nervosa. In the Middle Ages, however, holy mystics such as Catherine of Siena, Veronica Guiuliani, and the "Daughters of God" practised "holy anorexia" as a form of self-abnegation and piety. According to Bell (1985), half of the forty-two women in Italy who were recognized as saints in the fourteenth century exhibited anorexic behaviour, and many of them died of starvation. In this period, denial of the body for the sake of the soul was considered saintly. At a later period, such perverse self-control was opposed by the church as a form of willfulness.

Addiction

The use of addictive substances for pleasure or religious enlightenment, rather than for medical purposes, is sometimes accepted and sometimes condemned. Most societies regulate some forms of drugs, but not always the same ones. In Muslim societies, there is low tolerance for alcohol, but in some there is considerable social acceptance of other drugs, such as marijuana. In North American society, alcohol is not only tolerated but also hard to avoid, while marijuana use is criminalized. In Japan, amphetamine use—often by workers trying to increase their productivity—routinely brings two-year prison sentences. In North America, however, amphetamines are frequently prescribed by doctors and treated as a serious issue only when used by "speed freaks" and outlaw bikers, whose lifestyles are already disreputable.

The prohibition of a particular drug corresponds less to the physiological danger it poses than to the degree to which the groups that are believed to use it are accepted in society. Opiates and their derivatives were accepted—if not admired—until they became associated with "outsider" ethnic, racial, and occupational groups. Outlawing these drugs criminalized the undesirable groups that used (or misused) them, allowing for increased surveillance of "users" and increased stigmatization of their identities (Cook 1969; Blackwell and Erickson 1988). Yet tobacco kills far more North Americans each year than heroin does, even if we control for the number of people using each drug (Addiction Research Foundation 1980; Markle and Markle 1983; Clark 1988; Trebach 1982; Brown, Esbensen, and Geis 1991:18). Many (though by no means all) of the undesirable effects attributed to illegal drugs derive from the way these substances are regulated. The involvement of organized crime and its attendant violence, inflated prices that provoke users to theft and corruption, and an absence of quality control over supplies are just a few of the unwelcome consequences of making certain drugs illegal.

Child Abuse

All societies impose limits on the way in which adults may treat children. What is considered abnormal, unnecessary, and unacceptable child rearing varies over time and place. Many cultures prescribe that parents expose their children to hardships to prepare and strengthen them for adult life. Other cultures practise painful procedures that are deemed necessary to increase the child's attractiveness to prospective mates; these include tattooing, tooth-filing, and genital surgery (without anaesthetic).

A free, multicultural society is challenged to define child abuse in a way that respects the subcultures in the society while also protecting children. In Sweden, hitting children is illegal, and the state may take children into its care if their parents use disciplinary tactics that are quite common elsewhere. In many other countries, parents who *refuse* to discipline their children risk losing them to social welfare agencies. In Canada, many native children have been seized by the Children's Aid authorities primarily because the native cultural prohibition against "telling children what to do" is judged to be "negligent" rather than just "different" (Ross 1992). Although normative in many parts of the world, child marriage is treated as child abuse in the industrialized West. In England in 1986, the public was outraged over the report that an Iranian had been allowed to bring his 12-year-old wife into Britain. Changes in immigration regulations were demanded. The husband protested that he had done nothing wrong, and had not been warned that his actions would offend "British sensibilities" (West 1987:2).

The need to distinguish between legitimate cultural activities and child abuse becomes even more urgent with respect to such practices as genital mutilation—the ritual or medical circumcision of boys or the much more drastic clitoridectomy and infibulation of girls. The Western doctor who is asked to perform such operations may either comply or else report the parents as child abusers. In Canada some regulating bodies (such as the Ontario College of Physicians and Surgeons) prohibit doctors from performing "female circumcision," and in 1996 the California state legislature banned the practice.

Homosexuality

Same-gender sexual behaviour may be perceived as shocking, as required, or as something in between, depending on the rules of the society or subculture. The anthropological literature shows that societies with at least some institutionalized male-male relations (often surrounding male puberty) outnumber those without. Many of these societies believe that boys must receive sperm from adult males in order to become men themselves. Sapphic (lesbian) female-female relationships have been less institutionalized, but have long been tolerated or ignored in many societies (Stone 1990; Schur 1984:118–132).

The Christian church has traditionally condemned all forms of sexual expression that are not heterosexual ("missionary position") relations carried out for the purpose of procreation (West 1987:1; Masters, Johnson, and Kolodoy 1985). Islamic law also condemns homosexual behaviour. In many countries throughout the world, Christian and Islamic influences are found in laws that prohibit and punish homosexual relations. In Canada, homosexual behaviour (buggery) engaged in by not more than two consenting adults in private is legal, but the amount of disapproval, tolerance, or acceptance it meets varies considerably (West 1987:1; Kinsman 1987; Salamon 1988; Nelson 1992).

CORE ISSUES IN THE SOCIOLOGICAL STUDY OF DEVIANCE

Three core issues in the sociological study of deviance reflect the definitional concerns discussed above.

1. *The behaviour of people called deviant*—who does what? Before any reasonable explanation of deviance can be invoked, we need clear and accurate descriptions of what "deviants" actually do (if anything), as opposed to the images that are held about them. For example, people called witches rarely did the things for which they were tried and condemned. It should not surprise us too much that most persons found guilty of an offence do not readily fit into the standard cultural image of "that kind of person." These people, as Pfohl (1985:3) puts it, are "Losers are trapped within the vision of others," and therefore part of our role as researchers and students is to discover other views of the deviant.

2. *The rules or standards that define deviance*—made by whom, why, and with what effect? What are the social constructions of deviance that become labels for those called deviant? What effect do they have on those trapped in these definitions? What effect do they have on society as a whole? If a society is judged by the way it treats its least-valued citizens, then the study of deviance has important moral dimensions.

3. The methodology of deviance research—how we go about investigating deviance. Why do we use one methodology rather than another?

SUMMARY

Reasons for studying deviance include vicarious experience, a reforming impulse, self-protection and sophistication, understanding oneself and others, and intellectual curiosity. Each of these plays a role in the social scientist's approach to deviance. Various perspectives on deviance—student, public, and academic—have little in common when it comes to identifying deviant behaviours, beyond, that is, an agreement that most criminal behaviour is deviant. These perspectives reveal the diversity of ideas about deviance, but do not help us define it.

Defining deviance in a way that accommodates people with different cultural standards and political beliefs is difficult. A useful definition is one that meets the standards of objectivity, minimal assumptions, noncircularity, and distinctiveness. Most definitions of deviance, whether popular or academic, fail to live up to these standards, and may involve the criteria of rarity, harmfulness, and violation of normative standards, which are insufficient measures by themselves.

Deviance is best identified as a process in which a stigmatizing label is placed on people by others who claim (and usually believe) they are just enforcing social rules. This definition can be used by supporters and opponents of the stigmatization. It allows us to investigate not only the deviant but also the definers; that is, those who create and apply the labels of deviance. Deviance can be characterized by its universality, relativity, and situationality. These characteristics can be applied to specific behaviours, including cannibalism, murder, suicide, addiction, child abuse, and homosexuality.

REFERENCES

Addiction Research Foundation. (1980). *Facts About... Tobacco.* Toronto: Addiction Research Foundation.

Allen, Beverly. (1996). "Talking 'Terrorism': Ideologies and Paradigms in a Postmodern World." *Syracuse Journal of International Law* 22 (7): 7–12.

Allport, F.H. (1934). "The J-Curve Hypothesis of Conforming Behavior." *Journal of Social Psychology* 5:141–183.

America's Watch. (1993). *Urban Police Violence in Brazil.* New York: America's Watch.

Askenasy, Hans. (1994). *Cannibalism.* New York: Prometheus.

Barringer, F. (1993). "Sex Survey of American Men Finds 1% Are Gay." *New York Times,* April 15: A1, A18.

Beare, Margaret E. (1996). *Criminal Conspiracies: Organized Crime in Canada.* Toronto: Nelson Canada.

Bell, Daniel. (1961). "Crime as an American Way of Life: A Queer Ladder of Social Mobility." In Daniel Bell (ed.), *The End of Ideology: On the Exhaustion of Political Ideas in the Fifties.* Rev. ed. New York: Collier.

Bell, Rudolph. (1985). *Holy Anorexia.* Chicago: University of Chicago Press.

Blackwell, Judith C., and Patricia G. Erickson (eds.). (1988). *Illicit Drugs in Canada: A Risky Business.* Scarborough, Ont:. Nelson Canada.

Boorstin, Daniel J. ([1962] 1975). "Statistical Morality." In F. James Davis and Richard Stivers (eds.), *Collective Definition of Deviance.* New York: Free Press.

Boughy, Howard. (1973). Unpublished notes on a class experiment. Erindale College, University of Toronto.

Bowden, Mark. (1987). *Doctor Dealer.* New York: Warner.

Boyd, Neil. (1991). *High Society: Legal and Illegal Drugs in Canada.* Toronto: Key Porter.

Brown, Stephen E. (1986). "The Reconceptualization of Violence in Criminal Justice Education Programs." *Criminal Justice Review* 11:34–42.

Brown, Stephen E., Finn-Aage Esbensen, and Gilbert Geis. (1991). *Criminology: Explaining Crime and Its Context.* Cincinnati: Anderson.

Bryant, D. Clifton. (1979). *Khaki-Collar Crime: Deviant Behavior in the Military Context.* New York: Free Press.

Byers, Bryan. (1993). "Teaching About Judgement of Crime Seriousness." *Teaching Sociology* 21(1):33–41.

Cancian, Francesca. (1975). *What Are Norms? A Study of Beliefs and Action in a Maya Community.* New York: Cambridge University Press.

Chevigny, Paul. (1996). "Changing Control of Police Violence in Rio de Janeiro and São Paolo, Brazil." In Otwin Marinen (ed.), *Policing Change, Changing Police: International Perspectives.* New York: Garland.

Clark, Matt. (1988). "Getting Hooked on Tobacco: Is Nicotine as Addicting as Cocaine or Heroin?" *Newsweek,* May 30, 56.

Clarke, Ronald V. (1996). "The Distribution of Deviance and Exceeding the Speed Limit." *The British Journal of Criminology* 36(2):169–181.

Cook, Shirley. (1969). "Canadian Narcotics Legislation: A Conflict Model Interpretation." *Canadian Review of Sociology and Anthropology* 6(1):34–46.

Corelli, Rae. (1997). "The New Outlaws." *Maclean's* 110(15): 44–47.

Davis, Stephen. (1985). *Hammer of the Gods: The Led Zeppelin Saga.* New York: Ballantine.

DeKeseredy, Walter, and Ronald Hinch. (1991). *Woman Abuse: Sociological Perspectives.* Toronto: Thompson Educational Publishing.

Deutschmann, Linda B. (1991). Unpublished informal survey.

Douglas, John. (1995). *Mind Hunter: Inside the FBI's Elite Serial Crime Unit.* New York: Pocket Star (Simon and Shuster).

Durkheim, Emile. (1965). *The Rules of the Sociological Method.* New York: Free Press.

Eddy, Paul, with Hugo Sabogal and Sara Walden. (1988). *The Cocaine Wars.* New York: W.W. Norton.

Ellis, Desmond. (1987). *The Wrong Stuff: An Introduction to the Sociological Study of Deviance.* Don Mills, Ont.: Collier Macmillan Canada.

Empey, Lamar T. (1982). *American Delinquency*, rev. ed. Homewood, Illinois: Dorsey.

Francis, Diane. (1988). *Contrepreneurs.* Toronto: Macmillan Canada.

Geddes, Donald Porter (ed.). (1954). *An Analysis of the Kinsey Reports on Sexual Behavior in the Human Male and Female.* New York: New American Library (Mentor).

Gibbs, J. (1981). *Norms, Deviance and Social Control: Conceptual Matters.* New York: Elsevier.

Goode, Erich. (1978). *Deviant Behaviour.* Englewood Cliffs, N.J.: Prentice-Hall.

———. (1990). *Deviant Behaviour*, 3rd ed. Englewood Cliffs, N.J.: Prentice-Hall.

Gutman, Dan. (1990). *It Ain't Cheatin' If You Don't Get Caught: Scuffing, Corking, Spitting, Gunking, Razzing and Other Fundamentals of Our National Pastime.* New York: Penguin.

Hare, E.H. (1962). "Masturbatory Insanity: The History of an Idea." *Journal of Mental Science* 108:1–25.

Harris, Marvin. (1978). *Cannibals and Kings: The Origins of Cultures.* New York: Random House Vintage.

Hunt, C.W. (1988). *Booze, Boats and Billions Smuggling Liquid Gold.* Toronto: McClelland and Stewart.

Janeway, Elizabeth. (1987). *Improper Behavior: When and How Misconduct Can Be Healthy for Society.* New York: William Morrow.

Janus, Samuel S., and Cynthia L. Janus. (1993). *The Janus Report on Sexual Behavior.* New York: John Wiley.

Jimerson, Jason B. (1996). "Good Times and Good Games." *Journal of Contemporary Ethnography* 25(3):353–371.

Johnson, Holly. (1996). *Dangerous Domains: Violence Against Women in Canada.* Toronto: Nelson Canada.

Katz, D., and R.L. Schanck. (1938). *Social Psychology.* New York: Wiley.

Katz, Jack. (1988). *Seductions of Crime: Moral and Sensual Attractions in Doing Evil.* New York: Basic Books.

Kinsey, A.C., W.B. Pomeroy, and C.E. Martin. (1948). *Sexual Behavior in the Human Male.* Philadelphia: W.B. Saunders.

———. (1953). *Sexual Behavior in the Human Female.* Philadelphia: W.B. Saunders.

Kinsman, Gary. (1987). *The Regulation of Desire: Sexuality in Canada.* Montreal: Black Rose.

Knox, Paul. (1996). "Brazil's Image Tarnished by Acts of Police Brutality." *Globe and Mail,* June 26, A6.

Koch, Eric. (1980). *Deemed Suspect: A Wartime Blunder.* Toronto: Methuen.

Liazos, A. (1972). "The Poverty of the Sociology of Deviance: Nuts, Sluts, and Perverts." *Social Problems* 20:103–120.

Makihara, Kumiko. (1991). "Death of a Salaryman." *Health* (May/June):41–50.

Malarek, Victor. (1989). *Merchants of Misery: Inside Canada's Illegal Drug Scene.* Toronto: Macmillan Canada.

Markle, Ronald J., and Gerald E. Markle. (1983). *Cigarettes: The Battle Over Smoking.* New Brunswick, N.J.: Rutgers University Press.

Masters, W.H., V.E. Johnson, and R.C. Kolodoy. (1985). *Human Sexuality.* 2nd ed. Toronto: Little, Brown.

Merton, Robert. (1961). *Social Theory and Social Structure.* Rev. (enlarged) ed. Glencoe, Ill.: Free Press.

Mishima, Yukio. (1970). *Sun and Steel: Personal Reflections on Art and Action.* Tokyo: Kodansha International.

———. (1988 [1958]). *Confessions of a Mask.* London: Collins.

Mitchell, Broadus. (1957). "Hamilton's Motives in Meeting Burr." In Mitchell Broadus (ed.), *Heritage from Hamilton.* New York: Columbia University.

Molony, Paul. (1991). "Third Trial Expected Over Girl's Starvation." *Toronto Star,* July 19.

Murphy, B.A. (1972). *A Quantitative Test of the Effectiveness of an Experimental Treatment Programme for Delinquent Opiate Addicts.* Ottawa: Department of the Solicitor General of Canada.

Murphy, Judge Emily F. ([1922] 1973). *The Black Candle.* Toronto: Coles.

Nelson, E.D. (1992). "Homosexuality: Sexual Stigma." In Vincent Sacco (ed.), *Deviance: Conformity and Control in Canadian Society.* 2nd. ed. Scarborough, Ont.: Prentice-Hall Canada.

New Encyclopedia Britannica. (1984). Macropaedia: Vol. 2. Chicago: Benton.

Odean, Kathleen. (1988). *High Steppers, Fallen Angels and Lollipops: Wall Street Slang.* New York: Holt, Rinehart and Winston.

Opotow, Susan. (1990). "Moral Exclusion and Injustice: An Introduction." *Journal of Social Issues* 46(1) :1–20.

Pfohl, Stephen. (1985). *Images of Deviance and Social Control: A Sociological History.* New York: McGraw-Hill.

Pinguet, Maurice. (1993). *Voluntary Death in Japan.* Cambridge, U.K.: Cambridge University Press.

Proietto, Rosa, and James N. Porter. (1996). "Socrates: A Sociological Understanding of the Production of an Outcast" *Economy and Society* 25(1):1–35.

Ressler, Robert K., Ann W. Burgess, and John E. Douglas. (1988). *Sexual Homicide: Patterns and Motives.* New York: Lexington.

Rice, Berkeley. (1989). *Trafficking: The Boom and Bust of the Air America Cocaine Ring.* New York: Scribners.

Ross, Rupert. (1992). *Dancing with a Ghost: Exploring Indian Reality.* Markham, Ont.: Octopus.

Sabbag, Robert. (1990 [1976]). *Snowblind: A Brief Career in the Cocaine Trade.* New York: Random House.

Sagarin, Edward. (1969). *Odd Man In: Societies of Deviants in America.* Chicago: Quadrangle.

———. (1977). "Sex and Deviance." In Edward Sagarin and Fred Monanino (eds.), *Deviants: Voluntary Actors in a Hostile World.* Glenview, Ill.: Scott Foresman.

Salamon, E.D. (1988). "Homosexuality: Sexual Stigma." In Vincent Sacco (ed.), *Deviance, Conformity and Control.* Scarborough, Ont.: Prentice-Hall Canada.

Scher, Len. (1992). *The Un-Canadians: True Stories of the Blacklist Era.* Toronto: Lester.

Schur, Edwin M. (1984). *Labelling Women Deviant: Gender, Stigma, and Social Control.* Philadelphia: Temple University Press.

Scott, Robert A. (1969). *The Making of Blind Men.* New York: Russell Sage.

Sellin, Thorsten, and Marvin E. Wolfgang. (1964). *The Measurement of Delinquency.* New York: John Wiley.

Shkilnyk, Anastasia. (1985). *A Poison Stronger than Love: The Destruction of an Ojibwa Community.* New Haven, Conn.: Yale University Press.

Short, Jr., James F. (1975). "The Natural History of an Applied Theory: Differential Opportunity and Mobilization for Youth." In N.J. Demerath III, et al. (eds.), *Social Policy and Sociology.* New York: Academic Press.

Simmons, Jerry L. (1969). *Deviants.* Berkeley: Glendessary Press.

Simon, David R., and D. Stanley Eitzen. (1993). *Elite Deviance.* 4th ed. Boston: Allyn and Bacon.

Simpson, Brian A.W. (1984). *Cannibalism and the Common Law.* Chicago: University of Chicago Press.

Smyth, Mitchell. (1988). "Whatever Happened to ... Anita Bryant?" *Toronto Star,* Aug. 14, D4.

Snider, Lauren. (1992). "Commercial Crime." In Vincent Sacco (ed.), *Deviance: Conformity and Control in Canadian Society,* 2nd ed. Scarborough: Prentice-Hall, Canada.

Stone, Sharon (ed.). (1990). *Lesbians in Canada.* Toronto: Between the Lines.

Taylor, Ian, Paul Walton, and Jock Young. (1973). *The New Criminology: For a Social Theory of Deviance.* New York: Harper Colophon.

Toronto Star. (1989). "Headscarves of Muslim Schoolgirls Unveil a Culture Crisis in France," October 29.

Trebach, Arnold S. (1982). *The Heroin Solution.* New Haven, Conn.: Yale University Press.

Troyer, Ronald J., and Gerald E. Markle. (1983). *Cigarettes: The Battle over Smoking.* New Brunswick, N.J.: Rutgers University Press.

Visser, Margaret. (1991). *The Rituals of Dinner: The Origins, Evolution, Eccentricities and Meaning of Table Manners.* Toronto: HarperCollins.

Weisman, Richard. (1993). "Reflections on the Oak Ridge Experiment with Psychiatric Offenders, 1965–1968." Paper presented at the Canadian Sociology and Anthropology Association annual meeting, Carleton University, June (Copies available from Professor Weisman, Glendon College, York University.).

West, D.J. (1987). *Sexual Crimes and Confrontations: A Study of Victims and Offenders.* Cambridge Studies in Criminology. Aldershot; Brookfield, U.S.A.: Gower.

Weston, Greg. (1992). *The Stopwatch Gang.* Toronto: Macmillan Canada.

Winsor, Hugh. (1989). "Tories Urged to Recognize Riel as a Father of Confederation." *Globe and Mail,* August 28.

Yarrow, Marian Radke, Charlotte Green Schwartz, Harriet S. Murphy, and Leila Calhoun Deasy. (1987). "The Psychological Meaning of Mental Illness in the Family." In Earl Rubington and Martin S. Weinberg (eds.), *Deviance: The Interactionist Perspective.* 5th ed. New York: Macmillan. Originally published in 1955 in the *Journal of Social Issues* 11, (4):12–24.

UNDERSTANDING AND

TESTING THEORIES

OF DEVIANCE

In addressing the central issue of how we know what we know, this chapter raises a number of related questions. What kinds of evidence support our ideas about deviance? What is the right way to find (and use) evidence? How can we interpret the findings that are reported in academic journals?

MANY PATHS: MANY THEORIES?

From time to time, a popular book or enthusiastic researcher bursts on the scene with the claim that the one real cause of deviance has been found. Whether it is junk food, working mothers, the decline of religious observance, a disturbance of the genetic code, or even the contradictions of capitalism, the single explanation has appeal in that it holds out the possibility of a quick fix. Unfortunately, no single cause can effectively explain all kinds of deviant action, and no single theory has managed to stake out a monopoly on truth.

If deviance is a destination, many paths lead to it, some more heavily used than others (Nettler 1982:6). Consider, for example, the many paths that might lead to someone's committing arson. One path is marked by psychopathy (some people are pyromaniacs). Another points to fraud (burning property in order to claim insurance money). Yet another path to arson is by way of organized crime, in which it occurs as part of extortion rackets or terrorism. Fires may be set by jilted lovers or mischievous children. Taking yet another path the "Sons of Freedom" Doukhobors for many years had a reputation for burning not only their own property but also that of Orthodox Doukhobors in order to "help" free them from materialism. Some paths to deviance, such as psychopathy, are mainly motivated by the deviant, while others (e.g., scapegoating) are more strongly associated with the motivation of those in authority. For most paths, though, motivations are mixed.

THEORY AS EXPLANATION

Explanations have been described as "the stories we tell each other in attempts to produce some order in our lives" (Nettler 1970:175). Explanations outline the paths that lead to particular outcomes, whether arson, theft, sexual deviancy, or any other reality we wish to understand. They allow us to feel we know why something happened, and whether, or under what conditions, it is likely to occur again. Suppose that a professor notices that a large number of students in her class are half asleep. She may choose from a wide variety of "explanations" the one that appears to make the most sense. She may decide that the students should go to bed sooner, or that the air in the classroom is too stuffy. If she is honest enough to take a "reflexive" approach, she may conclude her lecturing style is soporific. Such ad hoc theories suffice for everyday life, but they are often either self-serving or incorrect. They are not developed into consistent models of reality or tested by appropriate and controlled observations. In the study of deviance within the social science disciplines, this same explanatory process occurs, but, when properly done, it is more systematic, comprehensive, and self-conscious (Chafetz 1978).

Theories can be classified in many ways. For our purposes, one of the most important distinctions is among theory that is empathetic, scientific, or ideological, or some combination of the three (Nettler 1970).

EMPATHETIC EXPLANATIONS

Empathetic explanations employ conventions that enable us to identify with the individual whose behaviour is being explained (Nettler 1970:v). As the philosopher Alfred Schütz noted, "I am able to understand other people's acts only if I can imagine that I myself would perform analogous acts if I were in the same situation" (Schütz 1960). When we hear of a woman who has killed her husband, we may be quite satisfied with the simple and direct explanation that he was sexually or physically abusive to her and her children. But the empathetic explanation, because it includes much of the subjective as well as objective "reality" of the event being explained, often seems more complete, and thus more satisfying, than a totally objective explanation.

There are, however, limits to empathy. Most of us cannot imagine any circumstances in which we would rape a child, rob a helpless old woman, or wear a blanket pin through an ear, yet these things occur. In addition, we may think that we understand the feelings of a homeless person, for example, only to have our assessment contradicted upon closer acquaintance.

In deviance studies, the subjective, empathetic approach is the one most keyed to understanding the actor's point of view and most likely to use it to explain the actor's decisions. This approach is found mainly in the so-called interpretive or interactive theories (the subject of Chapter 10), but it is also part of other approaches such as the Chicago School and functionalism (discussed in Chapters 7 and 8). It is opposed by theories that emphasize biology or social structure, which either do not take the actor's viewpoint into account or see the viewpoint as merely an epiphenomenon, produced by natural processes or by socially based interests or opportunities.

SCIENTIFIC EXPLANATIONS

Scientific explanations make use of the scientific method, or adaptations of it. This method, first developed in the study of the physical world, provides techniques for developing models of how the world works as well as hypotheses about the connectedness of things. The scientific method works best with inorganic and nonsocial realities, and theorists who apply it to human behaviour draw heavy criticism. Sociologists often enclose the word "scientific" in quotation marks to indicate that, in much of our work, science is an ideal, not an achieved reality.

Social data differ from physical data, and the difference is important. For example, we can understand objectively and dispassionately why a person with a chest cold sometimes coughs, but to understand coughing when it is used as an act of social communication is a different matter. Similarly, we can understand why people who are addicted to nicotine, smoke; more difficult to explain is why they take up smoking in the first place, and why they later try to quit.

The scientific method provides for controlling observations so that the knowledge gained will be tested and cumulative. In deviance studies, the scientific approach has been most fully developed in the area of biological explanations. Early biological positivists abused the approach and produced many invalid studies. The scientific method has been applied much more successfully in later biological and psychological research (see Chapter 6). As well, it has been used a great deal by functionalists and, even more extensively, by control theorists (see Chapters 8 and 11).

IDEOLOGICAL EXPLANATIONS

Ideological explanations are based on systems of ideas that are held as doctrine. They are not just tentatively proposed, in the manner of scientific theories, but rather are often a matter of passionate belief (Nettler 1970:178). According to this approach, if the data do not fit, something is wrong with either the data themselves or with the way in which they were collected.

A great many ideologies have assumed the status of "isms" (e.g., environmentalism, pacifism, socialism). When politics and religion are used as ideology, they explain all phenomena on the basis of a limited number of beliefs, and are almost impervious to new information or alternative interpretations.

In deviance studies, ideological explanations are found most openly in the work of radical conflict theorists (see Chapters 12 and 13). At the same time, they may be implicit (present, but not so obviously present) in work that claims to be purely scientific. Chicago School, social control, social learning, and functional theorists have tended to be tacitly conservative in their implications, while interpretive and group-conflict theorists admit to being mainly liberal. It is important to recognize that ideological positions that are not acknowledged may affect the attainment of knowledge as much as—if not more than—acknowledged doctrines.

When scientific explanations are held as doctrine, they may also take on "ism" status. An example of this is social Darwinism, whose advocates believed that inequality in the social order was a function of nature. Darwinists argued, for instance, that the wealthy could attribute their status to the fact that they were more "fit" than the poor; similarly, criminals were regarded as evolutionary throwbacks, less than fully human. Data that did not fit this theory were changed, misinterpreted, or ignored. Another form of science as ideology is *positivism*. Positivism as a doctrine in social science corresponds to the belief that truth or knowledge can be based only on scientifically verifiable evidence. The extreme positivist is likely to take the stand that if something cannot be measured and tested, it either does not exist or is irrelevant. Emile Durkheim's work has sometimes been called "sociological positivism" because it denies the significance of biological and psychological variables in its explanation of social behaviour.

THE FORMULATION OF THEORY

Consider the following cases:

1. J., age 16, lives in a rent-subsidized housing project, where there are few recreational facilities or opportunities for unskilled, legal employment. J. is arrested for attempting to sell cocaine to an undercover police officer. *(Social disorganization)*

2. M., a sole-support mother with three preschool children, experiences voices that tell her to do dangerous things. Several of her relatives have been diagnosed as schizophrenic. *(Stress; mental illness)*

3. H., a middle-aged male, comes from a culture in which playfully pinching unescorted females is considered normal masculine behaviour. In downtown Vancouver, he is arrested for sexual assault. Unable to speak English well enough to explain himself, or even to understand what the fuss is about, he is sent to a psychiatric hospital. When the hospital acquires a doctor who speaks his language and knows his culture, he is released. *(Culture conflict)*

4. A., a high-school student, feels tired. She feels that she cannot live up to the expectations of family, friends, school, and work. Just living requires great effort. *(Depression; illness)*

5. Joe, James, and Jack are suspects in the case of a violent act. Joe looks fat and slow. James is skinny, has a high-pitched voice, and wears glasses. Jack is wiry and athletic. Which of these suspects will be charged, found guilty, and sent to training school? *(Somatotypes; labelling)*

6. T.'s father is a successful, hard-driven businessman who admires only material success. T. escapes into drugs and alcohol. *(Stress)*

7. S. dreads the day her friends find out that her family takes holidays at a nearby nudist camp. *(Role conflict; labelling)*

8. G., a conscientious government-employed meat inspector, looks at the rule book and knows that if he follows all the procedures required by law, he will be fired for being too slow. He skips some of the less important rules, is caught, and faces criminal charges. *(Role strain)*

Each of the above cases suggests its own explanation—you can "understand" these scenarios (and probably think of alternative ones). In each case, a condition or circumstance precedes the deviance, without which the deviance probably would not have occurred. (Preceding conditions that our theories have not highlighted will not be considered for investigation.) In Case 1, J.'s delinquent behaviour is preceded by environmental conditions that may have caused or "potentiated" the delinquency. In Case 6, T.'s escape into drugs and alcohol is preceded by his father's rigid demands.

But have we missed the real variables (the actual causes) entirely? In each of the above examples, a single causal variable was proposed. In real life, however, many events may precede (and seem to have some role in producing) the behaviour we are studying. Theory helps us to select which events are worth investigating.

Theories are generally developed through alternating processes of inductive and deductive approaches. In an *inductive approach,* we look at many specific cases and then make generalizations about them. For example, we might make a list of all 15-year-olds who were suspended from school in a particular school district and year, or take a sample of such students. We could then ask them a great many questions about their friends, families, and schools. From this data, certain patterns of family life, academic performance, and relations with other students and staff might emerge (Reynolds 1979:140). Some of these patterns might be quite accidental, and would not be found again if the study were repeated on a different sample of students. Only through further research could we separate those patterns that generally operate in situations of this kind from those that are peculiar to a particular school at a particular time.

In *deductive approaches,* we derive specific expectations from general ones that have been suggested either by previous research or by the logical relations of an existing theory. For example, the study of suspended students might have produced some theories that are worth testing. Durkheim ([1897] 1951) deduced from his general theory of society that extremes of integration and regulation would produce higher suicide rates. When his predictions were confirmed by a wide variety of statistical evidence, his theory about the nature of the social order gained credibility.

Academics from many humanistic and scientific disciplines have weighed and tested explanations against logic and empirical evidence. A great deal of information about the nature of deviance, and about its connections with other forms of behaviour and social action, has been accumulated. Whether this represents progress is debatable, since the perfection of one kind of theory may be irrelevant to those who favour a different theory (Kuhn 1970). Nonetheless, within each branch of theory, we can plot a trajectory of work that shows an increase in both logical consistency and amounts of supporting evidence, leading us to believe that we have increased our understanding of "the facts" about deviance.

THE COMPONENTS OF THEORY

Whether an explanation is empathetic, ideological, or scientific, it will require the use of concepts, variables, and statements that hypothesize connections among them.

CONCEPTS

Theory-building involves developing sensitizing concepts. A concept identifies a class of experiences that have something in common. A sensitizing concept points to some aspect of reality and allows us to symbolize it in a way that other people can share. The study of deviance has seen the development of many sensitizing concepts. Such concepts highlight aspects of reality that may be important factors in the genesis or shaping of deviance. Using one set of concepts rather than another has a clear impact on what we are able to "see." Examples of concepts used in deviance theory are relative deprivation, marginal man/woman, disidentifier, secondary deviance, and white-collar crime.

Relative Deprivation

This concept refers to the state of discontent felt by people who have enough to get by on (they are not absolutely deprived), but less than they deserve when compared with others. Even quite wealthy individuals may experience relative deprivation if they compare themselves to even wealthier people who are (or seem to be) less deserving. For example, a student who receives a high mark on a test will be pleased until she discovers that less able and hardworking people achieved even higher marks. Relative deprivation has often been cited as a reason for actions such as looting during riots or cheating on tests.

Marginal Man/Woman

The marginal man or woman is a person whose life is rooted in two or more cultures at the same time. Such people experience difficulty in balancing the different demands of each culture, but have the advantage of being able to see beyond the boundaries of each. The deviant is often a marginal person who functions in a deviant subculture while at the same time appearing to live a full life in the main-stream of society. The homosexual, for example, may participate in the gay subculture while maintaining a "straight" identity in work and marriage. The petty thief may run a small business as a respectable "front" to hide less respectable activities. The "one percenter" (criminal) motorcycle gang member may wear a three-piece suit in court or when dealing with respectable business partners.

Disidentifier

Erving Goffman (1963) developed the disidentifier concept to designate the symbols that people use to contradict or counteract the impression that they unintentionally (or unwillingly) convey. For example, a midget may use a cane, or wear gloves and a hat, to avoid giving the impression of being childlike. When students are looking for jobs, they often dress in ways that "disidentify" them from the image of irre-sponsible youth.

Secondary Deviance

This concept was introduced by Edwin Lemert (1951) to call attention to the impor-tance of societal reaction in the creation and shaping of deviance. It refers to deviance that occurs because the deviant has acquired a deviant label and finds it easier to conform to the label than to try to change it.

White-Collar Crime

Edwin Sutherland's (1949) concept calls attention to crimes that are not "street crimes," but that have effects on society that are just as serious. White-collar crime is "crime committed by a person of high social status in the course of his occupation" (Sutherland 1949:9). Crimes committed by people who have an established base of respectability are often dealt with, and understood, differently than the crimes of street criminals or the "bad habits" of the poor. The corporate executive may cause death by making cost-saving decisions that compromise safety on the job or, perhaps, the safety of products. This type of killing differs from that carried out by the criminal "hit man," but it is more common.

VARIABLES

A variable is a concept that can be counted or measured. This is particularly important in scientific research, although it is also implicit in much anti-positivist work. Age, for example, is a concept that can be treated as a quantitative variable. Whether it is expressed in years or graded age categories, age is related to most kinds of deviance. We have very few elderly vandals, and very few 12-year-old embezzlers. Income is also usually treated as a quantitative variable. It may range from below zero (indebtedness) to infinite size, or it may simply be recorded as larger or smaller than some standard. Income is related to deviance, but not in a simple way. The poorest people are not the most likely to steal or riot.

In contrast to the quantitative variables, beauty is usually treated as qualitative. People can be ranked as more or less beautiful, but the idea of measuring someone's looks on a scale of 1 to 10 is (mostly) taken humorously. Some evidence, however, suggests that less attractive people are more likely to be accused of wrongdoing, and more likely to be convicted if they are accused.

Some variables, which are called dummy variables when used in equations, are measured only by their presence or absence. An example of a dummy variable would be a measure of whether or not a rioter has had previous contact with the police. It is a dummy variable if we simply record "yes" or "no" and ignore such issues as how often and why. Gender is a variable with only two generally recognized alternatives: male and female. In genetic research, of course, this variable may take on a variety of alternatives based on chromosomal evidence.

HYPOTHESES

In addition to taking on different values, variables are understood to differ in relationship to other variables. Normally, we conceive of one variable (or set of variables) as the causal or *independent variable,* while the outcome we seek to explain is the *dependent variable.* Other variables in the causal chain are known as intervening variables (see Box 2.1).

The relationship between variables is usually expressed as a tentative statement, or hypothesis. A hypothesis links two variables by asserting that they will be found to be regularly related to each other under specified conditions. If the hypothesis is correct, when one variable changes the other will change in the predicted way.

The selection of which hypotheses to test is normally guided by a theory that tells us which relationships are likely to be worth investigating. A biological theory of delinquency might stress variables such as genetic inheritance or blood-sugar levels, while a sociological theory of delinquency would likely emphasize aspects of the social environment (e.g., degree of adult supervision or availability of recreational facilities).

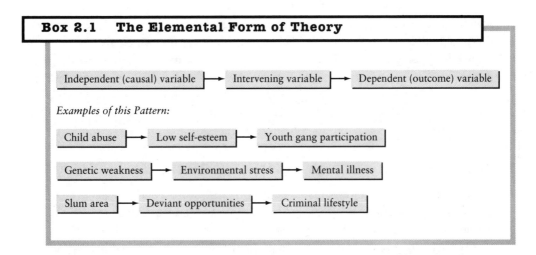

Box 2.1   The Elemental Form of Theory

Independent (causal) variable → Intervening variable → Dependent (outcome) variable

Examples of this Pattern:

Child abuse → Low self-esteem → Youth gang participation

Genetic weakness → Environmental stress → Mental illness

Slum area → Deviant opportunities → Criminal lifestyle

METHODS AND MEASURES FOR TESTING THEORY AND ITS COMPONENTS

Unlike journalists or independent authors, social scientists must test and evaluate, using established rules of research, the extent to which their findings either support or challenge competing theoretical explanations. Each discipline continually eliminates ideas that are not supported by evidence, and by doing so refines methods that produced research errors or ambiguities. This evolution should not be regarded as a straight line from ignorance to knowledge. A particular theory may become highly refined, only to be displaced by a different theory in much rougher form.

TESTS OF HYPOTHESES

Hypotheses state that particular relationships between variables will be found consistently, as long as conditions are the same. We can test these predictions (and the theories from which they may be drawn) by seeing whether or not observable evidence supports them. Evidence that is consistent with the hypotheses allows us to continue to hold the theory and test it further; evidence that is inconsistent with the theory forces us to reconsider it.

In the history of deviance studies, many hypotheses have been tested and discarded; even more have been tested and revised. The idea that beautiful theories are invariably killed by ugly facts is highly misleading. A theory can survive many incompatible results (assuming no alternative theory is proposed). For example, the hypothesis that the size of the brain is correlated with criminal behaviour has been thoroughly tested and rejected. However, the theory from which that hypothesis came—that genetic inheritance or body type may have something to do with deviance—is still very much alive. Thus, a theory is never entirely discredited, no matter how many facts refute it; by the same token, a theory is never entirely proven, no matter how many times the facts support it. But many theories have been forced into a new form by "ugly facts" (Chafetz 1978:3).

THE CLASSICAL EXPERIMENTAL DESIGN

The classical experimental design has evolved as the ideal type of research in science, the norm against which most research designs are evaluated. Very few, if any, studies in the field of deviance fully meet all of the criteria of this design, with the result that we are rarely presented clear, unequivocal results. Nonetheless, it remains our best hope for approaching understanding of the evidence.

Four steps or stages are typically followed in experimental research. Step 1 involves the selection of two groups that are virtually equivalent, particularly with respect to the dependent variable. For example, the two groups might be composed of youths who skip school more than once a week. One of these groups is designated the experimental group, while the other is called the control group. At the beginning of the experiment (referred to as "time one"), a measure of the dependent variable

Box 2.2 Developing a Hypothesis: Durkheim's Theory of Suicide

In Durkheim's (1951 [1897]) famous study of suicide, the independent variables were the integration and regulation of group membership; the dependent variable was the rate of suicide. As conceived by Durkheim, *integration* refers to the degree to which a person belongs in a group. In well-integrated groups, people tend to have similar values and to care about each other. If a group has too little integration, however, the individual is permitted to become "egoistic." The person who has weak or nonexistent attachment to the group is detached and thus not restrained from committing egoistic suicide. On the other hand, in groups characterized by too much integration, individual members may develop a selfless "altruism" that divests them of any sense of autonomous, personal value. Soldiers who sacrifice their lives on behalf of their "buddies" are committing a form of *altruistic suicide* in which the group takes precedence over individuality.

Regulation refers to the degree to which a person's life is subject to the rules of the group. If the group is unregulated, the individual is in a state of "anomie" or "normlessness." *Anomic suicide* is permitted by the breakdown of common rules for behaviour. In contrast, if there is too much regulation, the individual may give up trying to live an independent life and choose death. *Fatalistic suicide* tends to occur in prisons and other highly regulated settings.

According to Durkheim, conditions in modern Western society favoured egoistic and anomic suicide, while societies characterized by higher integration and regulation, such as Japan, were more likely to record fatalistic and altruistic suicides. Despite the crudeness of the information about suicide that was available in the late 1800s, he correctly predicted, across a wide variety of situations, the relationship between suicide and group membership. For example, he found (as predicted by his theory) that people who belonged to the more integrated, regulated religions (e.g., Catholicism and Judaism) had lower rates of suicide than did the less integrated and more independent Protestants. In addition, the suicide rate was higher among single people than among married people. Durkheim's generalizations also held true within groups. Thus, while Jews had lower suicide rates than did Protestant Christians (regulatory effect), highly educated, professional, and single Jews had higher rates of suicide than did their less independent co-religionists. Clearly, suicide is not just a matter of great unhappiness or despair: the social system also plays a role in people's decisions about their lives.

would show them to be virtually identical. (Sometimes, as in Durkheim's *Suicide,* no controlled experiment is performed, but the researcher takes advantage of the variations that occur naturally among people and groups in order to find appropriate experimental and control groups.)

In Step 2, the experimental group is subjected to the independent variable. The control group is treated in the same way except that it is not exposed to the independent variable. The experimental delinquent group, for example, might be exposed to a series of motivational films, while the control group might watch nature movies. In one American study, the experimental group put Black Panther (radical, anti-police) bumper stickers on their cars; the traffic violation tickets received by this group far exceeded those received by the control group, which did not use the stickers (Heussenstamm 1971).

Both groups are measured on the dependent variable in Step 3. At this stage (known as "time two"), the two groups will likely no longer be identical. In the case of the school truants, the two groups will reflect different rates of school absence. In Step 4, the difference between time one and time two (vis-à-vis the measure of the dependent variable) is computed for the control group and the experimental group. If there is any significant (greater than chance) difference between them, this can be attributed to the effect of the independent variable. Thus, if school absence declines in the experimental group more than in the control group, the motivational film (the independent variable) will be credited.

CORRELATION COEFFICIENTS

We can hypothesize that certain relationships will be found between groups that vary along specific dimensions, such as wealth or religion, and then observe whether, and how far, this prediction holds. Such a test often takes the form of a statistical measure called a correlation coefficient, which tells us to what extent, and in what ways, two variables are related to one another (Chafetz 1978:15). A direct or positive relationship is one in which both variables change in the same direction. If one increases, the other increases; if one decreases, the other decreases. For example, the number of privately owned handguns in an area is positively related to the number of homicides that occur each year. In the same way, illiteracy and street crime, or poverty and child neglect, are positively related. A negative or inverse relationship, in contrast, occurs when increases in one variable are regularly associated with decreases in the other. For example, we might expect that, as the level of supervision in a school increases, the amount of attempted cheating will decrease.

Correlations range from a potential +1.00 (perfect positive correlation) to –1.00 (perfect negative correlation). A correlation of +.85 is a high positive correlation indicating that two variables consistently co-vary, such that when one increases the other also increases (although not necessarily to the same degree). This correlation might be found, for instance, between a student's declared liking for a school subject and the grades he or she receives in that subject. A correlation of –.80 indicates that the variables are strongly, but inversely, related. Such a correlation might be found between hard drug use and the size of the police force and be used as support for increasing the size of the force. A correlation of +.32 indicates a much less predictable relationship, while a correlation of 0 would mean that knowing the changing measure of one variable would not be enough to enable the researcher to predict change in the other at all.

A strong correlation does not always mean a causal relationship exists between the two variables. It says only that they change together, which may be caused by a third variable that we have not considered. The number of storks and the number of babies may be correlated, but the causal variable is rural residence rather than the stork delivery service (Cole 1980:48). Nonetheless, correlations are often considered a part of the evidence of causal relationship.

CAUSALITY

Causality is a complex subject in both philosophy and science. Causality is considered established (or strongly supported) when three conditions are met. First, we must be able to show that, as long as other variables are held constant, when one variable changes, the other(s) change in predictable ways. For example, we might find a strong positive relationship between criminal records of adults and the delinquency of their children.

Second, we must show that the variable deemed to be the independent (causal) variable occurs, or changes, *before* the variable that is deemed to be caused undergoes change. Criminality of parents, for example, usually precedes criminality of children, and might therefore be more logically given causal status. Of course, just because something follows something else in time does not necessarily mean that the relationship is causal. If we were to take every variable in a study and test its relationship to every other variable (a dubious practice made possible by modern computers), many relationships would appear, some of which would be absolutely meaningless. For example, a single study might reveal a correlation of +.66 between living on a street that begins with the letter "A" and cheating on income tax returns. If this correlation has not been predicted on the basis of a guiding theory, it is probably meaningless. Thus, researchers place more trust in data when it supports ideas that have been drawn from theory.

Third, we must be able to rule out other variables that emerge as candidates for causal status. The finding of a high correlation between the number of fire engines sent to a fire and the damage to a burning building would best be interpreted by a third variable: seriousness of the fire (Cole 1980:48). Exclusion of rival causal factors is not always as obvious as this. If we find that there is a high inverse correlation between hours spent in video-game arcades and school grades received, we might want to interpret this as proof of the theory that video games turn the brain to mush. But there may be other variables that account for both game-playing and low school marks. Perhaps the kind of parents who permit their children to spend long hours in video arcades are also the kind of parents who fail to reward or encourage academic success, quite apart from any effects of the games themselves. If so, the causal variable is parenting, not excessive game-playing.

REPRESENTATIVENESS

A major goal of research is to find data that can be generalized beyond one study. Because we cannot study all criminals, nudists, or whomever, we examine representative members of these categories and then generalize from our studies to the groups in general. In the same way, the doctor who checks a patient's blood pressure at each annual visit assumes that the result is representative of the patient's customary blood pressure. Of course, if the patient is terrified of doctors, this measure may not be representative at all.

Compounding the problem of representativeness in deviance research is the fact that much deviance is hidden from view. For example, most studies of drug addicts have been based on small samples of individuals who are undergoing some form of rehabilitation; such persons may not, however, be representative of all other addicts (i.e., those in nontherapeutic settings). The "untreated" users may well have a less dependent relationship to the drugs they use than is found among those in treatment (Blackwell and Erickson 1988:63–68). In addition, our perceptions of deviance and crime are often distorted by the way we learn about them. Media accounts tend to be biased toward "newsworthiness."

The Crime Funnel

The problem of representativeness can be illustrated by the crime funnel (see Figure 2.1), which expresses the relationship between the total number of crimes that occur and the number of crimes that are represented by people who are at various stages in the criminal justice process.

Figure 2.1   The Crime Funnel

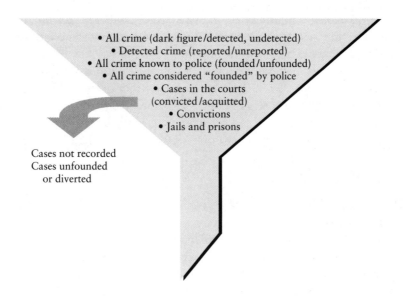

Source: Reproduced by authority of the Minister of Industry, 1997, Statistics Canada, *Juristat Service Bulletin,* 10, July 1990.

The top of the funnel represents all crime, whether detected or undetected. At this point, a great deal of information about crime is lost. We do not always know when we have been cheated or robbed. A broken window may be evidence of a windstorm, a neighbourhood baseball game, vandalism, or an attempted break-in. A missing wallet may be evidence of carelessness or a pickpocket.

The middle part of the funnel depicts all crimes reported to the police. In 1941, German criminologist Kurt Meyer suggested that for every reported homicide between 3 and 5 went unreported, and that behind every reported theft between 16 and 20 went unreported (Meyer 1941). Estimates by British criminologist Sir Leon Radzinowicz indicate an even wider gap (Radzinowicz and King 1977). If the police believe that an act took place and that it was a crime, it is considered "founded" (confirmed). Aggravated assaults are more likely to be considered founded than are reports of sexual assault, partly because the evidence is less susceptible to subjective interpretation. If the offence seems trivial, or if the "victim" does not cooperate with the police or is perceived as being undeserving of help, the offence may be treated as unfounded.

At the bottom of the crime funnel are those individuals who are incarcerated in a regular prison instead of diverted into community service, psychiatric care, or back to their families. Those who remain in the system may have a great deal in common with each other, but not so much in common with those criminals who are not caught or processed by the system. At the bottom of the funnel we find a considerable amount of information about a few unrepresentative cases (i.e., persons who were accused, convicted, and incarcerated), while at the top we find virtually no information about a great many cases (Hood and Sparks 1970:3–37).

RELIABILITY

Reliable measures are consistent measures that presumably reflect a regularity that occurs in nature. We may find in the course of one study that second-born children are more likely to be risk-takers than are first-born children. (Risk-taking tends to be associated with many forms of deviance.) To find out whether this is a reliable finding, we have to do further research under the same methodological conditions as existed in the earlier study. Achieving the same results will give us test-retest reliability. When there is a failure of replication (i.e., test-retest reliability is low), we place less faith in the original findings.

Durkheim's research permitted him to make generalizations about the relationship between group membership and suicide. Since he followed the rules of the scientific method as much as possible, other researchers have been able to replicate his work and show the reliability of his findings in additional settings. This replication adds support to the belief that Durkheim's hypothesis was, and continues to be, a reliable one.

VALIDITY

Validity raises the question "Are we measuring what we think we are measuring?" Measures can be accurate and consistent, but irrelevant. For example, activations of residential burglar alarms produce what are thought to be highly accurate statistics, and these numbers are sometimes used as indicators of crime attempts; in some jurisdictions, however, more than 90 percent of activated alarms are false alarms. Thus alarm records are statistically accurate, but are not valid measures of break-in attempts. Similarly, in the middle ages, warts and other bodily marks were seen as indications that people who had them were involved with the devil. The validity of this indicator was not effectively challenged until the 1700s.

Sometimes there is a wide discrepancy between the indicators typically used and the thing being measured. For example, decisions about granting parole often rest on measures of how well the convict has adapted to institutional life. Parole boards consider whether the applicant is respectful of authorities and expresses a convincing amount of remorse for his or her past offences. These characteristics are, in fact, very poor indicators of that person's ability to stay out of trouble *outside* the prison. Similarly, many programs that aim to rehabilitate juvenile delinquents regard such qualities as neatness and orderliness as indications of effective reform. There is, however, little evidence to suggest that the teen who has acquired bed-making skills will no longer seek out drugs at the earliest opportunity.

Validity is sometimes lost when our attempt to study people causes them to behave differently than they would if we were not watching them. It is difficult to test people without giving them some idea of our expectations or hopes, and thus influencing their responses. A videotape of a crowd taken by police cameras differs from videotapes of the same crowd taken by network TV stations. To some extent, we all gear our "performance" to our "audience." Like reliability, validity is partly a measure of trustworthiness.

Box 2.3   Validity of Information

In his research on an organized crime family, Ianni (1972:188–189) developed a scale of validity for the data he gathered. From highest to lowest, the assumed trustworthiness was ranked as follows:

1. data gathered by Ianni's team through personal observation;
2. data gathered through the personal observations of participants, who, though not members of Ianni's team, were trusted on the basis of their past accuracy;
3. interview information that could be checked against documented sources (e.g., records of arrest or business ownership);
4. data corroborated by more than one informant; and
5. data from only one source.

Source: Francis A. Ianni, "The Lupollo Family." In Francis A. Ianni, *A Family Business: Kinship and Social Control in Organized Crime.* New York: Russell Sage. Reprinted with permission of Russell Sage Foundation.

THE VALIDITY OF STATISTICS

Numerical measures are used in science to allow us to be more precise and rigorous than is possible with descriptive adjectives (Hagan 1982:1). It is often assumed that numerical data are more valid than qualitative data, but precision is not always the same thing as validity. Changes in the statistical rates of crime are sometimes due more to shifts in policing policies than to changes in the numbers of criminals or their activities. Prostitution arrests may increase immediately before a major tourist-attracting event, as the police act "to clean up the neighbourhood"; conversely, they may decline if police attention is directed elsewhere.

Furthermore, statistics can reflect attempts to deceive as well as to report real events. Insurance companies suspect that as many as 1 in 5 car thefts reported to police in Canada have in fact been arranged by the owners, as a form of insurance fraud (Picard 1990).

Social statistics have the following components:

1. *Real figure.* The real figure represents the actual number of people who engage in a particular kind of deviance, or the total number of deviant acts that occur in a specified time and place.

2. *Error component.* The error component is caused by over- or underreporting. Overreporting can be used to sell a book or to justify police budget increases. Underreporting may occur for several reasons. The victim may be too embarrassed to admit having been "taken in" by the criminal (e.g., consumer fraud) or, as is typical of rape victims, may be unwilling to undergo further suffering, this time at the hands of the criminal justice system. Finally, reporting may be seen as not worth the effort; for many people, the success rate for solving such crimes as minor theft is not high enough to warrant the bother of informing police.

3. *Random errors.* Random errors are generally accidental and self-cancelling: the honest but overworked cashier's errors may favour the customer as often as they favour the company. Random errors can creep into many parts of the counting process. Coders of interview data, for example, may make errors of judgment in classifying respondents' answers, and these, in turn, may produce errors in the final counts that are used to test theories.

4. *Systematic errors.* Systematic errors can be serious in that they do not cancel each other out and may create cumulative distortions in the data. If police focus on particular urban neighbourhoods in their investigations, crime statistics for these areas will be higher, thereby increasing the justification for more police

attention. The tendency to suspect people on the basis of such factors as race or occupation may similarly create systematic biases in the collection of data.

Social policies too may distort the recording of empirical realities. For example, in our society, all babies are recorded as either male or female shortly after birth. When anomalous cases occur (i.e., some babies are born with both male and female physical characteristics), surgery is performed to clarify the sex of the baby one way or the other; doctors and families do not demand that a third category be created for the child (Kessler 1990). Adults who find standard male/female gender choices too restrictive may simply invent their own, but they do so at great risk of being treated as deviants. Social policies also influence how many people are recorded as black, white, indigenous, or "other." The individual who has black, white, indigenous, and Asian forebears could be classified as belonging to any of these groups, depending on such factors as place of residence, colour of skin, economic position, or self-definition. Using race as a criterion for collecting statistics on crime and deviance thus poses problems.

Validity can be improved if we have multiple measures. For example, in establishing a valid assault rate estimate, we might consult official police records and hospital reports, and compare these sources with others, such as crime survey data (self-report and victim studies). When estimates based on several of these methods agree, we are inclined to accept their validity; when they disagree, we are alerted to possible sources of error.

OBSERVATION AND THE PROBLEM OF ACCURACY

A particularly acute problem in deviance studies is the failure to obtain an accurate description of the thing to be explained (the dependent variable). All too often it is assumed that "what is going on" is already known, and that all we need are explanations for why it is going on. Reality is mediated to us by our senses and by the messages that already exist in our minds. Consider, for example, how waiting for a bus can lead us to believe that more buses are travelling in the opposite direction, or how our suspicions concerning someone's motives may affect our interpretation of everything that person does.

The impressions we receive from "common knowledge" may lead us to explain realities that exist only in our minds. An example of this is the "mindless crowd" concept. For years collective behaviour specialists tried to devise theories about why people in crowds lost their individuality and became parts of a primitive, headless monster given to committing violent and senseless acts. But this perspective changed with the arrival of handheld cameras, participant-observation techniques, and less prejudiced observers, all of which allowed for a proper investigation of crowd behaviour. In most crowds, it was discovered, individuals do not behave uniformly, and the violent acts they commit are purposive, not mindless (McPhail 1991). When sociologists had a better description and conceptualization of the "what"—the dependent variable—their answers to why crowds do what they do became more accurate. We can see the same process occurring with respect to studies of urban youth gangs. Only when researchers freed themselves from the journalistic accounts of gang domination of drugs and violence, and the spread of gangs from major centres to smaller ones, could they see that most gangs are local, and most are only marginally criminal (Spergel 1995; Klein 1995).

DATA COLLECTION AS A SOCIAL ACTIVITY

An important consideration in all research is that the collection of data is itself a social activity. Social values intrude at every point in the research process. They affect decisions about which problems to investigate, which research tactics to use, and which research to publish. The social organization of research activity can introduce distortions that may have undesirable social consequences. For example, it is generally much easier to obtain research money to investigate alcoholism as a disease rather than as a learned behaviour. This has implications for the findings that will emerge from alcoholism research, and for the cures that will be proposed and funded on the basis of these findings.

MAJOR SOURCES OF DATA ON DEVIANCE

In order to make and test meaningful hypotheses, we need to gather information about deviance. The major sources of data on this subject are:

1. Self-report data (questionnaires, interviews, and victimization surveys)
2. Field observation
3. Secondary analysis of statistical data
4. Secondary analysis of biographical materials
5. Content analysis
6. Simulations
7. Journalistic accounts.

Box 2.4   Self-Report Survey Questions

Please indicate (as accurately as you can) how often in the past six months you did each of the following:

	Never	1 time	2 times	3 times	4 times	5 or more times
Told a lie in order to get something you wanted	___	___	___	___	___	___
Drunk enough alcohol to become drunk	___	___	___	___	___	___
Sold an illegal drug	___	___	___	___	___	___
Told a racist or sexist joke	___	___	___	___	___	___
Dyed your hair an unnatural colour	___	___	___	___	___	___
Used a weapon to threaten another person	___	___	___	___	___	___

SELF-REPORT DATA

Surveys and interviews have been used mainly to ask people what kinds of deviance they have participated in, are aware of, or have been victimized by. This material is called self-report data (SRD).

Questionnaires

A common form of SRD is the survey questionnaire, which consists of a series of questions to be answered by respondents, who are usually assured of complete anonymity. The questionnaire may be mailed to respondents, administered in a group situation such as a high-school classroom or prison cafeteria, or circulated at work or school. While this is convenient for both parties, it has the drawback of removing the subject from the setting in which deviance occurs.

The 1950s saw a steady production of data based on self-report questionnaires on delinquency, which were administered to juveniles and young adults. Most of these early surveys dealt with minor delinquency. For example, Ivan Nye's (1958) survey asked respondents if they had ever openly defied their parents; skipped school without a legitimate excuse; bought or drunk beer, wine, or liquor; or purposely damaged/destroyed public or private property. In this and other studies, middle-class teens admitted to far more delinquent behaviour than was ever recorded in the official statistics or recognized by the public (Porterfield 1946; Wallerstein and Wyle 1947; Short and Nye 1957; Nye 1958). Middle-class deviance was shown to be as frequent and as serious as that of the supposedly more dangerous lower classes. Using SRD from various communities and schools, Vaz (1965, 1969) and Tribble (1972) challenged the view that upper- and middle-class boys committed fewer serious delinquencies than did their lower-class counterparts, and, by extension, the theory that delinquency was caused by poverty or other aspects of "underclass" life.

Early delinquency studies were often criticized for: their sampling (they used available samples of high-school students, rather than random samples from the population as a whole); for their trivial nature (they rarely looked at the most serious forms of delinquency, and they had no provision for reporting how often an offence occurred); for their lack of reliability testing (they were rarely repeated in order to ascertain test-retest reliability); and for their failure to check for dishonest reporting or distorted recall. While some studies used polygraph (lie detector) results and found that the SRD were reasonably accurate (Clark and Tifft 1966; Hardt and Peterson-Hardt 1977), other observers saw a tendency for respondents to downplay, or not report, their most serious offences (Gold 1966).

By the late 1960s, however, many of these criticisms were met by better designs. The National Survey of Youth (NSY)—begun in 1967 by the Institute for Social Research at the University of Michigan—used probability samples of 847 boys and girls between 13 and 16 years of age. Among the behaviours addressed in this study were serious offences such as assault, violent gang activities, taking a car, and carrying a weapon. Every person in the sample admitted to at least one chargeable offence over a three-year period; a minority admitted to more than one (Williams and Gold 1972:213). Boys reported more involvement in delinquency than did girls, while older youth reported having committed more serious offences than did younger youth. As in earlier studies, it was found that social status was not an important difference between offenders and nonoffenders, and that the self-reporting strategy uncovered far more delinquency than was reflected in official statistics (Williams and Gold 1972; Hagan 1982:146).

Today, self-report studies are used to investigate vandalism, drug use, prostitution, and other forms of socially undesirable behaviour (Coleman and Moynihan 1996). They are also used to investigate the range of behaviour that people regard as "normal" or "normative." Studies on prostitution and on student drug use have been especially prevalent since the 1980s (Lowman 1992; Adlaf, Smart, and Walsh 1994). Self-report studies are still rarely used with respect to serious offences or white-collar crimes, although they are increasingly used by researchers in the "career criminal" area of research (Greenberg 1996; Shover 1996). Only recently has this method been used for international comparisons (Junger-Tas et al. 1994).

Interviews

Another form of SRD is the interview, which may be structured (following a set pattern for each respondent interviewed) or unstructured (exploratory). While most early interview work was done in connection with case studies of individuals or families, the Kinsey studies of human sexuality pioneered the technique of combining individual interviews with survey forms.

Kinsey and his colleagues attempted to maximize interview effectiveness by canvassing the community in question for ideal interview candidates. Thus, if the community was a prison population, the researchers would attempt to interview "the oldest-timer, the leading wolf, the kingpin in the inmate commonwealth, or the girl who is the chief troublemaker for the administration" (Kinsey, Pomeroy, and Martin 1948:39).

Kinsey used three trained interviewers (four, including himself). He provided them with an exhaustive list of sexual activities, and instructed them to ask subjects about their participation in each of them. "It is important to look the subject squarely in the eye," Kinsey advised, "while giving only a minimum of attention to the record that is being made" (Kinsey et al. 1948:48). Kinsey's interviewers were also taught to not be evasive: they never used euphemisms, nor did they avoid words like "masturbation" and "climax." Had they done so, Kinsey explained, the interviewee would have answered in kind, picking up on the message that it was not all right to admit to such things. Kinsey was very concerned to reduce the probability of deliberate deceit and willful or unconscious exaggeration (Bullough 1994:173).

Interviewers were, Kinsey wrote, to

begin by asking *when* [their subjects] first engaged in such activity. This places a heavier burden on the individual who is inclined to deny his experience; and since it becomes apparent from the form of our question that we would not be surprised if he had had such experience, there seems to be less reason for denying it. (Kinsey et al. 1948:53)

Finally, interviewers were advised to use rapid-fire questioning, not only because it would enable them to cover the maximum amount of material in a single interview but because it would also encourage spontaneous responses (Kinsey et al. 1948:54).

Kinsey's goal was to secure 100,000 sex histories. At the time of his death, some 18,000 interviews had been completed, 8000 of them recorded by Kinsey himself (Bullough 1994:173). Partly because of the expense, most interview studies involve far fewer respondents than Kinsey's did, and most do not incorporate the techniques Kinsey's researchers used to build rapport and undermine evasion. It is hardly surprising that later, attempts to duplicate Kinsey's work by researchers less determined to elicit openness have generally found slightly lower rates of participation in deviant forms of sexuality.

Victimization Surveys

Interviews and questionnaires have been used in victimization surveys to question victims, such as people who have been raped, robbed, cheated, injured, threatened, or deceived. The first major victimization studies, initiated in the United States in the 1960s, tended to be based on nationally representative samples that involved contacting thousands of households by telephone. The technique, while it has been criticized for underreporting such categories of victimization as family violence, suggests generally much higher rates of victimization than are indicated by police statistics. In a typical study of this kind, the victimization rate for rape is eight times higher than official figures based on police reports (Brown, Esbensen, and Geis 1991:153).

The first major victimization study in Canada, conducted for the Ministry of the Solicitor General and published in 1986, involved interviews with more than 61 000 Canadians over the age of 16. It found, as expected, that many forms of crime went unreported and that there were great variations in what kinds of crime were and were not reported. For example, the study showed that only 38.5 percent of sexual assault victims had reported the crime to police, compared with 45 percent of robbery victims and 89 percent of car theft victims. Statistics Canada conducted a victimization survey as part of the General Social Survey in 1988 and again in 1993. Another is scheduled for 1998 (Statistics Canada 1995:3).

Problems encountered in victimization studies parallel those found in other kinds of self-report material. Findings can be distorted by selective or faulty memory, deliberate deception, and reluctance to report. People may, for example, fail to report family violence or sexual assaults by acquaintances. In addition, unavailability or lack of interest on the part of some respondents may lead to unbalanced, nonrandom interviewing (e.g., more homemakers than commuters, more women than men). Another important consideration is that the subject's notion of being victimized may not correspond, in any simple way, to the formal or legal definitions of crime or deviance as understood by the researcher. For example, more assaults are reported by highly educated people than by those who are less educated. This may be more reflective of lower tolerance of assault than of greater numbers of assaults. These drawbacks notwithstanding, self-report and victimization data, when combined with official data, have enabled researchers to produce a more accurate picture of crime and other forms of deviance, one which tends to offset the panic-mongering of the mass media. There is simply not as much "offending" going on as most people think there is, and it seems to be declining.

FIELD OBSERVATION

Evidence about deviance may also be gathered through *participant observation* (joining in the activities of the people being studied), through *nonparticipant field research* (taking notes and asking questions but remaining an outsider), or through *staged activity analysis* (in which subjects are asked "to reconstruct and simulate" their past deviant activities as closely as possible, thus allowing the researchers to "participate" in the re-enactment) (Cromwell, Olson, and Avary 1991:15–16). Arguing on behalf of observation techniques, Polsky (1967) likens studying criminals in prisons to studying animals in the zoo: neither is nearly as valuable as watching them in their natural habitat. In Polsky's words,

> data gathered from caught criminals ... are not only very partial but partially suspect. These are data that are much too heavily retrospective; data from people who aren't really free to put you down; data often involving the kind of "cooperativeness" in which you get told what the criminal wants you to hear so you will get off his back or maybe do him some good with the judge or parole board; data from someone who is not behaving as he normally would in his normal life-situations; and, above all, data that you cannot supplement with, or interpret in the light of, your own direct observation of the criminal's natural behaviour in his natural environment.
>
> To put the argument another way: Animal behaviour has a narrower range of determinants than human behaviour, [and is therefore] much less complex and variable. And yet, in recent years, animal

ecologists have demonstrated that when you undertake a "free ranging" study of an animal in his natural habitat, you discover important things about him that are simply not discoverable when he is behind bars. (115–116)

An interesting study by Prus and Irini (1980) employed participant observation to produce an ethnographic description of the hotel and bar community in a Canadian city. The study documented the supportive relationships among prostitutes, strippers, underworld hustlers, bellhops, hotel desk clerks, security personnel, bartenders, performers, waitresses, taxi drivers, and many others who form a deviant community that is within, but generally invisible to, the straight community.

Participant observation can be *overt* (open) or *covert* (hidden). In an overt study, the observer announces his or her intentions and does not pretend to have other reasons for being on the scene. This technique was used by Whyte (1943), who befriended the leader of a street corner group and used this position to openly study

Figure 2.2   Victimization Data vs. Uniform Crime Reporting (Police) Data

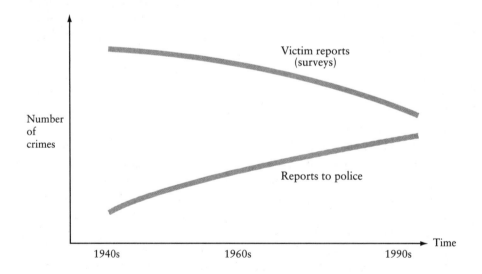

Note: Until recently, police reports showed increases, while victim surveys showed declines. In the 1990s, the curves are becoming more alike. Still, much "crime" is not reported to police.

the group members and the community in which they lived. The same technique was used by Wolf (1991) in his ethnography of an outlaw biker club. (Informing the bikers that he wanted to study them proved a delicate matter.)

A covert study of deviance is sometimes more objective than an overt one in that people who are unaware that their actions are being recorded will behave more naturally. However, this kind of study can be dangerous if those being studied become aware and defend themselves. Also, such tactics are ethically questionable. Consider the example of Humphreys (1970), who assumed the role of "watchqueen" (lookout) to study the behaviour of men who went to public washrooms ("tearooms") for quick, impersonal sexual encounters with other anonymous men. Humphreys kept records of the washroom activities and later interviewed some of the men involved (having located them through their licence plate numbers). He found that most were married and living with their wives; did not think of themselves as homosexual; did not participate in the gay subculture; and tended to be above average in their performance of home and community duties, often playing the role of the "perfect" neighbour with the immaculate lawn and the regularly washed car. Their participation in the tearoom trade, so drastically at odds with their public identity, was needless to say a matter of the greatest secrecy. Such men are likely to be suicidal if arrested and exposed (Deroches 1991:19).

At no point over the course of these interviews did Humphreys reveal to the subjects his true purpose, or indicate that he knew them from the washroom setting; he even changed his appearance to avoid recognition. While any other way of obtaining information about a group this secretive is difficult to envision, the Humphreys study nonetheless generated a good deal of controversy on the basis of its dubious ethics. A particular concern was how much damage might have been done had Humphreys' notes fallen into the hands of others, especially those of the police. The second edition of *Tearoom Trade,* Humphreys' book on the study, included a sixty-five-page "Retrospect on Ethical Issues."

In another controversial study, social psychologists pretended to join a religious cult to see what would happen when the group leader's prophecy about the imminent end of the world failed to materialize. Although the psychologists originally called it the Doomsday Cult, they later admitted that the group was a part of Reverend Moon's Unification Church (Festinger, Riecken, and Schachter 1956; Lofland 1981). These researchers did not reveal their true purpose, and their participation was extensive enough, involving more researchers than legitimate members, and in active roles, that it may have produced some of the behaviour that they were studying. It has been suggested—only partly in jest—that the membership lists of radical and fringe groups are filled with the names of sociologists, anthropologists, political scientists, and undercover police agents, all of whom are studying the others.

A final danger researchers engaging in participant observation face is that they will lose their objectivity by "going native" (i.e., becoming apologists for the deviant's lifestyle) or, conversely, that they will develop an intense aversion to the people under study. The anthropologist Bronislaw Malinowski, who was famous for his work on the Trobriand Islanders, published studies that were models of factuality and objectivity. Yet, as his posthumously published memoirs reveal, he despised the Trobriands and found their customs revolting.

SECONDARY ANALYSIS OF STATISTICAL DATA

Most official data used in studies of deviance and criminality come from various agencies of control, including police, courts, prisons, social agencies, and various government ministries at the municipal, provincial, and federal levels. Sir William

Figure 2.3   An Example of the Use of Uniform Crime Reporting Data in Combination with Other Sources of Information

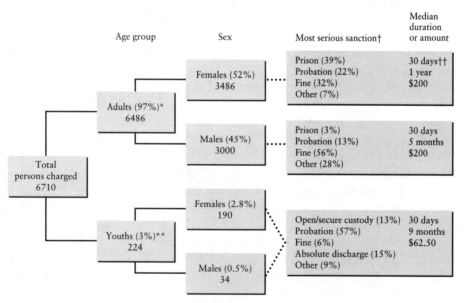

Source: Statistics Canada, "Uniform Crime Reporing Survey," from CANSIM database, Matrix No. 3302; "Youth Courts Survey," from CANSIM database, Matrix No. 3309; "Sentencing in Adult Provincial Courts: A Study of Nine Jurisdictions, 1993–94," Cat. No. 85-513. Reprinted with permission.

Petty, known as the father of English "political arithmetic," argued as early as 1670 that prisoner statistics should be collected and used as a measure of "vice and sin" in the nation, in roughly the same way that public health could be gauged by the number of deaths from contagious disease (Sellin and Wolfgang, cited in Gatrell, Lenman, and Parker 1980).

The Canadian Centre for Justice Statistics collects data through the Uniform Crime Reporting (UCR) system (Statistics Canada 1995). The UCR system contains information only about crimes that are officially known to police and reported (on a monthly basis) by them. Although the questions are periodically revised, UCR records are consistent enough to allow us to compare the crime rates of municipalities, provinces, and the country as a whole over more than a quarter century. Until recently, however, UCR data have been limited by the fact that detailed information about specific incidents was lost when it was coded in aggregate fashion for the report. For example, if four nonviolent offences occurred at the same time, only the most serious of them (usually the one with the longest possible prison sentence under the Criminal Code) was recorded. The "counting rule" for violent crime considers the number of victims. If two violent offences (murder/rape) involved only one victim, only one crime would be reported. For each victim, only the most serious offence is counted. If a murder and a rape occurred, the rape would be lost from the record unless it involved another victim involved in the same incident (a situation not very satisfactory for the researcher who is studying sexual assault).

A new version of the UCR has been launched, while the old one continues. The newer version (UCR Revised) addresses this serious flaw by taking an "incident-based approach" that allows researchers to access multiple aspects of the criminal event, including both accused and victim characteristics such as "age, sex, alcohol consumption, relationship, level of injury and weapon causing injury," as well as characteristics of the incident such as its location and "secondary violations" that may have occurred at the same time (Statistics Canada 1995:2). Although it has gradually been including more and more police departments over the past decade (it began with the Niagara Regional Police in 1988), the new UCR reports less than half of the crimes known to police in Canada (Statistics Canada 1995:2). Full implementation of the system is still a long way off.

Not all statistical data pertinent to deviance research come from the criminal justice system. Researchers have also made use of data collected by agencies such as hospitals (on injuries and death), schools (truancy and vandalism), coroner's offices (causes of death), and social welfare workers (drug abuse, family breakdown). Insurance data, while rarely directly available, is also useful for some kinds of research. The rates insurance companies are charging for different kinds of protection, for example, reflect evidence, collected by the companies, concerning either the deviance of the insured—drivers, boat owners, householders, and others—or the amount of crime that was perpetrated against them.

SECONDARY ANALYSIS OF BIOGRAPHICAL MATERIALS

Biographical material is often used in conjunction with other kinds of evidence as a way of seeing how real-life cases correspond to the models developed in the research process. We might, for example, read Jack Henry Abbott's autobiographical *In the Belly of the Beast* (1981) in order to see how Abbott's perceptions of his violent life flesh out or contradict the understandings that have been gained through other kinds of research. In the case study, however, biographical data predominates. Case studies are usually in-depth qualitative accounts of one or more illustrative individuals or families. They typically make use of personal documents (letters, diaries, autobiographies), as well as interviews with the subject and/or with people who know the subject. Even though a particular case study may have some unique features, it is usually presented as being representative of many other cases of the same sort. For example, Sutherland (1937) presents what he calls the autobiography of Chic Conwell along with a running commentary that places Conwell's life in the context of what was then known about professional thieves.

Case studies and autobiographical accounts have given us insight into the lives of members of street gangs and organized-crime groups (Keiser 1979; Maas 1968; Ianni 1972; Talese 1971; Anderson 1979; Theresa 1973), as well as into the lifestyles of "fences," who buy from thieves (sometimes after placing orders with them) and sell to anyone (Klockars 1974; Steffensmeier 1986); "jack-rollers," who steal from drunks (Shaw 1930; Snodgrass 1982); skid row alcoholics (Spradley 1970); safe-crackers, thieves, and pickpockets (Allen 1977; King and Chambliss 1975); and drug-addicted street youth (Rettig, Torres, and Garrett 1977).

While some autobiographies are highly reliable and reasonably objective, such accounts are often self-serving, selective, or fanciful, and should be approached with considerable caution. Micky McArthur's *I'd Rather Be Wanted Than Had* (1990), Roger Caron's *Go-Boy!* (1978), and Dwight Pichette's *The Diary of a Bank Robber* (1988) all show considerable commitment to underworld social values, even while professing a change of heart. A very different kind of quasi-autobiographical work is Malcolm Lowry's *Under the Volcano* (1948), which describes the experiences of an alcoholic diplomat living in Mexico. This book has inspired many other writers, among them Michel Foucault (Miller 1993:197, 250, 355), whose work is discussed in Chapter 12.

Although biographies tend to be less self-serving than personal accounts, they are also further removed from the reality of their subjects. Like autobiographies, they vary considerably in their usefulness to the social scientist. Literally hundreds of biographies are published every year, usually about people who are well known in the political, literary, artistic, or entertainment worlds. Almost without exception, they reveal aspects of their subjects' lives that might be regarded as deviant. They can, therefore, be useful as illustrations of the way in which deviance was understood by the subjects and those around them. At the same time, they reveal how deviance of certain kinds, and by certain people, may result in repression, notoriety, or celebration. The biography of cult leader/prophet Brother Twelve is a fascinating account of a man who attracted thousands of followers and created a saga of occult beliefs and unusual sexual practices (Oliphant 1991). Biographies of many creative people also reveal how deviance is a way of going beyond society's limits to feed the imagination. This is clearly shown in Miller's (1993) biography of Michel Foucault, a social philosopher who sought the "limit-experience" in sex and politics as a means of freeing himself from the mundane rigidities of normal thought, so that he could experience something beyond.

CONTENT ANALYSIS

Content analysis is any systematic procedure used to analyze materials such as written documents, films, audio recordings, and video presentations. Content analysis may involve simply measuring the amount of column space devoted to an issue in newspaper accounts (or, in the visual media, the amount of time allocated to a particular subject). Content analysis of this kind shows us that street crimes such as robbery and vandalism have always been given disproportionately greater amounts of space in the front pages of the newspapers than do harmful white-collar/corporate misdeeds. Similarly, the amount of space devoted to the Ben Johnson sports doping scandal far outweighed that given to reports about serious social problems such as the deaths of women at the hands of their husbands or former husbands. Content analysis also shows us that this imbalance has begun to right itself in recent years, as we are hearing more about crime in the suites and in the family than was true in the past.

Even suicide notes have been subjected to content analysis for the light they shed on some of the motivations for suicide (Schneidman 1976:203–280). Sometimes official documents, released under freedom of information regulations, provide useful information about the treatment of "deviant" populations. Kinsman's (1993) report, based on his analysis of the Canadian security force's internal memoranda, shows how the homosexual-as-security-risk idea was constructed out of partial facts (and a good deal of prejudice), and led to a purge of homosexuals from positions of power and responsibility in the Canadian federal civil service.

A unique form of content analysis is the study of people's garbage—"garbology" or "the archaeology of us" (Rathje 1996:158). This research exposes many unsuspected truths previously hidden behind our social fronts. Few people tell interviewers the truth about how much alcohol or how many cigarettes they consume, or how much they spend on "adult" video rentals and magazines. Most of us report food spending that conforms with our notions of a "balanced diet" and do not bother to mention such behaviours as recent binges on high-fat meats or desserts (Rathje 1996:169). The results of this research further underline the fact that when people are interviewed, they often underreport any behaviour that might be viewed negatively (Rathje 1996:166). Garbology is sometimes used by law-enforcement agencies to find out about people under surveillance. For example, as part of an FBI investigation, the home garbage of mobster Joseph ("Joe Bananas") Bonanno was collected for years. From it evidence was found that proved Bonanno was working on a revealing manuscript—evidence that was sufficient to convince a judge to permit a raid in which the manuscript was seized.

Michel Foucault's techniques, which are described in his *Archaeology of Knowledge* (1977), are a form of content analysis, but involve a very different conception of what knowledge means. Foucault's is a highly personalized form of social philosophy that makes use of archival documents to discover the forms of power/knowledge in the past and in the modern world. We will be looking at this work in Chapter 12.

SIMULATIONS

Simulations can be made with people (dramatizations and games) or with computers that are programmed according to the researcher's models of society (Hamburger 1979). Simulations allow researchers to manipulate the environment in a way that helps them to figure out how things work. As in the case of participant observation, the simulation may be covert or overt.

Most of the simulations reported in the literature have been "criminological"— that is, used by those researchers who are concerned with the study of criminal deviance and formal kinds of social control. Researchers have posed as both thieves and victims in order to find out what happens among passersby when an offence occurs (Stewart and Cannon 1977; Feldman 1968). Jury deliberations have been simulated in efforts to discover how a jury-like group arrives at a verdict (Haney, Banks, and Zimbardo 1973). Prison settings have been simulated in order to investigate the origins of aggressive guard-inmate behaviour, with undergraduate students taking on the roles of guards and prisoners; one such experiment had to be terminated when the "guards" got out of hand (Zimbardo 1972, 1973).

JOURNALISTIC ACCOUNTS

Investigative journalists have played an important role in uncovering evidence that has changed social theories. Many social scientists are made uneasy by the fact that journalists are not held to the same standards of proof and method as their academic counterparts, and are sometimes a good deal less committed to respectability and value neutrality. But this is often precisely why journalists can obtain data not available to academics.

There has been a long tradition of muckraking in journalism. One of the best-known muckrakers was Lincoln Steffens, who exposed the shameful and seamy underside of American government and business in the early 1900s (Kaplan 1974). Journalistic accounts that have helped us to develop a better knowledge of the inner workings of organized crime, outlaw motorcycle clubs, drug trafficking, and "laundering" of illegally obtained money include, respectively, James Dubro's *Mob Rule: Inside the Canadian Mafia* (1985), Mick Lowe's *Conspiracy of Brothers* (1988), Victor Malarek's *Merchants of Misery: Inside Canada's Illegal Drug Scene* (1989), and Jeffrey Robinson's *The Laundrymen: Inside the World's Third Largest Business* (1994). Journalists also provided an "insider perspective" on the Donald Marshall case (Harris 1986) and have written controversial accounts of the way in which the justice system works with respect to criminals and victims alike (Marshall and Barrett 1990; Stroud 1993; Marron 1992; Batten 1986; Birnie 1990; Callwood 1990).

Sometimes journalism and biography overlap, as in Brian Martin's *Never Enough: The Remarkable Frauds of Julius Melnitzer* (1993), Vernon Oickle's *Jane Hurschman-Corkum: Life and Death After Billy* (1993), and Anne Kershaw and Mary Lasovich's *Rock-A-Bye Baby: A Death Behind Bars* (1991). In a different vein, Diane Francis's *Contrepreneurs* (1988) provided a nonacademic perspective on stock market fraud, money laundering, and white-collar crime in Canada. And Marlene Webber's *Street Kids: The Tragedy of Canada's Runaways* (1991) is an excellent and well-documented survey of her topic. Thus, while journalists may not use the same methodology as social scientists, their very separation from the need for "respectability" allows them to raise valuable questions. In addition, they sometimes provide the social scientist with evidence that can be used in conjunction with data from other sources.

SUMMARY

This chapter introduced the elements of theoretical thinking, some of the ways in which theories are tested, and the principal sources of information on deviance. Much of the chapter dealt with issues that have emerged from attempts to conduct the study of deviance according to the standards of science. At the same time, recognition was given to the possibility of learning about deviance through alternative approaches and methods such as participant observation.

Throughout, the central issue has been "How do we know?" In order to assess the work of others and to ensure the validity of our own, it is important that we understand issues relating to concept formation, the development of hypotheses, and the nature of correlation and causation, and that we know which kinds of evidence will best test or illustrate our ideas.

REFERENCES

Abbott, Jack Henry. (1981). *In the Belly of the Beast* New York: Random House.

Adlaf, E.M., R.G. Smart, and G.W. Walsh. (1994). *Ontario Student Drug Use Survey.* Toronto: Addiction Research Foundation.

Allen, John. (1977). *Assault with a Deadly Weapon: The Autobiography of a Street Criminal.* New York: McGraw-Hill.

Anderson, Annelise Graebner. (1979). *The Business of Organized Crime: A Cosa Nostra Family.* Stanford, Cal.: Hoover Institute Press.

Bagley Committee (Committee on Sexual Offences Against Children and Youth). (1984). *Sexual Offences Against Children.* Ottawa: Department of Supply and Services.

Batten, Jack. (1986). *Judges.* Toronto: Macmillan Canada.

Birnie, Lisa Hobbs. (1990). *A Rock and a Hard Place: Inside Canada's Parole Board.* Toronto: Macmillan Canada.

Blackwell, Judith C., and Patricia G. Erickson. (1988). *Illicit Drugs in Canada: A Risky Business.* Toronto: Nelson Canada.

Brown, Stephen E., Finn-Aage Esbensen, and Gilbert Geis. (1991). *Criminology: Explaining Crime and Its Context.* Cincinnati: Anderson.

Bullough, Vern L. (1994). *Science in the Bedroom: A History of Sex Research.* New York: Basic/HarperCollins.

Callwood, June. (1990). *The Sleep-Walker: The Trial That Made Canadian Legal History.* Toronto: McClelland and Stewart.

Chafetz, Janet Saltzman. (1978). *A Primer on the Construction and Testing of Theories in Sociology.* Itasca, Ill.: Peacock.

Clark, John P., and Larry L. Tifft. (1966). "Polygraph and Interview Validation of Self-Reported Deviant Behavior." *American Sociological Review* 31:516–523.

Cole, Stephen. (1980). *The Sociological Method: An Introduction to the Science of Sociology.* 3rd ed. Chicago: Rand McNally.

Coleman, Clive, and Jenny Moynihan. (1996). "Self-Report Studies: True Confessions?" In Clive Coleman and Jenny Moynihan, *Understanding Crime Data.* Buckingham, England: Open University Press.

Cromwell, Paul F., James N. Olson, and D'Aunn Wester Avary. (1991). *Breaking and Entering: An Ethnographic Analysis of Burglary.* Studies in Crime and Justice, vol. 8. Newbury Park: Sage.

Deroches, Frederick. (1991). "Tearoom Trade: A Law Enforcement Problem." *Canadian Journal of Criminology* (January):1–21.

Durkheim, Emile. (1951 [1897]). *Suicide.* New York: Free Press.

Feldman, Roy E. (1968). "Response to Compatriot and Foreigner Who Seeks Assistance." *Journal of Personality and Social Psychology* 10:202–214.

Festinger, Leon, H. Riecken, and S. Schachter. (1956). *When Prophecy Fails.* Minneapolis: University of Minnesota Press.

Fraser Committee (Special Committee on Pornography and Prostitution). (1985). *Pornography and Prostitution in Canada.* Ottawa: Department of Supply and Services.

Gatrell V.A.C., Bruce Lenman, and Geoffrey Parker (eds.). (1980). *Crime and the Law: The Social History of Crime in Western Europe Since 1500.* London: Europa Publications.

Goffman, Erving. (1963). *Stigma: Notes on the Management of Spoiled Identity.* Englewood Cliffs, N.J.: Prentice-Hall.

Gold, Martin. (1966). "Undetected Delinquent Behaviour." *Journal of Research in Crime and Delinquency* 3:27–46.

Greenberg, David F. (1996). *Criminal Careers.* Vol.1. International Library of Criminology, Criminal Justice and Penology. Brookfield: Dartmouth.

Hagan, Frank E. (1982). *Research Methods in Criminal Justice and Criminology.* New York: Macmillan.

Hamburger, Henry. (1979). *Games as Models of Social Phenomena.* San Francisco: W.H. Freeman.

Haney, C., W.C. Banks, and P.G. Zimbardo. (1973). "Interpersonal Dynamics in a Simulated Prison." *International Journal of Criminology and Penology* 1:69–77.

Hardt, Robert H., and Sandra Peterson-Hardt. (1977). "On Determining the Quality of the Delinquency Self-Report Method." *Journal of Research in Crime and Delinquency* 14:247–261.

Harris, Michael. (1986). *Justice Denied: The Law Versus Donald Marshall.* Toronto: Macmillan Canada.

Heussenstamm F.K. (1971). "Bumper Stickers and the Cops." *Trans-action* 8:32–33.

Hood, Roger, and Richard Sparks. (1970). *Key Issues in Criminology.* London: Weidenfeld and Nicholson.

Hughes, Everett C. (1945). "Dilemmas and Contradictions of Status." *American Journal of Sociology* 50 (March):353–359.

Humphreys, Laud. (1970). *Tearoom Trade: Impersonal Sex in Public Places.* Chicago: Aldine.

Ianni, Francis A. (1972). "The Lupollo Family." In Francis A. Ianni, *A Family Business: Kinship and Social Control in Organized Crime.* New York: Russell Sage.

Junger-Tas, J., G. J. Terloun, and M. Klein (eds.). (1994). *Delinquent Behaviour Among Youth in the Western World: First Results of the International Self-Report Delinquency Study.* Amsterdam: Kugler.

Kaplan, Justin. (1974). *Lincoln Steffens: A Biography.* New York: Simon and Schuster.

Keiser, Lincoln R. (1979). *The Vice Lords: Warriors of the Streets.* Toronto: Holt, Rinehart and Winston.

Kessler, Suzanne J. (1990). "The Medical Construction of Gender: Case Management of Intersexed Infants." *Signs: The Journal of Women in Culture and Society* 16(11):3–26.

King, Harry, and William J. Chambliss. (1972). *Box Man: A Professional Thief's Journal.* New York: Harper and Row.

Kinsey, A.C., W.B. Pomeroy, and C.E. Martin. (1948). *Sexual Behavior in the Human Male.* Philadelphia: W.B. Saunders.

Kinsman, Gary. (1993). "'Character Weaknesses' and 'Fruit Machines': Towards an Analysis of the Social Organization of the Anti-Homosexual Purge Campaign in the Canadian Federal Civil Service, 1959–1964." Paper presented at the annual meeting of the Canadian Sociology and Anthropology Association, Ottawa.

Klein, Malcolm W. (1995). *The American Street Gang: Its Nature, Prevalence, and Control.* New York: Oxford University Press.

Klockars, Carl. (1974). *The Professional Fence.* New York: Free Press.

Kuhn, Thomas. (1970). *The Structure of Scientific Revolutions.* Chicago: University of Chicago Press.

Lemert, Edwin. (1951). *Social Pathology.* New York: McGraw-Hill.

Lofland, John. (1981). *Doomsday Cult: A Study of Conversion, Proselytization and Maintenance of Faith.* Rev. (enlarged) ed. New York: Irvington.

Lowman, John. (1992). "Street Prostitution." In Vincent Sacco (ed.), *Deviance: Conformity and Control in Canadian Society.* 2nd ed. Scarborough, Ont.: Prentice-Hall Canada.

Maas, Peter. (1968). *The Valachi Papers.* New York: Bantam.

Marron, Kevin. (1992). *Apprenticed in Crime: Young Offenders, the Law, and Crime in Canada.* Toronto: McClelland and Stewart.

Marshall, W.L., and Sylvia Barrett. (1990). *Criminal Neglect: Why Sex Offenders Go Free.* Toronto: Doubleday.

McMullan, J.L., and P.D. Swan. (1991). "Social Economy and Arson in Nova Scotia." In Robert A. Silverman, James J. Teevan, and Vincent F. Sacco (eds.), *Crime in Canadian Society*. Toronto: Butterworths.

McPhail, Clark. (1991). *The Myth of the Madding Crowd*. New York: Aldine de Gruyter.

Meyer, K. (1941). *Die Unbestraften Verbrechen*. Leipzig, Germany: G. Thieme.

Miller, James. (1993). The *Passion of Michel Foucault*. New York: Simon and Schuster.

Nettler, Gwynn. (1970). *Explanations*. New York: McGraw-Hill.

———. (1982). *Explaining Criminals*. Criminal Careers, Vol. 1. Cincinnati: Anderson.

Nye, F. Ivan. (1958). *Family Relationships and Delinquent Behavior*. New York: John Wiley.

Oliphant, John. (1991). *Brother Twelve: The Incredible Story of Canada's False Prophet and His Doomed Cult of Gold, Sex and Black Magic*. Toronto: McClelland and Stewart.

Picard, Andre. (1990). "Many Car Thefts Arranged By Their Owners." *Globe and Mail*, January 22.

Polsky, Ned. (1967). *Hustlers, Beats and Others*. Chicago: Aldine.

Porterfield, Austin L. (1946). *Youth in Trouble*. Fort Worth: Leo Potisham Foundation.

Prus, Robert, and Irini Styllianoss. (1980). *Hookers, Rounders And Desk Clerks: The Social Organization of the Hotel Community*. Toronto: Gage.

Radzinowicz, L., and J. King. (1977). *The Growth of Crime*. London: Hamilton.

Rathje, W.L. (1996). "The Archaeology of Us." *Science and the Future: 1997 Year Book*. Chicago: Encyclopaedia Britannica, 158–176.

Rettig, Richard P., Manual J. Torres, and Gerald R. Garrett. (1977). *Manny: A Criminal Addict's Story*. Boston: Houghton Mifflin.

Reynolds, Paul Davidson. (1979). *A Primer in Theory Construction*. Indianapolis: Bobbs Merrill.

Robinson, Jeffrey. (1994). *The Laundrymen: Inside the World's Largest Business*. London: Simon and Schuster.

Schneidman, Edwin S. (ed.). (1976). *Suicidology: Contemporary Developments*. New York: Grune and Stratton.

Schütz, A. (1960). "The Social World and the Theory of Social Action." *Social Research* 27 (Summer):203–221.

Shaw, Clifford R. (1930). *The Jack-Roller: A Delinquent Boy's Own Story*. Chicago: University of Chicago Press.

Short, James F., Jr., and F. Ivan Nye. (1957). "Reported Behavior as a Criterion of Deviant Behavior." *Social Problems* 5:207–213.

Shover, Neal. 1996. *Great Pretenders: Pursuits and Careers of Persistent Thieves*. Boulder, Col.:Westview/HarperCollins.

Snodgrass, Jon. (1982). *The Jack-Roller at Seventy: A Fifty-Year Follow-Up*. Lexington, Mass.: D.C. Heath.

Spergel, Irving A. (1995). *The Youth Gang Problem: A Community Approach.* New York: Oxford University Press.

Spradley, James P. (1970). *You Owe Yourself a Drunk: An Ethnography of Urban Nomads.* Boston: Little, Brown.

Statistics Canada (Canadian Centre for Justice Statistics). (1990). *Juristat Service Bulletin* 10 (10).

———. (1995). *Canadian Crime Statistics 1994.* Ottawa: Statistics Canada.

Steffensmeier, Darrell. (1986). *The Fence: In the Shadow of Two Worlds.* Totowa, N.J.: Rowman and Littlefield.

Stewart, John E., and Daniel A. Cannon. (1977). "Effects of Perpetrator Status and Bystander Commitment on Response to a Simulated Crime." *Journal of Police Science and Administration* 5:308–323.

Stroud, Carsten. (1993). *Contempt of Court: The Betrayal of Justice in Canada.* Toronto: Macmillan Canada.

Sutherland, Edwin H. (1937). *The Professional Thief.* Chicago: University of Chicago Press.

———. (1949). *White Collar Crime.* New York: Holt, Rinehart and Winston.

Talese, Gay. (1971). *Honor Thy Father.* Greenwich, Conn.: Fawcett Crest.

Theresa, Vincent. (1973). *My Life in the Mafia.* New York: Doubleday.

Tribble, S. (1972). "Socio-Economic Status and Self-Reported Juvenile Delinquency." *Canadian Journal of Criminology and Corrections* 14:409–415.

Vaz, Edmund W. (1965). "Middle Class Adolescents: Self-Reported Delinquency and Youth Culture Activities." *The Canadian Review of Sociology and Anthropology* 2:52–70.

———. (1969). "Delinquency and the Youth Culture: Upper- and Middle-Class Boys." *Journal of Criminal Law, Criminology and Police Science* 60(1):33–46.

Wallerstein, James S., and Clement J. Wyle. (1947). "Our Law-Abiding Lawbreakers." *Probation* 25:107–112.

Whyte, William Foote. (1943). *Street Corner Society.* Chicago: University of Chicago Press.

Williams, Jay. R., and Martin Gold. (1972). "From Delinquent Behavior to Official Delinquency." *Social Problems* 20:209–229.

Wolf, Daniel R. (1991). *The Rebels: A Brotherhood of Outlaw Bikers.* Toronto: University of Toronto Press.

Zimbardo, Philip. (1973). "A Pirandellian Prison." *The New York Times Magazine,* April 8, 38–60.

———. (1972). "Pathology of Imprisonment." *Society* 9:4–8.

PRESCIENTIFIC APPROACHES TO DEVIANCE

In this chapter, we will look at the ways in which deviance was understood before the great transition to rationalism and science ("the enlightenment") in the late 1600s. Early treatment of deviance was noncausal. It used stories to illustrate the character of deviance, and to warn people about the consequences of excessive control as well as excessive deviance. The spread and penetration of monotheistic religions—especially Christianity—led to a more causal, but still supernatural, explanation according to which the "devil" caused deviance and all other ills. Deviance no longer evoked feelings of ambivalence; it was evil, as were those who failed to oppose it. This chapter devotes considerable space to explaining the nature, origins, and consequences of the witchcraft craze that shook Europe from roughly A.D. 1400 to A.D. 1700.

Witchcraft is important for the study of deviance because it provides a paradigm of the processes whereby deviants are "created" by authorities. It is relatively easy, looking back through contemporary eyes, to see that "witches," as seen by the medieval authorities, did not really exist. Once this paradigm is understood, we can look at other kinds of deviance closer to our own time, and raise the same questions. For example, how much of both the glamour and the horror of the "drug trafficker" is real, and how much is a construct made up of some truths and many inaccuracies? What is the underlying reality, and why is distortion of that reality so common?

PAST AND PRESENT REPRESENTATIONS OF DEVIANCE

MYTHS, PARABLES, AND STORIES

Before the Enlightenment brought us science, rationality, and an empirically bound reality, people understood life in terms of myths, parables, and stories. These tales described their experiences and, in a nonscientific way, explained them.

Deviance has always been a powerful theme in religion, art, folklore, drama, and political life. The earliest perspectives on deviance, which persist in various forms to this day, take the shape of stories that provide examples of deviance and its consequences. While they may or may not also provide moral instruction, these stories give us an understanding of how deviance fits in the scheme of things.

The ethical message of each major religion is supported by collections of historical or mythical tales in which various kinds of offences against the powers of creation, or against social regulation, happen by accident or through carelessness. The offence is not always intended by—or even known to—the offender. The response of heaven and earth, however, is usually punitive unless mitigated by ritual reconciliation. The prodigal son, for example, may be welcomed home. For the most part, deviants are expelled from the garden, turned into pillars of salt, or condemned to perform eternal tasks. Temptation and its consequences is the theme of many stories of this kind. Eve was tempted into tasting the forbidden fruit of knowledge. Pandora's curiosity led her to open the box containing all the evils of the world. Buddha, Christ, Mohammed, and other important religious figures all had experience, at least in figurative terms, of demons or temptations.

Secular or magical stories also reinforce cultural images of deviance and control. In Heinrich Hoffmann's *Der Struwwelpeter*, a classic storybook for children, a little girl plays with matches, her dress catches fire, and soon all that remains of her is a pile of ashes, two shoes, and two cats whose tears flow like a stream across the page. In another story, a boy who insists on sucking his thumbs has them cut off by a tailor with huge scissors (Hoffmann n.d.). Many other children's stories have similar cautionary intentions. The boy who cried wolf when there was no wolf is denied help when he needs it. Little Red Riding Hood talks to a stranger in the woods and gets herself and her grandmother eaten. Cinderella's ugly stepsisters have their eyes plucked out and eaten by doves. These stories conform to the common cultural practice of warning and admonishing in order to induce polite language, table manners, caution, cooperation, and responsibility.

Trickster Legends

Despite the above examples, most of our secular tales are ambivalent about deviance in that they do not regard it as unconditionally "bad." Indeed, the deviant character is frequently more likable and sympathetic than the characters who teach and correct. This ambivalence about deviance and control is reflected in the culturally universal trickster legend (Radin 1972:iii). In trickster stories, the smart "little guy" outwits the stupid, greedy authorities. The trickster circumvents the usual rules in disrespectful ways.

> Unburdened by scruples, tricksters dupe friends, acquaintances, and adversaries alike in the pursuit of their selfish ends and blithely reward their benefactor's generosity with sometimes deadly betrayals. In addition, they have a pronounced weakness for food but are plagued by an inveterate aversion for work, a trait that forces them to rely on trickery to obtain food both in times of want and of plenty. (Owomoyela 1990:626)

Everything the trickster does is permeated with laughter, irony, and wit. The audience reaction is laughter tempered with awe (Radin 1972:xxiv).

The trickster takes many forms but is basically a smart, unethical, mischief-making character who shockingly violates many of the customary norms of honesty, mannerliness, and loyalty. In Anglo-American culture, Brer Rabbit, Roger Rabbit, and Bugs Bunny represent the amusing, human, and likable side of the trickster. Among natives, such as the Haida of the Queen Charlotte Islands, the trickster takes the form of Raven, or, in other native cultures, is sometimes Coyote (Wilkins 1994:73). The trickster also represents darker, uncontrolled, less human forces. Batman's archenemy, the Joker, is funny, in a campy way, but he is also violent, unpredictable, homicidal, and sadistic. The mean and mischievous imp Mxyzptlk in *Superman* comic books combines both comedic and demonic features. Thus, the trickster embodies the paradox of deviance—its attractiveness and dangers, and its many faces.

The trickster is found in many European picaresque tales where he/she (the form is gender-bending) represents "revolt against the rigidity of tradition" (Radin 1972:185). Thus Goethe's *Renard the Fox,* and Thomas Mann's *The Confessions of Felix Krull, Confidence Man,* also fit within this genre.

The trickster tradition continues in the form of certain modern entertainers and political figures.

Box 3.1   The Trickster in Native Mythology

The character of Nanabush [the Canadian Cree Indian version of the Trickster] is vital [in Tomson Highway's celebrated plays] *The Rez Sisters* and *Dry Lips Oughta Move to Kapuskasing.*

"The Trickster," known by different names in different languages, is a central figure in Native mythology. Indeed, says Highway, the Trickster is as important to Cree culture as Christ is to Western Culture ... Nanabush is funny, visceral, and may be of either gender. Because Nanabush is also mischievous and fallible, unlike Christ in the European tradition, the Native listener must exercise his own judgment to learn from Nanabush's adventures, whereas Christ's followers need only obey precept and example.

Source: Denis W. Johnson, "Lines and Circles: The 'Rez' Plays of Tomson Highway," in *Native Writers and Canadian Writing,* edited by W.H. New. Vancouver: University of British Columbia Press 1990, 254–264. Reprinted with permission.

Rock music, from Elvis Presley to Michael Jackson, regularly serves up androgynous, shaman-like figures who challenge cultural norms. In the late sixties, John Lennon consciously adopted the role of the holy fool as he and his wife Yoko Ono staged "bed-ins for peace" .... Prince (especially in his dualistic guise as Gemini) exemplifies the gender-bending, rule-shattering rock star ... The figures of the clown and holy fool played a large part in sixties counterculture politics as well, specifically in the persons of Jerry Rubin and Abbie Hoffman. (Santino 1990:662)

Cross-dressers (people who wear clothes designed for the opposite sex) sometimes fall into the trickster category. They make fun of the established order and question one of its most fundamental dichotomies, the great gender divide. Thus, the role of the fool as trickster is a contrary one that turns the accepted order of things on its head.

Contemporary Legends

Contemporary legends differ from legends of the past in that they claim to be factual rather than fantastic. These legends, it turns out, are based on hearsay rather than fact (Goode 1992:306). An example of this is the perennial legend of the poisoned (by strangers) Halloween candy, which stirs up parental anxieties each October (Best 1985; Brunvand 1989). In fact, the only proven cases of Halloween poisoning show this act to have been perpetrated not by strangers but by relatives or acquaintances. The story persists, however, supported by our fear of strangers in the urban environment.

Another urban legend is the story of the man who, accompanied by his child, went to Neiman Marcus for tea and cookies. He asked for the cookie recipe, was told it cost $2.50, and agreed to buy it. Later, he was shocked to find that $250 had been charged to his credit card. Unable to get the store to delete the charge, and angry about it, he sent the recipe out on computer networks—telling users to copy and circulate it—as a way of getting back at the store. The recipe spread among friends and relatives of the computer network users, and was even reprinted in many newspapers—only to be scotched when Ann Landers revealed that Neiman Marcus does not sell any such cookie recipe. This story recently resurfaced on a women's studies e-mail list as "Cookie Recipe E-mail Empowerment 101." This time it was a mother and daughter at Neiman Marcus but the price and the request for getting back at the store was the same.

Pearson (1984) recounts a Canadian urban legend, concerning someone who came to be known as "the North York [Ontario] banana man." This man, the story went, had been hit by a car after spending the evening in a singles' bar. The nurses at the hospital discovered a banana secured to his thigh with rubber bands. Jan Harold Brunvand, University of Utah English professor and folklorist, has collected hundreds of these tales, which always betray their spuriousness by being told far too many times, and with far too many embellishments and revisions. Urban legends deal with understandings of deviance and control. They tell us that certain ways of living (deviance) are likely to lead to grief or humiliation, and in the process they express our fears (and sometimes our sense of humour).

DEVIANCE AS A MEANS OF LITERARY INSPIRATION

Great literature has often had as its themes sin, crime, and disorder, and has treated them as central aspects of the human condition. Writers have been criticized for glamorizing or glorifying deviance in their works, and sometimes for even addressing it at all. In authors as diverse as Sophocles, Dickens, Dostoyevsky, and Shakespeare, we can trace common themes of transgression, punishment, remorse, and revenge. Other literary figures have written about adultery, incest, and homosexuality (Lawrence Durrell, Jean Genet, William S. Burroughs); about drug intoxication (Samuel Taylor Coleridge, Thomas de Quincey, Aldous Huxley, Malcolm Lowry); about pacts with evil or with the devil (Joseph Conrad, Bram Stoker, Robert Louis Stevenson); and about being an "outsider" (Camus).

Many well-known authors themselves lived on the fringes of acceptability and used their experiences in deviance as literary themes. The Beat Generation, exemplified by such writers as William S. Burroughs and Jack Kerouac, actively pursued deviant sexual and drug experiences as a way of shaping their public personas and inspiring their literary efforts (Morgan 1988). Malcolm Lowry "used" his alcoholic dreams to fuel his writing, as did Aldous Huxley with his mescaline-induced visions. Coleridge's "Kubla Khan" resulted from a dream inspired by the poet's use of laudanum, a form of opium. The French recognize a whole school of "criminal writers," including Jean Genet, a homosexual-pederast thief who did much of his writing in prison. The British, somewhat less extreme, produced the "Angry Young Men" writers who revolted against "good taste," the prevailing mores, and class distinctions during the 1950s.

Other writers may have owed their creativity to various forms of mental or physical illness (Gutin 1996). William Blake, John Keats, Edgar Allen Poe, Mary Shelley, and Robert Louis Stevenson, for example, were very likely manic depressives. Dostoyevsky suffered from epileptic seizures. Even syphilis and tuberculosis have been credited with creative inspiration (Gutin 1996).

The actual creative benefits to be accrued from illnesses or from perilous lifestyles are debatable. These writers might possibly have been even more creative had they not been afflicted or lived such dissolute lives.

DEVIANCE AND THE MEDIA

Deviance, especially bizarre or criminal deviance, is the bread and butter of modern journalism. This is not a new phenomenon. In the supposedly prudish Victorian era, newspapers teemed with "sensationalist" accounts of murder, suicide, child battering, and social disorder. As Boyle (1989) recounts,

> *The Times* of January 3, 1857, lay open before me. It featured an account of "The Double Murder of Children in Newington," a lead article on "Robberies and Personal Violence," an extended rendition of "A Week of Horror." Having consumed these tidbits, I decided to move on to something I assumed would be quite different. *The Miner and Workman's Advocate*—the other end of the journalistic social scale from the august *Times*—featured, on page 3 alone of the January 7, 1865, edition, "The Poisoning of Five Persons at Gresford," "Extraordinary Outrage in Ireland," "Horrible Murder at Aldershot by a Madman," "Steamer Runs Down and Four Men Drowned on the Clyde," "Shocking Child Murder," and "Horrible Death by Fire." (3-4)

The contemporary mass media give even greater attention to themes of deviance, which resonate with people's anxieties about their personal safety and about threats to the social order. A brief look at the front pages of almost any city or town newspaper will confirm that deviance is a major part of the messages we receive each day. Television increasingly carries true-crime and simulated crime stories that convey a similar message. Since the early 1970s, about 30 percent of prime-time TV in the United States has been devoted to reality-based crime and law enforcement shows (Dominick 1978:105). The figure would be much higher if dramatizations of these themes were included. As for commercial films, in Medved's words (1991):

> Indescribable gore drenches the modern screen, even in movies allegedly made for families. And the most perverted forms of sexuality—loveless, decadent, brutal and sometimes incestuous—are showing regularly at a theatre near you. (40)

Films shown on television follow the same pattern, and are even more heavily slanted toward images of the criminal and the law.

EARLY EXPLANATIONS OF DEVIANCE: THE DEMONIC PERSPECTIVE

The earliest recorded attempts to *explain* rather than describe the nature of deviance did not, as modern science does, seek causes in the empirical world. Deviance, like everything else, was deemed to be caused by forces in the supernatural realm. In theoretical terms, the independent variables were supernatural forces, often demons or devils of some kind, who acted through particular human beings to cause harm in the world. Thus, when floods came, crops failed, farm animals sickened, or women miscarried, people did not look for the causes in nature, physiology, or medicine. They did not understand that mould on the crops could produce hallucinations, miscarriages, and other problems. They looked instead to the supernatural—to witches, sorcerers, demons, and the like—as an explanation for these events. In this world, there were no coincidences: if a man walked along a path and something fell on him, someone else must have willed that event to happen by invoking the powers of the supernatural.

Over time, there have been many versions of the demonic perspective, each corresponding with the different ideas about the supernatural that were typical of the particular age and culture. Pantheistic religions each espoused a belief in gods and goddesses who had selfish, egotistical, or violent natures and a wide range of

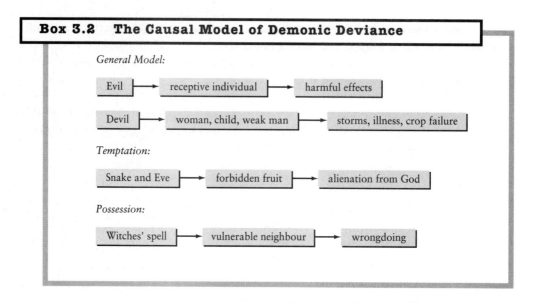

Box 3.2   The Causal Model of Demonic Deviance

General Model:

Evil → receptive individual → harmful effects

Devil → woman, child, weak man → storms, illness, crop failure

Temptation:

Snake and Eve → forbidden fruit → alienation from God

Possession:

Witches' spell → vulnerable neighbour → wrongdoing

supernatural powers. Such gods, although capable of goodness, were also capable of malice in their treatment of human beings. They could tempt them or put them into situations in which evil would result. Madness or other forms of punishment might be visited upon humans who crossed the will of a powerful god, even if they did so inadvertently or while serving the interests of another god. Pantheism encompassed the notion of demons or other evil beings, none of which, however, achieved the status of Christianity's Satan. Hinduism and Buddhism likewise recognize demons (although not in the form of a conspiracy theory, whereby the demonic is part of an extensive, sinister plot against the forces of good).

Monotheistic religions like Judaism, Christianity, and Islam have tended to see the goodness of an all-powerful Creator as offset by a single, purely evil power (sometimes personified as a type of devil) bent on wresting power from the Almighty. In the Judeo-Christian view (which is partially also the view of Islam and which has precursers in Manichaeism and Neoplatonism), the supernatural primarily reflects a cosmic struggle between evil and good, personified by God and the devil (Satan). In the battle for human souls, the devil turns people into deviants. Such people are bad not just because of what they do to others, but also because of their "treasonous" role in the battle between good and evil. The demonic deviant commits physically harmful acts that weaken the system, while at the same time challenging the order of things. In Shakespeare's *Macbeth,* for example, both Christian and pagan traditions are called upon to describe the cosmic effects of Macbeth's capitulation to his wife's ambition and greed. Macbeth's stabbing of Duncan is not just a killing on earth—it is also an event that disturbs cosmic forces, and as such is accompanied by thunder, screeching horses, and baying dogs.

THE PAGAN AS DEVIANT

In their efforts to discredit and displace other religions, monotheistic religions have demonized the other religions' gods, made "wizards and sorcerers" of their sages, and treated their times of ritual ceremony as occasions of demonic celebration (Simpson 1996). Witches Sabbath, a time when witches supposedly gathered to engage in sex with the devil and his demons, was a transformation of the celebration of the Celtic Samhain, a midpoint between the autumnal equinox and the winter solstice, which marked the new year. Similarly, Baal-Zeebub, the "lord of the flies," was a fertility god worshipped by the Philistines and other semitic groups. He was transformed by the Old Testament Israelites into Beelzebub, a powerful devil. Both the horned Celtic god Cerunnos and the Graeco-Roman Pan were remade into Judeo-Christian images of devils with horns and cloven hooves (Russell 1984:63). Other demonized residuals of pagan times include the immoral or amoral human-like creatures depicted as elves, fauns, trolls, satyrs, fairies, leprechauns, werewolves, dragons, ghosts, and jinn. Although now the stuff of children's storybooks, these creatures were once an accepted part of everyday life, both feared and respected. Anticipating retaliation if they failed to do so, people spoke kindly about fairies (Briggs 1978). "Bad" children are still sometimes seen as changelings—evil replacements for "good" children stolen by goblins or trolls; the deviance of such children is in no way the fault of their parents.

The pantheistic view of the world saw deviance and suffering as phenomena more or less beyond human control. The actions of both gods and hostile spirits were neither predictable nor always preventable. In the monotheistic cosmos, however, humans bear some responsibility for evoking, or giving in to, the forces of evil. The two main paths to deviance in this view are temptation and possession. The devil tempts or possesses weaker human beings such as children or morally weak (irreligious) adults. Sometimes the deviant contributes to the process by dabbling in the occult, indulging in heretical ideas, or living a lifestyle open to corruption.

EXAMPLES OF DEMONIC DEVIANCE: TEMPTATION AND POSSESSION

In the monotheistic tradition, Satan appears in multiple guises to promote our fall into the "seven deadly sins" of sloth, anger, lust, pride, envy, gluttony, and greed. In the Old Testament, the snake seduces Eve with promises of God-like knowledge. In the New Testament, the devil tempts Jesus to test God's love by jumping from the pinnacles of the temple, and Judas submits to evil when he accepts 30 pieces of silver in exchange for his loyalty to Jesus. In hundreds of folktales, the devil promises humans earthly pleasures in exchange for their eternal souls. This explanation gives humans a role in invoking the forces of evil, but still explains the wrongdoing in terms of supernatural powers.

Sometimes the person is not tempted into evil but experiences a sense of being "taken over" by destructive forces. These forces may be conceived as demons lying in wait for the unsuspecting passerby, or as evil spirits unleashed by witches or sorcerers by way of curses, spells, or enthralments, intended to make ordinary, good people do evil things. Possession has been reported in every society (Levack 1992a). Among North American Indians, the windigo was a spirit that could possess humans and entice them to their deaths or turn them into cannibalistic monsters. In many cultures, people who suddenly "run amok" and kill others are deemed to be possessed.

Thus, in the demonic perspective, mental illness, the birth of deformed children, repeated crop failures, and the like could be blamed either on violations of supernatural laws by humans or on the actions of supernatural beings engaged in possessing or tempting humans. Even mundane "vices" such as drinking or gambling could be blamed on the devil. In sixteenth-century Germany (a time in which few people could read), more than 100,000 copies of "devil books" were on the market. This popular literature singled out particular offences as proof of "how powerful and ubiquitous the devil and his followers were" (Coudert 1992:68). Misfortune and deviance were treated as evidence of possession or corruption by the devil. The two "solutions" to the problem were exorcism—cleansing the individual of demonic influence—or destroying the demonic influence by destroying the individual.

THE SOCIAL CONTROL OF DEMONIC DEVIANCE

Exorcism is a religious ritual designed to cast out—from either a place or a person—troublesome evil spirits, ghosts, demons, or other nonphysical, malign entities. Exorcisms persist to this day and are usually performed by teams (rather than individuals) led by a specially trained religious expert (e.g., a priest) or by a magical/occult adept, who acts as a kind of "ghostbuster." (Whether one believes in them or not, exorcisms are often extremely traumatic for the person being "cured" and may even result in death.) Some exorcisms have even been performed by psychologists and psychiatrists as a means of relieving patients of obsessive-compulsive symptoms (Peck 1983:182). Exorcism techniques range from the prayers, holy water, and confrontations of the Roman Catholic *Rituale Romanum,* to the laying on of hands practised in Pentecostal churches, to dances, trances, and the burning of animal dung of ritual paganism (Guiley 1991:192).

Alternatively, instead of casting out a spirit, the authorities could execute those who illegitimately invoked supernatural powers. It was also believed that the death of a convicted witch, if painful enough, would result in the salvation of that person's soul while at the same time driving the devil out. An added bonus was that such executions provided a highly educational (and sometimes profitable) form of entertainment for the people who came to watch.

THE WITCH CRAZE OF THE EUROPEAN RENAISSANCE, 1400–1700

HISTORICAL BACKGROUND

Virtually all societies have maintained some beliefs about witchcraft or sorcery. Before the witch craze, European beliefs were similar to those found on other continents. Witches and sorcerers were sometimes feared, sometimes persecuted, but they were often respected and recognized as people who served a useful role in the social order (e.g., by providing charms and amulets to protect people from harm or sickness, or by acting as oracles to decide the innocence or guilt of accused people). Magic directed against political leaders, however, was regarded as treason.

Belief in witches was "a continuing preoccupation of villagers, but not an obsession" (Garrett 1977:462; Thomas 1971; Cave 1995). The penalties for unauthorized or malicious practice of witchcraft were commensurate with those enforced for other kinds of assault on individuals or their property.

In the period before A.D 1000, church canon law (as reflected in the *Canon Episcopi* of about A.D 906, a compendium of popular lore on demons) tended to hold that it was both un-Christian and illegal to believe in the reality of witches (Webster 1996:77; Trevor-Roper 1969:13; Groh 1987:17). The Canon suggested that women who believed themselves able to use love incantations or to fly at night with the pagan goddess Diana were suffering from delusions planted by the devil. The Canon asserted that that the folkloric practice associated with such beliefs would disappear as all people became Christian (Ben-Yahuda 1985:34; Richards 1990:77). Catastrophes were sent by God to test humankind, and witches were deluded in believing that they could affect such things. In this period, attacks on presumed witches were regarded as superstitious pagan behaviour and sometimes resulted in protests to Rome.

In the period between 1000 and 1480, witches and sorcerers (along with other manifestations of supernatural beings) were redefined. Rather than harmless and misunderstood relics of pagan life, they became agents of the devil—a vast subversive conspiracy against everything that was right, orderly, and holy. In fact, many of the accusations made against heretics and witches in this period (incest, infanticide, sex orgies, and cannibalism) were the same as those that had been levelled against the early Christians by classical pagan writers (Richards 1990:78; Cohn 1976). The process whereby folklore, witchcraft beliefs, ritual magic, and devil worship became one overall and world-shattering conspiracy was neither smooth nor gradual: it was contested in some areas and embraced in others.

The witch craze has been described as a collective psychosis or mania (Trevor-Roper 1969). Although it has connections with modern fears of Satanism, its scale was much broader and its impact far more devastating. The exact number of victims is difficult to ascertain, given the widespread (but nonetheless local and episodic) nature of the witch-hunt. Episodes broke out repeatedly in towns, villages, and cities throughout Europe, the British Isles, and the American colonies, sometimes receding in one area only to break out in others. Events such as plagues, wars, and famines were likely to be followed by outbreaks of witch-hunting. In all, somewhere between 100,000 and 200,000 executions probably took place (Ben-Yahuda 1985:23), although figures as low as 60,000 (Levack 1987) and as high as 500,000 (Harris 1978:237), and even 9 million (Pelka 1992:7), have been cited.

CONTRIBUTING FACTORS: THE INQUISITION AND THE *MALLEUS MALEFICARUM*

While the witch craze can be seen as a symptom of the new dualist (monotheistic) way of looking at the world, its immediate sources were found within the dominant churches of the time, first among the Roman Catholic authorities, and then the Protestant ones. (When the dominant conformity is religious, the dominant deviance is likely to be antireligious.) The witch craze developed out of the work of the Roman Catholic Inquisition.

The Inquisition caught in its net not only heretics who challenged what the authorities felt were the appropriate forms of belief and behaviour with respect to church services, but also people who, like Galileo, put forward alternative interpretations of the empirical world (Redondi 1987; Christie-Murray 1989). The first Inquisition was set up in the eleventh century to combat heresy (false belief) by baptized Christians. It was followed in the late 1400s by the Spanish Inquisition, which directed its energies against residual Muslim and Jewish elements in Spain, and, in 1542, by the Roman Inquisition, which was established primarily to combat

Protestantism. All three inquisitions took the form of judicial bodies and operated under the assumption that witchcraft (which was seen to include the belief that the devil should be worshipped) was heresy of the worst kind and a special kind of crime (Larner 1980).

Witch-hunting received a considerable boost from the work of the Franciscan and Dominican brotherhoods. These "begging friars" were missionaries, healers, and preachers. Part of their mandate, which came directly from Rome, was to fight heresy in those areas not well controlled by the Church (towns, mountains, and outlying areas where feudalism had failed to take hold). Heresy was often interpreted as any resistance to the control of feudal authorities, and could also exist entirely in the minds of the people who were appointed, or appointed themselves, hunters of heretics. Conrad of Marburg, appointed first Inquisitor of Germany in

Figure 3.1   Heretics About to be Burnt to Death by the Inquisition at Valladolid in 1559

Source: Mary Evans Picture Library. Reprinted by permission.

1231, conducted a reign of terror, discovering "nests of devil-worshippers" until he was murdered in 1233. Like him, many of these witch-hunters, after killing hundreds, were themselves murdered. Peter of Verona, founder of the inquisition in northern Italy, was murdered in 1252. He was promptly the following year canonized as St. Peter Martyr (Richards 1990:57). The process by which such murders could take place is described in the book *The Name of the Rose*, later made into a film of the same name, by medievalist Umberto Eco. In this story Bernard Gui (a historically real Dominican inquisitor) meets a dramatic and sticky end.

Two Dominicans in particular—Heinrich Kramer (also called Institor) and Jakob Sprenger—played a major role in systematizing and giving shape to the definition of witchcraft as a conspiracy. Together they wrote a treatise on witchcraft called the *Malleus Maleficarum* (The Hammer of the Witches). Published in 1486, this was not the first book to codify all that was then known or believed of witchcraft—or even the first to set standards for the prosecution of witches—but it was the most systematic and complete. One of the first books to be printed on the newly invented printing press (Trevor-Roper 1969:101), it quickly became one of the first "bestsellers" in the history of books, outselling every book except the Bible (Russell 1988:166; Groh 1987:17). The "papal bull" that declared the jurisdiction of the authors to be the extirpation of witches in the Germanic countries, was issued in 1484 and reprinted with the *Malleus Maleficarum* in 1486. By printing the "bull" as an introduction to the *Malleus Maleficarum*, the book itself seemed carry Rome's blessing, as it eventually did. Sprenger and Kramer were unable to obtain the endorsement of the theological school at Cologne, so they forged the endorsement they wanted and published this with the book as well (Ben-Yahuda 1985:52). This act did a great deal to legitimize the legal persecution of witches.

The *Malleus* compiled all the existing sources of belief about witches and witchcraft, most of which were taken from common superstitions, biblical references, Greek and Roman writings, and the confessions of "witches." From this material the authors fashioned an impressive work that put witches in the worst possible light. Hailed for centuries as a work of great knowledge and scholarship, this book is now regarded as a compilation of pseudo-knowledge, fuelled by the fantasy projections of misogynistic and power-hungry men.

The book was divided into three parts. The first sought to convince readers that witches were dangerous heretics and that their gatherings *(sabbats)* were subversive. The ability of witches to raise hailstorms, cause crop failure, and emasculate men was only the tip of the iceberg. The real danger lay in the alliance with Satan. In contrast with previous church doctrine, the *Malleus* stated that those who rejected the reality of the witchcraft conspiracy were themselves part of it. The second section of the book was devoted to the identification of witches by "devil's marks" and other criteria, while the third section outlined the proper procedure for prosecuting a witch. This section included an extensive discussion of the kind of torture to be used at each point in the formal examination of accused witches.

TREATMENT OF THE ACCUSED

On the continent (Europe), torture was authorized in 1252 to elicit confessions from Albigensian heretics; in 1468, its use was extended to accused witches. Torture was needed to produce convictions because the Roman canon law of proof (valid in most European courts) required, for a conviction, the evidence of two eyewitnesses or a confession. Eyewitnesses were often impossible to find for something as conspiratorial as witchcraft, and thus confessions became crucial (Inverarity, Lauderdale, and Field 1983:251–254). As for the tortures used, Trevor-Roper (1969) provides a harrowing description:

> There were the gresillons ... which crushed the tips of the fingers and toes in a vice; the *échelle* or ladder, a kind of rack which violently stretched the body; and the *tortillon* which squeezed its tender parts at the same time. There was the *strappado estrapade,* a pulley which jerked the body violently in mid-air. There was the leg-screw or Spanish boot, much used in Germany and Scotland, which squeezed the calf and broke the shin-bone in pieces—"the most severe and cruel pain in the world," as a Scotsman called it—and the "lift" which hoisted the arms fiercely behind the back; and there was the "ram" or "witch-chair," a seat of spikes heated from below. There was also the "Bed of Nails," which was very effective for a time in Styria. In Scotland one might also be grilled on the caschielawis, and have one's finger-nails pulled off with the turkas or pincers; or needles might be driven up to their heads in the quick. But in the long run perhaps nothing was so effective as the *tormentum insomniac,* the torture of artificial sleeplessness, which has been revived in our day. (46)

In Anglo-Saxon territories (England, North America), torture was not as regular or systematic as that practised on the continent of Europe (Inverarity, Lauderdale, and Field 1983:251–25). In the American colonies, those who confessed to witchcraft in the Salem witch trials of 1692 were spared execution but were expected to name their co-conspirators. Whatever country we look at, however, we find that accused witches were regularly subjected to rough and humiliating treatment.

Under the pressure of torture (Scotland and the European continent) or rough treatment (England and America), the accused were expected to answer leading questions such as: When had they attended meetings with the devil *(sabbats)*? What had they eaten at the meetings? How had they had sex with the devil? Whom had they seen there? The resulting confessions were similar, whether they were made in France, Germany, Italy, Spain, or England. This apparent uniformity across widely separated places seemed to confirm the objective reality of the events described, which spurred the inquisitors to ever-greater industry (Trevor-Roper 1969:44). Those who understood what was going on were often silenced. For example, Father Friedrich von Spee, a Jesuit, was confessor to those condemned to die at the stake in the German city of Würzburg (Sagan 1995:407). He attempted to console more than 260 victims, many of them girls under ten years of age. He wrote an exposé, *Cautio Criminalis seu de Processibus contra Sagas Liber* (Precautions for Prosecutors)(1631), and as a result was lucky to escape the fires himself. He spent the rest of his life (cut short by the plague) in exile, writing mournful nature poetry (Cornwell 1991:359; Sagan 1995:407).

The examination process, while it assumed various forms, was generally self-reinforcing. Either a priest would ask for names of witches, or a witch-hunter (who was often paid on a per-witch basis) would name one. Almost any distinguishing behaviour or physical trait could be taken as an initial sign of a person's association with witchcraft. Being old and ugly, or even unusually beautiful or lucky, could necessitate further testing. If the woman was afraid, it meant her conscience was accusing her; if unafraid, then she was confident that Satan would rescue her. If she had led an exemplary life, that life was evidence of dissembling (only appearing to be virtuous); if she had not led an exemplary life, this was proof that she kept company with demons (Sagan 1995:406). Commonly, the accused would be thrown into water; sinking meant the person was innocent, while floating denoted guilt. This form of judicial torture almost always produced the desired effect of more names, and yet more confessions. The snowballing effect of each trial seemed to confirm the existence of an extensive, ever-growing, and terrifyingly conspiratorial underworld.

On the continent, the witch's property was usually confiscated by the court. The whole process became "an expense account scam" (Sagan 1995:120). The witch's family was often forced to pay for the services of the torturers and executioners, the wood for burning, and the banquet held after the burning. In England, where those who were found guilty were hanged rather than burned, and where any confiscated property went to the state, not the court, far fewer executions took place, and there were far fewer wealthy victims (Inverarity et al. 1983:251–254).

Figure 3.2   Trial by Water

Trial by water. The suspected witch was flung into a pond or stream with her hands and feet bound together. If she sank she was innocent; but if she floated she was found guilty of witchcraft and then had to endure an even more horrible death.

Source: Reproduced from *Fireburn: Tales of Witchery* by Ken Radford. London: Michael O'Mara Books Ltd.

EXPLANATIONS FOR THE CRAZE

The demonic explanation for the witch craze is complete in itself and cannot be refuted by any form of natural evidence. It is an explanation built on faith, one that teaches us nothing beyond the belief we started with in the first place.

More worldly interpretations of the causes of witch-hunting can be found by examining what kinds of people were accused of witchcraft, what kinds of people profited from their persecution, and when or under what conditions the accusations were made. All of these aspects are considered in the following list, which summarizes the characteristics of those selected for prosecution as witches.

Characteristics of the Accused

1. *Women.* By most accounts, at least 80 percent of those executed were women (Levack 1992b). Male victims were frequently related to—or were trying to protect—women who had been accused. Thus, to understand the witch-hunts, it is necessary first to "confront the deeply imbedded feelings about women—and the intricate patterns of interest underlying those feelings—among our witch-ridden ancestors" (Karlsen 1989:xiii).

    The *Malleus Maleficarum* attributed the fact that "a greater number of witches is found in the fragile feminine sex than among men" to women's moral and intellectual inferiority, their weakness, and, most especially, their sexual depravity:

    > All witchcraft comes from carnal lust, which is in women insatiable.... Wherefore for the sake of fulfilling their lusts they consort even with devils. (Kramer and Sprenger 1971:47)

    The selection of women as targets was hardly surprising given a patriarchal church that excluded women from all leadership roles and feared them as potential subversives (Worobec 1995:175). Women who stepped out of their assigned roles as bearers of children and servants to men were especially vulnerable. Thus, women who were "old maids," widows without family support, sexually promiscuous, or who were lesbians were likely to be targeted (Worobec 1995:176).

2. *Women who gave birth to deformed babies.* These infants were regarded as "Satan's spawn," the product of sexual orgies involving the mother and the devil or his demons.

3. *People seen in the dreams of others* (especially if in the form of a sexual partner).

4. *Men or women who claimed to have occult powers and played the role.* In every society, there have been people with "second sight," who have forecast the future, dispensed spells or charms, or threatened others with supernatural vengeance. In the 1692 Salem witch trials, the first accused was Tituba, a West Indian servant who entertained the local girls with stories of voodoo and with fortune telling by palmistry. When the girls began falling into unexplained fits, Tituba's employer, the Reverend Parris, beat a confession of witchcraft out of her. People such as Tituba are tolerated in normal times, when there is no anxiety about demonic conspiracies, but are often among the first condemned when such fears are raised.

5. *People believed to be involved in treasonous conspiracies.* When the inheritance of a throne could depend on the birth of a living male baby and when poisoning was a major factor in royal succession, the practice of witchcraft for political purposes was often suspected. This form of accusation was particularly common in the early witchcraft trials (around A.D. 1400). For example, under James III of Scotland, several witches were executed on the grounds that James's brother, the Earl of Mar, had been conspiring with them against the king. The earl was mysteriously murdered, presumably on his brother's orders (Larner 1980:53).

6. *People who did not fully accept Church dogma and practice.* Besides free thinkers and early scientists, this group consisted of people who continued to follow the customs of the earlier pagan religions. Among the evidence presented at the heresy trial of Joan of Arc was the fact that she had participated in ancient Celtic practices that were traditional in rural areas but forbidden by the Church, which saw such events as the equivalent of participating in *sabbats* with the devil. It should be noted, however, that the claim made early in this century by Margaret Murray that the "witches" were in fact members of a secret pre-Christian fertility religion is no longer supported by historians (Murray 1921; Larner 1980:59).

7. *Healers, herbalists, and naturopaths.* People involved in issues such as fertility, midwifery, and abortion were particularly vulnerable. Known as "cunning men" and "wise women" in England, and by equivalent names in Europe, they had "powers" that were not under the regulation of the authorities (Cassar 1993:319). To be an expert in sexual matters in a society dominated by the clergy was dangerous. Abortion, for example, was associated with beliefs that newborn babies were being used in obscene rituals with the devil. Curing people by "magical" means was also condemned. Both "white" (good) and "black" (bad) witchcraft were considered heretical. Female midwives and herbalists

were in competition with the rising all-male, university-based medical establishment, which relied more on logic and dogma than on practical experience (Watts 1984:28; Eastlea 1980). Finally, people knowledgeable about drugs were also suspect because the effects of drugs such as atropine, henbane, and thornapple, which have narcotic and poisonous properties, seemed to reveal supernatural powers (Worobec 1995:171). Vision-inducing drugs may lie at the root of beliefs about witches flying at night and being able to change shape (Harris 1978:190). Whether these drugs were given to people by women healers, or whether they simply came to them as mould on bread (some fungi that attack grain have LSD-like properties), they could be responsible for visions.

8. *People blamed for the misfortune of others.* Many accusations of witchcraft had their root in quarrels in which one party apparently threatened another, who later became sick or experienced some misfortune. Illnesses attributed to witchcraft or sorcery included "impotence, stomach pains, barreness, hernias, abscesses, epileptic seizures, and convulsions (Worobec 1995:166–67). Many cases involved beggars who seemed to be retaliating against those who had denied them assistance (Groh 1987:19), or people who *ought* to have been seeking revenge for some previous insult or harm (Worobec 1995:181) The most frequent cases were those in which someone repudiated a neighbour—usually an old woman seeking a favour—and then attributed personal misfortunes to her (Macfarlane 1970:196; Garrett 1977:462-63; Worobec 1995:182). Situations of this kind became increasingly common as the mutual-help systems typical of rural communities were disrupted by population growth and the arrival of early capitalist forms of economy; people who had some wealth began to feel threatened by the rising numbers of beggars and indigents.

9. *Exceptional people.* Sometimes personal characteristics like an unusual appearance, or perhaps extraordinary success or talent, were seen as the result of a Faustian bargain with Satan. The story of Faust, who sells his soul to the devil in exchange for knowledge and power, goes back at least to the ninth century. Niccolo Paganini, a composer and violin virtuoso of the 1800s, was treated as a Faustian figure, primarily because his playing was so extraordinary. Similarly, it was widely believed that Sir Francis Drake defeated the Spanish Armada with Satan's help (Russell 1984:82). Canadian fiddler Ashley MacIsaac has similarly been accused of having made a demonic pact. Unlike Paganini, MacIsaac will not have to worry about being harmed or refused burial rites.

10. *People named by accused witches under torture or persuasion.* Almost anyone could be named, but most confessing witches did not try to implicate court officials or other powerful people; such accusations, when they occurred, were often

suppressed by the court. In New England, people who denied the charges were often convicted and executed, while those who confessed and named others were set free; not surprisingly, then, a great many witches were named by the accused.

11. *People named by those suffering from illness or hardship.* In Salem in 1692, the young girls who showed signs of "possession" (screaming unaccountably, falling into grotesque convulsions, mimicking the behaviour of dogs) named everyone they had a grudge against (Erikson 1966:142). In total, 142 persons were named, ultimately resulting in the death by hanging of 21 men and women (and one dog). A man who refused to plead either guilty or not guilty was crushed to death under heavy stones; his refusal to enter a plea was interpreted as a denial of the legitimacy of the proceedings. Only when the accusations began to include prominent people (e.g., Lady Phipps, wife of the Massachusetts colony's governor) was the process seriously questioned and, ultimately, rejected. Similarly, in Europe, the craze began to die out as it threatened more powerful people.

12. *The mentally ill.* Allowed to wander freely in normal times, those suffering from mental illness were particularly vulnerable to being caught up in the witch-hunt. Also singled out were people with psychoneurotic symptoms (manifested, for example, in a failure to react when pricked with a pin) and "hysterics," who acted out because of physical or emotional stress. As Ben-Yahuda (1985) notes,

> While Freud himself virtually ignored the European witch-craze, it contains elements to warm any analyst's heart: cruel and destructive persecutions, women, sex, and violence. These could easily be integrated into psychoanalytic interpretations, emphasizing the projection of hostility, reaction-formation, incestuous wishes, and impulses of the id. (43)

13. *People with physical disabilities or neurological disorders.* Such individuals might be seen as victims of the witchcraft of others or as suitable partners for Satan. They were likely to be accused of giving others "the evil eye." Also included in this group were the elderly and the physically unattractive.

14. *Scapegoats for the system.* These were generally people who lacked the clout to defend themselves (although few individuals were absolutely safe from accusation). As long as people believed that plagues, wars, famines, and personal troubles were caused by demons, they did not expect their leaders to provide alternatives to scapegoating. More significantly, as long as they thought they

needed their leaders to combat witches, they would not rise up against them. The control of witchcraft became a very significant reason to pay tithes to church authorities and to obey their rules; only they knew how to diagnose and treat supernatural ills, and only they were powerful enough to oppose the devastating powers of Satan. Thus, the witch craze "divided the poor against each other in suspicion and fear" at the same time as it forced people to depend on the Church (Harris 1978; Erikson 1966).

The above list tells us a great deal about the conditions that informed the craze. Whether in Europe, England, or the American colonies, witch-victims represented resistance to the "sacred canopy" erected over society by their respective churches. Some of these victims were actually opposed to the system. Others served as scapegoats for the threat posed to churches by the fundamental changes that were taking place around the world. Events such as Columbus's voyage to Americas in 1492, the opening up of trade routes to the East, and the invention of the printing press all contributed to a growth in knowledge that had the potential to undermine Church rule. Scapegoats also provided a convenient explanation for plagues and famines, which were especially acute in the period between 1400 and 1700, as was social change (Watts 1984:7). Throughout the witch-craze period, most of the trials were held in the cultural "borderlands," where social diversity and religious conflict were the greatest, or in places where war and plague had created disorder (Coudert 1992:89; Thomas 1971). Even in later outbreaks, such as in prerevolutionary Russia (late 1800s), the background of the craze was anxiety-provoking social change and economic upheaval (Worobec 1995:168). Places that were sheltered from change did not develop the craze. For example, while the French in France were burning Huguenot heretics and witches, the stable French settlement in Canada was not affected; the belief in witches existed, but there was no panic associated with it (Morison 1955:248).

Only when rational and scientific ways of thinking developed to the point that the courts became fully secular did the craze finally wither away. The courts gradually ceased to treat witchcraft as a reality other than in its associations with criminal acts, fraud, extortion, or abuse (such as ritual child abuse). Witchcraft remains part of modern law, but only in this restricted sense. The Criminal Code of Canada, for example, makes it an offence to "pretend to exercise or use any kind of witchcraft sorcery, enchantment or conjuration." In December 1988, a Toronto court found a laboratory technician guilty of practising witchcraft because he had been treating a teenage girl's psychological problems with "herb drinks, candles and the laying on of hands," and had charged a fee for it (Kelly 1988). Similar legislation in Australia has resulted in criminal charges against tarot card readers and other fortune tellers (Hume, 1995:148). However, when an Ontario Supreme Court judge said to murderer Peter Demeter (sentenced to five life terms in 1988) "You certainly appear to ooze evil from every pore of your body," few people in the courtroom thought that Demeter was being told he was "possessed" or in the service of Satan (Claridge 1988).

MODERN VERSIONS OF WITCH-HUNTING

Although we no longer regularly consider the things we fear as being demonic, Satan remains a powerful metaphor for our fears of the unknown and dangerous, and for our awareness of the frightening and disgusting aspects of reality. Fundamental to this conception is the theory that a conspiracy exists against public order and decency. This belief has led to "witch hunts" aimed at finding and rooting out the "heretics" whose way of life threatens our own. What distinguishes the "moral panic" version of social menace conspiracy from real cases of conspiracy is that with the former there is an almost total lack of empirically verifiable evidence, along with cavalier treatment of the data that do exist. The story, spread through rumour, gossip, and innuendo, is accepted and passed on by credulous or ill-motivated people without being meaningfully "tested." The same pattern is found in the fears about Catholic "popish plots" in early England as in the more recent cases of the Hitler's campaign against Jews, McCarthy's persecution of "communists," or accusations that child-care workers can fly through the air, or would cannibalize babies.

THE HOLOCAUST

In Nazi Germany, the "witch-hunt" involved all those who seemed to oppose Hitler's new order. Like the witchcraft craze, it spread far beyond those who were a potential threat and served purposes other than those admitted to by authorities. As with witches, systems were set up to identify a hidden enemy and destroy it, and the web of suspicion grew ever wider until no one could feel entirely safe. A note published with *The Protocols of the Elders of Zion* (an anti-Semitic forgery) explicitly linked Jews with the antichrist:

> There is no room left for doubt. With all the might and terror of Satan, the reign of the triumphant King of Israel is approaching our unregenerate world; the King born of the blood of Zion—the Antichrist—is near to the throne of universal power. (quoted in Cohn 1981:255)

By thus characterizing Jews, the *Protocols* attempted to justify any action that might be taken against them. The *Malleus* had done much the same to the witches several centuries earlier.

THE RED SCARE

In the 1950s, there were people in both Canada and the United States who believed in communism and sometimes even secretly belonged to communist organizations. Nonetheless, the "red menace" notion greatly exaggerated their numbers and influence, and resulted in the harassment and blacklisting of thousands of citizens.

In the United States, "red scares" have occurred periodically. At these times people believed to be communists have been subjected to investigations, as were accused witches throughout the witch craze. Here, too, the belief that hidden conspirators were at work fuelled paranoia and turned people against one another. "McCarthyism" (named after Senator Joseph McCarthy, who made a career of communist-hunting) also spread into Canada. Most victims were deprived of their jobs, and many were also treated as social pariahs (Scher 1992). Leopold Infeld, a Polish-born University of Toronto professor, was denounced in the House of Commons and harassed by the RCMP. Ultimately he returned to Poland. The reason for the harassment was that when some of his friends' names turned up on the list of spies in Canada that Igor Gouzenko (a Soviet who defected to Canada in 1945) gave to the Canadian government, Infeld joined a small organization formed to defend them. For this "crime," he was dubbed a "fellow traveller" and suspected of abusing his knowledge of atomic energy. The fact that he was not an atomic scientist carried little weight at the time (Zeidenberg 1990).

DAY CARES AND NURSERIES: THE BUCKEY CASE

Other witch-hunting outbreaks concerned cases in which accusations of child molesting were made against day-care workers. Particularly notorious was the case of Peggy Buckey and her son Raymond, who in May of 1989 were together charged with 65 counts of child molestation. The Buckeys ran the McMartin Nursery School in Manhattan Beach, near Los Angeles. According to newspaper accounts, the first complaint came from a woman who later died from conditions often associated with alcoholism. This same accuser maintained that McMartin teachers had put staples in her child's ears, nipples, and tongue, and that her son (aged 2 1/2) had taken part in a human sacrifice ritual (Fukurai et al. 1994:47). She claimed that Ray Buckey "flew through the air." Following her complaint, police sent a form letter to each of the families of the children who attended the nursery. Parents were asked to question their children about possible criminal acts including "oral sex, fondling of genitals, buttocks or chest area, and sodomy" (Reed 1989). They were also informed that

> photos may have been taken of children without their clothing. Any information from your child regarding ever having observed Ray Buckey leave a classroom alone with a child during any nap period, or if they have ever observed Ray Buckey tie up a child, is important. (Reed 1989)

As a result of this highly suggestive letter, about 360 children who had attended McMartin were sent to a Los Angeles anti-child-abuse group. Therapists there elicited stories of activities that included sodomy, oral copulation, nude photography, and exhibitionism. Films of the interviews show that the children were praised if they reported abuse; if they did not report abuse, the therapist rephrased the question or repeated it. The therapists used dolls with adult-sized genitalia, which could have shocked the children and induced fantasies. The McMartin Nursery School and seven others were closed. Peggy Buckey, her son Raymond, and five other childcare workers were charged. Raymond Buckey spent four years in custody before the trial (Reed 1989). Costs for the prosecution's part of the trial alone amounted to $15 million (Fukurai, Butler and Krooth 1994:44). After six years, a destroyed business, and ruined reputations, the defendants were acquitted on all 135 charges that came before the court. Other charges (based only on the children's tainted testimony) were dropped.

Such cases, of which there have been many, began increasing in the mid-to-late 1980s and seem now to be decreasing. From 1985 on, various allegations about satanic elements in the murder of unbaptized children, ritual abuse, mutilation, sexual trafficking of children, human sacrifice, and cannibalism were publicized on network television programs such as ABC's *20/20*, specifically its story, "The Devil Worshippers" (1985); NBC's "1986"; and Geraldo Rivera's Halloween special "Devil Worship: Exposing Satan's Underground"(1986). Journalistic accounts appeared in newspapers and books, and an explosion of exposés, "recovered memory" autobiographies, and anti-cult organizations followed. Satanists were accused of sixty thousand Americans deaths each year, even though no evidence exists to support these repeated claims (Jenkins and Maier-Katkin 1992:54, 60).

A Canadian day-care satanism case took place in the small town of Martensville, Alberta (population about 3000), in 1992, in which 9 people, including 5 police officers, were charged with more than a hundred sex-related charges. Children reported that they were "cut with knives" and forced to take part in sex

---

Box 3.3   A Cautionary Tale

Five years later, the nightmare continues for Ron and Linda Sterling. Accused and ultimately acquitted of child-sex-abuse charges alleged to have occurred at the day care centre in their Martensville, Sask., home, the Sterlings have yet to put their shattered lives together. They have gone from being accused in a case that rivetted national attention, to being the victims of a justice system that seemingly went terribly wrong. "It has destroyed our lives completely," says Ron Sterling, who has been unemployed since he and his wife were found not guilty in February 1994. "We lost our home, our vehicle, and our reputation"...

Initially, nine people, including five police officers, were charged with 170 counts in what was said to be child-abuse ring operating out of the Sterlings' home in the quiet bedroom community 10 km north of Saskatoon. Only the Sterlings' then 25-year-old son, Travis, and a female young offender were found guilty. But the young offender's conviction was later reversed on appeal. Charges against five others were eventually stayed by the Crown due to a lack of evidence.

Ron Sterling remains adamant that his son, convicted on eight counts of physical and sexual assault, is also innocent. He is demanding a public airing of what happened to expose what he says was a misguided prosecution based on fabrications planted in the pliable minds of young children by incompetent police interrogation ... Five civil law suits are pending against the police, prosecutors and Saskatchewan government, including a suit launched by the Sterlings seeking $11.6 million in damages.

If there is a lesson from Martensville, it is that suggestions of sexual abuse, especially involving young children, must be handled with care and professionalism. The Martensville case rested almost exclusively on testimony of children aged 2 to 9, with no corroborating forensic or eyewitness evidence. Dr. David Raskin, a former University of Utah psychology professor who has studied roughly 500 child-abuse cases, testified for the defence at the Sterlings' trial. "The interview techniques used on the children were horrendous," Raskin told *Maclean's*. "They put extreme pressure on the kids who initially denied anything happened. In that sense, it was the worst case I've seen ...."

Source: Dale Eisler, "A Cautionary Tale," *Maclean's* February 10, 1997, 46. Reprinted by permission.

acts with dogs and flying bats. They claimed that they had watched a baby being skinned, roasted, and eaten. Other than the statements of seven youngsters who had been exposed to many intense and repetitive interviews in which "leading and suggestive" questioning techniques were used, there was no evidence to support the allegations. The lengthy trial resulted in only one conviction, which was for "fondling a 9-year-old-girl." Although fondling is a serious offence, it is a much different kind of offence than crimes of satanic ritual abuse. Several of the accused are now suing the Crown and police for malicious prosecution (Roberts 1996:A6).

MODERN BELIEFS ABOUT DEMONIC DEVIANCE

Despite the predominance of secular definitions of deviance, the demonic remains a theme recognized and sometimes used in our society. A 1978 Gallup poll reported that 1 out of 3 Americans believed that "the devil is a personal being who directs evil forces and influences people to do wrong," while another 1 out of 3 believed in the devil as an impersonal force. A 1990 Gallup poll of 1226 adults found that 55 percent of Americans believe in the reality of the devil, and that 14 percent believe that witches are real.

The belief that there is evil in the world does not necessarily result in accusations of demonism and panic over hidden conspiracies. When it does emerge in this form, however, the modern identifying label for those suspected of conspiring is "satanist" rather than witch, and the suspects are male as often as they are female. Indeed, the emphasis on female witches has receded, and the term "witchcraft" is rarely used in this sense. A huge divide has emerged between those who use the concepts of Satanism and those who speak of witchcraft. Contemporary witches consider themselves to be practitioners of faiths such as the Mother-Goddess religion. They neither believe in nor worship Satan, and they are usually (but not always) ignored rather than feared by people with different religious convictions (Marron 1989; Guiley 1991).

Belief in satanic deviance is, not surprisingly, found mainly (but not exclusively) in areas with a high degree of religious consciousness, such as the Bible Belt areas of Canada and the United States. Anti-Satanism, however, goes far beyond the usual religious explanations of deviance. It shares with the various examples of witch-hunts presented earlier a tendency to label people on the basis of very insubstantial empirical evidence.

THE INGRAM CASE

Following his arrest on charges of child abuse in 1988, Paul Ingram, a "zealous member of a born-again church" (Wright 1993) in Olympia, Washington, admitted to abusing his daughters and to years of participation in a Satanic child-abuse ring that practised pornography and ritual sacrifice. His confession implicated more than a dozen other people, two of whom were charged.

But there was a problem. No physical evidence of any kind existed to back up Ingram's confession: no videotapes or photographs of satanic, pornographic activities; no visible scars on the daughters (other than those resulting from acne and an appendectomy), even though both of them claimed they had been cut and burned. The alleged activities had left no traces at all, other than the wildly improbable and inconsistent—and increasingly horrifying—stories recounted by Ingram's daughters. Ingram maintained that he had no memory of the acts he was being accused of, but at the same time he did not deny doing them. His confession was elicited after four hours of interrogation in which detectives informed him that he was in denial, and that the only way he would ever remember the abuse would be to admit that he was guilty. People who heard the taped confession said Ingram sounded like someone in a hypnotic state, and that he was influenced by suggestions put forward by the interrogators.

The three accused men spent months in jail before their trials, were forced to pay for their defence ($90,000 in one case), and continue to be ostracized by others in the community (Watters 1991; Wright 1993). While charges against Ingram's two co-conspirators were dropped, Ingram himself pled guilty and was sentenced to twenty years in prison. His later efforts to withdraw his guilty plea have, to date, been denied (Wright 1993). In 1996, Ingram was still in a penitentiary, apparently well-adjusted and working on the prison newspaper. The parallels between this satanism-related case and the witchcraft craze are clear:

> One could say that the miracle of the Ingram case is that it did not go any further than it did. If Ingram's memories had not finally become too absurd for even the investigators to believe, if Rabie or Risch [Ingram's alleged co-conspirators] had accepted the prosecution's deals, if the alleged crimes of other people implicated in the investigation [some thirty in all] had occurred within the statute of limitations—if any of these quite conceivable scenarios had taken place, then the witch-hunt in Olympia would have raged out of control, and one cannot guess how many other lives might have been destroyed. (Wright 1993:76)

MORAL PANIC AND ROLE-PLAYING AS ASPECTS OF SATANISM

Two distinct aspects of satanist and antisatanist thinking exist. The first, moral panic, expresses the ideological pattern of the witch-hunt. Fears are raised that are out of all proportion to the empirical evidence. In role-playing, the second aspect, individuals recognize the pattern of deviance being described by authorities and proceed to become what others fear. They act out the role provided to them, sometimes developing it still further. The cases of murderers Leonard Lake, Sam Berkowitz, and cult leader Charles Manson, for example, for follow this pattern.

Thus, satanism as a modern phenomenon involves: (1) monsters in the mind (the innocent who are accused); and (2) monsters in reality (people who deliberately live up to the evil images of those who fear satanism). While some occult gang members engage in horrifying satanic acts, far more of them are playing a role (Korem 1994:171–197). In the following sections, we will look at both aspects of satanism—at the exaggerated claims of the antisatanists, which often entrap and destroy innocent people, and at the behaviour of people who call themselves satanists.

SATANISM AS MORAL PANIC

The 1980s witnessed a sudden increase in reports of satanic cult activities—reports that originated from religious groups in both England and North America. Other sources, however, reported no evidence of such activities (Marty 1990:308; Hicks 1991; Marron 1989). For example, while accusations of kidnappings and ritual murders rose, there were no corresponding increases either in missing people reports or in the discovery of places where such activities could have occurred. Just as in the witchcraft episode, the hidden nature of satanism induced "experts" to construct lists of partial evidence from which they could develop accusations against others.

On November 7, 1989, a group of probation officers met in Ingersoll, Ontario, with Rob Tucker, director of the Council on Mind Abuse (COMA), to discuss the issue of satanism among their teenaged clients. The resulting report (Bulthuis 1989) provided an A-list of suspected satanic cult involvement characteristics under the heading "Our Client Displays the Following Behaviours," and a B-list under the heading "Our Client Also Displays the Following Behaviours." The A-list included characteristics and behaviours such as social withdrawal; lack of trust in others; suicidal tendencies; self-mutilation; involvement in shoplifting, vandalism, or murder; interest in abnormal sexuality; manipulativeness with respect to authorities;

Box 3.4   The Construction of a Panic

In the case of a sensational panic like satanism, it is especially interesting to see the rhetorical devices used to dispel incredulity about these remarkable charges. A writer will commonly introduce a theme, and suggest that the occult might play "some" role in this particular problem. An example might be given to support this idea. Other quotes then gradually build up the scale of the occult role until the reader is convinced that the whole problem is in fact little more than a facet of the immense satanic menace.

These quotes are judiciously chosen, and few can be described as untrue in specifics. [One writer] for example, quite rightly notes that "Some cult watchers and police agree that a large number of missing children are victims of human sacrifice cults." Of course these "experts' may be utterly wrong in their belief, but his actual sentence is quite true; they do indeed agree on this. He then develops his argument as if the initial opinion is established as factual. "According to the few survivors, children are abducted and subjected to the terrible intimidation of drugs and brainwashing before being sacrificed." (We might note here that brainwashing a person one intends to kill anyway seems a massive waste of time and energy.) "Innocent children and guiltless babies are perfect vicitims." As a clincher, he then produces the remark of a police officer in Beaumont, CA, to the effect that "95 percent of all missing children are victims of occult-related abductions. The unwary reader may well leave the page with the impression that this is the opinion of a well-known or widely respected police authority, instead of one individual in a specific department."

Source: Kluwer Academic Publishers, *Crime, Law and Social Change* 17(1), 1992, pp. 53–75—excerpt from Daniel Malir-Katkin: "Satanism: Myth and Reality in a Contemporary Moral Panic," with kind permission from Kluwer Academic Publishers.

and lack of remorse (Bulthuis 1989:8). The more specific B-list produces a profile of a client who "has an obsession with images of horror"; likes the violence associated with heavy metal music; collects satanic paraphernalia; and draws, as graffiti, such things as the pentagram or the numbers 666 or 18 (Bulthuis 1989:9). Taken together, these indicators were proposed as soft (A-list) and hard (B-list) signs of satanic involvement. While no particular recommendations were made, probation officers were clearly expected to be more concerned about deviant acts with a satanic element than about similar acts without it.

Box 3.5   Police–Community Conferences on Satanism

The typical [police–community] conference runs from one to three days, and many of them include the same presenters and instructors ... Typical topics include the following:

1. Historical overview of satanism, witchcraft, and paganism from ancient to modern times
2. Nature and influence of fantasy role-playing games such as *Dungeons and Dragons*
3. Lyrics, symbolism, and influence of rock and roll, Heavy Metal, and Black Metal music
4. Teenage "stoner" gangs, their symbols and their vandalism
5. Teenage suicide by adolescents dabbling in the occult
6. Crimes committed by self-styled satanic practitioners, including grave and church desecrations and robberies, animal mutilations, and even murders
7. Ritualistic abuse of children as part of bizarre ceremonies and human sacrifices
8. Organized, traditional, or multigenerational satanic groups involved in organized conspiracies, such as taking over day-care centers, infiltrating police departments, and trafficking in human sacrifice victims
9. The "Big Conspiracy" theory, which implies that statistics are responsible for such things as Adolf Hitler, World War II, abortion, pornography, Watergate, Irangate, and the infiltration of the Department of Justice, the Pentagon, and the White House.

During the conferences, these nine areas are linked together with the liberal use of the word "satanism" and some common symbolism (pentagrams, 666, demons, etc.). The implication is that all are part of a continuum of behaviour, a single problem, or some common conspiracy. The information presented is a mixture of fact, theory, opinion, fantasy, and paranoia, and because some of it can be proven or corroborated (desecration of cemeteries, vandalism, etc.) the implication is that it is all true and documented....

Source: Reprinted with permission from *Out of Darkness: Exploring Satanism and Ritual Abuse*, by D.K. Sakheim and S.E. Devine. Copyright © 1992 Jossey-Boss Inc., Publishers. First published by Lexington Books. All rights reserved.

Another example of antisatanism can be seen in the furor that erupted over the traditional logo of Procter & Gamble (see Box 3.6) and over a flyer circulated about the company. The flyer (disseminated by fundamentalist churches and posted on

---

Box 3.6   Anti-Satanism in Action: The Procter & Gamble Logo

Procter & Gamble Co. is redesigning the traditional moon-and-stars symbol that critics charged linked it with the devil.

The consumer products grant is also adopting two corporate logos to complement the symbol of a bearded man in a crescent moon surrounded by stars, company spokesman Terry Lottus said.

Stationery, business cards and other materials soon will feature either a script-like "Procter & Gamble" or "P&G," the company said.

The moon and stars will continue to be the company's officially registered trade-mark, Mr. Loftus said. But the company is eliminating curly hairs on the man's beard that look like the number 6. For about a decade, the sixes helped fuel the rumours that P&G supports Satan, since the number 666 is linked with the devil in the Bible book of Revelation.

Cincinnati-based P&G has filed court lawsuits and issued repeated statements to deny the rumours since they began about 1981.

"The moon and stars remains an important company trademark, and we will continue to use it broadly," Mr. Loftus said. Of the new logos, he said: "We were looking to develop corporate identity symbols that would translate to consumers around the world."

Since 1985, Procter & Gamble has gradually removed the moon-and-stars mark from most of the company's products. The symbol probably will be limited to use in buildings and on awards and stationery, P&G said.

P&G managers presented the new logos to the company's board of directors Tuesday. Management is developing guidelines on when to use which symbols.

Source: "P & G Redesigns Moon/Stars Logo." *The Globe and Mail,* July 11, 1991. Reprinted by permission of The Associated Press.

supermarket bulletin boards first throughout the southern United States then through the midwest and into the northern states) claimed that on March 1, 1991, the president of Procter & Gamble had appeared on *The Phil Donahue Show* to announce that he was "coming out of the closet" with respect to his financial support for the Church of Satan, a substantial part of which consisted of profits from P&G products (Blumenfeld 1991; Victor 1993:13–14). As a final challenge to all Christians, the flyer claimed that the P&G president had claimed that satanism could not hurt his business, since there were "not enough Christians in the United States to make a difference." (The *Donahue* staff set up a voice-mail answering system in response that informed callers that the president of Procter & Gamble "never, ever appeared on the show." The message could be accessed by pressing the number 6 on a touchtone phone.) This campaign, which included a boycott of P&G products by all "right-thinking" Christians, exemplifies the conspiracy aspect of witch-hunts. No amount of empirical evidence is sufficient to undo the tight logical circle that produces both the deviant category and the deviant chosen to fill it.

SATANISM AS ROLE-PLAYING

The second aspect of satanism involves the way in which the socially constructed role of satanist is taken over by people, who then attempt to enact it in real life. One of these was Aleister Crowley (1875–1947), who called himself "The Great Beast" and was pleased to be known as "the wickedest man in the world" (Wilson 1987). Crowley deliberately cultivated his "beast" role and spent his life in devotion to the occult. He was described (in the liner notes from Colin Wilson's *Aleister Crowley: The Nature of the Beast* published in 1987), as an "insatiable ambisexual athlete, a pimp who lived on the immoral earnings of his girlfriends, and a junkie who daily took enough heroin to kill a roomful of people." In 1934, Crowley attempted to sue a biographer who had accused him of involvement in black magic and human sacrifice; the testimony given at the trial was so repulsive to both judge and jury that Crowley lost his case (Guiley 1991:131). On another occasion, a friend of Crowley's lost a libel suit mainly because the jury accepted the argument "that anyone who was a friend of Crowley's had no reputation to lose" (Wilson 1987:25).

Satanist elements have, in varying degrees, entered the personal lives of many well-known writers and performers. Horror novelist Shirley Jackson "played with" ideas of witchcraft and the occult in her own life, as well as in her novels (Oppenheimer 1988). Other writers have both sought out and felt "possessed" by occult forces. William Burroughs, for example, tried to explain how he came to shoot his wife, toward whom he felt no anger.

I live with the constant threat of possession, and a constant need to escape from possession, from Control. So the death of Joan brought me into contact with the invader, the Ugly Spirit, and maneuvered me into a lifelong struggle, in which I have had no choice except to write my way out." (quoted in Morgan 1988:199)

The writer-artist Jack Pollock also expressed the feeling that his "excesses" in life were somehow demonically caused.

I do have a "mad motor" and the brakes are very difficult to locate most of the time. If I don't keep positively active, then the negative takes over ... I feel possessed. Your enquiry whether I feel that there is a foreign power within me strikes a familiar chord ... (Pollock 1989:121)

Though few in number, some psychiatrists entertain the possibility that satanic possession may be real. M. Scott Peck, for example, has written about people he believes are demonically evil. In one such case, his patient (the brother of a suicide) received, as a birthday present from his parents, the weapon with which his brother had killed himself. Peck felt that parents who could do such a thing were evil, and he acted to rescue the boy from them. Another case involved a man who "made a pact with the devil" in order to rid himself of obsessive-compulsive thoughts. While Peck gives logical reasons for denouncing this man's behaviour (he should have been courageous enough to face, and deal with, the sources of his obsessions), he does not rule out the possibility that the devil may really have been involved. Finally, Peck describes two modern exorcisms at which not only demons but also the antichrist appeared (Peck 1983:31–35; 51–59; 185–211).

Those who are committed to a "bad" identity may acquire pentagram tattoos and other symbols of the occult, or they may seek to participate in occult rituals (Lowney 1995). In 1990, in North York, Ontario, two young men were arrested after a woman and her 3-year-old son escaped from their apartment. The woman reported that she had been attacked and threatened with death if she refused to join a coven. Inside the apartment, police found artificial human skulls, candles, a satanic bible, a sword, dagger, robes, and audiotapes and books on witchcraft (*Toronto Star* 1990b).

People may acquire their knowledge of the satanic role from religious authorities (by reversing or reframing their teachings) or by perusing Church documents such as the *Malleus Maleficarum* or Guasso's *Compendium Maleficarum*. As noted by Stephen Kent, "Readily accessible religious texts that often are central to our culture may provide inspiration to people who either want to sanctify their deviance or venerate the reputed god of this world (i.e., Satan) (Kent 1993a:229). Some may acquire this knowledge through other "deviant" religious traditions, such as the Masonic Order (Kent 1993b). Or they may discover it through popular culture (e.g., books and movies with Satanic themes). Jenkins and Maier-Katkin have found that most youths arrested for "satanic" crimes are "dabblers ... whose notion of the occult derived from horror films or the game '*Dungeons and Dragons*'" (1992:61). The controversial role-playing game Dungeons and Dragons, in the judgment of the Reverend John Torrell, as quoted on CBC's *Ideas,* provides teaching on

> demonology, witchcraft, voodoo, murder, rape, blasphemy, suicide, insanity, sex perversion, homosexuality, Satan-worship, gambling, Jungian psychology, barbarism, cannibalism, sadism, demon-summoning, necromantics, divination, and many more teachings brought to you in living colour direct from the pit of Hell. (Canadian Broadcasting Corporation 1991:1)

The people involved in role-playing games reject this viewpoint, and instead insist that these games have very positive effects on the players.

Heavy-metal music has assumed a satanic character in the public eye. In 1990, the families of two young men sued CBS Records and the rock band Judas Priest. The families claimed that subliminal messages in the band's *Stained Glass* album had prompted the pair to shoot themselves. The suit failed, largely because there was ample evidence that the youths had been self-destructive long before the album was released.

Sometimes satanism's primary aspects, moral panic and role-playing, overlap. This was evident in 1990 when the suicides of three Lethbridge, Alberta, teenagers were reported alongside accounts that they had been involved in devil worship. The story made front-page news across Canada. Completely unrelated suicides were interpreted by some newspapers as also being part of an overall satanic problem (Chruscinski and Gabor 1990). The media used the suicides as a basis for discussing allegations (mostly from American sources) that devil worshippers were kidnapping children and animals and using them for ritual rapes, pornographic films, and human sacrifices. Despite these allegations, police investigation failed to uncover any organized cult (Oake 1990; *Toronto Star* 1990a; Victor 1993:351).

EVIL AS METAPHOR

In modern times, the demonic has become more of a metaphor than an explanation when applied to deviance. Alcoholics speak of the "devil in the bottle," and many drug addicts see their addiction as a consequence of demonic-like trickery—the drug promises euphoria but delivers death. Some people even see evil behind the apparently secular surface of everyday life:

> The iniquitous roster of evil all around us is an unending list of dark powers that are proliferating: racism, genocide, monstrous crimes, drug gang wars, merciless and random slaughter of innocent civilians, gas bombing of cities, pestilence, famine and war, governmental policies of racial cruelty, death squads, violent or insidious suppression of human rights, forms of slavery, abuse of children, bestial military action against civilians, callousness to the homeless, the AIDS victims and the poor, abuse of the elderly, sexism, rape, wanton murder, cults, terrorism, torture, the unremitting aftermath of past holy and unholy wars, the Holocaust, heinous cruelty and hatred, and the seven deadly sins: wrath, pride, envy, sloth, gluttony, lust, and avarice.
>
> We go on polluting the air, the soil and the water. We think the unthinkable: atomic destruction of civilization and the earth itself. We trash outer and inner space. We literally are in danger of running amok. All the while we feed an unbridled and insatiable appetite for horror; demonic projections are made on enemies as "Evil Empire" and "The Great Satan," governments conspire with organized crime, assassinate and massacre, destroy the souls of people for power and money, arm nations and individuals, and, as a consequence human beings are now exploding in every corner of the globe. Such things as these are often nourished and cunningly abetted by the media: television, film, newspapers, and even art, literature and music. (Wilmer 1988:2–3)

SUMMARY

Long before academics attempted to understand deviance, it was the subject of folklore and mythology, which gave it a place in the social order. While many of the early formulations were moralistic and presented the deviant as a pitiful or evil creature, the dominant kind of story emphasized the multifaceted, frightening, and humorous aspects of deviance, and did not always side with the forces of control. These forms of understanding persist in their modern descendants—children's literature (and sometimes that for adults) and the oral tradition of the "urban myth," in which terrible or embarrassing things happen to people who engage in questionable activities.

The first attempt to provide a fully causal explanation of deviance was the demonic theory, which was rooted in the idea that powers of both good and evil cause all events in the world. The demonic explained not only deviance but other kinds of troubling events, including storms, crop failure, and plagues, as well as religious doubt.

In the late Middle Ages, beginning slowly in the 1100s and becoming a veritable holocaust by the 1600s, the idea that deviance resulted from supernatural causes was transformed into a terrifying conspiracy theory. Believers felt themselves surrounded by a swelling confederacy of witches who were in league with Satan to defeat the armies of Christ.

The dominant modern interpretation of the witchcraft craze is that the "witch" was a social construct, created and maintained by religious authorities in a manner that reflected the common beliefs of the people. Witches were invented by those who feared them (Erikson 1966) and by those who saw them as enemies of patriarchy and the extension of Church power (Daly 1978; Hester 1990). The witchcraft mania had its start in the challenge to church hegemony posed by mountain regions and residual cultures that empowered women, and it reached its peak in the period in which religious wars and the rise of secular thought and science seriously threatened Church authority. It continues to emerge in places where a powerfully positioned religious worldview is challenged by alternative ideas. Thus, witchcraft beliefs were both functional for the authorities and representative of the increasing conflict between a religiously validated patriarchy and alternative views of the world.

The witch-hunt provides a paradigm that can be applied to events such as the Nazi persecution of the Jews, the McCarthyite "red scare" in North America, and the overzealous search for child molesters and satanists. In modern times, demonology is used to explain deviance—generally in its most serious manifestations—only after all rational explanations have failed. However, the paradigm can also be applied to more mundane forms of deviance such as drug trafficking when those forms of deviance are "demonized" by political authorities.

REFERENCES

Ben-Yahuda, Nachman. (1985). *Deviance and Moral Boundaries: Witchcraft, the Occult, Science Fiction, Deviant Sciences and Scientists*. Chicago: University of Chicago Press.

Best, Joel. (1985). "The Razor Blade in the Apple: The Social Construction of Urban Legends." *Social Problems* 32(5):488–499.

Blumenfeld, Laura. (1991). "Procter and Gamble's Devil of a Problem." *Toronto Star*, July 18.

Boyle, Thomas. (1989). *Black Swine in the Sewers of Hampstead: Beneath the Surface of Victorian Sensationalism.* Harmondsworth, U.K.: Penguin.

Briggs, Katharine M. (1978). *The Vanishing People.* London: B.T. Batsford.

Brunvand, Jan Harold. (1981). *The Vanishing Hitchhiker.* New York: W.W. Norton.

———. (1989). *Curses! Broiled Again!: The Hottest Urban Legends Going.* New York: W.W. Norton.

Bulthuis, Jack. (1989). "The Teen Satanism Workshops—Ingersoll, Ontario." Unpublished report.

Canadian Broadcasting Corporation. (1991). "Dungeons and Dragons." *Ideas.* Toronto: CBC. Transcript of program aired May 29.

Cassar, Carmel. (1993). "Witchcraft Beliefs and Social Control in Seventeeth-Century Malta." *Mediterranean Studies* 3(2):316-334.

Cave, Alfred A. (1995). "The Failure of the Shawnee Prophet's Witch Hunt." *Ethnohistory* 42(3):445–475.

Christie-Murray, David. (1989). A *History of Heresy.* New York: Oxford University Press.

Chruscinski, Theresa, and Peter Gabor. (1990). "Meeting the Needs of Troubled Teens." *Globe and Mail,* March 28.

Claridge, Thomas. (1988). "You Ooze Evil, Demeter Told, as Judge Adds Two Life Terms." *Globe and Mail,* July 29: A1.

Cohn, Norman. (1976). *Europe's Inner Demons.* St. Albans: Dutton.

———. (1981). *Warrant for Genocide: The Myth of the Jewish World Conspiracy and the Protocols of the Elders of Zion.* Toronto: Scholar's Press.

Cornwell, John. (1991). *Powers of Darkness, Powers of Light: Travels in Search of the Miraculous and the Demonic.* London: Penguin.

Coudert, Allison P. (1992). "The Myth of the Improved Status of Protestant Women: The Case of the Witchcraze." In Brian P. Levak (ed.), *Witchcraft, Women and Society: Articles on Witchcraft, Magic and Demonology.* Vol. 10. New York: Garland.

Daly, Mary. (1978). *Gyn/Ecology: The Metaethics of Radical Feminism.* Toronto: Fitzhenry and Whiteside.

Dominick, Joseph R. (1978). "Crime and Law Enforcement in the Mass Media." In Charles Winick (ed.), *Deviance and Mass Media.* Beverly Hills: Sage.

Dunning, John. (1989). *Mystical Murders: True Murders of the Occult.* London: Arrow.

Eastlea, Brian. (1980). *Witch-hunting, Magic and the New Philosophy.* Brighton, England: Harvester.

Erikson, Kai T. (1966). *Wayward Puritans: A Study in the Sociology of Deviance.* New York: John Wiley.

Fukurai, Hiroshi, Edgar W. Butler, and Richard Krooth. (1994). "Sociologists in Action: The McMartin Sexual Abuse Case, Litigation, Justice, and Mass Hysteria." *The American Sociologist* 25(4):44–71.

Garrett, Clarke. (1977). "Women and Witches: Patterns of Analysis." *Signs: Journal of Women in Culture and Society* 3(2):461–470.

Goode, Erich. (1992). *Collective Behavior.* Fort Worth: Harcourt Brace Jovanovich.

Groh, Dieter. (1987). "The Temptation of Conspiracy Theory, Part II." In C.F. Grauman and S. Moscovici (eds.), *Changing Conceptions of Conspiracy.* Berlin: Springer-Verlag.

Guiley, Rosemary Ellen. (1991). *Harper's Encyclopedia of Mystical and Paranormal Experience.* San Francisco: HarperCollins.

Gutin, Jo Ann C. (1996). "That Fine Madness." *Discover* 17(10):75–82.

Harris, Marvin. (1978). *Cows, Pigs, Wars, and Witches: The Riddles of Culture.* New York: Random House.

Hester, Marianne. (1990). "The Dynamics of Male Domination: Using the Witch Craze in 16th and 17th Century England as a Case Study." *Women's Studies Institute Forum* 13(1/2):9–19.

Hicks, Robert D. (1991). *In Pursuit of Satan: The Police and the Occult.* Buffalo, N.Y.: Prometheus.

Hoffman, Sr. Heinrich. n.d. *Der Struwwelpeter.* Germany: Pestalozzi Verlag.

Hume, Lynne. (1995). "Witchcraft and the Law in Australia." *Journal of Church and State.* 37(1):135–144.

Inverarity, James M., Pat Lauderdale, and Barry C. Field. (1983). *Law and Society: Sociological Perspectives on Criminal Law.* Boston: Little, Brown.

Jenkins, Philip, and Daniel Maier-Katkin. (1992). "Satanism: Myth and Reality in a Contemporary Moral Panic." *Crime, Law and Social Change* 17(1):53–75.

Karlsen, Carol F. (1989). *The Devil in the Shape of a Woman: Witchcraft in Colonial New England.* New York: Random House.

Kelly, Francis. (1988). "Judge Convicts Lab Technician of Witchcraft." *Toronto Star,* December 8.

Kent, Stephen A. (1993a). "Deviant Scripturalism and Ritual Satanic Abuse Part One: Possible Judeo-Christian Influences." *Religion* 23:229–241.

———. (1993b). "Deviant Scripturalism and Ritual Satanic Abuse Part Two: Possible Masonic, Mormon, Magick and Pagan Influences." *Religion* 23:355–367.

Korem, Dan. (1994). *Suburban Gangs: The Affluent Rebels.* Richardson, Texas: International Focus Press.

Kramer, Heinrich, and James Sprenger. (1971). *The Malleus Maleficarum of Heinrich Kramer and James Sprenger.* New York: Dover.

Larner, Christina. (1980). "Criminum Exceptum? The Crime of Witchcraft in Europe." In V.A.C. Gatrell, Bruce Lenman, and Geoffrey Parker (eds.), *Crime and the Law: The Social History of Crime in Western Europe Since 1500.* London: Europa, 49–75.

Levack, Brian P. (1987). *The Witch-Hunt in Early Modern Europe.* New York: Longman.

———. (ed.). (1992a). *Possession and Exorcism.* Articles on Witchcraft, Magic and Demonology, Vol. 9. New York: Garland.

———. (1992b). *Witchcraft, Women and Society.* Articles on Witchcraft, Magic and Demonology, Vol. 10. New York: Garland.

Lowney, Kathleen S. (1995). "Teenage Satanism as Oppositional Youth Subculture." *Journal of Contemporary Ethnography* 23(4):453–484.

Macfarlane, Alan. (1970). *Witchcraft* in *Tudor and Stuart England.* London: Routledge and Kegan Paul.

Marron, Kevin. (1989). *Witches, Pagans, and Magic in the New Age.* Toronto: McClelland-Bantam Seal Books.

Marty, Martin E. (1990). "Satan and the American Spiritual Underground." In *Britannica Book of the Year,* 308–309.

Medved, Michael. (1991). "Popular Culture and the War Against Standards." *New Dimensions: The Psychology Behind the News* June:38–42.

Morgan, Ted. (1988). *Literary Outlaw: The Life and Times of William S. Burroughs.* New York: Avon Books.

Morison, Samuel Eliot. (1955). *The Parkman Reader: From the Works of Francis Parkman.* Boston: Little, Brown.

Murray, Margaret. (1921). *The Witch Cult in Western Europe.* London: Oxford

Oake, George. (1990). "Tales of Devil Worship Chill Albertans." *Toronto Star,* November 12.

Oppenheimer, Judy. (1988). *Private Demons: The Life of Shirley Jackson.* New York: Putnam's Sons.

Owomoyela, Oyckan. (1990). "No Problem Can Fail to Crash on His Head: The Trickster in Contemporary African Folklore." *The World and I* April:625–632.

Pearson, Ian. (1984). "The Cat in the Bag and Other Absolutely Untrue Tales from Our Urban Mythology." *Quest Magazine,* November.

Peck, M. Scott. (1983). *People of the Lie: The Hope for Healing Human Evil.* New York: Simon and Schuster.

Pelka, Fred. (1992). "The 'Women's Holocaust." *The Humanist* 52(5):5–9.

Pollock, Jack. (1989). *Dear M.: Letters from a Gentleman of Excess.* Toronto: McClelland and Stewart.

Radin, Paul. ([1956] 1972). *The Trickster: A Study in American Indian Mythology.* New York: Schocken.

Redondi, Pietro. (1987). *Galileo: Heretic.* Princeton, N.J.: Princeton University Press.

Reed, Christopher. (1989). "Diabolical Debauchery or Mere Stories from the Mouths of Babes?" *Globe and Mail,* May 20.

Richards, Jeffrey. (1990). *Sex, Dissidence and Damnation: Minority Groups in the Middle Ages.* New York: Barnes and Noble.

Roberts, David. (1996). "Study Ordered of Criminal Prosecutions." *Globe and Mail,* March 26, A6.

Russell, Jeffrey Burton. (1984). *Lucifer: The Devil in the Middle Ages.* Ithaca, N.Y.: Cornell University Press.

———. (1988). *The Prince of Darkness: Radical Evil and the Power of Good in History.* Ithaca, N.Y.: Cornell University Press.

Sagan, Carl. (1995). *The Demon-Haunted World: Science as a Candle in the Dark.* New York: Random House.

Santino, Jack. (1990). "Fitting the Bill: The Trickster in American Popular Culture." *The World and I* April:661–668.

Scher, Len. (1992). *The Un-Canadians: True Stories of the Blacklist Era.* Toronto: Lester.

Sherman, Josepha. (1990). "Child of Chaos, Coyote: A Folkloric Triad." *The World and I* April:645–650.

Simpson, Jacqueline. ([1973] 1996). "Olaf Tryggvason versus the Powers of Darkness." In Venetia Newall (ed.), *The Witch in History.* New York: Barnes and Noble.

Thomas, Keith. (1971). *Religion and the Decline of Magic.* New York: Charles Scribner's Sons.

Toronto Star (1990a). "Albertan Denies Suicide Link: Satanist Cult Cited in Trio of Teen Deaths," March 15.

———. (1990b). "Police Seize Satanic Objects," October 31.

Trevor-Roper, H.R. (1969). *The European Witchcraze of the Sixteenth and Seventeenth Centuries.* Harmondsworth, U.K.: Penguin.

Victor, Jeffrey S. (1993). *Satanic Panic: The Creation of a Contemporary Legend.* Chicago: Open Court.

Watters, Ethan. (1991). "The Devil in Mr. Ingram." *Mother Jones,* July-August.

Watts, Sheldon. (1984). *A Social History of Western Europe, 1450–1720.* London: Hutchinson University Library and Hutchinson University Library for Africa.

Webster, Charles. ([1982] 1996). *From Paracelsus to Newton: Magic and the Making of Modern Science.* New York: Barnes and Noble.

Wilkins, Charles. (1994). "The Bird the Haida Call the Trickster." *Canadian Geographic,* March/April:71–79.

Wilmer, Harry A. (1988). "Introduction." In Paul Woodruff and Harry A. Wilmer (eds.), *Facing Evil: Light at the Core of Darkness.* LaSalle, Il.: Open Court.

Wilson, Colin. (1987). *Aleister Crowley: The Nature of the Beast.* Northhamptonshire, U.K.: Aquarian Press.

Worobec, Christine. (1995). "Witchcraft Beliefs and Practices in Pre-Revolutionary Russian and Ukrainian Villages." *The Russian Review* 54:165–187.

Wright, Lawrence. (1993). "A Reporter At Large: Remembering Satan" (Parts 1 and 2). *The New Yorker,* May 17&24. Copyright 1993 by Lawrence Wright. Appeared originally in *The New Yorker.* Reprinted by permission.

Zeidenberg, Jerry. (1990). "Persecuted Professor: Celebrated Scientist Was Driven into Exile by Cold War Witch-Hunt in Canada." *Globe and Mail,* March 16.

CLASSICAL THEORIES OF DEVIANCE AND THEIR INFLUENCE ON MODERN JURISPRUDENCE

This chapter examines the long, slow process whereby demonic-supernatural theories of deviance were pushed aside by powerful new ideas about the nature of man and of reality. By the late 1600s and early 1700s the "sacred canopies" of Catholicism and Protestantism were no longer sufficient to explain everything that happened in the world. Travel, science, and newer philosophies challenged these religious perspectives with knowledge that simply would not fit religiously bounded cosmologies.

The new, "enlightened" classical view of deviance saw it as behaviour that detracted from the overall happiness or well-being of members of society. No longer was the deviant seen as a person in league with the forces of evil, or as a perpetrator of heretical thoughts. Heretics might still be "deviant" in the courts of the churches, but not in the civil courts. The deviant was one whose self-interest was not sufficiently constrained by his or her expectation of cost, so that he or she was willing to commit acts detrimental to the community as a whole. Since deviance was a rational calculation, the way to reduce it was to increase the swiftness, certainty, and severity of punishment precisely to the point at which the potential deviant would be deterred; that is, to the point at which the individual would decide whether the risk of deviance was worth it or whether conformity was the better choice.

The infliction of excruciating pain and violent death was no longer viewed as a means to salvation, but rather as an expression of the impotent and erratic rage of the system being displaced. The new thinkers devoted much of their attention to devising controlled systems of punishment that would warn would-be deviants that the cost of their offences would be higher than the pleasure they might gain. They argued that punishments beyond this were criminal in themselves, since they reduced happiness without contributing to the overall good. They defined "good" as "the greatest happiness for the greatest number" rather than adherence to moral codes. Classical theorists worked toward making the system of social control more reliable and accountable. Judges were no longer permitted to devise their own laws and sentences, and were to be restrained by legislation. As well, accused individuals were no longer to stand alone against the system. Measures of "due process" were instituted to ensure the right to a fair trial and, if convicted, to punishment that would not be "cruel and unusual."

RATIONAL CALCULATION IN AN IMPERFECT WORLD: THE ENLIGHTENMENT, 1680–1800

The Enlightenment was characterized by a new view of the world, one in which real world events were explained by real world causes and could no longer be satisfactorily explained by deduction from Scripture or from the actions of unseen spirits. Hell was no longer a physical place into which an unlucky sailor might accidentally fall (Jenkins 1984:126). The moral certitudes based on faith alone were also eroding. In this despiritualized, disenchanted world, the deviant person was seen as a rational human being who made self-serving choices, not as a creature driven by spirits, possessed by devils, or punished by God. Interest in deviance turned from the outrages of heresy and witchcraft to the disruptions of crime. The central tenets of the classical view were as follows:

1. People are *hedonistic*. They seek pleasure (gain) and avoid pain (harm).
2. People have *free will*. They choose whether to commit offences or conform to rules in solving their problems or meeting their needs.
3. Society represents a form of *social contract* whereby each individual gives up some of his or her right to hedonistic pleasure in order to partake of the greater good provided by social order.
4. *Punishment* is justified as a means of transforming the hedonistic calculation so that the performance of duty is more rewarding than following the criminal path. In classical utilitarian terms, the solution for all kinds of crime is to make the punishments sufficiently severe and predictable that the calculation is changed and conformity are preferred over crime.
5. Reform of the secular world is worthwhile and appropriate since the chief goal in life is not to achieve salvation, but rather to allow *the greatest good for the greatest number*. Armageddon is not imminent: abuses, injustice, and oppression are the chief evils to be fought against, not the armies of the antichrist.

With crime as the focus, other forms of deviance tended to be neglected, but the paradigm of the classical school can readily be extended to include the explanation of noncriminal forms of deviance (Gottfredson and Hirschi 1990:10). Just as we may weigh the likelihood of a fine or jail, we may also weigh the likelihood that our actions will cause our families to disown us, our best friends to express their disapproval, or some nasty disease to shorten our lives.

While the classical view is sometimes described as "noncausal" because of its emphasis on free choice (Henry and Milanovic 1996:127), it does implicitly invoke pain and pleasure as causal factors (Beirne 1991:807).

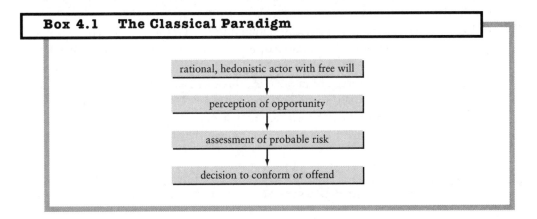

Box 4.1   The Classical Paradigm

rational, hedonistic actor with free will

↓

perception of opportunity

↓

assessment of probable risk

↓

decision to conform or offend

The classical view emerged only after several centuries of transition, during which the ideas of religion, rationality, and science overlapped and competed with each other in a violent, disruptive way. Those who first espoused these new ideas needed powerful friends if they were to avoid the fires of the Inquisition. Giordano Bruno (executed in 1600) and Galileo (sentenced to penance in 1633) argued that the earth moved around the sun, a position that was inconsistent with Church dogma. To accept the scholar's heretical ideas would have forced a rapid and unsettling change at every level of the medieval Church. Galileo survived only because he recanted. Both cases exemplify the dangers of progressive thought in this period (Lerner and Gosselin 1986; Redondi 1987; Peters 1989).

The Enlightenment was rooted in the rediscovery of early Greek and Roman prescientific writing (which had been preserved in monastic libraries), and in the work of the emerging geological, astronomical, and medical sciences, which were being aided by new technology—the telescope and microscope—and by improvements in transportation. Many of the discoveries were incompatible with established medieval cosmology, a cosmology based on a rigid, literal interpretation of

Scripture. If the world had been older than the 6000 years indicated by the Bible, and was not the centre of the universe, many other aspects of dogma might have been questioned as well (Russell 1988:212–213).

The strongest champions of the changing world view, the *philosophes,* often used material provided by scientists. Not just philosophers, these thinkers were advocates of a new faith in reason, toleration, materialism, and empiricism (Russell 1988:208). Nor were scientists the empiricists they have since become. In this period, the natural and supernatural worlds were not so clearly divorced. Paracelsus, a founder of clinical medical science, was, for example, a firm believer in some aspects of sorcery and demonology. His credulous description of the witch has been described as a "folklore classic" (Webster 1996:77). Newton's "science" was profoundly theological and mystical (Dobbs 1975; Figala 1977). The work of astronomists and astrologists overlapped, as did chemistry and alchemy, medicine and curative incantations, and mathematics and number mysticism. As the philosopher Immanual Kant observed of late 1700s, this was an age that aspired to enlightenment, but was not actually an enlightened age (Kant 1784). "It was an age whose literary spokesmen preached the virtues of reason and good sense and humane regard for one's fellow man. But it was not an age that had achieved these virtues (Gay 1966:53).

Box 4.2   Demonic and Classical Perspectives Compared

	Demonic	Classical
Time of Dominance	*1400–1700*	*1700–1800*
Conception of deviance	Evil	Violation of social contract
Explanation	Moral weakness, temptation	Free will and hedonism
Remedies	Exorcism, execution	Measured, swift, certain, severe punishment

---

Only gradually did Hume's idea that the universe was governed by immutable natural laws become the dominant assumption in science and philosophy. In the meantime, the classical thinkers discussed in this chapter occupied a middle ground. They rejected what they regarded as the superstitious, misguided oppression of the Church, but at the same time were disturbed by what they saw as the displacement of humanism by the forces of science. The scientific attempt to study man as one would any other phenomenon (rocks, trees, insects) seemed to downgrade humanity in that it left no room for man's essential qualities of morality, dignity, and faith (Becker 1968:7). The anguished, heartfelt writings of Jean-Jacques Rousseau, which are often interpreted as "anti-science," reflect the clashing and incompatible worldviews that characterized the period (Becker 1968:16; Dent 1988).

SOCIAL JUSTICE IN THE 1700S

The ideas of the Enlightenment arrived on a scene that was anything but enlightened. The practice of the courts was demonstrably irrational, corrupt, unjust, cruel, harsh, and arbitrary. Holy terror was the law of the times. Most forms of misbehaviour went totally unpunished, so that life for most people was unpredictable and hard. While few became entangled in the justice systems of government or Church, those who did were treated as terrible examples for everyone else. The process of selection was capricious at best and biased against the powerless at worst. Throughout Europe, courts accepted anonymous denunciations. In France, for example, a *lettre de cachet* (an anonymous letter to the King) was sufficient to send a person to prison. Those accused were imprisoned until tried, and investigation of the case often required that they be put to judicial (investigative, not punitive) torture. These painful investigations produced surprisingly few confessions, although it was not uncommon for a person's health to be irreparably damaged. In typical cases, judges answered to no higher authority, apart from the rich and powerful whom they feared to antagonize. They made up the law as they went along, and decided punishments according to their own interpretations of appropriate standards. Particularly when the accused was of low status, punishments were deliberately made as horrifying as possible, and often took the form of public rituals of pain, which attracted large crowds as a circus might do. The safeguards of due process, which we now take for granted, were completely absent.

Despite the terror, social control was not well maintained. The system was so unpredictable that the guilty might well escape punishment while the innocent were tortured into confessions and executed. In this period, there was growing fear of the "dangerous classes," a category that included all those who were not under the control of a master and who were thus free to commit crimes and engage in the actions of the urban mob.

Several factors contributed to the growing crime and disorder. Disastrous wars meant increases in taxation, and the periodic return of disaffected soldiers hardened by war and unsuited to peacetime employments. Typhus and cholera epidemics brought on by urban conditions affected the social balance. In England, gin became a staple for the poor because it was cheaper and more filling than nonalcoholic alternatives. *Gin Lane,* a painting by Hogarth, dramatically presents the depravity of people who were undernourished, drunken, and living in squalor. The response to all this social chaos was greater punishment. In England, law reforms in 1722 and 1758 added more than 350 crimes to the list of those already punishable by death. Most of these were meant to deal with concerns about the defence of property. Executions came to be scenes of drunken revelry or rioting. Ignatieff (1978) explains why:

> All such ritual punishments depended for their effectiveness as a ceremonial of deterrence on the crowd's tacit support of the authorities' sentence. Hence, the magistrates' control of the ritual was limited. In theory, the processional to the gallows and the execution itself were supposed to be a carefully stage-managed theater of guilt in which the offender and the parson acted out a drama of exhortation, confession and repentance before an awed and approving crowd. The parson's sermons were set pieces on social obligation, delivered at the gallows and subsequently hawked in the streets with an account of the offender's life and descent into crime.
>
> The trouble was that if the spectators did not approve of the execution, the parson would find his worthy sentiments drowned in the abuse welling up from the crowd. Moreover, the crowd had a highly developed sense of the rights due the condemned, and if any of these rights were abridged, they were quick to vent their wrath on the authorities, especially if the condemned also happened to contest the justice of the execution itself. This double sense of outrage, at rights ignored and offenders wrongfully sacrificed, drove the Tyburn crowd attending the execution of the silk weavers who cut looms during the Spitalfields agitation of 1769 to attack and destroy the sheriff's house after the execution. What irked them particularly, one of them told a gentleman bystander, was that the sheriff had not even had the decency to give the men time to say their prayers. This was a courtesy that the poor of London defined as one of the rights of the dying. (21–22)

Prisoners were sometimes rescued by the crowd, and the executioner (especially one who bungled the job) was sometimes killed. A legal system as disorderly as this one could not last long.

THE *PHILOSOPHES* AND THE CLASSICAL SCHOOL

The *philosophes* expressed anger and scorn over the inconsistencies, stupidities, and abuses of the social order; at the same time, they developed a new vision of how society could be if it were based on rational principles that would ensure the greatest happiness for the greatest number.

One of these courageous crusaders against the tyranny, bigotry, and cruelty of his time was François-Marie Arouet (1694–1778), who is usually known by his pen name, Voltaire. As a youth, he had experienced some of the inequities of the French justice system firsthand when an anonymous accusation landed him in the Bastille, an infamous prison later to figure as a symbol of tyranny. In his first book, *The Philosophical Letters* (1734), Voltaire took issue with the religious philosopher and mathematician Pascal, arguing that the purpose of life was not to reach heaven through suffering, but rather to assure the greatest amount of happiness through material progress in the sciences and the arts. In *Candide* (1759), he satirized almost every aspect of eighteenth-century life. At one point in his travels, Candide is shipwrecked off Lisbon on the eve of the great earthquake of 1755. Voltaire goes on to describe the event and, in the following passage, its aftermath:

> After the earthquake had wiped out three-quarters of Lisbon, the learned men of the land could find no more effective way of averting total destruction than to give the people a fine auto-de-fé [burning of heretics]. The University of Coimbra had established that the spectacle of several persons being roasted over a slow fire with full ceremonial rites is an infallible remedy against earthquakes. (quoted in Peters 1989:179)

Here Voltaire attacks the blind stupidity of those who regard natural disasters like earthquakes as religious phenomena and then proceed to punish and torture innocent people for them. In 1762, Voltaire led the successful lobby for "rehabilitation" (a postmortem declaration of innocence) on behalf of Jean Calas, a Protestant (Huguenot) merchant of Toulouse who had been convicted for the murder of his son. Calas's son had been mentally unstable and had committed suicide. The prosecutor maintained that the son had been about to convert to Catholicism. Although he continued to deny the charges, Calas was convicted and executed by being broken on the wheel on March 10, 1762. His family was arrested and his property confiscated by the state (Brown et al. 1991:215–16; Pfohl 1985:59–60).

Some of the *philosophes* joined other social-contract writers who maintained that the greatest good is served when each of us gives up some of our freedom to do as we please in order to preserve the safety and well-being of all, and that any law that goes beyond what is necessary to uphold the social order is oppressive and wrong. One of these social-contract writers, Thomas Hobbes (1588–1679), argued in his best-known work, *Leviathan,* that moral rules should have a purely secular basis. Hobbes (1881) describes human beings in their natural state as being engaged in a "war of all against all," a war fuelled by their desires for gain, safety, and reputation. In such a society there could be no industry or agriculture, no importation or building, no arts or letters because "the fruit thereof is uncertain." To escape this unpleasant condition, men make a social contract with each other to give up their freedom to the sovereign, whose sole obligation is to protect the people. Without this contract, there is neither justice nor injustice.

> To this warre of everyman against every man, this also is consequent; that nothing can be Unjust. The notions of Right and Wrong, Justice and Injustice have there no place. Where there is no common Power, there is no Law: where no Law, no Injustice. (Hobbes 1881:96)

The Leviathan (state), a huge, artificial monster made for our protection, establishes what is right and wrong and punishes in order to protect the common good (Hobbes 1881:91).

The two main representatives of the classical school—Cesare Beccaria (1738–1794) and Jeremy Bentham (1748–1832)—drew upon the work of many writers, particularly the *philosophes* and the social contract writers.

CESARE BECCARIA

Born of a noble Italian family, Cesare Beccaria was an indifferent student who often objected to the accepted notions of the day. He graduated with a degree in law from the University of Padua at the age of 20, was a professor of political economy for a brief period, and later enjoyed a reputation as a brilliant mathematician who found new applications for quantitative methods in social and political affairs. His famous essay *Dei delitti e delle pene* ("On Crimes and Punishments") (1764) was written as his contribution to the Society of Fists, a socially conscious literary club started by his friend Pietro Verri. Verri's brother, Alessandro, held the position of "protector of prisoners" in Milan, and gave Beccaria firsthand access to local penal institutions.

Beccaria was deeply disturbed by what he saw and heard in the penal institutions. While his essay did not express new ideas but rather those whose time had come, it did so with such eloquent logic that it was widely read and became a focal point for action against barbaric practices in criminal law and procedure in Europe, England, and the colonial settlements. Indeed, it may have had more practical effect than any other treatise ever written on the subject. It was highly praised by intellectuals of the time, including Voltaire, Diderot, Rousseau, and Hume. Its main points are summarized in the following list:

1. All people are motivated by pain and pleasure. They are rational pleasure/pain machines. Crime is reasonable behaviour and represents neither the devil nor illness. To reduce crime, it is necessary to make it less rational by changing social conditions.

2. The basis of all social action must be the utilitarian concept of the greatest happiness for the greatest number, not the salvation of the soul or preparation for Armaggedon (the end of the world).

3. The greatest happiness is ensured by the social contract whereby each individual gives up some of his right to hedonistic pleasure for the benefit of the whole. This is represented in the ruler (sovereign), who is thereby entitled, through the legislature, to make laws for the society.

4. The social contract is supported when the laws are openly made by the legislature, clearly written, widely known, and uniformly enforced.

5. Crime must be considered an injury to society, and the only rational measure of crime is the extent of this injury. Any act of authority of one man over another that is not justified by absolute necessity is tyrannical. The act, not the intent, is the measure of the crime. The most serious crimes are those "which immediately tend to the dissolution of society" (e.g., treason). Just below this are crimes that injure people and property. Least serious are crimes that disrupt public peace, such as being drunk in public. Punishment should be in proportion to the seriousness of the crime (hence banishment for treason, fines for property damage, and humane imprisonment for other crimes). Execution is not justifiable, especially since it cannot be reversed should an error later be found.

6. Punishment is justified only on the grounds that it helps prevent further criminal conduct. It does this by increasing the costs of unlawful conduct through such mechanisms as the law and a system of punishment that results in the minimum occurrence of crime. Imprisonment is one way of meting out "just enough" punishment to prevent further crime.

He did not put his name on the work at first, fearing repression by the Inquisition (Paolucci 1963:ix-xi). The inquisitors did commission an investigation of the book, and Beccaria was charged with sedition, sacrilege, and impiety. The provincial governor, however, interceded on his behalf (Maestro 1972:64; Brown et al. 1991). The Vatican denounced the book, and it remained on the index of proscribed books until that list was abolished in 1962 (Maestro 1973). As is often the case with censorship, however, the book, while it was banned only became more popular.

JEREMY BENTHAM

Like Beccaria, the English gentleman-of-means Jeremy Bentham found the law of his time an appalling mass of incongruities, absurdities, and barbarities. Justice went to those who could pay for it. Men were given the death penalty for stealing food to feed their starving children, and the majority of executions were for crimes against property.

Bentham spent most of his life obsessed with a vision of social reform that was based on utilitarianism, the principle that all things should be organized in such a way as to ensure the maximum happiness for the greatest number. He began with the premise: "Nature has placed mankind under the governance of two sovereign masters, pain and pleasure." From there he developed the idea of a "felicity calculus" whereby actions are evaluated on the basis of their tendency to produce either pleasure or pain. The calculus would include the pleasures and pains of wealth, benevolence, desire, hunger, and even piety (Rennie 1978:22).

According to Bentham's *Principles of Morals and Legislation* (1789), the law in particular needed to be totally reformed to meet utilitarian (i.e., useful) standards. The utility of any law could be measured by the extent to which it promoted the pleasure, good, and happiness of the people and the actions of individuals could be judged according to whether, on balance, they contributed to or detracted from the happiness and benefit of all. Criminal acts detracted from the collective happiness and therefore should be prevented. Acts that did not detract from the collective happiness should not be the subject of criminal law. Laws and punishments that were unnecessary were themselves evil. "All punishment is mischief: all punishment is in itself evil ... it ought only to be admitted in as far as it promises to exclude some greater evil" (Bentham 1988:170). Thus, in Bentham's system, people could do as they pleased, as long as it was not harming the overall happiness of the people around them.

Since humans were hedonistic, crime (harm to happiness) could be prevented if all citizens were made to understand that the punishment would be swift, certain, and slightly greater than the pleasure of the crime. Like Beccaria, Bentham argued that deviance could be controlled not by changing deviants but by changing the rules; not by terrorizing people but by showing them that conformity was the best way to be happy. Bentham believed that one day a sort of calculus would be devel-

Figure 4.1   Jeremy Bentham

Jeremy Bentham, a classical utilitarian, argued that the purpose of society was to produce the greatest happiness for the greatest number of citizens.

Source: New York Public Library Picture Collection. Reprinted by permission.

oped in which definite values would be assigned to pleasure and pain. If a thief gained X units of pleasure from a crime, it would be up to the court to assign X + 1 units of pain (Jenkins 1984:128). For each offence, it was appropriate to adjust the punishment so that:

1. The value of the punishment is not less than what is sufficient to outweigh that of the profit gained by the offence.
2. The more serious the offence, the more time and money should be invested to make sure that it is punished enough.
3. The punishment for the various offences should be set in such a way that, if a person decides to commit an offence, he or she will be induced to choose the less serious one.
4. If an offence has several aspects, the punishment should be set to discourage all parts of it, not just the most serious part.
5. The punishment should never be more than what is necessary to outweigh the value of the offence to the offender. Since punishment involves pain and is therefore intrinsically evil, it should only be used to exclude some greater evil.

6. The punishment should be generally consistent across similar offences but should take into account the differences between offenders that influence their sensitivity. (adapted from Rennie 1978:22)

This idea led to the invention of various kinds of punishment that could be meted out in measured doses. Typical of these were the treadwheel, on which men would be forced to keep walking uphill, as if on an endless staircase, and various gadgets that would count how many turns of a crank had been made (so many turns had to be made before earning a meal). The point of these boring, repetitive, and useless tasks was to make sure that the convict got no intrinsic pleasure out of the work. Bentham also attempted to develop a beating machine, which he felt would be preferable to the inconsistencies of the usual practice, whereby how much punishment the offender got varied by who was doing the beating. A modern revival of this kind of thought can be found in Graeme Newman's *Just and Painful: A Case for the Corporal Punishment of Criminals* (1983), in which Newman argues for the use of electric shock as an alternative to imprisonment or fine. Newman's argument is the same as Bentham's: the use of punishment can be scientifically controlled and precisely calibrated to fit the offence.

CLASSICAL THOUGHT WITHOUT SOCIAL CONTRACT: THE MARQUIS DE SADE

A contemporary of Bentham's was the infamous Marquis de Sade (1740–1814). While not a deep thinker, de Sade illustrated what happens to classical thought when the social contract element is rejected. De Sade went further than other thinkers in rejecting the moral force of the devil, God, and even laws of nature. For him, there were no absolute standards of right and wrong, nothing except the pursuit of the maximum self-gratification. In de Sade's view, the maximum pleasure was the maximum good, while virtue, kindness, and love were perversions because they restricted indulgence in pleasure (Russell 1988:211–212).

Because de Sade found his most intense self-gratification in demeaning and torturing not only prostitutes but also innocent boys and girls abducted from the community, his life was a series of imprisonments. He narrowly missed execution by the guillotine. His books were banned in France, a practice that (then as now) ensured them a readership far beyond that justified by their dull and repetitive style (Tannahill 1992:341).

Box 4.3   The Panopticon Prison

In Bentham's time, prison was rarely a punishment in itself. People were held in prisons until trial, and then subjected to capital punishment, a fine, the pillory, transportation (banishment), or short-term confinement in the prison hulks (Geis 1973:63; Radzinowicz 1948). Bentham felt that imprisonment was an ideal form of punishment since it would give the felon the opportunity to adjust his "felicity calculus" toward a belief in the value of conformity. Punishments could be meted out in measured days and years exactly proportionate to the seriousness of the offence. The panopticon was to be a different sort of prison.

Bentham envisioned the panopticon as a circular building with a tower in the centre. The tower would be designed for observation, with wide windows opening onto the inner side of the building, which would contain the cells. Each cell would have two windows, one permitting light from outside the prison to backlight the cell (thus revealing any activity on the part of its occupant), and the other permitting constant surveillance from the tower. In this arrangement, an omniscient prison inspector, himself protected from view, could observe any particular prisoner or prison employee. Visible to the supervisor and guards, the prisoner would be invisible, because of the side walls, to his fellow inmates. "He is seen, but he does not see; he is the object of information; never the subject of communication" (Foucault 1979:200).

The panopticon manager would derive income from the money earned by convict contract labour (which would enable convicts to develop useful work skills), but at the same time would be held financially liable to the government for failing to reform the convict or for an unusually high number of deaths among inmates over a given period. The panopticon was also to be placed close to a dense population centre, where it would be a visible reminder to those tempted to go astray (Geis 1973:64). Bentham campaigned vigorously, and ultimately unsuccessfully, for such a prison, and even imagined himself as its omniscient manager. Foucault (1979) turned Bentham's panopticon idea into a kind of symbolic representation of the omnipresent and omniscient forces of control in modern society.

NEOCLASSICAL THEORY

Classical ideas were quickly tested in the aftermath of the French Revolution. Beccaria's recommendations were used in the drafting of the French Declaration of the Rights of Man (1791). They also became an important part of the Constitution of the United States (1787) and were enshrined in the English Reform Act of 1832. Jeremy Bentham was honoured with citizenship in the French Republic in 1792. The classical approach, when tested by practical experience, however, proved too rigid and was gradually modified by neoclassical thinkers.

NEOCLASSICISM

The classical school of thought had maintained that all crimes were to be judged only in terms of their harm to the social fabric, and punished only according to the pain necessary to deter further offences. They were not to be judged in terms of what kinds of people committed them or in terms of the circumstances under which they occurred. The theft of a loaf of bread would be treated in the same way regardless of the thief's motivation. The person who killed in anger would receive the same penalty as the person who killed in a state of insanity. Dissatisfaction with this arrangement led to the French Declaration of Rights being modified in 1810 and 1819 to provide more discretionary power to the judge, although this discretion was still nothing like the unbridled power held by judges in the 1600s (Brown, Esbensen, and Geis 1991:229).

Three new concepts were introduced by the neoclassicists.

1. *Mitigating factors.* In the classical system, all assaults of a particular degree of seriousness were treated in the same way; under the neoclassical system, the judge could take into account, for example, whether the attack was perpetrated by a vicious bully, by someone engaged in self-defence, or by a person suffering delusions of persecution.

2. *Past record.* In the classical system, every offence was treated in the same way, whether it was a first-time, repeat, or a multiple repeat offence. The neoclassical system would punish the repeat offender more severely.

3. *Differences in free will.* It was increasingly recognized that the classical assumptions of free will and rational capability were not always corroborated by reality. Some classes of offenders—minors, the mentally impaired, the insane—were clearly not as capable as the average person of choosing between right and wrong. Neoclassical systems put into effect procedures for measuring the degree of responsibility possessed by the offender. This is seen in the separation of adult

and juvenile courts, and in the provision of legal defences, such as insanity, in criminal law.

To put neoclassical theory into perspective, it is useful to compare its approach to a specific offence, such as murder, with those characteristic of the demonic and classical systems.

In the demonic system, the treatment an offender receives depends on his or her social status and degree of influence over the judge. If a rich, powerful man murders a peasant, there will likely be no arrest, much less confinement and trial. Should the roles be reversed, however, the murderer will in all probability be arrested, treated very roughly before trial, subjected to judicial torture, and condemned to an extremely painful and public execution.

In the classical system, the offender's treatment depends solely on the nature of the murder, and on how much harm was done to the victim or to the social system as a result of it. It makes no difference whether the person who committed the murder was sane or whether the killing was an unintended result of some other action. The execution itself will be swift (if not painless), "a medical operation performed in an antiseptic environment by dispassionate experts" (Bowers 1974:29).

In the neoclassical system, the rich and powerful offender will receive greater punishment than the poor one if it can be determined that he or she had more choices in the situation or was motivated more by greed than by fear or rage. The accused is permitted to argue that he had no "free will" because of mental illness, duress, "mistake of fact," or any of the other mitigating circumstances specified in the law books.

CONTEMPORARY EXAMPLES

Since the 1960s, there has been a bifurcation of the neoclassical stream of thought into the "law and order" or "crime control" school and the "individual rights" school. The crime control school emphasizes determinate (fixed) sentencing—minimum sentences for particular offences—and both general and specific deterrence. The individual rights school emphasizes due process—that is, respect for the constitutional rights of offenders—and concern for incapacitation of offenders who are dangerous to the society (Schmalleger 1996:149).

Young Offenders Act

The laws of most Western countries have provisions for youthful offenders to be treated differently from adult offenders. In Canada, for example, the Young

Offenders Act (1982) provides that youth 12 to 17 years of age (as of the date of the offence) undergo a less punitive system of legal restraints. For most offences, the maximum punishment under the act is three years in a closed custody setting (detention centre or locked institution). The penalty for murder now allows three years of closed custody followed by two years of probation. Under some rare circumstances, involving very serious offences, the individual may be transferred to an adult court and given a longer sentence. The longest possible penalty for a young offender raised to adult court is a life sentence, with possibility of parole after ten years, while an adult can be declared a "dangerous offender" and locked up indefinitely, possibly for life. The constant pressure on authorities to introduce stiffer penalties for young offenders arises from a feeling among some observers that low penalties constitute a licence to offend.

Unlike the Juvenile Delinquents Act (1928), which it replaced, the Young Offenders Act clearly reflects the ideas of the neoclassical thinkers. Even though it recognizes the dependence and immaturity of youthful offenders, it emphasizes the offence that was committed rather than the overall character of the offender. Thus, Canadian law no longer has a general-status category called "delinquent," and youths cannot be imprisoned for being generally out of control but only for specific illegal acts. The Young Offenders Act also reflects classical and neoclassical thought in that it stresses the importance of *due process* (the rules concerning the rights of the accused at each point in the system) and of setting limits on the range of powers granted to legal authorities (Leschied, Jaffe, and Willis 1991; West 1984; Bala 1988; Griffiths, Verdun-Jones, and Hatch-Cunningham 1989).

Defences in Criminal Law

The provision of defences in law also reflects the neoclassical influence. The prosecution must show not only that a criminal act took place, but also that it was done without lawful excuse or defence. Defences that can be used either to prevent conviction or to moderate the seriousness of an offence include the following.

1. *Accident.* If I am chopping wood and the head of the axe comes off and decapitates someone I didn't like, I may be able to convince the court that it was an accident and thus avoid a murder conviction.

2. *Honest mistake.* The defence may argue that the crime resulted from an honest mistake. In one case, the parents of a 5-year-old diabetic, convinced that their son had been healed by the Holy Spirit, failed to give the child the appropriate medicine. Convicted of manslaughter at the first trial, the parents were later granted a new trial because the honest mistake issue had not been raised (*R. v. Tutton,* Ontario Court of Appeal, 1985).

"Honest mistake" is a defence often used in sexual assault cases. An example of this is the Pappajohn case, which occurred in 1976 and has been the subject of a radio play. The incident came to public attention when a woman, naked except for a bow tie wound around her neck and her hands tied by a bathrobe sash, ran out of a house and sought help at the nearby home of a Catholic priest. She claimed that she had been raped. The accused, a Mr. Pappajohn, claimed that it was a case of consensual rough sex. Since both sides agreed that sex had occurred, the only issue at trial was that of Mr. Pappajohn's honest belief that the woman had consented. The court did not believe Pappajohn, and he was convicted. The Supreme Court of Canada later overturned this conviction (Jonas 1983:21–248).

3. *Duress.* In a case in Victoria, British Columbia, a man was found not guilty of driving without due care and attention. Although he admitted to erratic driving, he convinced the judge that this had been caused when his driving companion dropped a live crab on his lap.

4. *Insanity.* This controversial defence is rarely invoked. From the accused's point of view, it is almost always preferable to be dealt with as a rational actor and suffer whatever penalty is provided in law.

While neoclassical thought modified the rigidity of classically based systems, it still emphasized that most offenders had made rational choices and could be deterred by rational levels of punishment. The punishment was directed at deterring individuals (and others like them) from committing offences. There was no interest in such issues as overall moral reform or the "cure" of character disorders.

TESTING CLASSICAL THOUGHT: THE MODERN LEGACY

Classical theory has continued into the present in a number of different ways. The principal theoretical forms of this continuation are deterrence theory (discussed below), routine activities/rational choice theory, and social control theory (discussed in future chapters).

DETERRENCE THEORY

The whole thrust of classical thought is based on the belief that preventing crimes is better than punishing those who commit them. Classical thinkers postulated that since human beings are rational, pleasure/pain calculators, who seek pleasure and avoid pain in a state of free will, the best way to prevent crime is to convince would-be offenders that committing the crime will not bring them enough reward to make the risk of punishment worthwhile. Cesare Beccaria enumerated the three principles of punishment that became the hallmark of classical deterrence doctrine. He argued that crime control is a function of *certainty, celerity* (speed), and *severity* of punishment. Taken together, these amounted to a fourth criterion, *exemplarity*—that is, the example set for would-be offenders.

Research has been directed toward finer analysis of what deterrence is, and of the circumstances under which deterrence succeeds or fails (Schneider and Ervin 1990). The following sections introduce six types of deterrence: absolute, relative, cross, general, specific, and restrictive.

Absolute Deterrence

Penalties are so sure, so soon in coming, and so terrible that no crime is committed. The authorities might create near-absolute deterrence for parking offences by raising the penalty to some amount greater than the value of the car—and enforcing it. This method would fail with respect to any infraction that was not calculated. Some people would still assault others or be unable to restrain their desire to say or do politically incorrect things. Generally speaking, absolute deterrence is prohibitively expensive and would not necessarily make a better world. One can imagine, for example, a world in which people lost in the woods would starve to death rather than break into a cottager's summer home, or in which parents would allow their children to be killed by wild animals rather than violate game laws.

Relative Deterrence

Reduced crime. Fewer crimes are committed if they become more difficult or risky. Raising the price of alcohol and reducing liquor store hours may have a general effect of reducing (though not eliminating) alcohol-related problems. Increasing the visibility of police (e.g., by using more marked cars or by making public announcements through the media) may reduce the number of drivers willing to risk speeding or racing as long as this surveillance is maintained. Increasing penalties for crimes without increasing surveillance is not always, or even usually, successful in reducing the crime rate, despite the "commonsense" belief that it should (Broadhurst and Loh 1993:251).

Cross-Deterrence

Fear of penalties for one crime may influence would-be offenders to commit another. Rates of regular car theft, for example, declined when newer cars were produced with antitheft devices, such as locking steering wheels, but the rate of cars being

Box 4.4 Deterrence Theory Helps Explain Why Some Toronto Smokers Don't Butt Out

The woman who owns the café is nervous—her customers are, after all, breaking the law. In a corner, about 20 nicotine cravers puff away in defiance of Toronto's tough new antismoking bylaw, which came into effect on March 3. The owner, exasperated, says she has asked smokers to butt out, only to have others light up. "Some of them are like my brothers and sisters—I see them more than my children," she says. "They say to me, 'Are you not ashamed?'"

So it was, last week, as Toronto the Good tried to live up to its name. Adopted last July, the hotly contested bylaw forbids smoking in all restaurants and bars. Businesses can build a costly enclosed and separately ventilated room for their smoking clientele—up to 25 per cent of seating capacity—though most are waiting to see if the bylaw survives the proposed megacity amalgamation of Toronto with five other municipalities. In the meantime, owners are posting the required no-smoking signs and, according to the bylaw, issuing verbal warnings to smokers. "All they have to say to them is 'It is my duty to inform you that you are smoking in a prohibited area'—it ends there," says Pamela Scharfe, Toronto's environmental health manager. "They don't have to say, 'Butt out, step outside, or I'm not going to serve you.'"

Which raises the issue of enforcement. About 25 inspectors plan to visit all 3,500 of the affected establishments by the end of this month, and issue owners notices detailing their degree of compliance. Those visits will be followed up with spot checks (the city also has a so-called snitch line). Fines range from $200 to $5,000. But as long as no-smoking signs are posted and warnings issued, establishments cannot be charged. As for smokers breaking the bylaw, health inspectors have no power to force them to produce identification. So, Scharfe concedes, "You can't give a ticket if you don't know who the person is" ...

Despite the ban on smoking, the air in Toronto has certainly not been cleared.

Note: The no-smoking bylaw was amended two months after it was implemented due to public refusal to obey the law. The new bylaw implemented tougher seating restrictions for smoking areas within establishments

Source: From Danylo Hawaleshka, "Smokeless in Hogtown," *Maclean's,* March 17, 1997. Reprinted by permission

forcefully taken away from their owners increased. Some thieves were deterred; others escalated their offences to include robbery. Similarly, the number of nighttime safe-cracking raids on banks decreased as security systems evolved and less money was kept overnight, but the number of holdups increased.

General Deterrence

Demonstration Effect. General deterrence is the effect seeing others punished has on people that causes them to desist from committing offences. The criminal court demonstrates how particular kinds of crime are treated, and parallels can be found in the "courts" of everyday life. Judges find themselves faced with a dilemma when the crime is serious but severe punishment would be unjust, as in a murder trial that took place on Canada's East Coast. In what at first appeared to be a clear-cut case of murder, Jane Stafford admitted to killing her husband while he slept. The evidence showed, however, that Billy Stafford had been an appallingly abusive father and husband—a man who made serious death threats against his wife and her children, and who blocked all avenues of escape. He was so violent that police were afraid to intervene, even when Jane Stafford begged for help. Although convicted, she served only two months in jail before being paroled (Jonas 1986:97–122). Some observers feared that her light sentence would bring on an "open season on imperfect spouses," but no such effect has been observed.

General deterrence is a controversial concept. Not only does it sometimes seem unjust to punish an offender so that others will not offend, but it is also not clear that general deterrence regularly occurs. Fattah (1976) reports on some historical cases in which it apparently failed. Charlie Justice, who devised the clamps used to hold condemned persons in the electric chair, was himself convicted of murder and electrocuted. Alfred Wills, a convict who helped install a prison gas chamber, later killed three people and was gassed. Similarly, in 1705, a burglar who was almost hung (he was strung up but given a timely pardon) returned to his former practices, only with a new name—"half-hanged Smith."

Specific Deterrence

Direct personal effect. Specific deterrence is achieved by the actual experience of punishment (Fattah 1976:13). The consequences of punishment, however, are much less understood at present than the consequences of reward. Some punishments actually increase the likelihood of further offences, for example, by giving the offender attention and recognition, or by cutting off legitimate work.

Restrictive Deterrence

Selective reduction of offending. A recent entry in the "deterrence" idea is the concept of "restrictive deterrence" (Gibbs 1975:33). Restrictive deterrence has occurred when the individual avoids punishable acts selectively. Jacobs provides the example of drug dealers who stay in business but who will not sell to people they perceive to be possible "narcs" (police) (Jacobs 1996:409–410). Fear causes them to reduce their activities but does not make them stop.

WHEN DOES DETERRENCE WORK?

Between actual penalties and offence rates is an actor who (1) perceives, or fails to perceive, the penalties; (2) calculates, or does not calculate, the risks and benefits that are involved; and (3) acts or does not act. While early classical theory assumed that the process of awareness and calculation would be the same for everyone, neoclassical theory recognized differences in the ability and willingness to know and evaluate the seriousness of penalties, as well as differences in their impact on people with differing sensibilities. As mentioned earlier, classical theorists proposed that the three main factors in deterrence were certainty, celerity, and severity. The main findings from the studies that test these ideas are treated in the following sections.

Box 4.2   Mechanical Moose Snare Poachers

Mechanical moose, electric elk, Styrofoam deer and rubber rainbow trout have become shock troops in a war against game poachers in the North American wild.

Game wardens across the continent, anxious to protect wildlife, are ecstatic over the success of sting operations in which they use decoy animals to catch illegal hunters.

In Manitoba, wardens place dummy elk, deer and moose in clearings near roadsides where illegal hunters are known to prowl. The conservation officers then take to the bush and lie in wait for their human prey.

"The guy comes along, he shoots the decoy, and we nab him," summarized Manitoba Natural Resources spokesman David Purvis.

In virtually all provinces and states it is illegal to hunt at night, or to shoot from a public roadway even in daylight. Apart from public-safety

---

Mechanical Moose Snare Poachers (cont.)

concerns (a bullet from a high-powered rifle can travel more than a kilometre), deer particularly are mesmerized by the 500,000-candlepower searchlights of "jack-lighters" who plunder game after dark for meat or mantelpiece trophies.

The decoy stings are efficient: game wardens in some jurisdictions have bagged 80 poachers for every 600 person-hours at a stake-out.

Decoys come in all shapes and sizes, from crude plywood elk covered in burlap to expensive remote-controlled deer and moose.

"At night we may only use a set of eyes that glow when the headlights hit them," Mr. Purvis said.

Canadian wildlife officers speak in envious tones when they describe decoys used in some parts of the United States. These mechanical creatures, with removable antlers, walk, wag their tails and wreak havoc on poaches—when they are not in the repair shop having lead removed.

In Manitoba "we can move the head, jiggle the ears and wag the tail," says Mr. Purvis, steadfastly refusing to elaborate for security reasons.

The results of the decoy program in Manitoba have sometimes been amusing, Mr. Purvis said. Officers have watched Dads emerge from crammed station wagons to shoot a photograph of a stuffed moose—thrilling the happy carload, who believe the sophisticated decoy is real.

But more often, it is a hunter intent on doing a different kind of shooting. "You see the vehicle come along. The guy sees the decoy. He slows down and stops. He backs up. He looks again. He waits. The gun comes out the window. Bang!

"You should see the look on his face when he knows he's hit a deer and it doesn't drop. Finally it dawns on him—he's been had."

It takes only seconds for wardens to seal off the area and make the arrest. The Manitoba fine: $1,056.

In Ontario, the penalty is much more serious. The maximum fine for hunting illegally has just been raised to $25,000, and convicted offenders' vehicles and weapons may also be seized.

Officials say the decoy programs have been able to withstand legal entrapment tests. Hunters who argue that the decoys are an invitation to break the law have had not had a sympathetic ear in court. "There's no sign hanging around the deer's neck saying, 'shoot me,'" an official noted.

Mechanical Moose Snare Poachers (cont.)

Jeff Thielen, a wildlife enforcement officer in St. Cloud, Minn., said jack-lighters there routinely end up in jail. The maximum penalty is $5,000 and/or one year behind bars.

He said Minnesota legislators were forced to revise state statutes this year to make it officially illegal to shoot decoys. One hunter successfully argued that a decoy is not, technically, a game animal.

Al Farrer, district enforcement officer in Kenora, Ont., said the decoy program has been a highly successful deterrent to would-be poachers in the area between Thunder Bay and the Manitoba boundary.

"We nailed one night-hunter a few years ago," he recalled. "The next year we put the same (deer) decoy out with a modification. The guy pulls up and the gun comes out. 'Na, it's a decoy,' he says. We wiggle the tail. Bang! He shoots. We get him again" …

Source: From David Roberts, "Mechanical Moose Snare Poachers," *The Globe and Mail*, October 9, 1991, pp. A1–2. Reprinted with permission of The Globe and Mail.

Certainty and Awareness

Beccaria argued that the certainty of punishment is much more important than its severity. Certainty can be measured either by actual rate of detection and punishment or by the beliefs about the rate of punishment held by the population.

The assumption of early classical theory that awareness of possible punishments and calculation of the risks is the same for everyone has proved to be untrue. An actual increase in the probability of punishment does not have a deterrent effect unless the potential deviant is aware of it (Green 1989), and thinks that it applies, specifically and personally. Some evidence suggests there is a "threshold effect" whereby most of us curb our behaviour when the chances of being caught and punished seem to us to be greater than 3 in 10 (Green 1989:799–800). Widely publicized criminal cases generate more public awareness of the penalties than do less well-known cases. Most us have a clearer perception of the likely penalties for theft than we have, say, for bigamy.

Some offences are much more likely to be detected, reported, and acted upon. In so-called victimless crimes (crimes-with-customers) such as prostitution, drug trafficking, and gambling, there is often no complainant and observers may be intimidated into silence. The risk of being apprehended is influenced mainly by police policies, which may range from ignoring the behaviour to targeting it for special surveillance. When proactive policing (increased patrols, targeting particular groups of offenders) increases the likelihood of apprehension and punishment, the offences will probably decline or become less observable, at least temporarily.

With respect to crimes such as murder, assault, kidnapping, and terrorism, changes in the level of policing can create deterrent effects. For instance, the number of airplane skyjackings dropped noticeably following several highly publicized failed attempts (Chauncey 1975:447–473). Similarly, there is considerable evidence to show that, in cases of family violence, the formal arrest of the offending partner by police has a greater impact on reducing further attacks than do other modes of control, particularly if the violence is not part of a long-established pattern (Pate and Hamilton 1992:691–697; Berk et al. 1992:698–708).

Chambliss (1966) describes a "natural experiment" he observed at a midwestern American university where parking regulations underwent a sudden and dramatic change. Before the changes were introduced, professors were among the most flagrant offenders. If caught, they seldom paid the one dollar, which was the penalty for violation. The new policy involved stiffer fines, towing, and rigid enforcement—in other words, a dramatic increase in certainty and severity. Thirteen professors in the sample were "frequent violators" before the new policy was introduced. After it went into effect, six of the professors stopped offending altogether, another six reduced their violations, and one began parking in an alley beside his office where he was less likely to be tagged (Chambliss 1966). In this case, increasing severity and certainty were effective. It is debatable, however, whether such a policy would work as well with offences motivated more by passion than by reason.

Personal Vulnerability

Offenders who believe they are not vulnerable to the penalties associated with a particular offence are less likely to take them seriously. For example, Claster's (1967) study of juvenile delinquents found that, while the delinquents in the sample assessed the likelihood of *anyone* getting caught in a hypothetical criminal act in about the same way as the nondelinquents did, they assessed their *personal chances* of getting caught as much less. Claster attributed this to a "magical immunity" belief that translated into a "delusion of arrest immunity" on the part of the delinquent (80–86). People who feel they are "lucky" or "above the law" are more likely to offend. In the highly publicized case involving the murder of JoAnn Wilson by her husband Colin Thatcher, the accused was frequently depicted in the media as a man who believed—and on the basis of previous experiences had some reason to believe—that he was "above the law" (Bird 1985).

A related finding concerning personal likelihood of getting caught is that people who have had more experience committing minor offences have lower estimates of the likelihood of being caught, even when they are interviewed in prison (Homey and Marshall 1992:575). This may be attributed to Claster's "magical immunity" theory, or it may reflect the actual experience of most small-time offenders. For more serious and repeated offences, however, a deterrent effect with increased penalties has been found (Homey and Marshall 1992:576; Blumstein, Cohen, and Nagin 1978).

Severity

People who park illegally often argue that the cost of the ticket is reasonable compared to the trouble of finding a legal parking space. Professional criminals often assume that the occasional bust is simply a cost of doing business. Many white-collar offenders are right in assuming that they will make more profit by breaking the rules, even if they get caught. Similarly, many young offenders believe, often correctly, that lawbreaking by juveniles carries with it only minor penalties. Increasing the severity of punishment may reduce the offence rate, as long as certainty is maintained. For example, a road traffic act introduced in Germany in 1962 provided very stiff penalties for drunk driving. The new regulations were widely publicized, and the number of reported offences immediately declined. However, as drivers became aware that police were not rigorously enforcing the law, violation numbers crept back up to former levels (Middendorf 1968). Similar down-then-up findings have been reported in Minnesota, where new laws promised stiffer drunk driving penalties, increased surveillance, and increased the speed of court processing but did not, in fact, deliver these things (Green 1989:785,799). A study by Phillips (1980) on the effects of well-publicized executions over the 63 years from 1858 to 1921 showed the same pattern: a decline in homicides for about two weeks, followed by an increase in the homicide rate over the next three weeks. Clearly, deterrence effects are not simply additive.

In the early 1970s, a delinquency prevention program called Scared Straight! was introduced by the Juvenile Awareness Project at Rahway State Prison in New Jersey. Fuelling the treatment program was the classical notion of deterrence. Youths were to visit prisons and be shown by convicts just how bad the consequences of delinquency would be, with the expectation that at least some of them would be shocked into abandoning their criminal lifestyles in order to avoid such a fate. The program, and those modelled after it, provided youths with a no-nonsense view of the humiliations and abuses typical of prison life. The programs were popular because they seemed to provide an inexpensive form of education. However, evaluation has failed to confirm their deterrent effects. In fact, Finkenauer (1982) found that youths who were exposed to the Scared Straight! program had higher rates of offending in the six months that followed than did control group members who were not exposed to it (Hagan 1982:31; Scared Straight! 1979).

Celerity (Speed)

A punishment or penalty that is immediate is expected to be more effective than one received long after the offence. In many European countries, traffic fines are levied on the spot. Classical theory would predict this to be a more effective deterrent than receiving notification of an offence in the mail. If, as in most cases, bank robbers are caught only after they have had time to enjoy some of the fruits of their offence, this pattern would tend to reinforce the offence rather than correct it. The clearest support for the importance of celerity has come from laboratory research on animals. Studies of human beings have been quite inconclusive, particularly with respect to punishment as opposed by rewards. Human behaviour is most predictably influenced by rewards (Verna 1977:621-624; Corman 1981:476; Selke 1983; Clark 1988).

Group Loyalties and Personal Commitments

Such factors as group spirit and loyalty, situational ethics, and passion may interfere with the operation of a rational cost-benefit analysis of participation. The assumptions of neoclassical theory hold that people are rational rather than emotional, and that they weigh the costs of gratifying their impulses in terms of material rewards and punishments. This is not always the case: gang members may count the gain in group prestige, in "being a somebody," as more important than the risk of prosecution. People who are furious with one another may not weigh the consequences of their actions (Brown, Esbensen, and Geis 1991:443), although increasingly evidence shows that even in cases apparently characterized by blind rage, deterrence is not completely irrelevant (Katz 1988).

Heavier Penalties for Alternative Choices

Making an offence such as kidnapping punishable by death may actually contribute to more serious crime, since the kidnapper has even more to lose should the kidnap victim be allowed to live and end up providing useful evidence to the police. In such a case, murder might be seen as a safeguard against this possibility. Similarly, witnesses in court cases may be harassed, intimidated, and even killed by offenders determined to avoid a heavy penalty for the crimes they have already committed. Heavy penalties may make juries reluctant to convict, thus reducing the certainty of punishment.

Brutalization

It has been suggested that state violence in the form of corporal punishment and executions has a brutalizing effect, actually increasing the likelihood of violent crime (Bowers and Pierce 1980). Parents who try to teach their children not to hit other children, but do so by spanking or hitting, provide a role model of violence as a means of solving problems.

On the whole, deviant behaviours that are engaged in for rational (instrumental) reasons (e.g., cheating, stealing, lying, and deceiving for economic gain) are more likely to be affected by changes in the likelihood of detection and punishment than are behaviours with less rationally controlled components (e.g., compulsions and addictions) (Brown, Esbensen, and Geis 1991:443). Deterrent sanctions also work best on individuals who have low commitment to crime as a way of life (they may have a job and family and be unwilling to risk losing them), and who are older, future-oriented, nonimpulsive, and pessimistic about their chances of criminal success (Brown, Ebsensen, and Geis 1991:451).

TARGET-HARDENING: THE ECONOMY OF DEVIANCE

While classical theorists concerned themselves mainly with the offender's calculation of risk, later theorists, particularly "rational choice" theorists, have expanded the idea of calculation to include the calculation of reward relative to effort—that is, they treat deviance as a form of utilitarian economic activity (Cornish and Clarke 1986; Yunker 1977). The economic approach considers not only the costs in terms of punishment, but also such factors as the skill and effort required by any particular deviant act relative to others. For example, small electrical appliances are more likely to be stolen than refrigerators (Gottfredson and Hirschi 1990:6).

In the late 1960s, a paper on the economy of deviance by Ernest Becker (1968) inspired a flood of articles that depicted criminals as being just like everyone else with respect to rationally maximizing "their own self-interest (utility) subject to constraints (prices, incomes) that they face in the marketplace and elsewhere" (Rubin 1980:13). The cost-benefit ratios of various crimes and infractions show that deviants often act as if they were the rational actors of the classical model, affected not just by penalties but by other kinds of costs and rewards.

> The notion of the criminal as a rational calculator will strike many readers as highly unrealistic, especially when applied to criminals having little education or to crimes not committed for pecuniary gain. But ... the test of a theory is not the realism of its assumptions but its predictive power. A growing empirical literature on crime shows that

criminals respond to changes in opportunity costs, in the probability of apprehension, in the severity of punishment, and in other relevant variables, as if they were indeed the rational calculators of the economic model—and this regardless of whether the crime is committed for pecuniary gain or out of passion, or by well or by poorly educated people. (Posner 1977:164–165)

In this view, it is possible to work out the cost-benefit ratios for particular acts (Lo 1994). On one side of the ledger, we can put the potential costs: risks (whether from other deviants, from victims, from the act itself, or from legal authorities); difficulty (distance, skills needed); lost opportunities (the deviant lifestyle may preclude certain legitimate activities); expenses (obtaining weapons, a getaway car, a stash of drugs, or supporting a particular lifestyle); and time (planning and executing a plan, recruiting others for group activities). On the other side of the ledger are the benefits, which may be material (property or money) or emotional (revenge, power, respect, excitement, acceptance). Any increase in the likelihood of detection (arrest and exposure) and punishment (imprisonment, societal rejection, job loss) changes the balance of the ledger. Simply making the behaviour harder to accomplish, through various kinds of target-hardening, may achieve the same effect (Posner 1977:164; Cohen, Felson, and Land 1980). Target-hardening may be physical (locking things up and creating obstacles for thieves) or educational (warning elderly people about the "bank inspector" scam and similar rip-offs directed at them by con artists, or teaching people to be wary of "free offers").

SUMMARY

Classical theory introduced a radically new view of the deviant as a person who rationally chooses to increase his or her pleasure by acting in a way that violates the rules of society, or, conversely, as a person who may rationally decide to abandon deviance in order to avoid predictable pain. Classical theorists argued that deviance was caused by an environment in which reasonable people would judge that breaking the rules was more attractive than conforming to them. They criticized the existing justice system for providing a social milieu that encouraged crime. Although punishments were severe to the point of being crimes in themselves, their erratic application precluded any deterrent effect.

The classical theorists devoted themselves to elaborate schemes to make punishment more predictable and consistent, and to calibrate it at a level severe enough—no more, no less—to counterbalance the rewards of crime. They argued for greater swiftness and certainty of punishment. As a consequence of their work, horrifying public executions began to give way to punishments, such as imprisonment, that could be administered in precisely measured doses.

Classical theorists focused more on crime than on other forms of deviance, more on the criminal justice system than on informal social controls. Their interest in deterrence is shared by many researchers today, just as their view of crime as a rational choice has been revitalized by modern economic criminologists. However, while classical theory (especially as adjusted by the neoclassical thinkers) enjoyed considerable support when applied to the actions of apparently rational predators and cheaters, it seemed less able to deal with deviance in which rationality seemed absent or diminished. The theory's fundamental assumption of human rationality came under increasing attack as biological science and the emerging fields of psychology and sociology began to provide alternative assumptions and explanations.

REFERENCES

Bala, Nicholas N. (1988). "The Young Offender's Act: A Legal Framework." In J. Hudson, J. Homick, and B. Burrows (eds.), *Justice and the Young Offender in Canada.* Toronto: Thompson Educational Publishing.

Becker, Ernest. (1968). *The Structure of Evil: An Essay on the Unification of the Science of Man.* New York: Free Press.

Beirne, Piers. (1991). "Inventing Criminology: The 'Science of Man.' In Cesare Beccaria's *Dei delitte della Pene (1764)." Criminology* 29(4):777–820.

Bentham, Jeremy. (1988). *An Introduction to the Principles of Morals and Legislation.* Buffalo: Prometheus Books.

———. (1995 [1787]). *The Panopticon Writings.* Edited and introduced by Miran Bozovic. London: Verso.

Berk, Richard A., Alec Campbell, Ruth Klapp, and Bruce Western. (1992). "The Deterrent Effect of Arrest in Incidents of Domestic Violence: A Bayesian Analysis of Four Field Experiments." *American Sociological Review* 57(5):698–708.

Bird, Heather. (1985). *Not Above the Law: The Tragic Story of JoAnn Wilson and Colin Thatcher.* Toronto: Key Porter.

Blumstein, Alfred, Jacqueline Cohen, and Daniel Nagin (eds.). (1978). *Deterrence and Incapacitation: Estimating the Effects of Criminal Sanctions on Crime Rates.* Washington, D.C.: National Academy of Sciences.

Bowers, William J. (1974). *Executions in America.* Lexington, Mass.: D.C. Heath.

Bowers, William J., and Glenn L. Pierce. (1980). "Deterrence or Brutalization: What is the Effect of Executions?" *Crime and Delinquency* 26(October):453–484.

Broadhurst, Roderic, and Nini Loh. (1993). "The Phantom of Deterrence: The Crime (Serious and Repeat Offenders) Sentencing Act" *Australia and New Zealand Journal of Criminology* 26(3):251–271.

Brown, Stephen E., Finn-Aage Esbensen, and Gilbert Geis. (1991). *Criminology: Explaining Crime and Its Context*. Cincinnati: Anderson.

Chambliss, William J. (1966). "The Deterrent Effect of Punishment." *Crime and Delinquency* 12:70–75.

Chauncey, Robert. (1975). "Deterrence, Certainty, Severity and Skyjacking." *Criminology* 12(February):447–473.

Clark, Richard D. (1988). "Celerity and Specific Deterrence: A Look at the Evidence." *Canadian Journal of Criminology* 30(2):109–20.

Claster, Donald S. (1967). "Comparison of Risk Perception Between Delinquents and Nondelinquents." *Journal of Criminal Law, Criminology and Political Science* 58 (March):80–86.

Cohen, Lawrence E., Marcus Felson, and Kenneth C. Land. (1980). "Property Crime Rates in the United States: A Macrodynamic Analysis 1947–1977, With Ex-Ante Forecasts for the Mid-1980s." *American Journal of Sociology* 86 (July):90–118.

Corman, H. (1981). "Criminal Deterrence in New York: The Relationship Between Court Activities and Crime." *Economic Enquiry* 19:476–487.

Cornish, Derek B., and Ronald V. Clarke (eds.). (1986). *The Reasoning Criminal*. New York: Springer.

Dent, N.J.H. (1988). *Rousseau: An Introduction to His Psychological, Social and Political Theory*. Oxford: Basil Blackwell.

Dobbs, B.J.T. (1975). *The Foundations of Newton's Alchemy*. Cambridge, Mass.: Cambridge University Press.

Fattah, Ezzat A. (1976). "Deterrence: A Review of the Literature." In *Fear of Punishment*. Law Reform Commission of Canada. Ottawa: Minister of Supply and Services Canada.

Figala, Karen. (1977). "Newton as Alchemist." *History of Science* 15:102–137.

Finkenauer, James. (1982). *Scared Straight! and the Panacea Phenomenon*. Englewood Cliffs, N.J.: Prentice-Hall.

Foucault, Michel. (1979). *Discipline and Punish*. New York: Vintage.

Gay, Peter. (1966). *Age of Enlightenment*. New York: Time Inc.

Geis, Gilbert. (1973). "Jeremy Bentham." In Hermann Mannheim (ed.), *Pioneers in Criminology*. 2nd ed. Montclair, N.J.: Patterson Smith.

Gibbs, Jack P. (1975). *Crime, Punishment and Deterrence*. New York: Elsevier, North Holland.

Gottfredson, Michael, and Travis Hirschi. (1990). *A General Theory of Crime*. Palo Alto, Cal.: Stanford University Press.

Green, Donald E. (1989). "Past Behavior as a Measure of Actual Future Behavior: An Unresolved Issue in Perceptual Deterrence Research." *The Journal of Criminal Law and Criminology* 80(3):781–804.

Griffiths, Curt T., Simon Verdun-Jones, and Alison Hatch-Cunningham. (1989). "The Canadian Youth Justice System." In Curt T. Griffiths and Simon Verdun-Jones (eds.), *Canadian Criminal Justice*. Toronto: Butterworths.

Hagan, Frank E. (1982). *Research Methods in Criminal Justice and Criminology*. New York: Macmillan.

Henry, Stuart, and Dragon Milovanovich. (1996). *Constitutive Criminology: Beyond Postmodernism*. London: Sage.

Hobbes, Thomas. (1881). *Leviathan*. Oxford: James Thornton.

Homey, Julie, and Ineke Haen Marshall. (1992). "Risk Perceptions Among Serious Offenders: The Role of Crime and Punishment." *Criminology* 30(4):575–594.

Ignatieff, Michael. (1978). *A Just Measure of Pain: The Penitentiary in the Industrial Revolution, 1750–1850*. New York: Columbia University Press.

Jacobs, Bruce A. (1996). "Crack Dealers and Restrictive Deterrence: Identifying Narcs." *Criminology* 34(3):409–431.

Jeffrey, C. Ray. (1990). *Criminology: An Interdisciplinary Approach*. Englewood Cliffs, N.J.: Prentice-Hall.

Jenkins, Philip. (1984). *Crime and Justice: Issues and Ideas*. Monterey, Cal.: Brooks/Cole.

Jonas, George (ed.). (1983). *The Scales of Justice: Seven Famous Criminal Cases Recreated*. Montreal: CBC Enterprises.

Jonas, George (ed.). (1986). *The Scales of Justice: Ten Famous Criminal Cases Recreated*. Vol. 2. Toronto: Lester and Orpen Dennys/CBC Enterprises.

Kant, Immanual. (1784). "What Is Enlightenment?" In H. Reiss (ed.), *Kant's Political Writings*. Cambridge, U.K.: Cambridge University Press, 1977.

Katz, Jack. (1988). *Seductions of Crime: Moral and Sensual Attractions in Doing Evil*. New York: Basic Books.

Lerner, Lawrence S., and Edward A. Gosselin. (1986). "Galileo and the Specter of Bruno." *Scientific American* 255(5):126–133.

Leschied, Alan W., Peter G. Jaffe, and Wayne Willis (eds.). (1991). *The Young Offenders Act: A Revolution in Canadian Juvenile Justice*. Toronto: University of Toronto Press.

Lo, Lucia. (1994). "Exploring Teenage Shoplifting Behavior: A Choice and Constraint Approach." *Environment and Behavior* 26(5):613–639.

Maestro, Marcello. (1972). *Voltaire and Beccaria*. New York: Octagon.

———. (1973). *Cesare Beccaria and the Origins of Penal Reform*. Philadelphia: Temple University Press.

Middendorf, W. (1968). *The Effectiveness of Punishment Especially in Relation to Traffic Offences*. South Hackensack, N.J.: Fred E. Rothman.

Paolucci, H. (1963). "Translator's Introduction." In Cesare Beccaria, *On Crimes and Punishments*. New York: Bobbs Merrill.

Pate, Antony, and Edwin Hamilton. (1992). "Formal and Informal Deterrents to Domestic Violence: The Dade County Spouse Assault Experiment." *American Sociological Review* 57(5):691–697.

Peters, Edward. (1989). *Inquisition*. Berkeley: University of California Press.

Pfohl, Stephen. (1985). *Images of Deviance and Social Control: A Sociological History.* New York: McGraw-Hill.

Phillips, D.P. (1980). "The Deterrent Effect of Capital Punishment: New Evidence on an Old Controversy." *American Journal of Sociology* 86:139–148.

Posner, Richard. (1977). *Economic Analysis of Law.* 2nd ed. Boston: Little, Brown.

Radzinowicz, Leon. (1948). *A History of English Criminal Law from 1750:* Vol. 1. *The Movement for Reform.* London: Stevens.

Redondi, Pietro. (1987). *Galileo: Heretic.* Princeton, N.J.: Princeton University Press.

Rennie, Ysabel. (1978). *The Search for Criminal Man.* Lexington, Mass.: Lexington Books.

Rubin, Paul H. (1980). "The Economics of Crime." In Ralph Andreano and John J. Siegfried (eds.), *The Economics of Crime.* New York: John Wiley.

Russell, Jeffrey Burton. (1988). *The Prince of Darkness: Radical Evil and the Power of Good in History.* Ithaca, N.Y.: Cornell University Press.

"Scared Straight! found Ineffective Again." (1979). *Criminal Justice Newsletter* 10(Sept. 10):7.

Schmalleger, Frank. (1996). *Criminology Today.* Englewood Cliffs, N.J.: Prentice-Hall.

Schneider, Anne L., and Laurie Ervin. (1990). "Specific Deterrence, Rational Choice, and Decision Heuristics: Applications in Juvenile Justice." *Social Science Quarterly* 71(3):585–601.

Selke, W.L. (1983). "Celerity: The Ignored Variable in Deterrence Research." *Journal of Police Science and Administration* 11:31–37.

Tannahill, Reay. (1992). *Sex in History.* Lanham, Md.: Scarborough House.

Verna, G.B. (1977). "The Effects of Four-Hour Delay of Punishment Under Two Conditions of Verbal Instruction." *Child Development* 48:621–624.

Vold, George B. (1979). *Theoretical Criminology.* 2nd ed. New York: Oxford University Press.

Webster, Charles. (1996 [1982]). *From Paracelsus to Newton: Magic and the Making of Modern Science.* New York: Barnes and Noble.

West, W. Gordon. (1984). *Young Offenders and the State: A Canadian Perspective on Delinquency.* Toronto: Butterworths.

Yunker, James A. (1977). "An Old Controversy Renewed: Introduction to the Journal of Behavioral Economics Capital Punishment Symposium." *Journal of Behavioral Economics* 6:1–32.

BIOLOGICAL AND PHYSIOLOGICAL EXPLANATIONS OF DEVIANCE

It is difficult to explain some kinds of deviance in classical terms. Consider the following cases, for example:

> A Calgary man, accused of hoarding stolen garden implements, was put on six months probation yesterday for stealing part of a hose from a neighbour's home. Csaba Goczan, 48, who was arrested in June, still faces trial on 21 other charges laid after a search of his home. The search turned up about $16,000 worth of implements missing from neighbourhood yards, including four lawnmowers, 108 shovels, 109 garden hoses, 148 extension cords and 316 sprinklers. (*Toronto Star* 1988).
>
> Steve Fonyo, the one-legged runner who ran across Canada for cancer research, has lost his leg to a thief [while] taking part in the ninth annual Terry Fox run in Edmonton ... After doing his part in the run, Mr. Fonyo put his artificial leg in the car and later discovered it missing ... Mr. Fonyo, who lost his leg to cancer, ran across Canada in 1985 to raise money for research. (*Globe and Mail* 1989)

Positivism is based on the belief that the methods of natural science should be adapted to the study of human beings. Positivist theory assumes that knowledge can be discovered only through sensory experience, observation, and experiment. Its early proponents claimed, sometimes only half-truthfully, that they employed the scientific method of sampling, controls, and analysis. When the assumptions and techniques used in the scientific study of rocks, plants, and insects were applied to human affairs, the result was an entirely new view of our species, one that seemed to address kinds of deviance not well explained by classical theory.

Although classical thinkers frequently invoked the spirit of science, most of their work was not "scientific," either because it was untested by empirical data, or because no effort was made to collect empirical data in a disciplined, systematic, manner. Thus, positivism—and the "positive school of criminology" it gave rise to—represents what Kuhn (1970) terms a "paradigm shift." It constituted a new kind of lens through which human nature and human behaviour could be understood.

Box 5.1   Comparison of Classical and Positivist Schools

Time of Dominance	*1700–1800*	*1800–1900*
Conception of deviance	Violation of social contract, crime	Pathology, constitutional inferiority, sickness
Explanation	Free will, balance of punishment	Determinism, symptoms of constitutional faults
Remedies	Swift, certain, severe punishment	Treatment, separation, elimination.

This paradigm achieved dominant status as an explanation of deviance in the late 1800s and the early 1900s, when sociological positivistic approaches challenged it with yet another paradigm. Sociology still competes vigorously, and sometimes quite acrimoniously, with the biologically oriented paradigms. Students should be aware that this competition causes many biologically oriented theorists to deny the importance of sociological insights, and many sociologists to deny the relevance of biology to social action. Sociology texts quite customarily deal only with the "fame, fortune, and fudged data" period of biological positivism, before going on to discuss sociological research.

While some of the early attempts to discover the biological level of social action really *were* crude and fraudulent, this should not discredit the probability that a final "theory of social action" will have to incorporate biological perspectives. In the meantime, these biologically rooted theories constitute the main alternatives to sociological approaches, and must be taken into account. This is particularly important given the fact that the average citizen is bombarded with this type of explanation in newspapers, television documentaries, soap operas, films, and other media. Whether we agree with biological theories or not, it is important to understand and evaluate them. As we will show, none of the nonsociological theories explains so much that no room remains for sociological contributions, and some do not deserve the popularity they enjoy.

The early positivists followed the lead of natural science by assuming that underlying all empirical reality were discoverable laws that could be used to explain everything in nature, including human behaviour. The hedonistic self-directed actor depicted in classical thought was replaced by a person whose every action was a symptom of dark, biological impulses, evolutionary position, and environmental forces. This view of human beings stressed the extent to which all behaviour is determined by forces no individual ever fully controls. "Free will," in this view, is nothing but an illusion through which human beings try to establish their superiority over other animals.

> The illusion of a free human will (the only miraculous factor in the eternal ocean of cause and effect) leads to the assumption that one can choose freely between virtue and vice. How can you still believe in the existence of a free will when modern psychology, armed with all the instruments of positive modern research, denies that there is any free will and demonstrates that every act of a human being is the result of an interaction between the personality and environment of man? And how is it possible to cling to that obsolete idea of moral guilt, according to which every individual is supposed to have the free choice to abandon virtue and give himself up to crime? The positive school of criminology maintains, on the contrary, that it is not the criminal who wills; in order to be a criminal it is rather necessary that the individual should find himself permanently or transitorily in such personal, physical and moral conditions, and live in such an environment, which become for him a chain of cause and effect, externally and internally, that disposes him toward crime. (Enrico Ferri 1885, quoted in Grupp 1968)

If a person's misbehaviour is not willed, it is no longer appropriate to expect guilt or remorse (the demonic view), or to believe in the efficacy of punishment as a form of deterrence (the classical position). Just as the classical theorists satirized the practice of curing earthquakes by burning heretics, so the positivists ridiculed the classical notion that deviance was willed and thus could be deterred by punishment.

Box 5.2   Crime and Punishment in Erewhon

The illogic of punishing sickness was parodied by the English humorist Samuel Butler in his 1872 novel *Erewhon* (an anagram for "nowhere). In Erewhon, criminals receive treatment while sick people are punished.

> *Prisoner at the bar, you have been accused of the great crime of labouring under pulmonary consumption [lung cancer or tuberculosis], and after an impartial trial before a jury of your countrymen, you have been found guilty ... I find that though you are now only twenty-three years old, you have been imprisoned on no less than fourteen occasions for illnesses of a more or less hateful character; in fact, it is not too much to say that you have spent the great part of your life in jail. It is all very well for you to say that you came of unhealthy parents, and had a severe accident in childhood which permanently undermined your constitution; excuses such as these are the ordinary refuge of the criminal ... You are a bad and dangerous person, and stand branded in the eyes of your fellow-countrymen with one of the most heinous known offenses ... had not the capital punishment for consumption been abolished, I would certainly inflict it now. (1967:77–78)*

Butler simultaneously attacks and pokes fun at the practice of sentencing criminals, who were seen as being no more responsible for their actions than were sick people for their symptoms.

SOCIAL DARWINISM

The English philosopher Herbert Spencer (1820–1903) coined the phrase "survival of the fittest" to describe the implications of evolutionary theory for human society. Spencer argued that every field—industry, art, science, or human biology—reflected a pattern of development from lower to higher, from less complex to more complex, from inferior to superior. He took from Darwin's *Origin of the Species* (1859) and *Descent of Man* (1871) the notion that the development that occurred in human societies followed the principles of natural selection through competition. The more fit competitors win, survive, and procreate, while the less fit die out—unless, of course, the fit commit race suicide by not breeding, or the unfit are artificially supported by well-meaning but misguided people. Social Darwinists believed that those living organisms—whether human, plant, or animal—best able to adapt to a particular set of living conditions were the ones with the greatest chances of survival. Darwin's concept of evolution was used by Social Darwinists such as the wealthy industrialist Andrew Carnegie to justify political and social conditions that made life very hard for the poor.

Social Darwinists reasoned the powerful and rich were that way because they were more "fit" than those less well off. If England dominated the world with her imperialist system, it was because the English were a superior race who had to carry the "white man's burden" of responsibility for those less fit to govern themselves. Fitness became a synonym not only for "healthy" but also for "deserving." The higher socioeconomic classes were regarded as better "stock" and encouraged to have children. Social Darwinists felt that while "survival of the fittest" occurred automatically in nature, it was being interfered with in human societies, where "defectives"—criminals, the poor, ethnic and racial minorities—were being artificially supported, allowed to procreate, and survived to bite the hands that fed them.

MENDEL AND THE DISCOVERY OF GENETIC INHERITANCE

Gregor Mendel (1822–1884) studied plant seeds and discovered the genetic principles whereby variations of colour and size are transmitted by heredity. Before Mendel's work, it was assumed that changes in an organism's physical traits reflected its adaptation to the environment. Mendel found that inheritance of many plant characteristics occurs through mutation and combination of genes. This finding was often misinterpreted as meaning that environment played no role in determining individual traits. Consequently, there were those who attributed "feeblemindedness" and criminal behaviour entirely to heredity (Jeffery 1990:181); for them, heritable was synonymous with inevitable and immutable (Gould 1981:156).

The popularity of Social Darwinist and Mendelian genetic explanations grew throughout the 1800s and reached its apex by the early 1900s. In the 1930s, Hitler used these theories to establish breeding programs for the "Aryan" race, including the infamous *Lebensborn* program, and to justify the mass execution and abuse of millions of Jews, Gypsies, homosexuals, Jehovah's Witnesses, and others whose politics or physical traits were interpreted as signs of degeneracy and unfitness.

BORN CRIMINAL THEORY

The idea that criminality was not only inborn but also was revealed by a person's appearance was common in antiquity. The rise of science gave it a new immediacy.

Box 5.3   Better Breeding

Fairly or not, modern genetics research is still haunted by the history of eugenics. "It offers a lot of cautionary lessons," says Daniel J. Kevles, a historian and author of the 1985 book *In the Name of Eugenics.* The British scientist Francis Galton, cousin to Charles Darwin, first proposed that human society could be improve "through better breeding" in a 1865 article entitled "Hereditary Talent and Character." He coined the term "eugenics," from the Greek for "good birth," in 1883.

Galton's proposal had broad appeal. The American sexual libertarian John Humphrey Noyes bent eugenics into an ingenious argument for polygamy. "While the good man will be limited by his conscience to what the law allows," Noyes said, "the bad man, free from moral check, will distribute his seed beyond the legal limit."

Francis Galton in 1864
Source: Mary Evans Picture Library. Reprinted with permission.

A more serious advocate was the biologist Charles E. Davenport, founder of Cold Spring Harbor Laboratory and of the Eugenics Record Office, which gathered information on thousands of American families for genetic research. After demonstrating the heritability of eye, skin and hair colour, Davenport went on to "prove" the heretability of traits such as "pauperism," criminality, and "feeble-mindedness." In a 1919 monograph, he asserted that ability to be a naval officer is an inherited trait, composed of subtraits for thalassophilia, or love of the sea, and hyperkineticism, or wanderlust. Noting the paucity of female naval officers, Davenport concluded that the trait is unique to males.

Better Breeding (cont.)

Beginning in the 1920s the American Eugenics Society, founded by Davenport and others, sponsored "Fitter Families Contests" at state fairs across the United States. Just as cows and sheep were appraised by judges at the fairs, so were human entrants ...

No nation, of course, practiced eugenics as enthusiastically as Nazi Germany, whose program culminated in "euthanasia" ("good death") of the mentally and physically disabled as well as Jews, Gypsies, Catholics and others.

Source: John Horgan, "Trends in Behavioral Genetics: Eugenics Revisited," *Scientific American* (June 1993) 268(6):122–131.

If criminals could be detected at an early stage, they might be terminated or confined before committing any offences.

The earliest researchers sought to find statistical connections between external characteristics such as facial features, skull size, and body shape. Later, science would move into the less visible realms of genes, blood-sugar counts, and neurochemical markers. In roughly chronological order, the early efforts took the form of physiognomy, phrenology, craniometry, atavism, and degeneracy.

PHYSIOGNOMY

Physiognomy, the study of facial features, was based on the idea that outward appearance indicated inner character. As far back as Aristotle, facial features were used to draw analogies between humans and animals. If a person looked like a bull he would be stubborn and tenacious; if he looked like a lion he would be brave.

The "science" of judging character based on facial features had widespread support and appeal in the late 1700s and early 1800s. John Caspar Lavater (1741–1801) produced a detailed, four-volume map of the human face, which associated various shapes and structures with specific personality traits. In this work, entitled *Physiognomical Fragments* (1775), criminals were characterized as tending to have shifty eyes, weak chins, and large, arrogant noses. A physiognomist's report on Lizzie Borden, said to have murdered her parents with an axe in 1892 (but acquitted in court), was typical of a number of them done at the time in diagnosing from her face that she "[is] high tempered, secretive, and fond of property," among other strong-willed characteristics that strongly suggest she committed the crime

Figure 5.2   The Brain as Seen by Phrenologists

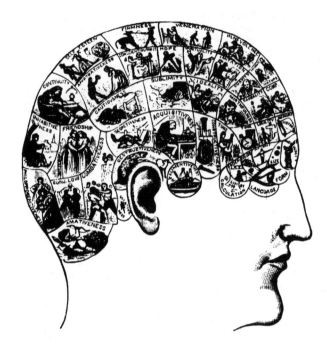

Source: Reproduced by permission of the Bettmann Archive.

(Lane 1992:467, from *Phrenological Journal* 1892). While physiognomy may be used as a quick indicator of conditions like Down's syndrome, its value today is negligible.

PHRENOLOGY

Phrenology, which was most popular in the mid-1800s, was based on the theory that "functions" such as cautiousness, firmness, benevolence, mirthfulness, and their opposites were located in distinct parts of the brain and that the stronger the functions, the larger their physical manifestations. These enlarged parts would push the skull out so that a trained technician could feel the slight bumps and thus "read" the person's character. Phrenologists (nicknamed "skullfeelers") judged personality by measuring the skull shape and its irregularities (Brown, Esbensen, and Geis 1991:231).

In the early 1800s, Franz Joseph Gall (1758–1828) and his student and colleague, Johann Caspar Spurzheim (1776–1832), published a two-volume work on phrenology, presenting it as a new science (Leek 1970). Gall catalogued 26 bump-producing psychological characteristics, and Spurzheim expanded the list to 35. Whether a person were characterized as cruel or benevolent, the dominant quality would appear as a bump in the contour of the skull in the appropriately mapped area. In the normal person, the higher faculties of friendship, religion, and intellect were dominant, but deviant behaviour, in the form of crime or violence, could occur if the lower propensities came to dominate the personality; thus arson or murder might result if destructiveness became dominant (Fink 1938:1–19; Leek 1970). In the mid-1800s, it was customary to make a cast of the head of executed criminals, so that such features of skull and brain could be measured and interpreted (Lane 1992:463).

A phrenological analysis of Adolf Hitler by Alfred Richter, which was published in the late 1930s with the approval of Hitler's National Socialist Party, claimed that Hitler's facial expression was that of "a genius, a creative, spiritual leader, powerful, tenacious, filled with great love, unspeakable pain, and renunciation," while the upper part of his head showed "universal love, lofty religion, beauty and nobility of nature" (Richter 1938, cited in Fest 1970).

Widely accepted in popular culture, phrenology was used by authors as diverse as Balzac and Hawthorne for characterization, in much the same way that a modern novelist would incorporate insights from modern psychology. Long since discredited as a science, phrenology booths can be found today at "psychic fairs," along with those offering palmistry, astrology, tarot cards, and other forms of fortune telling.

CRANIOMETRY

Craniometry was a system of classifying human types on the basis of skull measurement. Leading practitioners like Swedish anthropologist Anders Rolf Retzius thought of themselves as objective observers who merely recorded and honestly interpreted the weights and volumes of the brains and skulls they studied. At first, larger brains were believed to indicate greater brain activity (and thus the superiority of the individual). While the data usually corroborated prevailing social, racial, and gender biases, there were anomalies:

A study by T. Bischoff on the brains of 119 assassins, murderers, and thieves found that their average weight exceeded the mean of honest men by 11 grams. While only three men of genius topped 1600 grams, 5 of the criminals did. The largest female brain ever weighed (1,565 grams) belonged to a woman who had killed her husband. (Gould 1981:94)

The French surgeon and anthropologist Paul Broca argued that execution might give the brain spuriously high weights, but it was finally decided (Gould 1981:94; Topinard 1888:15) that too much weight might be as bad as too little. The social import of the "science" of craniology can be illustrated by looking at one aspect of the popularized version, as put forth by Gustave Le Bon, a French sociologist and follower of Broca:

> In the most intelligent races ... there are a large number of women whose brains are closer in size to those of gorillas than to the most developed men's brains ... All psychologists who have studied the intelligence of women, as well as poets and novelists, recognize today that they represent the most inferior forms of human evolution and that they are closer to children and savages than to an adult civilized man. They excel in fickleness, inconstancy, absence of thought and logic, and incapacity to reason. (quoted in Gould 1981:60–61)

The limits of craniometry were soon reached, as anthropologists, realizing that many other factors (including nutrition) influenced brain and skull size, turned to more defensible and reliable indicators of human characteristics.

LOMBROSO'S THEORY OF ATAVISM

The controversial theories of Cesare Lombroso (1835–1909) have inspired more commentary, praise, and condemnation than those of any other criminologist (Wolfgang 1972:232). Though often credited with being the "father of criminology," his biological approach to crime causation, sometimes called forensic anthropology, proved to be full of unlikely assumptions and questionable statistical tests. Central to Lombroso's conception of crime was his theory of biological atavism. According to this theory, criminals possessed atavistic characteristics that were indicative of an accidental reversion to a more primitive stage in human evolution. The criminal was an evolutionary throwback. Physical characteristics ("stigmata") such as sloping foreheads, bushy eyebrows, and protruding jaws and cheekbones were evidence of atavism, and thus criminal propensity. Different kinds of criminality were indicated by head and body size, hair colour, and abnormalities of the ears, nose, arms, and body. "Ravishers," for example, "have short hands, medium-sized brains, and narrow foreheads; there is a predominance of light hair with abnormalities of the genital organs and of the nose" (Lombroso 1895; Lane 1992:161). Lombroso's follower Enrico Ferri coined the term "born criminal" to describe the biologically determined criminal type (Brown, Esbensen, and Geis 1991:233).

Just as Beccaria turned against the theological and supernatural theories that were part of his education, Lombroso found himself, as a result of his medical training, increasingly at odds with the classical ideology of "free will," dominant in Italian academic circles of this period. He was influenced by evolutionary theory through the work of Auguste Comte (1798–1853), who argued that society goes through evolutionary stages just as the human species does; by the biological work of Gall; and by the French alienist (psychiatrist) B.A. Morel, who argued that degeneracy was expressed in epilepsy, insanity, mental deficiency, and crime (Wolfgang 1972:234, 242).

Lombroso's earliest research involved the study of cretinism, a type of physical stunting and mental deficiency now understood to be produced by prenatal thyroid deficiency, and pellagra, a disease characterized by skin rashes that is now known to be caused by nutritional deficiencies (Brown, Esbensen, and Geis 1991:254). While working as a physician in the Italian army, Lombroso systematically measured and observed some 3000 soldiers (Wolfgang 1972:245). One of his early observations was that many of the most disruptive soldiers had tattoos, and he, therefore, came to believe that tattooing reflected primitive man's insensitivity to pain and love of adornment.

This early work inspired Lombroso to test the theory that physical and psychological traits were correlated. Soon he was conducting anthropometric studies of inmates and inmate cadavers in Italian prisons. In one of these prisons, he uncovered the skull of a notorious brigand, which he repeatedly used in public lectures to illustrate the idea of the atavistic criminal.

> This was a revelation. At the sight of that skull I seemed to see all of a sudden, lighted up as a vast plain under a flaming sky, the problem of the nature of the criminal—an atavistic being who reproduces in his person the ferocious instincts of primitive humanity and inferior animals. Thus were explained anatomically the enormous jaws, high cheek bones, prominent supercilliary arches, solitary lines in the palms, extreme size of the orbits, handle shaped or sessile ears found in criminals, savages and apes, insensitivity to pain, extremely acute sight, tattooing, excessive idleness, love of orgies, and the irresistible craving for evil for its own sake, the desire not only to extinguish life in the victim but to mutilate the corpse, tear its flesh, and drink its blood (Lombroso-Ferrero 1911:xiv-xvi).

In addition, he used the case of a young Italian soldier, suitably named Misdea, who was subject to epileptic fits, as an illustration of the epileptiform nature of criminality. Misdea had suddenly attacked and killed eight officers and men. He then fell into a deep sleep for twelve hours and awoke with no memory of his deed (Wolfgang 1972:248). Lombroso classified all criminals as "epileptoids" on a scale in which epileptic was at the top, followed by criminal moral imbecile, born criminal, criminaloid (occasional criminal), and criminal by passion (Lombroso 1897, cited by Wolfgang 1972:254). Such ideas added fuel to the arguments of eugenics experts about restricting the procreation of inferiors, epileptics, and the mentally ill.

Lombroso did not claim that all criminals were "born" criminals. He adjusted his argument repeatedly to meet the criticisms of other researchers. He finally proposed that about 30 to 40 percent of criminals took this form while the rest (i.e., those without epilepsy, mental illness, or atavistic stigmata) were brought to crime by force of circumstance (Gould 1981:132). Lombroso believed, however, that born criminals were the most serious and chronic offenders. When, over the course of his research, Lombroso discovered that most of his noncriminal samples possessed some atavistic characteristics, he decided that as many as five of these anomalies in a single individual could be taken as evidence that the person was a born criminal (Brown, Esbensen, and Geis 1991:256).

The Female Offender

In every country that keeps records of such things, women have much lower rates of criminality than do men. To be logically consistent, Lombroso should have concluded from this that women were more evolutionary advanced than men (Hagan 1985:76–78). Instead he argued that women were nearer to their atavistic origins than were men, but that criminal propensities in women were neutralized by their natural passivity, which he attributed to the "immobility of the ovule [egg] compared with the zoosperm [sperm]" (Lombroso 1895:109). The typical woman, Lombroso claimed, was characterized by piety, maternal feelings, sexual coldness, and an underdeveloped intelligence. Criminal women, on the other hand, were either born with masculine qualities (intelligence and activeness) conducive to criminal activity, or encouraged to develop these qualities through such things as education and exercise. Furthermore, Lombroso wrote, "[Women's] evil tendencies are more numerous and more varied than men's, but generally remain latent. When they are awakened and excited they produce results proportionately greater" (quoted in Wolfgang 1972:255).

Lombroso argued that when not restrained by religious sentiments, maternal feelings, and stupidity, the "innocuous semi-criminal present in the normal woman" emerges as a born criminal "worse than any man" (Lombroso-Ferrero 1895, quoted in Wolfgang 1972:255).

For the most part, Lombroso found that women escaped the "atavistic laws of degeneration." He felt that prostitutes were the one exception, and that they were the closest to the typical representative of criminality, even to a greater extent than the male homicidal robber (Wolfgang 1972:254). Autopsies of women from Italian prisons showed criminal women were more masculine, exhibiting darker skin, and had a more "virile cranium" and excess body hair. These results, used to support Lombroso's theory, would now be interpreted as the result of researchers finding what they were looking for, of the hard lives lived by women who ran afoul of the law, and of prejudice against migrant Sicilians, who were, on the whole, darker than northern Italians.

Lombrosian Theory and Social Control

Lombrosian theory became a factor in determining guilt or innocence in the court-room and in deciding how a convicted criminal should be treated. Called as an "expert witness" in a case in which the court was trying to determine which of two stepsons had killed a woman, Lombroso testified that one of them was the perfect type of born criminal. In *Criminal Man* (1911), he described this man (who was convicted) as having had "enormous jaws, frontal sinuses and zygomata, thin upper lip, huge incisors, unusually large head, tactile obtuseness with censorial manicin-ism" (436). The precise meanings of these terms is lost to us, but it is clear that the signs of atavism had replaced warts, black cats, and unusual abilities as indicators of criminality.

When it came to social control of the born criminal, relatively few options existed. Neither "suffering for salvation" (the demonic approach) nor the manipulation of free will (classical theory) were appropriate for the born criminal; this left as possible solutions elimination, isolation, or treatment. At the time, few treatments were available, especially if the problem was seen as congenital. Lombrosians tended to favour the death penalty; long, indefinite sentences; or isolation in institutions for the insane. Mussolini supporters Raffaele Garofalo (1852–1934) and Enrico Ferri, both followers of Lombroso, argued for the elimination of the unfit in terms similar to those invoked by the Nazis (Brown, Esbensen, and Geis 1991:236).

The Displacement of Lombrosian Theory

Paul Topinard, a contemporary of Lombroso, observed that Lombroso's collection of atavistic criminals looked much like his own friends (Brown, Esbensen, and Geis 1991:237). This observation hits at the main problem with atavistic explanations of criminality: no matter how accurate Lombroso's measurements of ears, noses, and brains were, this evidence did not support the conclusion that particular sizes, weights, and shapes of anatomical parts were associated with particular criminal proclivities. The research, in other words, was not valid. It did not measure what the researchers claimed to be measuring (criminal propensities). In addition, Lombroso was severely criticized for using ill-defined measurements, unwarranted deductions, and inadequately chosen control groups, as well as for relying too frequently both on reasoning by analogy and anecdotal illustration.

Charles Buckman Goring (1870–1919), a doctor and medical officer in the British prison system, accepted Lombroso's challenge to do a real test of the theory of atavism. With the help of the well-known statistician Karl Pearson, he collected, beginning in 1902, "biometric" data on more than 3000 English convicts chosen on the basis of chronic recidivism (convicted more than once). In comparing these convicts with control groups made up of hospital patients, Cambridge and Oxford students, and British Royal engineers (military), Goring found that the physical and mental constitutions of both criminal and law-abiding persons of the same age, stature, class, and intelligence were virtually identical with respect to Lombroso's atavistic stigmata. (Goring did not rule out "the existence of a 'physical, mental, and moral type of person who tends to be convicted of crime'" (quoted in Pick 1989:187), but he concluded that Lombroso's "anthropological monster" did not exist (Goring 1913). Nonetheless, aspects of the "criminal man," from his "bulbous fingertips" to his "malformed ears," continue to surface in modern works on criminal profiling (Lane 1992:165).

Lombroso's chief long-term contribution to criminology and the study of deviance was not his now-discredited theory of atavism, but rather the fact that he stimulated others to observe at first hand what criminals looked and sounded like, what they had in common, and how they differed from others. Using far superior research techniques, post-Lombrosian studies brought about a dramatic increase in our knowledge about criminals and other rule breakers.

THEORIES OF DEGENERACY

Robert Dugdale and the Jukes

In 1875, a year before the publication of Lombroso's *Delinquent Man,* an American investigator for the Prison Association of New York named Robert Dugdale (1841–1883) published a study of a "degenerate family" entitled *The Jukes: A Study in Crime, Pauperism, and Heredity.* During his prison inspections, Dugdale had been struck by the number of inmates who were related to each other. In 1873, he had been present in a Kingston, New York, police court when a youth was being tried for receiving stolen goods. Five of the youth's relatives were present, and the group struck Dugdale as a particularly depraved-looking clan. The family, it turned out, lived in caves in a nearby lake region and had a reputation for all sorts of criminal and moral wrongdoing (Adams 1955:41). Although the accused youth was acquitted, Dugdale's opinion was already formed. He made inquiries about relatives of the youth who were in court, and concluded that one was a burglar, two had been involved in pushing a youth over a cliff, and two were "harlots" (defined by Dugdale as any woman who had ever experienced a "lapse"). Dugdale investigated other relatives, and came up with the mathematically unsound finding that 17 of the 29 adult males were criminals, while 15 others had been convicted of some degree of offence.

Dugdale traced the family back to its beginnings 150 years earlier in the person of Max Jukes, who became "exhibit A in the Dugdale rogues' gallery, although nothing criminal appears in his record" (Adams 1955:42). Dugdale spent a year hunting through prisons, almshouses, asylums, and public records in search of Jukes. He uncovered approximately 1200 of Max Jukes's descendant progeny, of whom only 709 could be fully traced. More than 25 percent of these (180) were paupers, while about 20 percent (140) were "criminals" (including 7 murderers, 60 thieves, and 50 prostitutes) and about 30 others had been charged with the crime of "bastardy."

As a result of Dugdale's report, the name Jukes became a synonym for depravity. The author claimed he had proven the existence of hereditary criminality, pauperism, and degeneracy. He felt that the environment might be adjusted to eliminate these problems, but his work played an important role in the eugenics movement, particularly with respect to its policy of sterilization for "undesirables." In Canada, A.P. Knight, a professor at Queen's University, spread the word about how the Jukes had cost New York more than a million dollars in public expenses, in this way providing a clear indication of how Dugdale's flawed information could be used (McLaren 1990:41).

Henry Goddard and the Kallikaks

Psychologist Henry Herbert Goddard (1866–1957) was part of the ferment that surrounded a revival of Mendel's work on genetic heritability (Gould 1981:162). As director of research at the Vineland Training School for Feeble-Minded Boys and Girls in New Jersey, Goddard used the newly developed Binet intelligence scale to identify "high-grade defectives." Goddard assumed not only that intelligence was inborn and inherited, but also that it was a measure of many other aspects of human worthiness, especially human morality.

Goddard published the "pedigrees" of hundreds of people (many of them Vineland Training School residents) who would not have existed had their feeble-minded ancestors been prevented from breeding (Gould 1981:168). One family study that became particularly well known concerned the history of Martin Kallikak, a respectable young soldier in the colonial army at the time of the American Revolution. Goddard coined the name from the Greek words *kallos* "beautiful" and *kakos* "bad" (Gould 1981:168).

Kallikak, a normal soldier, had a sexual liaison with a feebleminded barmaid, which resulted in a family tree full of hopeless ne'er-do-wells (as Goddard characterized them) who were living in great poverty in the pine barrens of New Jersey. Later, Kallikak returned home, married a respectable Quaker woman, and started another family line. In contrast to the previous union, all but three of the 496 descendants from this match were "normal." The validity of Goddard's research has been called into question. Stephen Gould has shown conclusively that photographs of the "degenerate" Kallikaks in Goddard's book were amateurishly doctored to make the family members appear unintelligent and vaguely diabolic (Gould 1981:171).

Convinced that feeblemindedness was a cause of delinquency, Goddard administered IQ tests to Vineland training school residents and compared their scores with those of inmates in several New Jersey jails and prisons. Since none of the inmates at Vineland scored higher than a mental age of 13 on the Binet scale, he set the cutoff point for feeblemindedness at the mental age of 12. When he found that a median of 20 percent of the prisoners scored below this point, he interpreted the result as support for his theory of delinquency. As intelligence tests became more widely used, however, this interpretation was challenged. Carl Murchinson's 1926 study, *Criminal Intelligence,* showed that more than 47 percent of recruits to the United States Army in World War I were below the mental age of 13, while more than 30 percent were below the mental age of 12. In comparison with Goddard's numbers, Murchinson found that the rate of feeblemindedness was higher in the army than it was in the prisons (Pfohl 1985:93). Thus, while intelligence may be related to some kinds of crime, crime is not the inevitable outcome of mental disability.

BORN CRIMINAL THEORY REVISITED

Body-type theory was revived in the work of two Americans: anthropologist Earnest Albert Hooton and psychologist William Sheldon. Both men continued in the Lombrosian tradition of using flawed research methods and relying on unrepresentative data to support questionable public policy decisions, such as sterilization of the poor.

EARNEST ALBERT HOOTON AND THE HIERARCHY OF DEGENERATION

Harvard anthropologist Earnest A. Hooton (1887–1954) described the biological component of criminal behaviour as "degeneracy" rather than "atavism." Hooton argued that crime was the result of normal environmental stress upon low-grade organisms (humans). He conducted, over a twelve-year period, a massive study of more than 17,000 people (including about 14,000 prisoners), which was published as the three-volume *The American Criminal* in 1939; a shorter version, *Crime and the Man,* appeared the same year.

Hooton made 107 distinct measurements of each subject. Despite the fact that his statistics actually showed there were more differences among prisoners than between prisoners and the noncriminal controls, Hooton concluded that prisoners were distinctive and inferior, and, moreover, said he had discovered a natural "hierarchy of degeneration."

> If one considers in order, sane civilians, sane criminals, insane civilians and insane criminals he finds that each succeeding group tends to manifest greater ignorance, lowlier occupational status, and more depressing evidence of all-round worthlessness. The same hierarchy of degeneration is evidenced in physical characteristics. The lower class civilian population is anthropologically fair to middling, the sane criminals are vastly inferior, the insane civilians considerably worse than sane criminals, and insane criminals worst of all … The specific criminal proclivities found in certain races and nationalities among the sane prisoners are carried over, to a great extent, into the offenses committed by insane criminals of the same ethnic or religious origin. (Hooton 1939:382)

Hooton presented his data by racial and national-origin groups. He argued that while race did not affect whether a person would be a criminal or not, it *did* affect what kind of crime would be committed. Thus, he divided Caucasians into nine different groups, including the "pure nordic" type, which he characterized as "an easy leader in forgery and fraud; a strong second in burglary and larceny and last or next to last in all crimes against the persons." "Negroids," he maintained, "commit a great deal of homicide, are parsimonious in sex offenses, and perpetuate [sic] a modest amount of robbery" (Hooton 1939:249, 382).

It should come as no surprise that Hooton was an enthusiastic supporter of eugenics. He argued that, in all racial groups, it is the inferior organisms that succumb to the adversities of natural temptations in their environment, and that it is impossible to correct the environment to the point "at which these flawed and degenerate human beings will be able to succeed in honest social competition" (Hooton 1939:388). Hooton believed that both crime and war could be ended for all time by a stringent policy that would either extirpate the physically, mentally, and morally unfit or else segregate them into a "socially aseptic" environment (Hooton 1939:309).

Hooton was criticized by other academics for improperly selecting (and using) his control samples, for suppressing data that did not fit his hypotheses, and for making the very basic research error of defining as "inferior" all characteristics found most often among prisoners and then proceeding to show that the data demonstrated how inferior prisoners were—an example of "circular reasoning" (Sutherland 1939; Reuter 1939; Merton and Ashley-Montague 1940; Gould 1981:109). Nonetheless, the work enjoyed instant and widespread success among the general public, confirming as it did popular prejudices of the day against blacks, immigrants, various ethnic groups, and the lower classes in general (Moran 1980:220). As late as 1959, a book by Clyde Kluckhohn entitled *Mirror for Man* postulated Hootonian associations between biological characteristics and criminal behaviour. ("For example," writes Kluckhohn, "among criminals as a group, those convicted of burglary and larceny are likely to be short and slender; those convicted of sex crimes are likely to be short and fat.") Even when the research has been badly done, the ideas may live on.

WILLIAM H. SHELDON AND SOMATOTYPING

William H. Sheldon (1898–1977), a colleague of Hooton's at Harvard, took the ideas of the German psychiatrist Ernst Kretschmer, who had identified three distinct body types—asthenic (frail, weak), athletic (muscular), and pyknic (short, rotund)—and associated them with different behavioural styles.

In *Varieties of the Human Physique* (1940), Sheldon mapped out the relationships among human physique, personality, and criminal propensity. His method of making objective bodily measurements is called somatotyping. The basic divisions or somatotypes are *endomorph* (soft, round, easygoing, sociable, self-indulgent); *mesomorph* (hard, rectangular, restless, energetic, insensitive); and *ectomorph* (lean, fragile, introspective, sensitive, nervous). Sheldon argued that the human embryo comes with three forms of skin tissue—the endoderm, the ectoderm, and the mesoderm. The endomorph was a person in whom the organs associated with the endoderm (e.g., the digestive system) were most highly developed relative to the other two tissue types. Mesomorphs had a preponderance of the muscle- and bone-related mesoderm tissue, while ectomorphs had relatively little body mass and relatively great surface area.

Each individual in Sheldon's sample would be assigned a score from 1 to 7 for endomorphy, mesomorphy, and ectomorphy. Anyone who scored an average of 4 for the three measures would be classified as average. If, however, the score was close to 7–1–1 (or 1–1–7), the person was mainly an endomorph (or an ectomorph) (Brown, Esbensen, and Geis 1991:263). In *Varieties of Delinquent Youth* (1949), Sheldon reported on an eight-year test in which he had compared 200 boys from the Hayden Goodwill Inn (a reform school for delinquent boys) with a control group of 200 nondelinquent college students. He developed a "D" scale (D = disappointingness) and tried to show how it was related to somatotype. His D scale brought together measures such as IQ insufficiency, medical problems, psychotic problems, psychoneurotic traits, cerebrophobic delinquency (alcoholism, drug use), gynandrophrenic delinquency (homosexuality), and primary criminality (legal delinquency). Sheldon found that his delinquents not only had a much worse rating on the D scale, but also had an average mesomorphically dominated somatotype of

Figure 5.3   Sheldon's Somatotypes

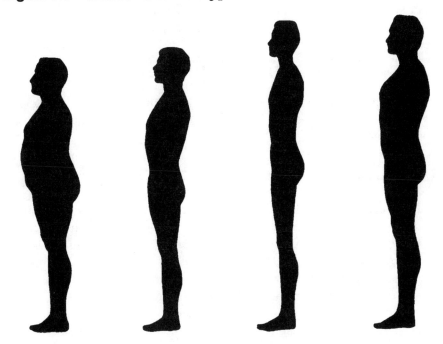

From left to right: endomorph, mesomorph, ectomorph, normal.

Source: Reproduced by permission of *The Encyclopedia of Sociology: New & Updated,* Second Edition, by Dushkin Publishing Group. Copyright © 1981, The Dushkin Publishing Group/Brown & Benchmarks Publishers, a division of McGraw-Hill Higher Education Group, Guilford, CT. All rights reserved.

3.5–4.6–2.7. The nondelinquents scored much lower on mesomorphy, which led Sheldon and his associates to conclude that physical inadequacy was the basic cause of crime, and that eugenics should be practised as the best long-term solution to crime (Sheldon, Hartl, and McDermott 1949).

Sheldon's work, like Hooton's, entered into the popular imagination without being particularly well received by the academic community. Sutherland (1951) reanalyzed Sheldon, Hartl, and McDermott's (1949) data using what he thought was a more meaningful criterion of delinquency (conviction in a court of law) than the D scale. He found no significant differences between seriously delinquent and nondelinquent boys. Although later research has confirmed the finding that those found guilty of delinquent behaviour tend to be more mesomorphic than in control groups (Glueck and Glueck 1950; Corte and Gatti 1972), biological explanations have given way to sociological ones. Thus, the relationship between mesomorphy and delinquency may be a reflection not of biological determinism, but rather of opportunity (the mesomorph is better able to carry out delinquent acts), labelling (the mesomorph is more likely to be suspected of delinquent acts), and incarceration (in a prison environment controlled food intake and incentives for muscular development the ectomorph and endomorph take on mesomorphic features).

BIOLOGICAL POSITIVISM REVISITED

As studies of degenerate families and body types ran their course, new approaches were being developed, the most important of which involved the use of twin and adoption studies.

TWIN STUDIES

> If I had any desire to live a life of indolent ease, I would wish to be an identical twin, separated at birth from my brother and raised in a different social class. We could hire ourselves out to a host of social scientists and practically name our fee. For we would be exceedingly rare representatives of the only really adequate natural experiment for separating genetic from environmental effects in humans—genetically identical individuals raised in disparate environments. Few investigators have been able to rustle up more than 20 pairs of twins. (Gould 1981:235)

The nature versus nurture debate has dogged the efforts of those who wanted to prove that behaviour, whether criminal or conforming, was determined by inborn characteristics. For example, the finding that one of the best indicators of antisocial behaviour in a young boy is his father's criminal record can be interpreted as supporting either a genetic-inheritance argument or a social-learning argument. Twin studies have been looked upon as a means of sorting out these conflicting interpretations.

In nature, monozygotic (identical) twins are formed from one egg and have virtually identical chromosomes; in contrast dizygotic (fraternal) twins share about half the same chromosomes, as do brothers and sisters born apart. The differences among the three groups (ordinary brothers and sisters, fraternal twins, and identical twins) provide opportunities to test the importance of inheritance and environment. If behavioural traits are largely inherited, then identical twins, whose genetic makeup is exactly the same, are more likely to have similar traits than are fraternal twins, who share on average half of their genes. Thus, a greater concordance between identical twins than between fraternal twins could be taken as evidence of a genetic factor in the behaviour. *Concordance* is defined as similar outcome, such that if one twin is convicted of an assault, the other will face a similar conviction. *Discordance* is defined as contrasting outcomes, such that if one twin is a heterosexual Casanova, the other is monogamously homosexual.

Twin studies began in 1929 with the publication of German geneticist Johannes Lange's *Crime as Destiny*. Lange had obtained the cooperation of the Bavarian State Ministry of Justice in locating 30 pairs of twins, at least one of whom was in prison. Lange divided his sample into 13 apparently monozygotic (identical) pairs and 17 dizygotic (fraternal) pairs. Of the 13 identical pairs of twins, 10 were both in prison, compared with only 2 of the 17 fraternal twins. Fraternal twins were only slightly more likely than ordinary siblings to both be criminals (Moran 1980:219; Christiansen 1977a; 1977b).

Later studies have found a concordance between identical twins that is higher than that for fraternal twins, but significantly less high than that reported by Lange. One of the most authoritative of these studies was conducted in Denmark by Christiansen (1977a; 1977b). Christiansen was able to use the Danish twin register (a full listing of all twins born in Denmark between 1870 and 1920) and the Danish national register of criminal behaviour to establish the criminal or noncriminal paths of 14 344 twins (7172 pairs). He found prison, police, or court records on 926 people, involving 799 of the twin pairs (Wilson and Herrnstein 1985:94). Concordance was found for 35 percent of the identical twins, compared with 13 percent of the fraternal twins.

Studies by English psychologist Sir Cyril Burt (1883–1971) on genetically identical twins who had been raised apart initially seemed to constitute strong support for the argument that heredity was more important than environment with respect to both measured intelligence and delinquency (Samuelson 1992). Burt's findings were used as recently as 1969 by Arthur Jensen to support his belief that IQ differences between blacks and whites were inherited and ineradicable. Burt's work is an interesting (and extreme) example of wishful, prejudiced thinking and fraudulent data. Despite the recent publication of two books intended to vindicate him (Joynson 1989; Fletcher 1991), it seems quite clear that Burt not only fabricated his twins, but even invented research associates and research papers authored by these phantom assistants (Gould 1981:Chap. 6).

To date, twin studies have consistently shown that identical twins are approximately two to three times as likely as fraternals to be similar with regard to their criminal record, or lack thereof. But even among identical twins who are raised together (i.e., those with both genetic and environmental commonalities), if one twin is psychopathic it is still reasonably possible that the co-twin will not be (Bohman 1996). As Lykken (1982) observes, "Even among persons as close as twins, individual unshared experiences often play a decisive role"(26). Thus, while the findings of twin studies provide some support for the inherited-predisposition (genetic) argument, they have not yet been able to fully exclude an environmental interpretation. Nonetheless, studies have found that identical twins who were raised apart tend to exhibit similar physical and mental traits, including habits and fears, brain waves, and heart patterns (Bouchard 1984; Bouchard et al. 1986; Langinvainio et al. 1984). In some cases, this includes similar patterns of deviant behaviour.

ADOPTION STUDIES

In an early adoption study, Crowe (1972) compared fifty-two adopted children whose natural mothers had criminal convictions with a sample of adopted children whose mothers had no convictions. The groups were matched in terms of age, sex, race, age of separation from the mother, and type of adopting family. As expected, the rate of arrests and convictions was higher in the first group than in the control group.

Most of the large-scale adoption studies have been done in Scandinavian countries like Sweden and Denmark, which have relatively small, immobile, and homogeneous populations, and are noted for their excellent records on births and adoptions, arrests and convictions, treatment for alcoholism, and other social data (Brennan, Mednick, and Jacobsen 1996). One Swedish study, Goodwin et al. (1974), showed that adopted men whose biological parents had a history of alcohol abuse were more likely to become alcohol abusers than those whose parents had no such problem, even though they had been adopted before the age of six weeks. Similarly, men whose biological parents were criminals were four times more likely to have criminal records than were men whose biological parents had no record.

In another Swedish study, Cloninger, Sigvardsson, Bohman, and von Knorring (1982) showed that adopted men whose biological parents had a history of alcohol abuse were much more likely to become alcohol abusers, while men whose biological parents were criminals were four times more likely to have a criminal record. Cloninger's study distinguished between "milieu-limited alcoholism" and "male-limited alcoholism." The first type was found among both men and women, was usually not severe, and seemed strongly influenced by environmental conditions. The other type of alcoholism was less common but more serious. It was found among boys whose biological relatives displayed the same characteristic heavy-drinking pattern, and it was not influenced by the drinking habits of the adoptive parents (Wilson and Herrnstein 1985:361–362).

While both of the above studies maintain that there is a connection between the behaviour of biological relatives and the behaviour of adopted-away children, the relationship is far from deterministic. In fact, most of these youths do not follow in their biological parents' footsteps. For example, Mednick and his colleagues studied parents and children involved in all nonfamilial adoptions in Denmark between 1927 and 1947. If either of the biological parents (mother and father) had a criminal record, the parents were counted as criminal. Table 5.1 shows Mednick's findings for the sample of 4065 male adoptees for whom records could be found. Rather than genetic determinism, these studies support the idea of genetic influence that is strongly influenced by environmental factors. Even in the highest category, approximately 70 percent of those with criminal parents are not offenders themselves.

Table 5.1   Conviction Rates of Adopted Youths

		Birth Parents Convicted	
		Yes	No
Adoptive Parents	Yes	24.5%	14.7%
		(of 143)	(of 204)
Convicted	No	20%	13.5%
		(of 1226)	(of 2492)

Source: Sarnoff A. Mednick, Wiliam F. Gabrielli, and Barry Hutchings. (1984). "Genetic Influences in Criminal Convictions: Evidence from an Adoption Court." *Science* (May 25), pp. 891–989.

Box 5.4   The State of Behavioural Genetics

CRIME: Family, twin and adoption studies have suggested a heritability of 0 to more than 50 percent for predisposition to crime. (Heritability represents the degree to which a trait stems from genetic factors.) In the 1960s researchers reported an association between an extra Y chromosome and violent crime in males. Follow-up studies found that association to be spurious.

MANIC DEPRESSION: Twin and family studies indicate heritability of 60 to 80 percent for susceptibility to manic depression. In 1987 two groups reported finding different genes linked to manic depression, one in Amish families and the other in Israeli families. Both reports have been retracted.

SCHIZOPHRENIA: Twin studies show heritability of 40 to 90 percent. In 1988 a group reported finding a gene linked to schizophrenia in British and Icelandic families. Other studies documented no linkage, and the initial claim has now been retracted.

ALCOHOLISM: Twin and adoption studies suggest heritability ranging from 0 to 60 percent. In 1990 a group claimed to link a gene—one that produces a receptor for the neurotransmitter dopamine—with alcoholism. A recent review of the evidence concluded that it does not support a link.

INTELLIGENCE: Twin and adoption studies show a heritability of performance on intelligence tests of 20 to 80 percent. One group recently unveiled preliminary evidence for genetic markers for high intelligence (an I.Q. of 130 or higher). The study is unsubstantiated.

HOMOSEXUALITY: In 1991 a researcher cited anatomic differences between the brains of heterosexual and homosexual males. Two recent twin studies have found a heritability of roughly 50 per cent for predisposition to male or female homosexuality. These reports have been disputed. Another group claims to have preliminary evidence of genes linked to male homosexuality. The data have not been published.

Source: From *Scientific American*, "Behavioral Genetics: A Lack of Progress Report," June 1993, 125. Copyright © 1993 by Scientific American Inc. All rights reserved.

MODERN BIOLOGICAL EXPLANATIONS OF DEVIANCE

As research continues and knowledge of organic processes accumulates, more sophisticated biological paradigms have emerged, mainly focusing on the operation of the human brain. The resulting explanatory maps often combine the study of inherited genetic conditions with consideration of how noninherited genetic abnormalities, brain damage, and the ingestion of chemicals (food or drugs) combine to increase the likelihood that specific kinds of behaviour may be "programmed" to occur. Modern psychological research often builds on the findings of the biological sciences, particularly with respect to the origins of persistent differences in individual temperament and behaviour.

THE XYY MALE

Chromosomes are thin threads of genetic material (DNA) that contain hereditary instructions (genes) for the growth of every living cell in an organism. They have been implicated in a number of syndromes, both physiological and behavioural. One of the earliest attempts to link genetic anomalies to criminal deviance is contained in the swift rise and fall of the "XYY monster myth" between 1969 and 1977. Normal cells have 46 chromosomes, two of which determine the gender of the individual. In the normal female, the two chromosomes are both X's (hence XX equals female), while in the normal male, the two chromosomes are XY. Different combinations are possible, however. Ever since it became possible to test for these anomalies, researchers have attempted to establish syndromes of behaviour and their accompanying physical traits. One such anomaly is the XYY male.

In 1965, Patricia Jacobs and her colleagues at a maximum-security prison hospital in Edinburgh published their findings concerning 197 mentally disabled male patients who had been institutionalized because of "dangerous, violent, or criminal propensities." Seven of these inmates (3.5 percent) were XYY genotypes (Jacobs et al. 1965). Given that the estimated frequency of XYY in the general population is about 1.3 percent (or one case per 1000), this finding led researchers to speculate that XYY might predispose a person toward the kind of behaviour that results in imprisonment. Underlying this research was the assumption that, since the Y chromosome is the male hormone, the XYY genotype must be some kind of "supermale."

> The Y chromosome is the male-determining chromosome; therefore, it should come as no surprise that an extra Y chromosome can produce an individual with heightened masculinity, evinced by characteristics

such as unusual tallness, increased fertility ... and powerful aggressive tendencies. (Jarvik, Klodin, and Matsuyama 1973:679–680)

Box 5.5   Genetic Explanations and Racism

While the XYY myth seems to have run its course, attempts to find genetic roots for various kinds of behaviour continue. Genetic explanations often merge into the racist ideologies of the society. When they do, common prejudice is bolstered and science is discredited. Claims that intelligence and law-abidingness are racial traits have not been supported by research that has been properly concluded and interpreted with the appropriate statistical controls.

For example, the evidence cited by Philippe Rushton (a research psychologist at the University of Western Ontario) concerning differences in intelligence among Asians, whites, and blacks does not stand up because the IQ tests he used were culturally biased toward lifestyle experiences of Asians and, to a lesser extent, whites.

Moreover, Rushton's evidence about the relative brain size of men, women, and different racial groups suffers from the same logical handicaps that characterized Paul Broca's work. It is a huge jump from the size of the skull to the size of the brain, and an even greater leap from the size of the brain to the capability of the individual person. As the followers of Broca eventually learned, a large brain does not necessarily mean an intelligent or law-abiding individual. Rushton's assertions that there are genetically based racial differences in law-abidingness are not supported by his data, since he does not control for environmental differences or to take into account cross-cultural evidence (e.g., the low crime rate among blacks in many African nations).

The ideas of Philippe Rushton, like those of Earnest Hooton before him, are not just part of an intellectual controversy. If not challenged, they can quickly lead to discriminatory and segregationist policies. A professor at the City University of New York (located in Harlem) has recently argued that blacks are less intelligent than whites and more likely to commit crimes; therefore, they should be confined to police-patrolled subway cars and subjected to curfews. Such views go far beyond any credible genetic evidence, and show more about the nature of the people proposing them than they do about the advance of science.

Stories and reports about "XYY men" began to appear in the scientific literature (often based on a single case), and in newspaper accounts of criminal cases in which defendants would enter a not-guilty plea on the basis of the XYY chromosomal "disorder." The controversy even had implications for social policy. In 1970, Dr. Arnold Hutschnecker, a medical adviser to President Nixon, suggested a program whereby every 6-year-old in the United States would be screened for chromosomal or psychological abnormalities; those testing positive would be sent to "therapeutic camps." The policy was, however, abandoned on the grounds that it was "not feasible" at the time (1973). The image of the XYY violent supermale has subsequently proved to have been a great exaggeration (Sarbin and Miller 1970; Fox 1971; Owen 1972; Borgaonkar and Shah 1974; Pyeritz et al. 1977). Most XYY males have nonviolent and noncriminal life histories.

GENETIC LOADING

Certain types of predatory aggression and seemingly senseless, explosive violence may be related to physical damage or malfunction in specific parts of the brain. Recent biologically based explanations are more open than their precursors were to the role of environmental factors. In the hypothetical case of a man who commits sudden, unpredictable acts of violence against women, this perspective would seek some inherited genetic condition or biological malfunction that is "loading" him toward aggression. Environmental factors such as his use of drugs, alcohol, or pornographic material, and stress at work or in his home would be seen as "triggers" that precipitate his violent episodes. This pattern can be diagrammed as in Box 5.6

Box 5.6 A Biological Model of Deviance

Heredity (Genetic Loading) →	*Biological Process* →	*Environmental Stress* →	*Deviance as Symptom*
Detective Genes	Nutrition Needs	Available Diet	
High Sensory Threshold	Allergies	Pollutants (Air, Noise)	
Hormones (Testosterone	Exercise	Work Demands	
Levels)		Family Demands	
Somatotype			

Thus, the person with an inherited predisposition is like a loaded gun, with the environment serving as a trigger. (This conceptualization differs from the typical social science viewpoint, which sees the environment as a factor *shaping* the behaviour rather than merely releasing it.) Men with high (genetically based) levels of the hormone testosterone are more likely than other men to commit aggressive acts, although only when they are in a situation with an appropriate target (i.e., they usually don't attack their employers or people twice as big as they are) (Booth and Osgood 1993). Similarly, women who suffer hormone imbalances after childbirth are more likely to kill their babies if they are simultaneously experiencing severe stress in the home. Many researchers regard mental illnesses like schizophrenia as pathological conditions that result from an interplay between genetic loading and an environmental trigger such as complications at birth, viral infection, head trauma, or severe stress. In the same way, anorexia nervosa, an increasingly recognized eating disorder, may have a genetic basis but emerge only in stressful social environments that strongly favour a cultural norm of thinness. Also supporting this idea is the finding that persons who become addicted to heroin while under conditions of stress free themselves from it quite readily when the stress is removed (Robins 1993).

A wide variety of sexually deviant behaviours called paraphilias, in which individuals are "turned on" by exposure to unusual or forbidden stimuli, have been blamed on the functioning of the limbic system of the brain. According to Money (1983), the particular need is "programmed" and the program is released when the opportunity is found, sometimes following cultural prescriptions found in the reading of pornography, but often "invented" in response to the situation. Paraphilias range from the need for a sexual partner who is an amputee (acrotomophilia), or dead (necrophilia), or unwilling (rapism or raptophilia) to involvement in "dirty talk" (scatophilia or narratophilia), or actual dirt (mysophilia), or human waste (coprophilia or urophilia) (Money 1983:169–170). Paraphilias can lead to serial homicide, as in the case of Jeffrey Dahmer, a cannibalistic necrophiliac who killed several young men; or to activities such as armed bank robbery, as in the case of Ronald Keyes, whose masochistic paraphilia "made" him act in ways that were dangerously illegal and wrong as part of his girlfriend's sexual domination over his life (Keyes and Money 1993).

Seeing drug use or other "addictions" as inborn characteristics is less easy. While some evidence supports the view that some people have an inborn predisposition to explore and take risks, it is difficult to deduce from this that some of them have a specific, inborn need for cocaine, heroin, or alcohol. It has been argued, however, that although the initial use of a drug like crack cocaine is mainly voluntary and very much influenced by the environment, once ingested the chemical properties of the drug trigger a continuing physiological disorder characterized by craving for the drug. In this view, the brain is either temporarily or permanently altered by the continuing use of the drug, such that withdrawal symptoms persist for hours or days when the drug is withheld, while craving for the drug may continue long after its use is terminated—sometimes even permanently. It follows from this that the best cure would be some new drug intervention to reverse the brain pattern established by the original drug. Mounting evidence shows, however, that the physiological aspect of addiction is not the only—or even the most important—factor in the continuing use of recreational drugs (Blackwell 1988). Studies of addictive behaviour have shown that, for many people in treatment, breaking away from the drug-using culture is at least as, if not more, difficult than breaking free of the physical need for drugs (Blackwell and Erickson 1988).

Whether we look at evidence from genetic inheritance studies, or focus on other sources of chemical or structural differences in brain functioning, such differences do seem, under certain conditions, to be related to offending behaviour. "If you have low levels of a certain neurotransmitter in your brain *and* an alcoholic father, your chances of being able to live a normal life are worse than if you simply had a drunken father *or* a chemical deficit (Moir and Jessel 1995:2 [authors' italics]). The causal pattern between such factors and actual behaviour is not direct and deterministic. You can inherit a predisposition toward particular kinds of behaviour based on one abnormality, or an even stronger predisposition based on several, but you will not necessarily act upon it.

SOCIOBIOLOGY AND THE SELFISH GENE

In the early 1970s, a rather different angle on the question of genetic influence on behaviour was put forward in the controversial book *Sociobiology* by entomologist E.O. Wilson. The main focus of sociobiology has been on the genetic origins of selfishness and altruism, and only indirectly on inborn causes of specific behaviours like suicide, marital infidelity, and homosexuality (along with religion, war and peace, slavery, and genocide). Sociobiologists argue that all living bodies are driven by an innate need to ensure that their genetic material survives, and, furthermore, that their behaviour is often unconsciously "programmed" toward this end (Crippen 1994:318–319). Organisms (individuals) are always seeking "inclusive fitness," defined as the sum of the individual's own reproductive success plus the reproductive success of others who carry that person's genes (his children, for example). Humans, like insects and animals, strive to enhance the number of genes they leave behind, "whether directly through their own offspring, indirectly through the offspring of their relatives, or through a reciprocal exchange of services with nonrelatives" (Maryanski 1994:381).

The theory is used to explain/justify many characteristics imputed to be immutable in humans, including gender roles (mainly male promiscuity, rape, aggression, warfare), status hierarchies, racial bigotry, cheating, and lying (Freese 1994:347; Maryanski 1994:380). According to Dawkins, each of us is primarily a walking container for the genes that use us. In other words, we are "survival machines"—robot vehicles blindly programmed to preserve these selfish molecules (1976:19). This does not mean that every detail of cultural life is genetically programmed. Most sociobiologists allow for considerable variation in the expression of biological imperatives, and "for a dynamic coevolution of genetic, behavioral and cultural traits" (Freese 1994:347).

Preservation of the gene pool does not always mean that the survival of the individual. When a person altruistically undertakes a suicide mission and in doing so saves others, the gene is preserved more effectively than if all members of the group exposed themselves to extreme danger. As the central sociobiological concept of "inclusive fitness" predicts, we are most likely to sacrifice ourselves if the people we are saving are kinfolk or people so like ourselves that they may be carriers of the same genes (Dawkins 1976:97). Similarly, sociobiologists feel that marriage laws restricting people to one partner violate the innate demand that the genes be passed on through a maximum number of partners. Adultery is a natural consequence of this form of sexual restriction. (Sociobiologists have claimed that males "profit" more by such behaviour than do females.) Similar arguments have been used to explain why stepchildren are more likely than biological children to be abused or killed (Daly and Wilson 1994; Daly 1996; Dawkins 1976:Chap. 9).

How might sociobiologists explain lifestyles that are *not* driven by reproductive needs, in particular homosexuality? It has been pointed out in response to this question that homosexuals have often filled the "altruistic" roles of shaman, diplomat, artist, and artisan, and are frequently found in human-service occupations where their social roles serve to improve the fitness of the group (Wilson 1975:555).

The idea that there might be a gene that specifically programs those who possess it to be homosexual remains speculative and controversial (Bailey et al. 1993; Burr 1993). Some observers, hostile to homosexuality, think that it takes away the moral blame that homosexuals somehow deserve; while others, who see homosexuality as a valid choice, argue that it pathologizes them, or could result in massive screening or genetic engineering to eliminate them (Bullough 1994:231).

Most researchers today feel that we should be looking for combinations of genes rather than single genes, and that the influence of genes on behaviour is more like "open programming" than determinism. Mapping of the three to six billion chemical components that make up the human genetic code has only just begun, and it will be a long time before genetic researchers are able to isolate particular genes or genetic combinations that control specific behavioural events in the body. Nor should it be forgotten that the leap from these inner events to behaviour is wide; one can feel rage without necessarily acting on it, just as one can feel a craving without having to engage in consummatory behaviour.

Most sociobiologists have explicitly disavowed the idea that "biology is destiny." In arguing that a particular genetic inheritance makes certain kinds of behaviour more likely, they do not deny that environmental factors may play a deciding role in whether the behaviour manifests itself. Nonetheless, some observers are concerned that sociobiological views lend support to unacceptable controls such as involuntary sterilization, abortion, and genetic screening for criminological or insurance purposes.

SUMMARY

The rise of natural science, particularly the biological sciences, provided a new model of explanation for deviance theorists that seemed better able than the classical model to account for all kinds of behaviour. The biological positivist approach denied free will and saw human beings as puppets whose strings were pulled by the bodies they inhabited.

Early biological positivism drew together the Darwinian evolutionary model and the Mendelian genetic model to create the science and the social movement of eugenics, which was grounded in the assumption that Caucasian males were the fittest of the species, and which led to the search for the "hereditary degenerate" and policies designed to eliminate crime, poverty, and war by eliminating "inferior" specimens of humanity. The search for the "born criminal" began with consideration of external characteristics such as facial features and body shape, and gradually progressed to the less visible features of the mind, such as brain chemistry. Family studies of hereditary degeneracy gave way to more scientifically appropriate twin and adoption studies. These were soon supplemented by the discovery of chromosomes, which led to premature and exaggerated claims about the relationship between single genes and specific behaviours, as exemplified by the characterization of XYY males as "supermales."

The search for connections between the genetic level of human existence and behaviour continues. It is possible that both the shape of our institutions, and the pattern of typical deviations from institutional expectations, may be influenced by (but probably not determined by) genetic codes that underlie both the genetic and the cultural evolution of humankind.

REFERENCES

Adams, Samuel Hopkins. (1955). "The Juke Myth." In E.A. Schuler, T.F. Hoult, D.L. Gibson, and W.B. Brookover (eds.), *Readings in Sociology.* 5th ed. New York: Thomas Y. Crowell.

Bailey, Michael J., Richard C. Pillard, Michael C. Neale, and Yvonne Agyei. (1993). "Heritable Factors Influence Sexual Orientation in Women." *Archives of General Psychiatry* 50(3):217-223.

Blackwell, Judith. (1988). "Sin, Sickness, or Social Problem? The Concept of Drug Dependence." In Judith Blackwell and Patricia Erickson (eds.), *Illicit Drugs in Canada: A Risky Business.* Scarborough, Ont.: Nelson Canada.

Blackwell, Judith, and Patricia G. Erickson. (1988). *Illicit Drugs in Canada: A Risky Business.* Scarborough, Ont.: Nelson Canada.

Bohman, M. (1996). "Predisposition to Criminality: Swedish Adoption Studies in Retrospect." *Genetics of Criminal and Antisocial Behavior.* Ciba Foundation Symposium 194. New York: John Wiley and Sons, 99–108.

Booth, Alan, and D. Wayne Osgood. (1993). "The Influence of Testosterone on Deviance in Adulthood: Assessing and Explaining the Relationship." *Criminology* 31(1):1993.

Borgaonkar, D., and S. Shah. (1974). "The XYY Chromosome, Male—or Syndrome." *Progress in Medical Genetics* 10:135–222.

Bouchard, T.J. (1984). "Twins Reared Together and Apart: What They Tell Us About Human Diversity." In S.W. Fox (ed.), *Individualism and Determinism: Chemical and Biological Bases.* New York: Plenum.

Bouchard, T.J., D.T. Lykken, N.L. Segal, and K.J. Wilcox. (1986). "Development in Twins Reared Apart: A Test of the Chronogenetic Hypothesis." In A. Demirjan (ed.), *Human Growth: A Multidisciplinary Review.* London: Taylor and Francis.

Brennan, P.A., S.A. Mednick, and B. Jacobsen. (1996). "Assessing the Role of Genetics in Crime Using Adoption Cohorts." *Ciba Foundation Symposium 194.* New York: John Wiley and Sons, 115–122.

Brown, Stephen, E. Finn-Age Esbensen, and Gilbert Geis. (1991). *Criminology: Explaining Crime and Its Context.* Cincinnati: Anderson.

Bullough, Vern L. (1994). *Science in the Bedroom: A History of Sex Research.* New York: (HarperCollins Basic Books).

Burr, Chandler. (1993). "Homosexuality and Biology." *Atlantic Monthly,* March, 47–65.

Butler, Samuel. (1967 [1923]). *Erehwon: Or Over the Range.* New York: New American Library.

Christiansen, K.O. (1977a). "A Preliminary Study of Criminality Among Twins." In S.A. Mednick and K.O. Christiansen (eds.), *Biosocial Bases of Criminal Behavior.* New York: John Wiley.

————. (1977b). "A Review of Studies of Criminality Among Twins." In S.A. Mednick and K.O. Christiansen (eds.), *Biosocial Bases of Criminal Behavior*. New York: John Wiley.

Cloninger, C. Robert, Soren Sigvardsson, Michael Bohman, and Anne-Liis von Knorring. (1982). "Predisposition to Petty Criminality in Swedish Adoptees: II. CrossFostering Analysis of Gene-Environment Interaction." *Archives of General Psychiatry* 39:1242–1247.

Corte, J.B., and F. Gatti. (1972). *Delinquency and Crime: A Bio-Psychological Approach*. New York: Seminar Press.

Crippen, Timothy. (1994). " Toward a Neo-Darwinian Sociology." *Sociological Perspectives* 37(3):309–335.

Crowe, Raymond R. (1972). "The Adopted Offspring of Women Criminal Offenders." *Archives of General Psychiatry* 27(November):600–603.

Daly, Martin. (1996). "Evolutionary Adaptationism: Another Biological Approach to Criminal and Anti-Social Behavior." *Genetics of Criminal and Antisocial Behavior. Ciba Foundation Symposium* 194. New York: John Wiley and Sons, 183–247.

Daly, Martin, and Margo Wilson. (1994). "Some Differential Attributes of Lethal Assaults on Small Children by Stepfathers versus Genetic Fathers." *Ethology and Sociobiology* 15:207–217.

Dawkins, Richard. (1976). *The Selfish Gene*. New York: Oxford University Press.

Fest, Joachim. (1970). *The Face of the Third Reich*. New York: Pantheon.

Fink, A.E. (1938). *The Causes of Crime: Biological Theories in the United States, 1800–1915*. Philadelphia: University of Pennsylvania Press.

Fletcher, Ronald. (1991). *Science, Ideology, and the Media: The Cyril Burt Scandal*. New Brunswick, N.J.: Transaction.

Fox, Richard G. (1971). "The XYY Offender: A Modern Myth." *The Journal of Criminal Law, Criminology and Police Science* 62(March):71–72.

Freese, Lee. (1994). "The Song of Sociobiology." *Sociological Perspectives* 37(3):337–373.

Glueck, Sheldon, and Eleanor Glueck. (1950). *Unravelling Juvenile Delinquency*. Cambridge, Mass.: Harvard University Press.

Goodwin, D.W., F. Schlusinger, N. Moller, L. Hermansen, G. Winokur, and S.B. Guze. (1974). "Drinking Problems in Adopted and Nonadopted Sons of Alcoholics." *Archives of General Psychiatry* 31:164–169.

Goring, Charles. (1913). *The English Convict: A Statistical Study*. Montclair, N.J.: Patterson Smith.

Gould, Stephen Jay. (1981). *The Mismeasure of Man*. New York: W.W. Norton & Co.

Grupp, Stanley E. (ed.). (1968). *The Positive School of Criminology: Three Lectures by Enrico Ferri*. Pittsburgh: University of Pittsburgh Press.

Hagan, John. (1985). "The Assumption of Natural Science Methods: Criminological Positivism." In Robert Meier (ed.), *Theoretical Methods in Criminology*. Beverly Hills, Cal.: Sage.

Hooton, Earnest A. (1939). *Crime and the Man.* Cambridge: Harvard University Press.

Jacobs, Patricia A., Muriel Brunton, Marie Melville, R.P. Brittain, and W. F. McClermont. (1965). "Aggressive Behavior, Mental Subnormality, and the XYY Male." *Nature* 208(December):1351–52.

Jarvik, Lissey F., Victor Klodin, and Steven S. Matsuyama. (1973). "Human Aggression and the Extra Y Chromosome: Fact or Fantasy?" *American Psychologist* 28:674–682.

Jeffrey, C. Ray. (1990). *Criminology: An Interdisciplinary Approach.* Englewood Cliffs, N.J.: Prentice-Hall.

Joynson, Robert B. (1989). *The Burt Affair.* London: Routledge.

Keyes, Ronald W., and John Money. (1993). *The Armed Robbery Orgasm.* Buffalo: Prometheus Books.

Kuhn, Thomas. (1970). *The Structure of Scientific Revolutions,* 2nd ed. Chicago: University of Chicago Press.

Lane, Brian. (1992). *The Encyclopedia of Forensic Science.* London: Headline.

Langinvainio, H., J. Kaprio, M. Koskenvuo, and J. Loanqvist. (1984). "Finnish Twins Reared Apart: III. Personality Factors." *Acta Geneticae Medicae et Cemellologlae: Twin Research* 33:259–264.

Leek, Sybil. (1970). *Phrenology.* New York: Macmillan.

Lombroso, Cesare. (1885). *The Female Offender.* London: Unwin.

———. (1895). "Criminal Anthropology Applied to Pedagogy." *Monist* 6:50–59.

Lombroso-Ferrero, G. (1911). *Criminal Man: According to the Classification of Cesare Lombroso.* Montclair, N.J.: Patterson Smith.

Lykken, David T. (1982). "Fearlessness: Its Carefree Charm and Deadly Risks." *Psychology Today* (September). 20–28.

Maryanski, Alexandra. (1994). "The Pursuit of Human Nature in Sociobiology and Evolutionary Sociology." *Sociological Perspectives* 37(3):375–389.

McLaren, Angus. (1990). *Our Own Master Race: Eugenics in Canada, 1885–1945.* Toronto: McClelland and Stewart.

Mednick, Sarnoff A., and J. Volavka. (1980). "Biology and Crime." In N. Morris and M. Tonry (eds.), *Crime and Justice.* Chicago: University of Chicago Press.

Mednick, Sarnoff A., Jan Volavka, William F. Gabrielli, Jr., and Twan, M. Ital. (1981). "EEG as a Predictor of Antisocial Behavior." *Criminology* 19(2):19–22.

Merton, Robert K., and M.F. Ashley Montague. (1940). "Crime and the Anthropologist." *American Anthropologist* 42(3):384–408.

Moir, Anne, and David Jessel. (1995). *A Mind to Crime: The Controversial Link between the Mind and Criminal Behaviour.* London: Michael Joseph.

Money, John. (1983). "Paraphilias: Phyletic Origins of Erotosexual Dysfunction." In S. Giora Shohan (ed.), *Israel Studies in Criminology.* New York: Sheridan House.

Moran, Richard. (1980). "The Search for the Born Criminal and the Medical Control of Criminality." In Peter Conrad and Joseph W. Schneider (eds.), *Deviance and Medicalization: From Badness to Sickness*. St. Louis: Mosby.

Owen, David R. (1972). "The 47, XYY Male: A Review." *Psychological Bulletin* 78:209–233.

Pfohl, Stephen. (1985). *Images of Deviance and Social Control: A Sociological History*. New York: McGraw-Hill.

Pick, D. (1989). *Faces of Degeneration*. Cambridge: Cambridge University Press.

Pyeritz, R., H. Schreier, C. Madansky, P. Miller, and J. Beckwith. (1977). "The XYY Male: The Making of a Myth." In Ann Arbor Science for the People Editorial Collective (compiler), *Biology as a Social Weapon*. Minneapolis: Burgess.

Reuter, E.B. (1939). Review of *Crime and the Man*, by E.A. Hooton. *American Journal of Sociology* 45:123–126.

Robins, Lee. (1993). "Vietnam Veterans Rapid Recovery from Heroin Addition: A Fluke or a Normal Expectation?" *Addiction* 88:1041–1054.

Sarbin, Theodore R., and Jeffrey E. Miller. (1970). "Demonism Revisited: The XYY Chromosomal Anomaly." *Issues in Criminology* 5(Summer):197–207.

Sheldon, William, Emile Hartl, and Eugene McDermott. (1949). *Varieties of Delinquent Youth*. New York: Harper and Row.

Sutherland, E.H. (1939). Reviews of *Crime and the Man* and *The American Criminal: An Anthropological Study*, Vol. 1, by Earnest Hooton. *Journal of Criminal Law and Criminology* 29:911–914.

———. (1951). "A Critique of Sheldon's Varieties of Delinquent Youth." *American Sociological Review*. 16:10–13.

Topinard, Paul. (1888). "Le poids de l'encephale d'après les registres de Paul Broca," *Memoirs*. 2nd ser., vol. 3. Paris: Société d'Anthropologie, 1–41.

Wilson, Edward O. (1975). *Sociobiology: The New Synthesis*. Cambridge, Mass.: Belknap Press.

Wilson, James Q., and Richard J. Herrnstein. (1985). *Crime and Human Nature*. New York: Simon and Schuster.

Wolfgang, Marvin E. (1972). "Cesare Lombroso." In Hermann Mannheim (ed.), *Pioneers in Criminology*. 2nd. ed. Montclair, N.J.: Patterson Smith.

PSYCHOANALYTIC AND PSYCHOLOGICAL EXPLANATIONS OF DEVIANCE

PSYCHOANALYTIC EXPLANATIONS OF DEVIANCE

FREUDIAN AND POST-FREUDIAN THEORIES

The psychoanalytic theories of Sigmund Freud (1856–1939) and his followers have had—and continue to have—a substantial impact on explanations of deviance. Freud's conception of the human personality as a three-part structure of *id, ego,* and *superego* is a useful conceptualization of how biological and social factors come together in the individual mind. The *id,* the only part of the personality present at birth, is the completely selfish, biologically rooted drive for the gratification of instinctual needs such as food and sex (Freud's *pleasure principle).* The *superego,* in contrast, is developed through the process of socialization and incorporates within itself the expectations of society, as taught by significant others (parents and role models). It is the cornerstone of what most of us call "conscience" and controls whether we feel proud or guilty about our actions. It demands that the primitive urges of the id be channelled, curbed, or repressed. The *ego* stands between the id and the superego, balancing their conflicting demands and keeping the individual in touch with both inner reality and the reality of the environment (Freud's *reality principle).* Freud also postulated the existence of the life instinct *(Eros),* which consists of impulses and drives toward self-preservation and reproduction, and the death instinct *(Thanatos),* which consists of an individual's impulses toward self-destruction, and which may be expressed as aggression and hostility toward others.

Deviant behaviour of almost any kind may be blamed on the id, the superego, the ego, or some combination of all three. Aggressive behaviour like murder or rape may express the transformed death wishes of the uncontrolled id. Neurotic behaviour like self-mutilation or nervous habits might be the consequence of an overly repressive superego. Aichen (1935) uses classical Freudian theory to explain the origins of delinquency. Some delinquents are love-deprived and fail to develop a strong superego. Others are overindulged and their id impulses are not restrained. Still others develop a criminal superego by identifying with criminal parents (in organized crime families, for example) or by identifying with other youths in criminal groups. Redl and Wineman (1951) similarly explain delinquent aggression as the product of inadequate ego and superego development caused by the lack of close relationships with adults.

In the Freudian system, the deviance that emerges is related to the stage of psychosocial development at which the individual experienced some kind of difficulty, such as a traumatic event or sustained abuse. Freud outlined the stages of development as a sequence, moving from the oral stage through anal, genital, and eventually phallic stages. A person who did not receive enough nurturing or experienced trauma during the oral stage of development might be more likely to engage in smoking, drinking, or compulsive shopping. Trouble in later stages of psychosocial development might result in disturbances of gender identity, such as homosexuality, transsexualism, transvestism, or prostitution.

Not all psychologists and psychiatrists accept Freud's concept of biologically based reasons for human behaviour. Psychiatrists such as Eric Erikson, Alfred Adler, Harry Stack Sullivan, Karen Horney, and Eric Fromm place far more emphasis on environmental factors than did Freud.

There are many variants of psychoanalytic interpretation. In courtrooms, lawyers are frequently heard attempting to explain that their clients' behaviour was not willfully chosen but rather caused by forces they neither understood nor were able to control. Freud (1948:52) suggested that some criminals are driven by an unconscious desire to bring punishment down upon themselves, either as a way of retaliating against their unacknowledged, forbidden desires (e.g., sexual feelings toward a parent), or as a means of justifying the sense of guilt produced by those desires. Similarly, people who engage in destructive, but noncriminal, behaviour such as compulsive spending may be trying to fill an inner emptiness, which may be the consequence of parental failure to provide unconditional love during infancy, or childhood sexual abuse. Compulsive spending may also reflect conflict within a marriage, as one partner makes the other "pay" for mistreatment of some kind (Lieberman 1991).

FRUSTRATION–AGGRESSION THEORY

Freud (1948) argued that civilization engenders frustration by restricting the primal urges of the id. Since the ultimate source of the frustration either is not recognized or cannot be directly attacked without negative consequences, the resulting aggression is likely to be displaced onto more accessible, "safe," or vulnerable targets. This idea was developed and dubbed "frustration–aggression theory" by psychologists in the late 1930s. Dollard et al. (1939 [1987]) proposed that all aggression was in some sense the consequence of frustration, which occurred whenever goal attainment was blocked.

Box 6.1   Gender and Psychiatric Explanations: Are Women Morally Better than Men, or Just Sneakier?

Freud, echoing the dominant patriarchal notions of his time, maintained that normal women exhibit feminine traits of passivity, masochism, and narcissism that lead them into self-destructive forms of deviance, or compulsive nonrational actions such as kleptomania. In his view, deviant women were a biological perversion or were expressing a psychiatric rebellion against their biologically natural female role. They were people who had developed a "masculinity complex" out of their jealousy of males' anatomical advantages.

Otto Pollack (1950) has argued that women are more deviant than men, even though statistics on most forms of misbehaviour, apart from prostitution and neonatal infanticide, seem to indicate that the reverse is true. According to Pollack, girls are not more moral than boys, just sneakier. The "normal" girl learns to resolve her problem in passive–dependent ways, while the male resolves his in aggressive–competitive ways. Women learn trickery and manipulation; men learn fighting and pushing. Pollack linked the female's ability to hide her feelings about the sex act from her husband and her sexuality from her children to her greater ability to get away with deceit. He argued that women are more devious when they commit offences (using poisoning instead of a gun, for example) or they use feminine wiles to induce men into committing offences for them. They also, in Pollack's view, get treated leniently by the authorities because they evoke male chivalry. This sort of explanation, which is not well supported by any available evidence, helps to explain the feminist view that "psychoanalysis is to sexism what that Klan is to racism" (Miller 1973).

Frustration–aggression theorists have documented an increase in the amount of aggression against out-groups (underdogs and minorities) when the political or economic system fails to meet expectations. One of the strengths of this approach, therefore, is that it helps explain that when minorities are attacked or buildings vandalized, the "real" cause may be frustrating social conditions. Displaced aggression in the form of *reaction formation* may also explain attacks on particular kinds of people (Hughes and Dagher 1993:302). Gay bashers, for example, may be unsure of their own sexual identity and express this by attacking those who, through reaction formation, represent the part of themselves they have disowned (Dollard et al. 1939 [1987]). Economic frustration was the explanation given by Quebec's justice minister after two hate slayings in Montreal:

> In a difficult economic period [the minister stated] there is more and more violence and hostility towards anyone who is different religiously, socially, culturally and sexually. It's the same anywhere all over the world. (Picard 1992)

The Austrian psychiatrist Alfred Adler (1870–1937) introduced the term "inferiority complex" to describe people who compensate for their feelings of inferiority by attempting to control and dominate others. Using a similar idea, Halleck (1971) sees criminality as a symptom of feelings of hopelessness and oppression. In this view, the criminal act imbues troubled, frustrated individuals with a sense of positive action and control, and gives rise to feelings of freedom and excitement. A substantial anecdotal record supports the view that juvenile delinquents tend to be people with low self-esteem.

Psychoanalytic explanations can help deviants understand how their behaviour is related to unmet needs, and thus provide them with the opportunity to find more acceptable ways of meeting those needs. And yet some observers feel that what psychoanalytic explanations really provide deviants with are excuses for their behaviour—excuses that free them from feelings of guilt, place the guilt on parents or society, and thus enable them to commit more offences. Criminals who "use" psychiatry in this fashion look upon punishment as further persecution and become bitter instead of reformed. Psychiatry has also been used as a means of controlling people. In the former Soviet Union, political dissidents were "treated" for their political views in psychiatric hospitals. Women still complain on occasion that psychiatry tries to coax them back into dependent roles.

PSYCHOLOGICAL THEORIES OF COGNITIVE DEVELOPMENT AND MORAL JUDGMENT

Cognitive theories of moral judgment are based on child-development studies that show how a person's understanding of the meaning of rules develops, in a fixed sequence, at various stages in his or her life. Piaget theorized that there were two main stages of moral development, the first characterized by an acceptance of rules as absolute, unchangeable, and valid in all circumstances, and a second, more mature stage in which the spirit of the law takes precedence over the letter of the law, and in which factors such as the motivation and intention of the rule breaker are considered.

LAWRENCE KOHLBERG'S STAGES OF MORAL DEVELOPMENT

In a more complex version of Piaget's formulation, Kohlberg (1969, 1986) presented his subjects with "story problems" (moral dilemmas) and recorded their solutions, classifying their responses into three major stages of moral development: preconventional, conventional, and postconventional. Each stage has an early and late phase, making six phases altogether. In the early preconventional stage (Stage 1), which is characteristic of young children, behaviour is dictated by the desire to gain reward and avoid punishment. It is the physical consequence of actions, not their meaning or value, that is important in this stage. Obedience to the rules is not indicative of a belief either in them or in the rule makers. In the late preconventional phase (Stage 2), rules may be used to meet one's own needs, sometimes by manipulating others. Right action is whatever serves one's ends. Sometimes this means taking others into account ("I'll scratch your back, if you scratch mine").

Early conventional behaviour (Stage 3) is characteristic of the "good person" who tries to win social approval and acceptance, and is affected by what the majority think about things. This is "moral majority" thinking, the stage at which the abilities to empathize and to feel guilt begin to emerge. Late conventional reasoning (Stage 4) sees rules as necessary for the smooth functioning of society. Even if a particular rule is not particularly justifiable, it will be supported. This is a "law and order" mentality.

Early postconventional behaviour (Stage 5) is characteristic of people who have the intellect to see rules in more than black-and-white terms, and to judge them in relation to their own personal standards and values. People who engage in late postconventional morality (Stage 6) judge rules according to universal principles of justice, and may go so far as to break rules they see as wrong or unjust. This thinking is most clearly embodied in the genuine political offender, who finds the present social system so intolerably corrupt that he or she either refuses to go along with it or actively attempts to destroy it. Robert Merton (cited in Denisoff and McCaghy 1973) calls such people "nonconformers" and describes them as those who:

1. announce their dissent publicly;
2. challenge the legitimacy of the specific norms of laws they break;
3. attempt to substitute illegitimate norms or laws with rules that have a sound moral basis;
4 are clearly motivated by disinterested purposes rather than hopes for individual personal gain; and
5. adhere to a higher morality—one justified by ultimate values—rather than to particular social norms. (53–55)

Political offenders paradoxically break the rules in the name of higher rules, in contrast to nonpolitical offenders, who break rules they usually support. Political offenders may commit exactly the same offences as their nonpolitical counterparts, but they do it for a cause. Their reward is not personal gain but the cause itself.

Kohlberg found that most American adults reached Stages 3 or 4 (conventional), but that very few moved beyond this. Common criminals were found to be significantly lower in their moral-judgment development (mainly Stages 1 and 2) than were noncriminals from the same social background (mainly Stage 3 or 4) (Henggeler 1989).

THE CRIMINAL-MIND PERSPECTIVE

Another psychological approach, this one with an implicit biological slant, is that put forward by psychiatrist Samuel Yochelson and his psychologist colleague Stanton Samenow, who argue that the criminal is distinctive in his or her "thought patterns" (Yochelson and Samenow 1976). This perspective recalls Lombroso's assumption that the criminal is "a different breed of person" (Yochelson and Samenow 1976:31), only in this case the distinctive traits are not physical but cognitive. Samenow (1984) maintains that when ordinary people enter a drug store, they assess how easy it will be to find what they want and then pay for it. In contrast, the criminally minded assess how the cash register is protected and where the store's exits are; they do this automatically, even if they are not currently planning to rob the store. According to Samenow, this kind of thinking can be traced to the criminal's earliest consciousness. As children, they are deceitful and rebellious, and constantly lie as a means of disarming other people. As adolescents, the criminal-to-be uses school as a training ground for "fighting, lying, stealing and engaging in power plays against teachers and other pupils" (Samenow 1984:14).

According to the criminal-mind perspective, the criminal is an abuser of family, school, and employer, not a victim of these institutions. Crime is not caused by bad neighbourhoods, inadequate parents, television, schools, drugs, or unemployment. If it were, Samenow argues, we would have far more criminals than we do (Samenow 1984:6–13). People with criminal minds can be trained to behave normally, he suggests, but just as the recovering alcoholic will always be an alcoholic, so the criminal will always be a criminal, although he or she can learn to avoid engaging in criminal activity.

Yochelson and Samenow's work was based primarily on a twelve-year study of 240 inmates at St. Elizabeths Hospital for the criminally insane in Washington, D.C. Critics have pointed out that offenders at St. Elizabeths are not typical criminals. Yochelson and Samenow provide no explanations as to why these criminal thought patterns emerge in the first place (Nettler 1982:110–111) and here have been few tests of this theory (Cry et al. 1991).

PSYCHOLOGICAL THEORIES OF LEARNING

Psychological studies of the learning process provide an important underpinning for sociological theories of learning. Sociologists have integrated psychobiological findings into theories that focus on *what* is learned rather than on *how* it is learned. Most psychologists would agree with Hebb (1980) that learning is "a changed pattern of conduction in the brain that results from experience and makes a change of response potential" (81). Thus, the capacity to learn is affected by differences in the capacity of the brain to receive and hold the changes produced in the learning process.

TEACHING, TRAINING, AND MODELLING

Human beings learn in several ways. The most significant of these are teaching, training (operant and classical conditioning), and modelling. The most obvious way we learn is through *teaching*, which is the conscious transmission of information and techniques that may be used to solve problems (Nettler 1978:315; Nettler 1982:114). Teaching tends to be intellectual and cognitive, and the learner is virtually always aware of the process. *Training,* on the other hand, need not always be obvious, aware, or even intended. One mode of training is *classical conditioning*. An experiment conducted by Ivan Pavlov (1849–1936) is the best-known example of this. In it, dogs were placed in an experimental situation in which food was paired with the ringing of a bell. Eventually, the sound of the bell was seen to trigger a salivation response among the dogs, even in the absence of food. The dogs had learned to associate the bell with food and responded accordingly. Humans also can learn in a comparable fashion by associating something new with something that is strongly liked or disliked. This kind of learning is the root of our preference for the familiar.

Classical conditioning can also be used to reverse an acquired behaviour in a process known as *desensitization*. In simple terms, this technique involves removing the negative feelings associated with an object or event and replacing them with positive ones. People who have a phobia (extreme fear reaction) can be desensitized by repeatedly pairing the feared thing (whether it be snakes, flying, or open or enclosed spaces) with something that they like or that has a calming effect on them. The technique has also been used to deal with feelings closely associated with such behaviours as problem drinking, sexual exhibitionism, chronic kleptomania (due to anxiety), reckless driving, racial hostility, and aggression in general. It is sometimes argued that the constant deluge of images of deviance we receive from the media and other sources has desensitized people—not to mention the deviants themselves—to the real meaning of acts like murder, rape, and child abuse.

The second important mode of training is called *operant* or *instrumental conditioning,* so named because the learner operates on the environment to produce the effect. While classical conditioning involves pairing a new stimulus with an existing response, in operant conditioning the individual learns to associate a particular behaviour with a particular consequence. If the individual finds the consequence of an action rewarding (positive reinforcement), the behaviour will continue, and may increase.

The only limits on this type of learning are the biological capability of the organism to perform the behaviour and the cognitive ability of the organism to link the consequence with the act. If a pleasurable consequence is not forthcoming, or is felt to be unrewarding, the behaviour will probably be extinguished and replaced by other kinds of actions. When an action has been repeatedly associated with unwanted consequences, the autonomic nervous system (which is not under conscious control) responds by increasing heart rate, blood pressure, and the production of hormones in a way that creates feelings of anxiety. Thus, most of us would feel acutely uncomfortable with the idea of picking a pocket or assaulting someone in order to rob them (Moffitt 1983; Fishbein 1990).

Psychological research has shown that the timing, intensity, and consistency of rewards and punishments have strong effects on how well a particular kind of behaviour is learned. Bank robbers, for example, are usually not caught immediately, so that they reap the rewards for their behaviour (excitement and the chance to spend money) long before their eventual punishment. In terms of reinforcement, the prison term comes much too late to be very effective.

Many things affect operant conditioning. For example, in prison there may be different rewards and styles of punishment, ranging from simple slaps to electric shocks, and from money, food, tokens, and praise to more complex forms such as the negotiation of an earlier parole date. The effects of rewards and punishments on individuals can differ as well. While rewards of money or pleasurable experiences are usually positive reinforcers, punishments are more difficult to evaluate in this respect. A child may well prefer punishment to being ignored, and members of a delinquent gang may gain status (positive reinforcement) as a result of the punishment they risk or stand up to. Nonetheless, "contingency management" or "reality therapy" programs use operant conditioning to influence behaviour in a wide variety of contexts in psychiatric institutions (Glasser 1965; Schaefer and Martin 1966; Atthowe and Krasner 1968; Cotter 1967); homes for the mentally disabled (Lent, LeBlanc, and Spradlin 1970); classrooms (O'Leary and Becker 1967); reform schools; prisons; and many other settings (Ulrich, Stachnik, and Mabry 1970; McKain and Streveler 1990).

The third major way of learning is through *modelling* (imitating the behaviour of others). In many languages, the verb "to teach" is the same as the verb "to show," and our awareness of this lies behind such things as the media policy not to publicize suicides that occur in places like subway systems or Niagara Falls. In modern life, each of us is exposed to a wide range of alternative models of behaviour, and we select from them those that attract us or suit our interests and capabilities. Seeing other people rewarded, apparently for behaving in particular ways, is part of this, as is admiring people who are higher than ourselves in one or all of life's hierarchies and identifying with their behaviour. It is this aspect of learning that makes the misbehaviour of popular entertainment figures particularly distressing to parents. The intentional shock tactics of performers like Madonna or Michael Jackson disturb many observers, who see them as role models for the young.

The influence of modelling is suggested by studies that show a high correlation between physical punishment for aggressive behaviour and increased physical aggression (Goldstein 1986:37). Children learn even more quickly from their parents' aggression than they do from the operant conditioning that the parents attempt to produce.

TEMPERAMENT AND LEARNING

Temperament refers to an individual's mental, physical, and emotional characteristics. Many psychologists argue that temperament is formed through a combination of genetic predisposition and perinatal environment (e.g., drug use on the part of the mother), and that its basic components are in place at the time of our birth. From earliest infancy, children display differences in terms of activity level, rhythmicity (regularity), distractibility, and responsiveness (Eysenck 1960, 1964; Cattell 1979). The baby who is very slow to establish routines of sleep and bowel movements is more likely to be the child who has difficulty adjusting to the routines of school, and the adult who struggles with the routines of work.

Mounting evidence shows that temperament does not change a great deal during an individual's life unless brain damage occurs (or is "repaired") or the immediate environment changes drastically and for a long time (Nettler 1982). For example, people can change dramatically when they are cut off from their roots, brainwashed, and kept in an environment that sustains the change. Even so, the person who compulsively sought drugs may become a person who compulsively does good deeds. The A+ student who drops out of school to join a cult may become the cult's best fundraiser or most devout member. An example of this kind of consistency of temperament despite an apparent transformation of behaviour can be found in the case of Patty Hearst. Prior to her kidnapping in 1974 by an ultraleftist urban guerrilla group, Hearst—a California college student and granddaughter of publishing magnate William Randolph Hearst—was a compliant individual who lived very much according to the ideas of her boyfriend and family. Although the public was shocked by a photograph of Hearst (as group member "Tanya") holding a machine gun during a bank robbery undertaken in the name of the "revolution," her change of behaviour was consistent with her compliant temperament. What had changed—traumatically—was the nature of the people who had authority over her (the kidnappers). Following her release, Hearst returned to a conventional lifestyle.

AROUSAL THEORY

While work on temperament and learning is diverse, considerable convergence is found in the area of differences in the responses of individuals to environmental stimuli. According to arousal theory, some people are "augmentors." They see colours as brighter than other people see them, noises as louder, pain as more painful, and excitement as more exciting. Others are "reducers" who perceive stimuli but do not react to them as much as average people do. These differences have been found to be associated with typical modes of behaviour, including types of deviance. Augmentors quickly find a given level of stimulation "too much" and attempt to retreat from it. They are more likely to be seen as introverts, who seek quiet pastimes and prefer to avoid risk-taking situations. If born into a crime family, they are likely to seek the role of bookkeeper rather than enforcer. If they become

---

**Box 6.2   From Troublemakers to Patients:
Attention Deficit Disorder (ADD)**

At home or in the classroom, the boy cannot sit still. He fidgets constantly and jumps up repeatedly from his seat. His teacher says he seldom follows instructions, rarely completes a task, and often interrupts lessons. Outside school, he chatters nonstop, breaking into conversations, asking questions and not waiting for the answers. He rushes to pick up a game and then, just as quickly, leaves it for something else.

Such children—who might simply have been labeled in the past as troublemakers—more often are diagnosed today as suffering from attention deficit disorder (ADD), a complex condition marked by poor concentration, impulsive actions, and, usually, hyperactivity. In the United States and Canada, 3% to 5% of all school-aged children may have ADD. That figure has risen steadily since the condition was identified in the 1970s. And increasingly, treatment for ADD includes powerful psychostimulant drugs. Use of Ritalin (methylphenidate), the most widely prescribed drug, grew 150% in North America from 1990 to 1995. This increase was sharp enough to prompt a United Nations (UN) report, released in February 1996, expressing concern about possible misuse and overuse of the drug.

The report added fuel to a controversy over ADD and its treatment. Drug therapy has proved an enormous help to many ADD suffers. But some experts charge that doctors, teachers and parents are too quick to blame behavior on ADD—and too quick to turn to drugs to quiet unruly children. As one Iowa pediatrician told *Newsweek* magazine, "It takes time for parents and teachers to sit down and talk to kids. It takes less time to get a child a pill."

Source: From Elaine Pascoe, "Attention Deficit Disorder," *World Topics Yearbook 1997,* 349. Copyright © 1997 by Grolier Incorporated. Reprinted with permission of the publisher.

criminals, it will be in the less exciting, less risky forms of crime. Reducers, on the other hand, perceive the same stimulus as less stimulating than the average person, and are easily bored. Reducers take longer to "get the message" from pain or pleasure (they are harder to train) and are more likely to enjoy the physical sensations that accompany risk-taking actions.

Eysenck (1960) produced scales that differentiate individuals from each other along a dimension of "neuroticism" (degree of stability/instability of behaviour) and "extraversion/introversion" (impulsive, outgoing behaviour versus controlled, withdrawn behaviour). In a psychiatric hospital, virtually all patients scored high on neuroticism (instability of behaviour) but differed in the kind of disturbance they showed. Those who scored high on introversion as well as neuroticism tended to suffer from depression, phobias, and compulsions, while those who scored high on extraversion and neuroticism were more likely to have been hospitalized because of personality disorders, manias, and hysteria. Various studies using the Eysenck scales have found deviant behaviour (car accidents, unwed motherhood, repeated criminal conviction, psychopathy) to be concentrated in the high-neuroticism/high-extraversion (NE) quadrant formed by the two scales (Eysenck 1960, 1964; Andry 1963).

The taste for risk taking or avoidance appears to be at least partly inborn, although culture and training can channel and modify it. Football players and soldiers, for example, undergo rigorous training in which they learn, among other things, to reduce their responsiveness to pain. Insensitivity, whether inborn or trained, may impede socialization in two ways. First, children who are less sensitive may be relatively unresponsive to the threats or promises that are an important part of socialization, and thus less likely to learn the rules. Second, the slower reaction to stimuli might be experienced as boredom, giving rise to a craving for danger and excitement. According to arousal theory, some deviants do not learn good behaviour because "normal" socialization doesn't get through to them, and they seek out stimulation because time seems so much longer to them than it does to other people (Lykken 1982). Those deviants for whom a normal amount of stimulation is "too much" may isolate themselves or take drugs to achieve the same effect.

Evidence supporting arousal theory comes from a wide variety of sources. Studies of brain-wave activity show that children who have slow alpha-wave patterns are more likely than other children to become delinquents (Mednick et al. 1981:219–229). The same pattern is shown for similar measures of nervousness and arousal, including galvanic skin response, electrodermal recovery rates, heart rates, and chemicals in the blood stream. People with a history of serious delinquency and criminality tend to have lower "resting levels" of arousal, are less likely to show physical signs of stress when provoked in test conditions, and when aroused show a slower return to resting level of arousal than do matched controls (Mednick and Volavka 1980; Furnham 1984; Raine and Venables 1984). An example of this kind of theorizing is found in the work of Anne Moir and David Jessel (1995:76):

> The conventional psychological wisdom—that bullies are motivated by
> an underlying lack of self-esteem—is simply not the case. A boy with

typically low levels of cortical arousal suffers from a stimulus hunger, a sort of craving for sensation. He becomes easily habituated, and therefore easily bored with his environment. Strong stimuli are not experienced as unpleasant and to be avoided—rather they can be exciting and engaging. The cycle becomes self-reinforcing; a child in a deprived community with nothing to do, and no hope of a creative stimulus, satisfies his hunger for sensation and novelty by an ever-increasing spiral of danger and impulsiveness. As he grows older, he associates this satisfaction with acting out of antisocial behavior. He has, indeed, become dependent on it in stronger and stronger doses. It's no use offering this boy a jigsaw or a bicycle—he'll get bored; it's no use offering him a dinghy or a skiing holiday to "let off steam"—the novelty soon wears off. He can be satisfied only with wrecking the regatta or crashing down the off-piste suicide runs.

Many researchers have taken arousal theory one step further and argued that low arousal is characteristic of both the hero and the psychopath, who, as Lykken (1982) says, "are twigs from the same branch" (22). The terms "psychopath" and "sociopath" both refer to a reasonably intelligent person, with no obvious mental illness, who is characterized principally by a lack of conscience (Cleckley 1964). Besides lacking a sense of guilt, remorse, or empathy, the psychopath is shallow and impulsive, seeks thrills, and fails to learn from experience (Bogg 1994). Psychopaths tend to have no meaningful social relationships, preferring instead to lie to and manipulate others. They are often able to conceal their pathology by adopting a socially acceptable front. The disparity between social image and inner pathology was especially jarring in the case of serial killer Paul Bernardo and his equally attractive partner, Karla Homolka. Although Bernardo indulged in several paraphilias (deviant sexual urges such as enjoying feces), abused alcohol, and had a narcissistic personality disorder, he was always "in full touch with reality" according to evidence presented at his trial (Jenish 1995:18).

MEDICALIZATION: USING AND MISUSING BIOLOGICAL EXPLANATIONS

What do the following accounts have in common?

A farmer from Blumenhof, Saskatchewan, became obsessed with singer Anne Murray and began a systematic campaign of harassment. He spent more than four years in custody and almost twenty years under various probation orders to stay away from Murray. After violating probation again, he was brought to court, declared unfit to stand trial, and committed to psychiatric care. He suffers from a rare mental disorder called erotic paranoia, which leads him to believe that he and the singer are involved in a secret affair.

Dan White, a Vietnam veteran, former policeman, and strong supporter of moral-majority values, was experiencing difficulties in his work as a member of the San Francisco Board of Supervisors. He resigned his position, but then had second thoughts and four days later tried to retract his resignation. Backed by Harvey Milk—the man who brought homosexual politics to City Hall—Mayor Moscone refused to reinstate him. At City Hall, White sought out and killed both Moscone and Milk. He had entered the building carrying a police .38 revolver and 10 dumdum bullets. In each case, he fired first to bring the victim down, and then shot him in the head. At the trial, White's lawyer argued that his client was suffering from depression exacerbated by his intake of snack food, in what came to be known as the "Twinkie defense." The jury apparently agreed that White had been temporarily insane, and convicted him of manslaughter, not murder. Shortly after he was released on parole, White committed suicide. (Miller 1987)

Accompanied by her three children, an orthopaedic surgeon was driving her BMW when she was stopped by police. She failed a breathalyzer test and was charged with drunken driving. It was reported that she used abusive language and tried to kick a state trooper in the groin. Her defence in court was that she was suffering from premenstrual syndrome (PMS).

In October 1992, a postal employee who had stolen a credit card from the mail was conditionally reinstated in her job by an arbitrator who accepted a psychiatrist's report that the theft was caused by post-traumatic stress disorder (PSD).

Stories like these are common in the media. In each, the behaviour in question has been explained in terms of a _medical model,_ only here the behaviour itself is the disease (or the only evidence of the disease). The medicalized interpretation of the behaviour becomes a substitute for moral interpretations, thereby lifting the burden of responsibility from the perpetrator (Conrad and Schneider 1980:272). Thus, they are all examples of _medicalization,_ a term that refers to the application of "disease" explanations to certain types of deviant behaviour. These behaviours would include excessive drinking (alcoholism); overeating or undereating (obesity, anorexia and bulimia); addictions (drugs, sex, cleaning, shopping, exercise, work); and compulsions (hair-pulling, nail-biting, child and spousal abuse).

Opponents of the medical model of deviance point to cases in which it has been flagrantly abused. One extreme example concerns the work of S.A. Cartwright, a prominent medical doctor in the American South during the period of slavery. Cartwright "discovered" pathological conditions among the slave population and used them as explanations for why slaves could not look after themselves or work properly without "treatment." A slave's "dysthesia," which was Cartwright's term for inadequate decarbonization of blood in the lungs, could be "cured" by such treatments as whippings and hard, out-of-doors labour. Another of Cartwright's "conditions" was "drapetomania," a mental disease characterized by an "insane" urge to run away (Gould 1981:70–71).

Revisionist psychiatrists like Thomas Szasz and R.D. Laing believe that our modern tendency to medicalize life is just as misguided as Cartwright's efforts. Szasz (1970) sees an analogy between the concept of mental illness and that of witchcraft:

> [T]he concept of mental illness has the same logical and empirical status as the concept of witchcraft; in short … witchcraft and mental illness are imprecise and all-encompassing concepts, freely adaptable to whatever uses the priest or physician (or lay "diagnostician") wishes to put on them … [Furthermore] the concept of mental illness serves the same social function in the modern world as did the concept of witchcraft in the late Middle Ages; in short … the belief in mental illness and the social actions to which it leads have the same moral implications and political consequences as had the belief in witchcraft and the social actions to which it led. (xix)

Szasz's argument that mental illness does not exist is echoed by Sarbin and Mancuso (1980), who claim that schizophrenia is just another name for a kind of rule-violating behaviour, and only a disease in a metaphorical sense. Most observers, however, do not completely reject the claims of the medical model, even if they remain skeptical about some of its applications.

Conrad and Schneider (1980) draw together several separate studies that trace the path by which particular kinds of deviance have come to be treated as medical problems. Individual chapters of their book describe and analyze how madness became mental illness, drunkenness became alcoholism, opiate users became addicts, delinquency became hyperactivity, discipline became child abuse, and homosexuality became a psychiatric illness. In each case, while the behaviour changed little, if at all, over time, the explanation for it changed from "moral

Box 6.3   Researchers to Cure Shortness: Is Skin Colour Next?

Short People: Target of a Growth Industry?

It was songwriter Randy Newman who shot to the top of the charts some years ago with his tongue-in-cheek song Short People (Got No Reason to Live). Apparently the National Institutes of Health and its advisers agree.

The NIH, in an effort to see whether shortness is indeed a disease in search of a cure, has been recruiting healthy boys and girls aged 9 to 15 for experiments. Half will be injected thrice weekly for seven years with a genetically engineered human-growth hormone; the other half will get a placebo.

An NIH advisory committee explained the controversial experiments this way: "Children and adults with extreme short stature may experience difficulty with physical aspects of the culture generally designed for individuals taller than themselves (e.g., driving a car). They may also be harmed by deeply ingrained prejudices, resulting in stigmatization and impaired self-esteem."

The controversy over curing shortness gives us some idea of what is in store from genetic engineering. At first blush, it would not seem too difficult to decide what medicine should seek to cure—what is sickness or disease and what is not. When we stay home from work to get over the flu or keep the kids with measles home from school, we know what we mean when we say we are "sick."

Yet sickness and disease are more than mere biological concepts. Labelling something a disease has always had profound political, economic and social consequences. Notions of disease vary. The same condition may be considered diseased, immoral, distasteful or even criminal.

For example, during the 18th or 19th centuries, masturbation was transformed from a moral offence into a disease. It was believed to lead to epilepsy, blindness, vertigo, loss of hearing, headache, impotence or even nymphomania. Homosexuality, too, was classified as a disease by the psychiatric establishment until 1973.

How does shortness measure up as a disease or condition to be subject to treatment? For some time, doctors have been using a genetically engineered version of the growth stimulant produced naturally at the base of the brain to treat children who are not expected to grow to more than four feet tall as adults.

Researchers to Cure Shortness: Is Skin Colour Next? (cont.)

The new round of experiments about to get under way will include otherwise healthy children who would grow up to 5 feet 6 inches as men or 5 feet as women.

The NIH experiment raises profound questions about the limits of medicine. Proponents of the experiment say it is designed to determine whether the growth hormone makes a child grow taller or just faster. They say it is no more controversial than cosmetic surgery or breast implants.

Critics, including the Physicians Committee for Responsible Medicine and the Foundation on Economic Trends, are seeking a court injunction to stop the experiments. Jeremy Rifkin, founder of the latter group and a long-time opponent of genetic engineering, believes NIH has no business experimenting on healthy children merely because they are victims of social discrimination.

If children are helped over what they or society perceive as a problem by seeking medical intervention, should you and I care? Yes. The question of who deserves medical intervention is not of interest merely to the individual, the doctor or the therapist. Treating disease invariably involves third-party payers, private and governmental.

What we have here is the very definition of a growth industry. If concerns about long-range side effects prove unwarranted, the commercial market for human growth hormone could approach $4-billion a year; a single year's treatment currently goes for approximately $20,000 (U.S.).

It is not merely Luddite anxiety that should give us pause about this experiment and the future it portends. Will certain skin colours be deemed a social disadvantage worthy of "treatment?" Short people may bear the brunt of social stigma and discrimination, but searching for a drug that makes them taller attacks the problem from the wrong direction.

Being short is not a disease. Shortness does not need a cure; there are plenty of diseases that do.

Source: Jeff Strycher, "Researchers Plan to Treat Short Stature Like a Disease," originally published in *The San Francisco Examiner;* reproduced by *The Globe and Mail,* July 15, 1993, p. A23. Used with permission.

badness" to "pathological illness." Conrad and Schneider use a sociohistorical sequential mode to describe the process common to all of these cases. The model has five broad stages:

1. definition of behaviour as deviant;
2. prospecting (medical discovery);
3. claims-making (medical and nonmedical interests);
4. legitimization (securing medical turf); and
5. institutionalization of a medical deviance designation. (Conrad and Schneider 1980:266–267)

In the first stage *(definition),* a particular type of behaviour is defined as highly undesirable. This definition may have been part of the "common sense" understanding embedded in the culture for a long time. For example, although masturbation had been negatively viewed since at least biblical times, it was not "medicalized" until the 1800s. Similarly, restless inattentiveness in school children was regarded as "bad" long before it was diagnosed as hyperkinesis or "attention deficit disorder." In other cases, the definition of behaviour as deviant may have developed after a long period of not being noticed very much. For example, anorexia nervosa has had a long history (at one time, it was even associated with holiness), but only recently has it come to be recognized as a medical problem.

In the second stage *(prospecting)* a medical perception of a problem is first proposed to a professional audience, usually in a medical journal or at a conference. This stage is called prospecting because it is tentative; the proposal may or may not be picked up by others. Prospecting tends to take one of three forms: new diagnosis, new physical cause, or new treatment. The most common of these, the proposal of a new diagnosis, is spelled out as a series of symptoms that add up to a physically based "syndrome." The second most frequent form of prospecting is the proposal of a new physical cause for the behaviour. Third, a new treatment—new application of an old treatment—may be proposed.

An example of the prospecting of a *new diagnosis* or recently "discovered" syndrome is fetal alcohol syndrome (FAS). The physical and cognitive abnormalities that characterize victims are attributed to heavy drinking on the part of the mother during the pregnancy. Although the condition must have occurred fairly often in the gin-soaked slums of nineteenth-century England, and in other places characterized by cheap, available, and culturally mandated use of alcohol, it has become a medically recognized syndrome only in recent years. Similarly, although some women no doubt experienced the symptoms associated with PMS, just as some men appear to have symptoms associated with testosterone-induced aggression, the definition of the symptoms as forming "syndromes" continues to be controversial (Siegal 1995:143; Moir and Jessel 1995:4).

Sometimes a proposed diagnosis is unambiguous and specific. Other times it is quite vague. Ysseldyke and Algozzine (1982) found that official definitions of "learning disabilities" were so diverse and nonspecific that over 90 percent of the students in public schools could be classified as learning disabled.

A *new etiology* (cause) has recently been proposed for homosexuality. In 1991, neuroscientist Simon LeVay published a report with the controversial finding that a cluster of neurons known as INAH 3 (the third interstitial nucleus of the anterior hypothalamus) is more than twice as large in heterosexual males (about the size of a grain of sand) than in homosexuals and women (LeVay 1991). The study involved a very small sample of cadavers (19 gay men, 16 apparently heterosexual men, and 6 women) with minimal knowledge of their history. It has not, thus far, been replicated.

Of the *new treatments* constantly being prospected, only a few catch on and become the treatment of choice. The discovery that the drug Ritalin had calming effects on disruptive children preceded an adequate understanding of the definition or explanation of hyperactivity. Similarly, the use of estrogen to combat problems associated with menopause preceded the definition of menopause as a kind of deficiency disease.

In 1989, the *New England Journal of Medicine* published a report on a new antidepressant drug called clomipramine, which was being used to treat trichotillomania (compulsive hair-pulling). The journal's editorial on the report included some typical prospecting when it suggested that clomipramine might also be used to control other compulsive behaviours such as nail biting, kleptomania, gambling, nymphomania, smoking, and obsessive shopping (Okie 1989). Historically, similar claims about controlling compulsive behaviours have been made for cocaine and methadone, as well as for treatments like psychosurgery.

The third stage *(claims-making)* is the key stage in the process of medicalization (Conrad and Schneider 1980:267). Medical definitions are sometimes not accepted if they compete with strongly held beliefs and interests. An interesting example of this is provided by Daniels's (1970) study of mental illness under combat conditions, which shows that the definition of this disease changes according to the circumstances and context in which it occurs. At the claims-making stage, pre-existing explanations for the behaviour are bypassed or discredited, and new claims are made and disseminated by people who are usually first drawn from among four groups: medical specialists who are researching the behaviour in question; administrators of institutions or clinics that deal with the behaviour; providers of the "cure" (e.g., pharmaceutical companies or makers of therapeutic devices); and self-help or support organizations.

Those who take up the cause of the new deviance designation are often beneficiaries of the programs that result: the "experts" gain both prestige and funding for their research; the administrators increase their resources for treatment services; the drug companies sell their pills and tonics; and the support groups gain interest, sympathy, and services for their area of interest (Horowitz 1981).

Box 6.4   Gender and Medicalization: A Case of Inequality?

"I can't help it," a character on the television show Designing Women once said of her nasty behaviour, "I have obnoxious personality disorder."

That was meant to be funny, but sometimes matters aren't so clear. Recently [c. 1989] two psychologists from the Ontario Institute for Studies in Education, Paula Caplan and Kaye-Lee Pantony, submitted a proposal to the *DSM (Diagnostic and Statistical Manual of Mental Disorders)* authorities suggesting that a condition called "delusional dominating personality disorder" (DDPD) be included in the new edition. Their aim was explicit: to correct the perceived sexist imbalance of the DSM, and of psychiatric diagnosis generally, by including a category that describes aggressively *male* behaviour as pathological.

Included in Caplan and Pantony's proposal was a table of behavioural traits, any six of which indicate the presence of DDPD. Among them were "an inability to establish and maintain meaningful interpersonal relationships," "an inability to derive pleasure from doing things for others," and "a tendency to feel inordinately threatened by women who fail to disguise their intelligence." The proposal discussed traits and diagnosis in the usual academic fashion, complete with extensive footnotes and replies from other scholars.

Whether or not DDPD makes it into the *DSM-IV,* it will have achieved its purpose if it does two things. First, it should remind us that a good deal of socially accepted—or at least socially unpunished—behaviours is essentially destructive: far more social violence results from raging testosterone than from the (mostly imaginary) crazed witches of PMS. Second, it should force us to remember that the line between normal and pathological is far from firm.

Source: From Mark Kingwell and Gail Donaldson "Who Gets to Decide Who's Normal?" *Globe and Mail,* May 18, 1993. Reprinted by permission.

The fourth stage *(legitimization)* is characterized by attacks on former explanations and cures, and by continued proselytizing on behalf of the new medicalized approach to the problem behaviour. The claims-makers exert pressure on medical associations and relevant government agencies (legislators, investigatory committees, and the courts) in order to gain official recognition and support for the new view while displacing the old. Success in the fourth stage is exemplified when a judge refuses to send a convicted person to prison because no appropriate treatment facilities are in place there for his or her particular disorder.

The fifth stage *(institutionalization)* is a direct outcome of successful work in the previous stages. It includes both acceptance of the diagnosis by medical authorities and the establishment of treatment programs based on the medical model. Thus, the establishment of programs for sex offenders has followed the demand of the courts that such people be "treated," even though there is little evidence that such programs are successful.

THE CONSEQUENCES OF MEDICALIZATION: THERAPEUTIC TYRANNY OR THE ABUSE EXCUSE?

In the early 1950s, there was increasing recognition of the way in which designations of sickness or badness were related to social control in society. As the sociologist Talcott Parsons observed in that period, both crime and illness are designations for deviant behaviour (Parsons 1951:428–479). Crime and illness both involve violation of the norms that structure role performance. Parsons argued that the "sick role" is a culturally available mechanism that minimizes the disruptiveness of deviance to the system as a whole. The sick role has four components: two exemptions from normal responsibilities and two new obligations. (The exemptions are conditional upon the performance of the obligations.)

1. The sick person is *exempted* from role obligations. The certifiably sick person does not have to write exams, show up for work, or even have a job if his or her illness is sufficiently serious.

2. The sick person is *exempted* from negative judgment *as well as the penalties* that normally attend failure to perform customary duties. (There may be some negative judgment if the illness is deemed to be self-induced.)

3. The sick person is *obligated* to recognize that illness is undesirable, and to want to get well. It is not acceptable to embrace the illness or to abandon oneself to it.

4. The sick person is *obligated* to seek and cooperate with a competent treatment agent. This may mean taking medication with unpleasant side effects, participating in behavioural modification programs, or submitting to psychosurgery.

Medicalized explanations of deviance that establish a "sick role" (instead of a "deviant" or "criminal" one) can have positive, negative, or mixed effects for the individuals involved. On the positive side, the person who is assigned a "sick" as opposed to a "bad" label is spared guilt and punishment, and is sometimes helped by being able to hope that a cure or effective control will be found.

However, the sick role has its dark side. First, calling someone's behaviour sick means that the behaviour is seen neither as rationally willed nor as worthy of serious attention beyond its status as a symptom of illness. Not uncommonly, the behaviour of rebels and nonconformists is labelled "mental illness" and thus demeaned.

In 1885, when Louis Riel was charged with treason for leading the Northwest Rebellion, he rejected his lawyers' advice that he plead "not guilty by reason of insanity" on the grounds that, although it would spare his life, it would cost him his dignity; that is, his claim to "the moral existence of an intellectual being" (Bliss 1974:212). Even when found guilty and sentenced to hang, he continued to dispute not his innocence but the imputation that he was mentally ill.

Second, the fact that a diagnosis or label for a particular behaviour exists would seem to imply that an effective treatment for that behaviour also exists. Often this is not the case, or is only partly the case. The individual may, in fact, be forced to endure appalling treatment in the name of therapy. Psychosurgery has helped some marginal deviants (e.g., epileptics) but turned others into functional zombies. Similarly, electroshock therapy has helped some depressives but left others damaged and bitter. It may seem that any treatment is better than none with respect to violent, habitual criminals, but even here, some "treatments," particularly those aimed at sex offenders, would appear to violate one of the major principles of Western democracy, which is the dignity and worth of each individual (Pellegrino 1985).

Third, while some medical diagnoses, such as hyperactivity, include a prediction that the individual will outgrow the problem, many others come with the assumption that the condition is permanent. When this expectation is coupled with the assumption that the individual lacks control over the behaviour in question, the medicalized diagnosis may very well constitute a self-fulfilling prophecy in which the person who might otherwise have outgrown a problem, or taken charge of it, or gathered with others to make the behaviour legitimate, instead suffers repeated and lifelong "relapses."

Fourth, the use of medicalization to control criminal behaviour has, according to some observers, brought about the "therapeutic state," in which the state bypasses the due process rights of the accused (i.e., those established under the classical model of the responsible criminal), substitutes diagnoses based on evidence that would not be acceptable in a courtroom, and sentences individuals to enforced treatment, for the

> ## Box 6.5   Almost Anything Can Be Pathologized: Coffee Drinkers' Syndrome
>
> The essential feature is a characteristic withdrawal syndrome due to the abrupt cessation of, or reduction in, the use of caffeine-related products after prolonged daily use. This syndrome includes headache and one (or more) of the following symptoms: marked fatigue or drowsiness, marked anxiety or depression, or nausea and vomiting. These symptoms appear to be more prevalent in individuals with heavy use (500 mg/day) but may occur in individuals with light use …
>
> *Source:* The American Psychiatric Association, *Diagnostic and Statistical Manual of Mental Disorders,* 1994, 708. Reprinted by permission.

"good" of the accused person (Kittrie 1971). At its most extreme, the substitution of treatment for punishment can result in "selective incapacitation" whereby those who are most likely to offend are identified *before* they commit any offence, and are either subjected to treatment or contained in an institution of some kind.

Finally, by focusing on the individual, illness models cause us to look inside the body rather than at the environment surrounding it. The medicalization of menopause, for example, results in emphasis on hormone therapy that tends to exclude any serious analysis of the social position of middle-aged women. Similarly, homosexuality becomes an "illness" rather than a lifestyle choice. The next chapter follows an alternative thread of explanation, one that emphasizes the social environment as the source of deviance.

SUMMARY

Many psychiatric and psychological theories are based on the Freudian idea that biological urges reside in the id portion of the mind and that these are subject to control or mismanagement by the ego and superego, both of which are influenced by environmental factors. Freudian theory has been used to explain violence against out-groups, as well as self-destructive forms of deviance.

Psychologists have also developed theories of cognitive and moral development that help to distinguish people who commit "common" offences from those who engage in political and morally motivated criminal activity. Psychological theories of temperament and learning also throw light on how deviants may learn deviant behaviour and deviant motives as a result of conditioning or social modelling in their environment.

Biological, psychological, and sociological research all converge in arousal theory. This theory predicts that people who are overstimulated in the normal environment will retreat, while those who are bored and insensitive to pain will take both legal and illegal risks. Arousal theory has particular relevance for sensation-seeking forms of deviance, especially with respect to those who fit the label "psychopath."

According to the medical model, deviant behaviour is a symptom of disease or, in some cases, is the disease itself in the sense that there are no other symptoms or obvious physical manifestations of illness. This model has been controversial when applied to mental illness, hyperactivity, and addictive-compulsive behaviours such as alcoholism, drug abuse, gambling, compulsive spending, and kleptomania. The medical model has been criticized on several fronts, most generally for addressing nonconformity as a symptom and treating it with drugs and psychosurgery, and by failing to consider the social conditions that may have contributed to the deviance.

REFERENCES

Aichen, August. (1935). *Wayward Youth*. New York: Viking.

Andry, R.G. (1963). *The Short-Term Offender*. London: Stevens.

Atthowe, John M., Jr., and Leonard Krasner. (1968). "Preliminary Report on the Application of Contingent Reinforcement Procedures (Token Economy) on a 'Chronic' Psychiatric Ward." *Journal of Abnormal Psychology* 73:37–43.

Bliss, Michael (ed.). (1974). *The Queen v. Louis Riel*. Toronto: University of Toronto Press.

Bogg, Richard A. (1994). "Psychopathic Behavior as Perpetual Gaming: A Synthesis of Forensic Accounts." *Deviant Behavior* 15(4):357–374.

Caplan, Paula. (1995). *They Say You're Crazy: How the World's Most Powerful Psychiatrists Decide Who's Normal*. Reading, Mass.: Addison Wesley.

Cattell, R.B. (1979). *Personality and Learning Theory*. Vol. 1. New York: Springer.

Cleckley, H. (1964). *The Mask of Sanity*. 4th ed. St. Louis: Mosby.

Conrad, Peter, and Joseph Schneider. (1980). *Deviance and Medicalization: From Badness to Sickness*. St. Louis: Mosby.

Cotter, Lloyd H. (1967). "Operant Conditioning in a Vietnamese Mental Hospital." *American Journal of Psychiatry* 124(July):23–28.

Cry, Mireille, Sheila Hodgins, Pierre Lamy, and Jean Paquet. (1991). "Research Note: La théorie de la personnalité criminelle: Résultats d'une expérience de réhabilitation." *Canadian Journal of Criminology* 33:83–92.

Daniels, Arlene K. (1970). "Normal Mental Illness and Understandable Excuses: The Philosophy of Combat Psychiatry." *American Behavioral Scientist* 14:2:167–184.

Denisoff, Serge, and Charles H. McCaghy (eds.). (1973). *Deviance, Conflict and Criminality.* Chicago: Rand McNally.

Dollard, J., L.W. Doob, N.E. Miller, O.H. Mowrer, R.R. Sears, and C.S. Ellis. (1987). "Criminality, Psychopathy, and Eight Other Behavioral Manifestations of Sub-Optimal Arousal." *Personality and Individual Differences* 8:905–927.

Eysenck, Hans. (1960). *The Structure of Human Personality.* London: Methuen.

———. (1964). *Crime and Personality.* London: Routledge and Keegan Paul.

Fishbein, Diana H. (1990). "Biological Perspectives in Criminology." *Criminology* 28 1:27–72 .

Freud, Sigmund. (1948). "The Ego and the Id." In *The Complete Psychological Works of Sigmund Freud.* Vol. 19. Translated and edited by James Strackey. London: Hogarth.

Furnham, A. (1984). "Extroversion, Sensation Seeking, Stimulus-Screening and Type A Behavior Pattern: The Relationship Between Various Measures of Arousal." *Personality and Individual Differences.* 5:133–140.

Glasser, W. (1965). *Reality Therapy: A New Approach to Psychiatry.* New York: Harper and Row.

Goldstein, Jeffrey. (1986). *Aggression and Crimes of Violence.* 2nd ed. New York: Oxford.

Gould, Stephen Jay. (1981). *The Mismeasure of Man.* New York: W.W. Norton & Co.

Halleck, Seymour. (1971). *Psychiatry and the Dilemmas of Crime.* Berkeley: University of California Press.

Hebb, Donald Olding. (1980). *Essay on Mind.* Hillsdale, N.J.: Erlbaum.

Henggeler, Scott. (1984). *Delinquency in Adolescence.* Beverley Hills, Cal.: Sage.

Horowitz, Allan. (1981). "Review of Medicalization of Deviance by Conrad and Schneider." *Current Sociology* 10(6):750.

Hughes, Gerald, and Douglas Dagher. (1993). "Coping with a Deviant Identity." *Deviant Behavior* 14:297–315.

Jenish, D'Arcy. (1995). "Heart of Darkness." *Maclean's,* September 11, 18–23.

Kittrie, Nicholas. (1971). *The Right to be Different: Deviance and Enforced Therapy.* Baltimore, Md.: Johns Hopkins University Press.

Kohlberg, L. (1969). *Stages in the Development of Moral Thought and Action.* New York: Holt Rinehart and Winston.

———. (1986). "The Just Community Approach to Corrections." *Journal of Correctional Education* 37(2):54–58.

Lent, James R., Judith LeBlanc, and Joseph E. Spradlin. (1970). "Designing a Rehabilitative Culture for Moderately Retarded, Adolescent Girls." In Roger Ulrich, Thomas Stachnick, and John Marbry (eds.), *Control of Human Behavior: From Cure to Prevention.* Vol. 2. Glenview, Ill.: Scott, Foresman.

LeVay, Simon. (1991). "A Difference in Hypothalamic Structure Between Heterosexual and Homosexual Men." *Science* 253 August:1034–1037.

Lieberman, Carole M.D. (1991). "Shopping Out of Control." *Britannica Medical and Health Annual.* Chicago: Encyclopaedia Brittanica, 342–346.

Lykken, David T. (1982). "Fearlessness: Its Carefree Charm and Deadly Risks." *Psychology Today,* September, 20–28.

McKain, Sally Joy, and Anthony Streveler. (1990). "Social and Independent Living Skills in a Prison Setting: Innovations and Challenges in Behavior Modification." *Behavior Modification* 14:4:490–518.

Mednick, Sarnoff A., and J. Volavka. (1980). "Biology and Crime." In N. Morris and M. Tonry (eds.), *Crime and Justice.* Chicago: University of Chicago Press.

Mednick, Sarnoff A., Jan Volavka, William F. Gabrielli, Jr., and Ital, Turan M. (1981). "EEG as a Predictor of Antisocial Behavior." *Criminology* 19(2):19–22.

Miller, Jean Baker (ed.). (1973). *Psychoanalysis and Women.* Baltimore, Md.: Penguin.

Miller, Jeffrey. (1987). "Is There Really a 'Twinkie' Defence?" *Lawyers Weekly,* January 16.

Moffitt, T.E. (1983). "The Learning Theory Model of Punishment: Implications for Delinquency Deterrence." *Criminal Justice and Behavior* 10:131–158.

Moir, Anne, and David Jessel. (1995). *A Mind to Crime: The Controversial Link between the Mind and Criminal Behavior.* London: Michael Joseph.

Nettler, Gwynn. (1978). *Explaining Crime.* 2nd ed. New York: McGraw-Hill.

———. (1982). *Explaining Criminals.* Criminal Careers. Vol. 1. Cincinnati: Anderson.

Okie, Susan. (1989). "Study Shows New Drug Can Help Compulsive Behaviours." *Toronto Star,* August 25.

O'Leary, K. Daniel, and Wesley C. Becker. (1967). "Behavior Modification in an Adjustment Class: A Token Reinforcement Program." *Exceptional Children* May:637–642.

Parsons, Talcott. (1951). "Deviant Behavior and Mechanisms of Social Control." Chapter 7 in Talcott Parsons, *The Social System.* New York: Free Press.

Pellegrino, Edmund. (1985). "Oedipus, Original Sin and Genetic Determinism." In Frank H. Marsh and Janet Katz (eds.), *Biology, Crime and Ethics.* Cincinnati: Anderson.

Picard, André. (1992). "Five Charged in Second Montreal Hate Slaying." *Globe and Mail,* December 18, A10.

Pollack, Otto. (1950). *The Criminality of Women.* Westport, Conn.: Greenwood.

Raine, A., and P.H. Venables. (1984). "Tonic Heart Rate Level, Social Class and Antisocial Behavior in Adolescents." *Biological Psychology* 18:123–132.

Redl, Fritz, and D. Wineman. (1951). *Children Who Hate.* Glencoe, Ill.: Free Press.

Samenow, Stanton. (1984). *Inside the Criminal Mind.* New York: Times Books.

Sarbin, Theodore R., and James C. Mancuso. (1980). *Schizophrenia: Medical Diagnosis or Moral Verdict?* New York: Pergamon.

Schaefer, H.H., and Patrick L. Martin. (1966). "Behavioral Therapy for 'Apathy' of Hospitalized Schizophrenics." *Psychological Reports* 19:1147–1158.

Siegal, Larry J. (1995). *Criminology: Theories, Patterns and Typologies.* 5th ed. Minneapolis: West.

Szasz, Thomas S. (1970). *The Manufacture of Madness: A Comparative Study of the Inquisition and the Mental Health Movement.* New York: Harper and Row.

Ulrich, Roger, Thomas Stachnik, and John Mabry (eds). (1970). *Control of Human Behavior: From Cure to Prevention.* Vol. 2. Glenview, Ill.: Scott, Foresman.

Yochelson, Samuel, and Stanton E. Samenow. (1976). *The Criminal Personality.* Vol. 1, *Profile for Change.* New York: Jason Aronson.

Ysseldyke, J., and B. Algozzine. (1982). *Critical Issues in Special and Remedial Education.* Dallas: Houghton Mifflin.

THE SOCIAL

DISORGANIZATION

PERSPECTIVE

In the summer of 1963, the federal government's Indian Affairs office in Kenora, Ontario, administered the relocation of the Ojibwa of Grassy Narrows from their old reserve to a new one, five kilometres away, where they would be more easily served with the benefits of modern life (an on-reserve school, medical care, electricity, and the like).

The move to the new reserve was not the first well-intentioned intrusion of government into this community: it was preceded by a long history in which the native way of life and religion had been weakened by white-run residential schools and regulations. This move, however, dealt a severe blow to the old community ways. The new reserve was laid out according to standards appropriate to a non-native population. It cut across the social boundaries of the native community and placed homes too close together and too far from the natural environment. In 1970, it was discovered that the Wabigoon River, which provided commercial fishing for the community, had been irreversibly poisoned by methyl mercury. As a result, the fishery shut down and, despite the provision of welfare support, the community began to self-destruct.

In the four years prior to the move, 91 percent of deaths in Grassy Narrows were due to natural causes. Between 1974 and 1978, 26 persons or almost one-fifth of the population in the 11-to-19 age group, had made suicide attempts. Public disorder and criminal offences, such as assault, break-and-enter and theft, vandalism, and gang rape had reached crisis levels. Many of these offences were attributed to pre-teen boys and girls. Young people were particularly affected by community and family breakdown. Many experienced severe neglect and physical abuse as their

---

**Box 7.1   Rebirth of a Nation: A Dispossessed People
Comes Home**

OUJE-BOUGOUMOU, Que.—For the better part of the past 25 years, John Shepacio-Blacksmith has wallowed in the mire of alcohol and drug addiction, one of the many lost souls among a dispossessed people.

Two weeks ago, he came home, literally and spiritually, to set down roots in Oujé-Bougoumou. Since taking possession of his new house with his wife and six children, Mr. Shepacio-Blacksmith has not had a drink, and he has rediscovered his culture and people....

The people of Oujé-Bougoumou were forcibly relocated at least seven times since 1927, and scattered into small camps consisting of rundown shacks along the highway. Their hunting grounds, still littered with the remnants of 25 gold and copper mines and, in large part, clear-cut by forestry companies, were plundered.

They were denied band status by an administrative error, and later left out of the James Bay and Northern Quebec Agreement, a treaty that resolved the land claims of other Cree Indians in the province.

But, against all odds, they persevered.

The 400-plus people of Oujé-Bougoumou, dubbed the Forgotten Crees, elected a chief and became squatters on their own land. Using lawsuits, roadblocks, political pressure and sheer determination, they won. In the past few years, the Indian Affairs Ministry recognized them as a band. They became signatories to the James Bay Agreement, and secured exclusive hunting, fishing and trapping rights over a 167-square-kilometre territory, along with more than $75 million in federal and provincial financing....

"This will be our first Christmas together [in the new community], said band member Lisa St-Pierre. "We are a family again." Not long ago, the holiday season here was associated with different feelings. It was a time of the year when drinking, and hence domestic violence and suicide, peaked; when the loneliness and hopelessness of the struggle was palpable....

If the people of Oujé-Bougoumou feel empowered by their new home, it is because they played an intimate part in its conception, creation and construction, and because the village is a living reflection of their culture and lifestyle.

Rebirth of a Nation (cont.)

The elders chose the site, on the shores of Lake Opémisca, close to all the traditional trap lines. They also sat down with the architect and explained the science underlying the traditional Cree dwelling, a rectangular structure dug into the ground, with poles covered with animal skins and moss, and the interior bathed in natural light from a fire hole at its apex.

From these "dreaming sessions" [the architect] fashioned modern Cree dwellings: energy-efficient houses where the roof is the dominant feature, and where light and open spaces define the interiors. A similar process was used to shape the band council office, the school, the healing centre, day-care centre, elder's home and community centre....

The results, when you put the village into its cultural context, are striking. The village design is circular, with the *shaptuwan* (traditional meeting place for feasts) central and at the top of the hill. The inner two rings are lined with community buildings, reflecting the culture of sharing. The homes are built in clusters, just like the old camps.

The people of Oujé-Bougoumou have, in large part, purchased their homes with a geared-to-income purchase plan. This is in stark contrast to Indian reserves, where land ownership is forbidden as part of the premise of the Indian Act that native people are wards of the state....

"The irony of all this is that Oujé-Bougoumou, as beautiful and culturally appropriate as it is, is a lot cheaper than a reserve," Mr. Bosum said. "It's real proof that transferring resources to native people is the way of helping us out of misery, that just continuing handouts solves nothing."

Source: André Picard, "Rebirth of a Nation: A Dispossessed People comes Home," *Globe and Mail,* December 4, 1993, A1, A6. Reprinted with permission from The Globe and Mail.

---

parents' alcoholism deprived them of food, clothing, and family support. Many were taken into custody by the Children's Aid Society. Anastasia Shkilnyk, who studied the community from 1977 to 1978, reported that:

[W]ithin the community, no blame is attached to acts of violence committed by children. One sixty-eight-year-old band member was beaten so viciously by a gang of children that he required lengthy hospitalization. Yet he did not press charges. When asked why, he said that he was very ashamed that the old way of life had gone, "because this would never have happened on the old reserve ... the kids, they had been drinking, and when a person is drinking, he is not himself." Most people forgive the youngsters, even for atrocious offenses, because they know that their violence is both a symptom of the general disorder in the community and an effect of the breakdown of the Indian family. (Shkilnyk 1985:34)

The above incident introduces the first of several distinctly *sociological* approaches to the understanding of deviance. Crime and deviance at Grassy Narrows cannot reasonably be blamed on genetic inheritance, since earlier generations of these families did not display exceptional levels of violent or self-destructive behaviour. It is also very unlikely that the problems found there were directly caused by mercury poisoning, since other cases of mercury poisoning (in Japan, for example) have not been associated with this kind of disruption. Most observers see the outbreak of alcoholism, murder, vandalism, and suicide at Grassy Narrows as symptomatic of a failure of the social order. The cultural beliefs and structural organization characteristic of the older Ojibwa community were disrupted to the extent that the new community was no longer able to integrate and regulate the lives of its members.

The idea that "pathology" can exist at the social level is characteristic of the social disorganization perspective. This view dominated the sociology of deviance from the 1890s to the mid-1930s, and later formed the basis for interactionist, social learning, and control theories, all of which will be discussed in later chapters.

ORIGINS OF THE SOCIAL DISORGANIZATION PERSPECTIVE

The idea that some kinds of deviance might be caused by social conditions was not new or unique to the 1800s; philosophers had long engaged in debates about which forms of government, and which social institutions, would be most conducive to higher public morality. What was new in the 1800s was the attempt to combine the idea of social causation with the investigative methods of science. Sociological positivism emerged when thinkers from various backgrounds (philosophy, theology, political science, and natural science) began to look for regularities in social life, just as natural science had sought regularities in plant and animal life.

Beyond a desire to follow the example set by the natural sciences, these early sociologists were motivated by the historical changes that had led to increasing concentrations of deviance among people in particular social classes and groups. The Industrial Revolution created entire new social classes of people, including the urban middle class and the so-called "dangerous and perishing classes" of the poor, unemployed, and criminal, who lived in the unsanitary and overcrowded urban slums of rapidly growing cities. It seemed evident to many thinkers that the unhealthy physical conditions, such as those documented by Charles Dickens in *Oliver Twist,* were matched by the unhealthy moral condition of the slums' inhabitants, which was reflected in high rates of deviance and crime (Pearson 1975:161; Tobias 1972; Adler 1994).

Religion, which had been largely irrelevant (if not antagonistic) to classical theory, now served as a motivating factor in the scientific study of society. Science was to be the tool for bringing about a better, more moral society. Those who were relatively well off were encouraged by their religious leaders to concern themselves with the quality of the physical, spiritual, and moral life around them. In part, this took the form of Social Gospel, a movement that became particularly strong along the eastern seaboard of the United States and in Canada's Maritime settlements.

In England and North America, many of the early sociologists had training in theology, and shared a commitment to religious views of social responsibility. Methodist Wesley College in Winnipeg was the first college to offer sociology courses (in 1906), followed by the Baptist colleges, Acadia and McMaster, in 1907. McGill University in Montreal shares this Baptist background. Its sociology department (established in 1922) was headed by Carl Dawson, who had trained for the Baptist ministry.

Other precursors of sociological study took the form of cartographers' maps and public welfare surveys. The cartographical school, which emerged in the 1820s, used statistics about social issues to create social maps that showed that crime, dependency, and other social problems regularly occurred in some areas at a higher rate than in other areas, and that these rates changed when social conditions changed. The cartographers established that there was stability over time in the statistics for suicide, crime, and public health from society to society, and from area to area. Through their work, it became possible to graph the progress of all kinds of social problems, and to demonstrate the predictability of overall rates of rule breaking, in a way that underlined the fact that crime was not just an individual, psychological fact.

Statistical studies of the early 1800s located the mass of social unrest, crime, and immorality in the slum areas of industrializing countries. The earliest studies made use of government statistics when these were available, but a tradition of independently sponsored social surveys soon grew up, as various agencies for public welfare and reform went into the slums to document conditions and to propose solutions. The predominant view was that the urban masses were ignorant and irreligious, without any sense of moral duty, and, especially if touched by radical

---

Box 7.2   Description of Field-Lane 1850

Let the inspector of the London prisons—after emptying all his outer pockets, and buttoning-up his coat to secure his watch, pocket-book and handkerchief—penetrate this celebrated receptical for stolen goods. The lane is narrow enough for him to reach across from house to house, and the buildings so lofty that a very bright sun is required to send light to the surface. The dwellings on either side are dark. In some of them candles or gas is burning all day long. The stench is awful. Along the narrow lane runs a gutter, into which every sort of poisonous liquid is poured. This thoroughfare is occupied entirely by receivers of stolen goods, which goods are spread out for sale. Here you may re-purchase your own hat, boots, or umbrella; and unless you take special precaution, you may have one of the importunate saleswomen ... attempting to seduce you into the purchase of the very handkerchief which you had in your pocket at the entrance ... Let him pause for a moment to contemplate this *hot-bed of crime and demoralization* [author's italics]. Here is one of the great dunghills on which society rears criminals for the gallows, as on other dunghills it rears melons for the table ... The flavour of the fruit depends upon the quality of the soil; and here we have some of the richest rankness in the world.

Source: W.H. Dixon, *The London Prisons,* edited by J.J. Tobias, David & Charles Publishers (Newton Abbot, Devon.: 1972 [1850]), 31–33. Reprinted by permission.

---

economic beliefs, a danger to the society in which they lived. A variety of people took up the challenge to understand the sources of urban squalor and to do something about them. These included:

1. Religious (frequently evangelical) "do-gooders" who saw the "moral uplift" of the lower classes as a spiritual duty, and who considered overcrowding, epidemics, infant mortality, crime, and other social problems as the consequences of inadequate moral training.

2. Humanitarian philanthropists from the industrial middle class who saw social problems as a matter of improper "social engineering," and who felt that impulsive and unsystematic charity was ineffective, even counterproductive, in that it maintained rather than relieved poverty and dependency. The industrialists were inclined to think that better means of dealing with poverty would result in a healthier and more motivated work force.

3. Journalists who produced descriptive accounts for newspaper articles or books, or muckraking investigative reporters who exposed the sources of corruption at the political and economic level. There was a ready market for stories of the depravity of the poor and the corruption of officials, whether they were "real life" versions in such books as W.H. Dixon's *The London Prisons* (1850), Charles Booth's *Life and Labour of the People in London* (1891), and Charles Loring Brace's widely read *The Dangerous Classes of New York* (1872), or fictionalized accounts as in the novels of Charles Dickens (Tobias 1972:30–33).

4. Officials hired by city governments to oversee public health and welfare. An example of this was Toronto's medical officer of health in the early 1900s, Dr. Charles Hastings. Dr. Hastings produced one of the earliest studies of the Toronto slums.

5. Social reformers, like John Howard, Charles Booth, and Beatrice Webb, who studied society in order to improve it; and radicals, like Karl Marx, who hoped to end urban poverty (and its attendant problems) by overthrowing the entire system.

The combined efforts of these groups resulted in an outpouring of studies that utilized the "social survey" form in one way or another. A distinct division existed between those who used these surveys to argue for repressive, coercive measures to outlaw "vice" (e.g., prostitution, intemperance, and gambling), and those who felt

---

Box 7.3   The City Below the Hill

One of the earliest sociological studies in Canada was *The City Below the Hill* (1897), by Sir Herbert Brown Ames, a successful industrialist and reformer. Like many of his contemporaries, Ames believed in the message of Social Gospel. He sought to use objective and scientific methods of study in order to identify problems and provide for effective social reform.

Ames organized a house-to-house canvass of a lower-class district of Montreal. Residents were systematically questioned about employment, family composition, housing, rent, ethnic background, and so on. The results were organized and transferred to a series of maps. Of particular concern to Ames was his discovery that drunkenness, crime, disease, death, and poverty were concentrated in the "rear tenements" of this area of Montreal, and he made numerous proposals for improving the area (Ames [1897] 1972; Campbell 1983:20).

that moral life would look after itself if the environment could be improved. The sociologists of the period were generally affiliated with the liberal, "environmental" group.

EMILE DURKHEIM AND SOCIOLOGICAL POSITIVISM

The founders of sociology—Auguste Comte, Herbert Spencer, Vilfredo Pareto, Emile Durkheim, Ferdinand Tonnies, Karl Marx, and Max Weber—were, in varying degrees, all influenced by Darwinist evolutionary theory. They saw societies as organisms that could adapt to their environments and evolve over time; and, like the social Darwinists discussed in Chapter 5, they felt that understanding the laws of evolution might enable them to influence its course.

Although Emile Durkheim (1858–1917) wrote in the same period as Cesare Lombroso, he was strongly opposed to Lombrosian thinking. Durkheim argued that "social facts are explained by social facts," and firmly rejected any explanation that invoked psychological or biological variables. So adamant was he in his rejection of such variables that his approach is sometimes criticized for being "sociologistic."

If society is seen as an organism that in some sense attempts to maintain itself, then deviance is either "natural" to the organism or it is a "pathology" of the organism. It was Durkheim's view that most deviance is natural and actually helps society to function effectively. Conversely, pathological forms of deviance emerge when the social organism fails to maintain deviance at a beneficial level.

Durkheim believed that societies, like other organisms, evolve from simple to more complex forms. The nature of deviance—and the way in which it is contained—differs according to the stage of development characteristic of the society. In the earliest societies (exemplified by small, tribal groups), most members of the community did the same kind of work and shared similar daily experiences. The congruence of their lives fostered common ideas and beliefs. When a rule was broken, it offended virtually all members of the society equally, and the offender's punishment was likely to be severe, repressive, and approved by all. In Durkheim's terms, the members of a society share a common conscience that holds them together in a state of *mechanical solidarity*. Little individualism or real freedom exists in such a society, but the people do not feel repressed, because they are in agreement with the rules.

Mechanical solidarity is transformed into *organic solidarity* when population pressure leads to an increasingly complex division of labour. The new specialization and diversity that characterizes members of a society is accompanied by a considerable diminishment of the common conscience. Police officers, bartenders, carpenters, priests, bankers, and others develop a slightly differing consciousness of moral

Figure 7.1   Durkheim's Forms of Solidarity

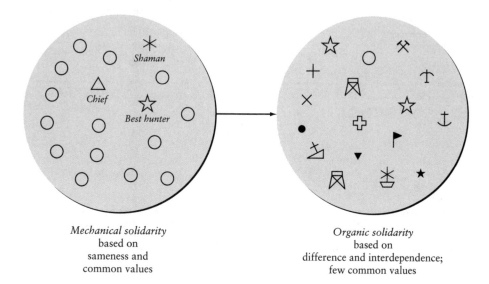

Mechanical solidarity
based on
sameness and
common values

Organic solidarity
based on
difference and interdependence;
few common values

issues, such that few deeds—among them not even violent murder—offend all groups equally or compel them to respond in identical fashion. There are even places in society where deviants can live without fear of repression. The moral outrage, which invariably led to repressive punishment in early society, now applies only to the most extreme offences (e.g., the torture of children). Durkheim thus equated organic solidarity with greater variety in human expression, more freedom, and less moral outrage. But accompanying this was a danger of too much freedom, and therefore too little control.

Although Durkheim accepted the normalcy and desirability of the social change from mechanical to organic solidarity, he argued that excessively rapid social change (e.g., urbanization and industrialization), or inconsistencies produced by crises of war, famine, or illness, could disrupt the natural adaptive processes of society, weaken its levels of integration and regulation, and thereby allow the development of socially harmful (pathological) forms of deviance.

As discussed in Chapter 2, Durkheim felt that social change in his time had created a society characterized by "anomie" (lack of integration in the group) and "egoism" (lack of regulation by the group), both of which led to high rates of suicide, mental illness, and crime. In anomic situations, people lack the firm moral values and commitments required to "hold" them in society, while lives that are not regulated or supervised allow the excessive development of egoism (Durkheim [1897] 1951). This analysis can be used today to interpret the evidence that crime rates are lower in countries such as Bahrain (which is characterized by a high degree of integration based on adherence to Islamic values, and is more highly regulated) than any North American countries (Helal and Coston 1991).

SOCIOLOGY IN AMERICA: THE EMERGENCE OF THE CHICAGO SCHOOL

When sociological ideas crossed the Atlantic to the United States, they found a mixed reception. In the established educational centres of the eastern seabord, sociology was regarded as an upstart discipline with a "bastard name and a barbarian terminology" (Matthews 1977:88). The discipline was seen as tainted by radicalism (i.e., socialism and feminism) and was often treated as subordinate to the more established disciplines of economics, political science, and theology. Sociologists in these departments had little independence and little access to departmental budgets for research. Many of these early sociologists considered themselves ministers, journalists, or natural scientists first, and there was no clear line between their professional sociology and their other activities. Thus, sociological work tended to be an uneasy combination of social ethics, social problems, and social science, and was sometimes funded by philanthropic or political reform groups, churches, or government. Similar conditions prevailed in Canada even longer than in the United States.

The University of Chicago, which opened in 1892, was different in almost every way. The city of Chicago was particularly well suited to be a centre for ideas about the influence of rapid change on the social order. The site that in the 1830s had held only Fort Dearborn, a small log fort on the prairie-urban frontier, had evolved into a boom town that gathered into its core a growing stream of migrants from both urban and rural areas, and waves of immigrants from Ireland, Sweden, Germany, Poland, and Italy. Chicago's population expanded from 4470 people in 1840 to 1,099,850 by 1890 and 3,375,329 by 1930 (Burgess and Newcomb 1931:5; Bulmer 1984:13). Bulmer (1984) describes the Chicago of 1890 as a "boiling, turbulent, industrial metropolis that knew what it meant to be great, but hardly had time to absorb the knowledge" (14). Two years later, the University of Chicago began its work under the threat of serious urban disorder. In 1886, someone had thrown a bomb that killed seven policemen in Chicago's Haymarket Square, and the police had responded by firing on the crowd. This event, which came to be known as the Haymarket Riot of 1886, was followed by similar outbreaks in other American cities. The apparent threat of class warfare, alien radicalism, and urban mass violence sent shock waves through the social classes that supported the university, and lent urgency to their desire for effective urban research. Exacerbating the social unease was the 1893–97 depression, during which unemployment ran as high as 20 percent. Downtown streets in these years were flooded with both the jobless (who "got by" in various, often illegal, ways) and opportunists eager to take advantage of the relative lawlessness that characterized the urban centre.

The university itself was not a tradition-bound outgrowth of long development and social-establishment support, but was created almost overnight with the assistance of $35 million in grant money from John D. Rockefeller and substantial gifts from the community, particularly from other local Baptists and industrialists (Pfohl 1985:144; Christakes 1978:15). Right from the beginning this gave the University of Chicago a reformist, liberal, and practical slant, providing a sharp contrast to both the elitist and pedantic style that characterized the eastern universities, and the radical and revolutionary complexion of European schools.

The University of Chicago's first president, William Rainey Harper, instructed staff "not to stock the student's mind with knowledge of what has already been accomplished in a given field," but instead to "train him that he himself may be able to push out along new lines of investigation" (Bulmer 1984:15; Goodspeed 1928:145).

Particularly important was the fact that Chicago had an independent sociology department, which meant the weight of traditional thought would not impede newer ideas. In addition, the university's enviable economic position enabled the first sociology head, Albion Small, to lure the best young minds away from other universities at salaries close to double those offered elsewhere, and then to encourage their research (Downes and Rock 1981:53). Though officially independent, the sociology department was in the early years closely associated with the social service-oriented (Baptist) divinity school and the departments of political science and philosophy. All of these departments were linked by the common objective of improving the social conditions of industrial America (Matthews 1977:89).

Also important to the development of the Chicago approach to sociological explanation was the close association between the sociology department and Hull House, a settlement house that provided social services in the Chicago slums. In this period, many North American universities were involved in work of this kind, following the model established by England's Toynbee Hall in London's East End. In England, settlement institutions were mainly seen as vehicles for helping the exploited working class to improve its socioeconomic position. In Chicago, Hull House was dealing with immigrants rather than with the established working class that characterized the British model. While it had its share of radicals, Hull House concentrated its efforts on helping both immigrants and the "rootless" poor surmount the barriers created by social disorganization, so that they could become successful participants in the American Dream.

Hull House also initiated much of the collection of statistical data and community mapping that informed the work of Chicago School academics. A pathbreaking and influential book by Jane Addams (co-founder of Hull House) was *The Spirit of Youth and the City Streets* (1909). One of the first academic books to examine youth gangs, it dealt with how the urban environment distorted "the spirit of youth," by which Addams meant the need for play, adventure, and idealism. Another important contribution was *Hull-House Maps and Papers,* produced by a women's collective within Hull House. This book used detailed maps of community social life to analyze the effects of social disorganization, immigration, and the economy on Chicago's South Side. And, as Deegan (1990) notes, "this book established the major substantive interests and methodological technique of Chicago Sociology that would define the School for the next forty years" (24). Much of this history, and with it, the history of the contribution of women to the Chicago School, however, was suppressed either purposefully, or simply as a by-product of Robert Park's drive for a sociology that would be "scientific" and not contaminated with social reform and social work viewpoints (Orcutt 1996:242; Deegan 1990; Hughes 1973).

The Chicago Department of Sociology was also associated with state-supported organizations such as the Institute for Juvenile Research, in which Ernest Burgess played a leading role. Among the Chicago School studies published by the Institute was Shaw and McKay's *Social Factors in Juvenile Delinquency* (1931). Clifford R. Shaw was a major force in founding and supervising the Chicago Area Project in the mid-1930s. This program, which provided a setting for the work of Chicago School theorists, was an innovative attempt to bring "organization" to "disorganized" areas. It employed local youths (often gang members) to work in recreation programs, community-improvement campaigns, and projects devoted to reaching and assisting delinquent youngsters and ex-convicts. The Chicago Area Project also spearheaded local improvements in education, sanitation, safety, and law enforcement, while providing recreational outlets and summer camping for youth.

As a result of these particularly favourable conditions, a "Chicago School" of sociology emerged. Although it involved collaborative and mutually supportive work that came to be characterized by a distinctive paradigm of interpretation (Bulmer 1984:2), the Chicago School was never a doctrine or an ideology. On the contrary, it was quite diverse in its expression. What its distinctive parts had in common was a tendency toward focused, grounded studies of observable social scenes.

Since graduate studies were only in their infancy in America, most of the original staff of the Chicago School had done at least some of their training in Germany, and the stamp of the German "research seminar" became part of the Chicago tradition. Many staff members also shared a very strong rural or small-town Baptist background, which fit well with the idea of social science as a way of fulfilling one's responsibility toward disadvantaged groups by improving their quality of life, both materially and morally. Their origins also inclined them toward viewing the seeming chaos of the city as something that contributed to vice, crime, and personal demoralization, especially when contrasted with the apparent stability, order, and harmony of rural life.

From the beginning, the Chicago School emphasized research in the community over abstract analyses of global statistics. The School was reformist and positivist rather than radical or revolutionary. The kinds of deviance it described and explained were street crimes and deviant lifestyles, not white-collar crimes or the "exploitation of the masses." Students were assigned class exercises that took them outside the university and into the community. Dissertations, research projects, and (eventually) books documented almost every aspect of Chicago life. Studies were made of gangs, organized crime, prostitution, real-estate offices, local newspapers, the rooming-house district, the community known as Hobohemia, the central business district, and taxi-dance halls (where men came by taxi and paid women to dance with them). There were also studies of the ethnic groups that made Chicago a vibrant (albeit sometimes conflict-ridden) mosaic. Many of these studies reported on deviants and deviant lifestyles, largely because of their proximity and accessibility to the university. Wealthier, more organized neighbourhoods tended to be "defended communities" that were largely inaccessible to researchers (Suttles 1972:35). In fact, Chicago School sociologists did not concern themselves with the deviance of the "stable" middle and upper classes, concentrating instead on deviance as it was expressed among immigrants, bohemians, and the rootless poor.

Chicago sociology became the sociology of Chicago, and then, in the 1920s as its reputation spread, the sociology of urban forms of social life, the frontier, and the relations between metropolitan centres and hinterland regions. Practitioners of Chicago School sociology became well known and influential. From 1915 to the mid-1930s, the University of Chicago dominated sociology in North America and, particularly in Canada, had a substantial influence on political science and history (Bulmer 1984:xiii). Many Canadian academics were drawn to the university. Roderick McKenzie, a Manitoban, entered the Ph.D. program in 1913. Having studied in Winnipeg, McKenzie brought with him an awareness of ethnic heterogeneity, the dominance of some groups over others, and the exploitation of the hinterland by the city, all of which entered into his work on natural areas and patterns of dominance. McKenzie became a leader of the Chicago School, and other

Canadians like Carl Dawson brought these ideas back to Canada, particularly to McGill, where they fit well with the Baptist traditions and the utilitarian emphasis of that university. For these sociologists, the city was a laboratory for the study of social order and social process.

THE CHICAGO SCHOOL AND SOCIAL DISORGANIZATION THEORY

While there were variations within the mainstream of Chicago theorizing, certain common threads can be identified. The main argument holds that rapid social change leads to a breakdown of common values and regulation in certain parts of society, thereby allowing anomic forms of deviance like suicide and mental illness to emerge. The Chicago School theorists regarded the following kinds of change as particularly germane to social disorganization:

1. *Urbanization:* transition from a relatively simple rural social order to a complex, crowded urban arrangement.
2. *Migration:* the movement of people from a close-knit, homogeneous rural society into an anonymous, heterogeneous urban setting.
3. *Immigration:* the movement of people with a wide variety of social backgrounds and customs, often European, into the American "melting pot."
4. *Industrialization:* the transformation of employment patterns and the development of the industrial working classes and underclasses.
5. *Technological change:* runaway change that outstripped adaptation, thereby producing a "gap" in which social disorganization occurred.

"Disorganization" tended to include anything that, when compared with the ideal of stable, small-town life, was negative or "pathological." Chicago theorists in the early period often overlooked the possibility that "disorganization" might really be another form of organization. They were aware, however, that the breakup of one form of order provided the basis for the growth of new forms. As the School developed, it paid increasing attention to the emergence of traditions and subcultures within the "disorganized" areas.

The social disorganization perspective argues that the breakdown of conventional institutions frees people to engage in unconventional or disapproved of behaviours (behaviours that are particularly concentrated in the inner-city reception areas, where the changes are most dramatic). Over time, a tradition or subculture may emerge that is characterized by a deviant or nonconformist lifestyle.

PRIMARY AND SECONDARY RELATIONS

Chicago School theorists such as Charles Horton Cooley emphasized the importance of "primary relations" (informal, face-to-face, personal interactions) over "secondary relations," which are formal, direct, and less personally involving. According to the Chicago School perspective, the less someone is integrated and regulated by involvement in personally meaningful interdependent relationships, the more likely it is that he or she will engage in unregulated or deviant behaviour. In small towns, the individual is enmeshed in primary relations that impose limits on behaviour; surveillance and gossip provide strong controls. In the urban setting, anonymity cuts these ties. In small towns, people might engage in homosexual behaviour at their peril; in the urban setting, there are niches in which this behaviour is accommodated in a relatively safe manner (Laumann et al. 1994; Rogers and Turner 1991).

HUMAN ECOLOGY

Ecology can be loosely defined as a science that deals with the relationships of organisms to one another and to other factors that make up their environment. Human ecology is the study of spatial and temporal relations between people, and how they are affected by social and economic competition for space and other resources; it views ethnic groups, occupational cultures, and various other users of "social space" as "species" seeking individual and group survival in a competitive environment.

From ecology, Chicago sociologists borrowed and adapted many concepts to form what was sometimes called a "human ecology theory of urban dynamics." The most important of these concepts are outlined below.

1. *Invasion:* the introduction of a new group or culture ("species") into the territory, not necessarily involving any force. A racial group may "invade" a district formerly dominated by another group, or a new use for land may push out incompatible elements, as may occur when a central business district expands into the residential areas that surround it. A modern example of invasion called gentrification takes place when upper-middle-class people buy properties in inner-city residential areas and transform them into areas in which the poor cannot afford to live.

2. *Segregation:* the separation of "species" (ethnic, racial, or business categories) from each other, so that each tends to be concentrated in some areas and absent in others. Various groups and institutions tend to settle in separate and distinct parts of the city, or even in distinct parts of a neighbourhood. Ethnic and racial

groups often tend to be segregated, either voluntarily or (due to economic or political circumstances) involuntarily. Some land uses mutually profit from being close to each other, whereas others (factories and upscale residential communities, for example) have a detrimental effect on each other; for the latter group, segregation may be the result.

3. *Natural areas:* unplanned processes like segregation help to produce "natural areas" with boundaries that are rarely entirely consistent with official administrative territorial units such as census tracts. As Park ([1916] 1967) observed, "Every large city has its occupational suburbs, like the stockyards in Chicago, and its residential enclaves, like Brookline in Boston, the so-called Gold Coast in Chicago, Greenwich Village in New York, each of which has the size and character of a completely separate town, village or city, except that its population is a select one" (10).

4. *Conflict:* intense competition between groups over the use of territory. Conflict often occurs when an area is first invaded by a new group or new land use. An example of conflict is gang warfare over street territory, or racially motivated rioting.

5. *Dominance:* the strength of one group relative to others. The dominant group may lack the authority or right to command, but nevertheless manages to exercise control through its ability to influence the conditions of life (Bogue 1949:10–11). Dominance may be expressed between ethnic or racial groups, between land uses, or between urban centres and their dependent hinterlands.

6. *Accommodation:* the process whereby different "species" (groups or land uses) achieve a nonconflictual adjustment. This often means that the weaker groups have adjusted to the dominance of others.

7. *Assimilation:* the complete absorption of one group into the way of life of another, as exemplified by the incorporation of new immigrants into the American melting pot. Chicago School theorists generally approved of assimilation (i.e., as a sign of adjustment to the emerging urban order).

8. *Succession:* takeover by a new group. Invasion may be followed by succession in a repeated pattern as group after group moves through an area. Succession may occur, for example, as wealthier residents move to better districts and the housing they leave behind is divided into rooming-house accommodation for a different social class or new immigrant group.

9. *Symbiosis:* interdependence among groups, as when one ethnic group provides restaurants, another specializes in carpet cleaning, and another does auto repair—each serving the needs of the other communities.

In the eyes of the Chicago School theorists and their followers, the well-organized community is a kind of symbiotically integrated superorganism. When invaded by new groups or new land use, it responds by attempting to regain "biotic balance." Conflict and competition occur, possibly on a level sufficient to disrupt the superorganic controls of the community. Eventually, the community either goes into a final decline, or accommodation and assimilation around a new dominant form occurs and order is restored.

LOCATION

The reliance of the Chicago sociologists on the ecological model made them more sensitive than later theorists to the locations of social activity. Location *as a geographical concept* refers to position on a land surface. Location *as an ecological concept* refers to the distribution of people in social as well as geographical space.

The Ecological Fallacy

The ecological analogy sometimes led to a confusion between the characteristics of an area and those of its individual residents. The "ecological fallacy" is exemplified by the assumption that, if a high-crime area has a large number of immigrants, transients, or students, then these people are the criminals (Robinson 1950). An alternative explanation is that the area is "undefended," which is to say it lacks the kind of social organization that can restrain violent or highly objectionable forms of deviance, and therefore attracts opportunists. People in public housing projects are often victims of the ecological fallacy. They lack the power to prevent criminals (who may not live in the area) from using their stairwells and lobbies for illegal purposes. They may be denied jobs or treated unfairly because others assume that area residents are the main perpetrators of crime.

Slum areas may be similarly stigmatized as places where only undesirable people live. Seeley (1959) classifies slum dwellers into four types.

1. permanent necessitarians (social outcasts and long-term poor);
2. temporary necessitarians who are poor for the short term (e.g., students and recent immigrants);
3. permanent opportunists (e.g., prostitutes who work there, fugitives, and criminals); and
4. temporary opportunists (e.g., short-term sellers and purveyors of illegal goods or services). (7–14)

Most likely to be criminal or seriously deviant are the opportunists (both permanent and temporary) who use the disorganized area but do not always live in it. Stokes (1962:187–197) makes a similar distinction between "slums of hope," which are inhabited by newcomers and recent immigrants looking for a better life, and "slums of despair," which show different kinds, and higher levels, of deviance.

RESEARCH METHODS OF THE CHICAGO SCHOOL

ECOLOGICAL MAPPING

The research method most closely associated with the Chicago School is ecological mapping. In this procedure, detailed maps of a particular city or district are used to show where deviant activities and social problems are concentrated. An ecological map might be constructed by plotting on a census tract map the home addresses of people charged with criminal offences, receiving psychiatric care, or being treated for sexually-transmitted diseases. Alternatively, the map might record which parts of the city experience the most break-ins, murders, or brawls, or have the highest concentration of brothels or drug dens.

The foremost exponent of the ecological approach was Canadian-born Roderick McKenzie. In the 1920s McKenzie developed the *zonal approach* to the study of cities, and contributed to the extension of ecological ideas into the study of the Canadian and U.S. frontier. This has provided a unique perspective on the path and pattern of vice and disorder in the newly formed communities (Shore 1987:xvi).

The best known of the ecological maps derived from McKenzie's work was published by Robert Park and Ernest Burgess, and was developed still further by Frederic M. Thrasher. Thrasher's version of this map is presented in Figure 7.2. The map presents the city as a series of five concentric circles or zones (Burgess 1925; Harris and Ullman 1945:12–13). Zone 1, the central business district, is characterized by large businesses, stores, banks, commercial offices, places of amusement, light industry, and transportation. Busy in the daylight hours, this area is deserted at night. It has few residents of any kind apart from those living in large hotels. Few criminals or deviants live here, but they may find within it crime targets or places conducive to deviant activities. Zone 1 tends to expand into the residential zone next to it.

Zone 2 is variously called "the transitional area," "zone in transition," and "interstitial area." It is characterized by rooming houses, flats, and hotels that are home to unskilled day workers, recent immigrants, and students. As the central business district expands, land values in Zone 2 rise, encouraging speculators to buy residential properties and convert them into rental housing. Speculators have no incentive to maintain the buildings, which quickly degenerate into slum housing. In Zone 2,

Figure 7.2   The Place of Chicago's Gangland in Urban Ecology

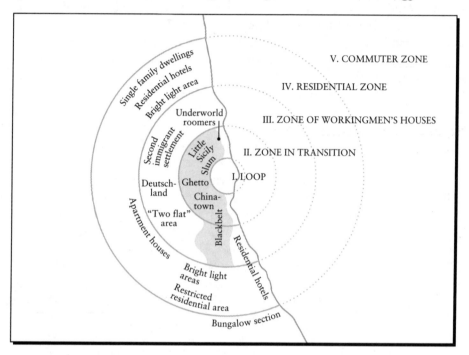

Source: Reprinted from *The Gang* by Frederick Thrasher by permission of the University of Chicago Press. Copyright © 1927.

marginals like hobos, alcoholics, and prostitutes find their own space; transvestites, gays, and others can find places to meet without censure; and various kinds of criminals are able to operate without much concern about interference from the law or their neighbours. Zone 2 is overwhelmingly the part of the city characterized by social problems, including school truancy, mental disorder, suicide, infant mortality, venereal disease, and poverty. The problems of Zone 2 are compounded by the fact that it is the "area of first settlement" or immigrant reception area. With the arrival of each new group, the social order is freshly disrupted as the older, more established groups leave for better housing in other parts of the city.

Zone 3 is the area settled by the stable working class and the second generation of immigrants. Its carefully tended homes are small, similar in design, crowded together, and frequently accommodate more than one family. Zone 3 is much more stable than Zone 2, but not as stable as Zone 4.

Zone 4 is the suburban middle-class area, settled mainly by white-collar workers and executives. Homes are larger, less similar, and less densely situated than those in Zone 3, and apartments are likely to be upscale. People tend to own their own homes, to move infrequently, and to share a sense of community values and norms.

Zone 5 is "exurbia," a commuter-zone characterized by large residential properties belonging to the relatively affluent. The area may also contain pockets of other kinds of use such as heavy industry or old rural slum.

Within the concentric zones are further subdivisions called "natural areas." Harvey Warren Zorbaugh's *The Gold Coast and the Slum,* first published in 1929, focused on the natural areas of the Near North Side of Chicago. This small territory just north of the central business district included a wide range of lifestyles. Lake Shore Drive was one of the most desirable living areas in Chicago (it was also known as the "Gold Coast"), where most of the people listed in the social register made their homes. Next to it was a less-favoured but still upper-class neighbourhood (although on its edge some houses had been converted to rooming houses).

Beyond this neighbourhood were the distinct communities of Hobohemia, Towertown, the rooming-house district, the North Clark Street strip, and the many small communities (like "Little Sicily") that were home base for at least 26 ethnic and immigrant groups. Hobohemia was "the last resort of the criminal and the defeated" (Madge 1963:95), an area in which individuals lived without any kind of meaningful attachments. Towertown was a run-down artist's colony and an "immigrant reception" neighbourhood that attracted the latest arrivals. Here Zorbaugh (1929) found a population of "egocentric poseurs, neurotics, rebels against the conventions of Mainstreet or the gossip of the foreign community, seekers of atmosphere, dabblers in the occult, dilettantes in the arts, or parties to drab lapses from a moral code which the city has not yet destroyed" (92). Towertown was a place where people who were not married to each other might live together without fear of censorship, and where homosexuality was said to be widespread.

In studying the rooming-house area, Zorbaugh documented how the lifestyles of the roomers were almost totally unregulated by any conception of communal life. The rooming-house keeper did not question the morality of the roomers, and the roomers had no control over each other. Zorbaugh contrasted this with the boarding house, in which people met over meals and established connections with each other. He also fleshed out his statistical and observational material with personal documents, including the story of a "charity girl" (prostitute) who had come to Chicago intending to become a pianist, only to end up a part of the lonely, unsettled, rootless population of the rooming-house world.

North Clark Street supplied the needs of the rootless population, "the hobos, the radicals, the squawkers [street vendors], the stick-up men, panhandlers, prostitutes, dopeys, jazz hounds, [and] gold diggers" (Madge 1963:100). In the slum area behind North Clark Street were many ethnic communities. Zorbaugh describes a community of young single Persian [Iranian] men who worked mainly as hotel help or janitors, a small Greek colony that focused on restaurant work and exuded a strong ethnic solidarity, and a small but growing community of blacks from rural Georgia, Mississippi, and Arkansas, who were displacing the Sicilian population. Altogether he found within the slum 28 distinct nationalities living side by side, with comparatively little friction. The only regular external contacts these communities had were with social service agencies and the law. The agencies were treated by residents as a resource to be exploited, while the law was regarded as a source of constant interference and oppression (Madge 1963:103).

Comparative studies of Philadelphia, Boston, Cincinnati, Greater Cleveland, Richmond (Virginia), Montreal, and even cities in England found the same zonal patterns. In the 1940s, Hoyt's (1939) sector model of residential differentiation and Harris and Ullman's (1945) multiple-nuclei model joined the concentric zone model as the main forms of ecological mapping (Bantingham and Bantingham 1984:312). In Canada, Toronto follows the Chicago concentric zone pattern, while Winnipeg is characterized by multiple nuclei (natural areas). Another Canadian application of Chicago School ideas has involved research on single-resource communities. More recent work in Canada and the United States has documented the massive changes in city organization brought about by the shift of business and commercial activities from the central business district to the suburbs. In many cities, suburban malls have become hangouts for those with time on their hands. These studies have generally confirmed the idea of "natural crime areas" in the sense that certain parts of the city, particularly its "undefended" neighbourhoods, tend to become places where crime and deviance concentrate.

Neighbourhoods rarely change from high-crime to low-crime areas (or vice versa) unless there has been change in the stability of the neighbourhood and its ability to organize for social control. When change does occur it may take the classic "Chicago" form of central business district expansion or immigrant pressure (Schuerman and Kobrin 1983, 1986), but in modern times it is more likely to be caused by public policy decisions such as slum clearance, subsidized housing, or urban redevelopment projects. Owen Gill (1977) describes how Luke Street, a stable, working-class neighbourhood in an English city, was transformed into an area characterized by aggressive, unemployed youth on the streets, heavy police attention, and high crime rates. Primarily responsible for the change was a housing policy that directed large, low-income families into the area, thereby overloading facilities like schools and playgrounds, undermining local community organizations, and creating stigmatization of the area.

Box 7.4 Canadian Single Resource Communities and Deviant Service Centres

Canada's wilderness frontier has been characterized by the rise and fall of small communities that are created for the purpose of exploiting a single economic resource. Such communities grow up around a mine or a mill, for example, or the building of a railway, pipeline, or dam. They rise suddenly as the resource is discovered or the project is begun, and they last until the project either loses its economic viability or the resource is exhausted. These temporary communities are small centres of suburban life dropped into the bush or other isolated areas. The urban centre may be thousands of miles away, connected only by air routes or summer roads. Some look like regular suburbs, while others are little more than trailer camps. There are three main periods in the lives of these communities.

In the initial phase, large numbers of mostly single young men are brought together to build the town and prepare the area for economic exploitation. During this phase there is some regulation and integration—revolving around a demanding work routine—and deviant opportunities are limited. The absence of women increases the likelihood of opportunistic forms of homosexuality (i.e., homosexual behaviour among men who would prefer to associate with women were they available). There are few controls such as family, church, or the mixing of generations to restrain behaviour. Social unrest at this stage is likely to take the form of alcohol abuse, brawls, and individual forms of violence. Organized strikes are unlikely, although wildcat strikes may occur in response to specific incidents.

The second phase has its "boom town" and its "model town" version. The gold rush encampment is an example of boom-town conditions. In the boom town, people attracted to the town by job or prospecting opportunities flood in. Historically, most have been relatively young males able to do the physical labour involved, and to hold their own against others' claims. They may be followed by women and older people who hope to provide services (bars, brothels, hotels) to those who are earning a great deal of money but have little time to look after their own needs. The boom town is initially characterized by confusion, disorder, and severe strains on the availability of provisions and accommodation. Services such as policing, medical care, sanitation, and fire control are only gradually achieved. The number of

> ### Canadian Single Resource Communities and Deviant Service Centres (cont.)
>
> shared problems, however, tends to lead to community organization, and eventually these towns develop social controls that stabilize the community.
>
> The model town emerges when the company (or the government) sets out formal plans for the community and controls who lives there and how they live. Issues such as housing for workers, middle management, and executives are settled in advance. Model-town plans rarely if ever include vice areas. As a result, the model town almost always develops a "parasite" community that provides prostitution, alcohol, drugs, gambling, and other "vice" activities. The parasite town may grow up "across the river" from the planned community, or it may take the form of ribbon growth along the highway leading into the community (e.g., Elliot Lake, Ontario). In cases where the company is able to prevent either of these developments, the vice centres of the most accessible free town or city will expand to meet the demand created by residents of the model town.
>
> Phase three occurs if a town lasts long enough to achieve stability. Then it takes on the characteristics of an urban centre, and may seem indistinguishable from other places, as long as the company or industry that is its primary support does not fail. Resource exhaustion or changes in the prices of resource products on the world market may turn such places into expensive ghost towns.

ETHNOGRAPHY

A frequently used tool of the Chicago School was urban ethnography, a "field enquiry" technique first developed by anthropologists in their study of tribal societies. Ethnography involved continuous monitoring of events as they unfolded in their natural setting. Chicago School ethnographies documented social worlds and ways of life within city neighbourhoods through a combination of field work (participant observation), techniques such as door-to-door surveys, and the collection of publicly available data on sex ratios, age structures, and racial/ethnic residential segregation and interaction. Even such data as the sale of streetcar tickets could be used to enrich the picture of how people lived and communicated and interacted within the city.

Ethnography looked at each group (prostitutes, hobos, delinquents, drug users) as if it were an urban "tribe" with unique characteristics that reflected its place in the urban order. Studies of vocational types—the shopgirl, the policeman, the vaudeville performer—laid the basis for understanding the interactive network in which these people lived, as well as the typical pattern that their careers followed. The Chicago School produced many studies showing how the city provided niches in which deviant lifestyles were able to flourish.

Nels Anderson's *The Hobo: The Sociology of the Homeless Man* (1923) was an early ethnographic study that pioneered the use of participant observation, as its author collected the "life stories" of some 60 men who lived in Chicago's Hobohemia area. In a work that exemplifies the classic perspective of social disorganization theory, Anderson—himself a mule driver ("skinner") and hobo before he entered the University of Chicago—depicted the "hobo" as a migratory worker who moves from place to place seeking temporary, often seasonal, work, the "tramp" as a migratory nonworker, and the "bum" as a nonmigratory nonworker (Anderson [1923] 1962).

LIFE DOCUMENTS

Other members of the Chicago School used "life documents," such as diaries and letters, to reveal how people experienced the transition to city life, and how their ideas and behaviour changed in response to the urban environment. The principal example of this approach is *The Polish Peasant in Europe and America* (1920) by W.I. Thomas and Florian Znaniecki.

Thomas and Znaniecki (1920) gathered data for their study by advertising for letters, diaries, and other personal documents of rural Polish peasants who had migrated to large U.S. cities in the early 1920s. Although they were particularly interested in what they called "undesigned records," such as letters that had not been written for publication (Bulmer 1984:51), Thomas and Znaniecki also made use of newspapers, records of court trials, sermons, and pamphlets issued by churches and political parties. Their analysis of these materials revealed a clear pattern whereby the second generation found Old World customs to be incompatible with participation in America. While the first generation could choose to insulate itself in a community of fellow immigrants, the second generation was obliged to participate in school and work that took them away from this closed community. Their experience of conflicting values and norms often led to an "anything goes" attitude, and the emergence of a stage in which the immigrant family was unable to prevent drift into forms of anomic deviance such as prostitution, delinquency, divorce, and mental disorder.

Another "life document" approach was the "life history," a story of one person or several individuals that could assume the form of an autobiography or a series of interviews. Exemplifying the genre is Shaw's (1930) account of a delinquent named Stanley. Here the autobiography is framed by Shaw's chronological record of his subject's brushes with authorities, behavioural problems, and criminal convictions. Shaw felt that such stories should be supported by the use of outside sources of data, including "the usual family history, the medical, psychiatric and psychological findings, the official record of arrests, offences, and commitments, the description of play-group relationships, and any other verifiable material which may throw light upon the personality and actual experiences of the delinquent in question" (Shaw 1930:2). While each life story was unique, Shaw and others believed that an overall picture of particular deviant lifestyles could be obtained through comparative analysis of similar studies.

SOCIAL DISORGANIZATION THEORY IN CANADA

McGILL UNIVERSITY

The centre of social disorganization theory and research in Canada was Montreal's McGill University. Like the University of Chicago, McGill was shaped by its affiliation with the theological and industrial concerns of its benefactors, as well as by the personal and scientific aspirations of its faculty. McGill's strong utilitarian and social service ethos was in part a natural expression of the university's roots, and in part a response to the conditions produced by World War 1. Montreal experienced severe strains both during and after the war, including widespread work stoppages in 1919 and a panic over Bolshevism, fuelled by the Russian Revolution of 1918. There was widespread concern about the quality, health, discipline, and loyalty of the working classes. This, and preoccupation with the process of "human efficiency," motivated the city's business and social welfare leaders to support the university in finding better ways than "charity" to deal with social problems (Shore 1987:xiv).

McGill's sociology department fought much harder than its American counterparts—but with less success—for recognition and funding. The service-oriented Department of Social Services was created in 1918, and only in 1924 did sociology emerge from it to form an academic department. By that time, McGill had developed an international reputation for scientific and medical achievements, and sociologists there found themselves under considerable pressure to imitate the methods of science and dissociate themselves from the more practically oriented, "unscientific" aspects of social work. Nonetheless, sociology at McGill was neither subordinated to political economy nor rejected as a shallow "American" discipline. (The same could not be said of other Canadian universities at the time; the University of Toronto, for example, offered courses in sociology, but did not have its own sociology department until the 1960s.)

Under the leadership of Carl Dawson, who had come to McGill in 1922 with a background in divinity studies and Chicago School sociology, the McGill sociologists produced studies of Montreal that detailed patterns of physical growth, the impact of industries, residential and occupational patterns, and sequences of race relations. When mapped in Montreal, Burgess's concentric circles became concentric "kidneys," with many natural areas within them and, as previously mentioned, a clear divide between French- and English-speaking areas. McGill sociology went beyond the city—and beyond the Chicago School—into the study of frontier settlement, and the processes whereby the interdependence of metropolis (major cities) and hinterland (resource-based communities) create new patterns of urban growth. Few of these studies dealt specifically with deviance, but some touched on the way in which social disorder is concentrated in specific parts of the city.

SOCIAL DISORGANIZATION IN THE ZONE OF TRANSITION

The Dufferin District

In the early 1900s, the part of Montreal that corresponded most closely with the Chicago School idea of "zone in transition" was the Dufferin District, an area studied by Robert Percy, a master's student at McGill University (Shore 1987:139–143). Dufferin District had originally been settled by English, Irish, Scottish, and French members of the stable working class: skilled workers, artisans, teachers, and merchants. But with the expansion of the commercial district, it was invaded by machine shops, warehouses and manufacturing establishments, and by successive waves of immigrants, including Chinese, Russian Jews, Russians, Greeks, Italians, Germans, Poles, and blacks. The original families departed, and their homes were remodelled into rental units and commercial places.

Percy found the Dufferin District riddled with noise, dirt, vice, despair, and conflict. Its many brothels (which competed with open street prostitution), gambling establishments, and drug dens attracted disreputable "johns," dope peddlers, and gamblers (Shore 1987:142–143). In line with the Chicago School theorists, Percy attributed the racial and ethnic tensions he observed to excessive cultural diversity, excessive stimulation, and the absence of institutions conducive to integration.

Africville

> Of all the black communities in Nova Scotia the most well-known—
> certainly the most notorious—was Africville. A black ghetto, it served
> as an illustration of how Canada handled the "race problem."
> Africville was an enclave or community, technically within the city of
> Halifax; but in terms of city services, positive concern shown by offi-
> cials, and the residents' own perception of the situation, it was "in" but
> not "of" the city. (Clairmont and Magill 1974:30)

Clairmont and Magill's (1974) study of Africville is based on their observations
of the forced relocation of its residents in the late 1960s and early 1970s. Africville
was not situated in the centre of the city, but otherwise shared the characteristics of
an interstitial area. What had begun as an idyllic rural village was caught up in the
expansion of Halifax. The residential area was surrounded and divided by industrial
enterprises and various institutions, including a prison, a hospital, and a sprawling
open dump that was used for the disposal of night soil (sewage). Africville became
a depressed shack town scheduled for future industrial and harbour development. It
was home to people who had little education, low and uncertain incomes, and
uncertain legal claim to the land on which they lived (Clairmont and Magill
1974:19–20).

Africville was distinguished by what Clairmont and Magill (1974:30) call its
"elaborately exaggerated" reputation as a deviance service centre. As a disorganized
and poorly policed area, it had become identified as a place where whites and blacks
alike went for bootleg booze, commercial sex, and unrestricted fun. Partly because
of the neglect afforded it by the city government, Africville enjoyed "functional
autonomy"; that is, residents had "freedoms" (such as the freedom to ignore building codes) that were not available in other parts of the city. This absence of external control was not compensated for by internal controls.

Over the years, the small, once cohesive community had lost its ability to unite
and achieve community goals. From the 1930s on, the population was characterized
by a shifting kaleidoscope of black and white drifters, many attracted by the low
rents, relative freedom, and deviant opportunities. High achievers and stable families began to move out, and the community's negative image scared off potential
replacements. As Clairmont and Magill see it, the cycle of deterioration began with
the encroachment of the city and the failure of city authorities to provide minimal
services to the community. Allowing Africville to deteriorate to the point at which
its residents would accept relocation was, for the city at least, a convenient solution
to the deviance problem.

FROM SOCIAL DISORGANIZATION TO DEVIANT TRADITION

EARLY SUBCULTURAL THEORY

By the end of the 1930s, the ideas of the Chicago School had begun to shift from an emphasis on how disorganization permits deviance to occur to an emphasis (which came to be known as "subcultural theory") on how deviant traditions in a community contribute to the maintenance of deviance in "delinquency areas." The new emphasis (partly a result of the aging of the transition zone, and the slowing of immigration and migration) made one of its first appearances in Thrasher's (1963 [1927]) study of 1313 Chicago gangs.

Thrasher begins *The Gang* in typical Chicago School style by noting the impact on society of immigration, urbanization, rationalization (secularization), social and geographical mobility, and industrialization. Along with prosperity and progress, these forces brought about gang delinquency, particularly in the zones of transition. Thrasher notes that when institutions are weakened by rapid social change, there are two main effects. First, effective legitimate regulation disappears, leaving children and youths "free" to create their own (unconventional) forms of order. Second, weakened institutions in disorganized environments do not work effectively, which means they are not meeting basic needs. Together, these two effects set a favourable context for the emergence of delinquent gangs.

According to Thrasher, the gang begins with the play group. While play groups are a natural and spontaneous childhood phenomenon in all communities, those in organized and disorganized areas differ from each other. In organized areas, institutions are strong and the play groups are supervised and channelled into legitimate activities such as sports. In disorganized areas, however, there are fewer opportunities for the kind of supervised play that integrates the participants into conventional social worlds. Thus, the play group in this area is likely to evolve in the direction of nonconformity. Because it is "free," the unconventional playgroup is able to provide "the thrill and zest of participation in common interests, more especially corporate action, in hunting, capture, conflict, flight and escape" (Thrasher [1927] 1963:32–33). As Thrasher puts it, "Gangs represent the spontaneous effort of boys to create a society for themselves where none adequate to their needs exists" (32). What distinguishes the nonconforming play group or "gang in embryo" from the delinquent gang is the presence of "tradition, unreflective internal structure, esprit de corps, solidarity, morale, group awareness, and attachment to territory" (Thrasher [1927] 1963:32–33). What transforms the unconventional play group into the more organized, self-aware gang is conflict between the play group and the conventional social order, and between groups who battle for control of "turf" within the neighbourhood.

Thrasher related many of the differences between gangs to the degree of disorganization around them, and to the kinds of opportunities for "action" that their communities offer them. For example, an area with poorly guarded rail yards might provide the delinquent gang with the opportunity for adventurous theft, followed by contact with local criminal elements, such as the fence, who will buy what they steal. Such contacts can draw the mischievous gang into a more criminal mode.

Another example of early subcultural theory from the Chicago School was provided by Clifford Shaw and Henry McKay, who between 1929 and 1942 published a series of massive studies in which they mapped and analyzed delinquent neighbourhoods in Chicago and in many other American cities. Shaw and McKay ([1942] 1969) used data from police and juvenile court records for the years between 1900 and 1940 to produce ecological maps. They found, as expected, that rates of crime showed a regular decrease as one moved from the centre of Chicago to its periphery. They also reported that:

1. areas characterized by low economic status tend to have high population turnover, heterogeneity (many groups), and poor self-regulation;
2. zones with high juvenile delinquency also have high adult crime;
3. recidivism (relapse into criminal behaviour) is highest in areas that have a high rate of delinquency;
4. each population group, regardless of racial or ethnic composition, experiences high rates of delinquency when it occupies areas of first settlement—rates that decline following a move to more stable areas; and
5. patterns of behaviour characteristic of each zone maintain themselves even as different groups pass through them. (Communities with high delinquency rates in 1900 also had high delinquency rates in 1940, despite an almost complete transformation in ethnic composition.)

But Shaw and McKay went beyond the traditional focus of the Chicago School on the disorganized nature of the delinquency area to develop the "cultural transmission theory of delinquency." According to this theory, within a delinquency area, particular forms of vice, crime, or deviance became a "tradition" that is transmitted from one generation to the next. Youth in such neighbourhoods are not only pressured by their peers to engage in deviant activity, but also are in contact with older offenders who pass down the traditions of behaviour in the same way that language and other aspects of culture are transmitted from generation to generation (Shaw and McKay 1931:256; Fitzgerald, McLennan, and Pawson 1981:13). When they are successful in their criminal activities, older offenders often engage in extravagant displays of affluence and power, and thereby become role models for youths living in areas with limited legitimate routes to wealth and influence. The cultural transmission theory thus explains delinquency not just in terms of social disorganization, but also in terms of learning and culture.

THE CONTINUING ROLE OF SOCIAL DISORGANIZATION THEORY

By the 1950s, social disorganization was no longer the dominant explanation of socially undesirable behaviour, largely because the social forces that had driven it— rapid and uncontrolled industrialization, urbanization, and immigration—had become increasingly regulated and routine.

However, social disorganization theory continues to play a role in the explanation of deviance (Harries 1980; Esbenson and Huizinga 1990; Handelman 1995). Today's disorganization perspective work has three main directions. The first of these develops from Durkheim's position that there is such a thing as "just enough" deviance to keep a social system integrated. This can be described as the "defining deviance up or down" argument. The second thread is a continuation of the ecological concerns of the Chicago School, and the third is found in recent "network" approaches.

DEFINING DEVIANCY DOWN (OR UP)

This extension of Durkheim's work emphasizes the role of deviance in establishing the moral boundaries of society, and the role of regulators in establishing just how much deviance is recorded and processed for this purpose. The first work along this path was Kai Erikson's *Wayward Puritans* (1965), which argued that the Puritan society experienced "crime waves" at times when moral boundaries were threatened by changes in the external environment, or by development of new problems within the society. Erikson noted that the amount of crime recognized fit rather nicely with the supply of stocks and whipping posts, and was just enough to serve the needs of the society for examples of defended morality. This number seemed only loosely connected with the actual numbers of people behaving in rule-violating ways. The Puritans were defining deviancy "up" in order to meet their needs for integration and regulation. This idea has been used by Ben-Yehuda to explain the role of witchcraft, the occult, science fiction, science hoaxes, and other forms of nonconformity as means of boundary management in society (1985).

The definition theme was picked up again by U.S. Senator Daniel Patrick Moynihan (1993) who argued that in the United States, a similar process was occurring. Only this time, instead of raising the standards to produce higher crime rates, the agencies of social control were choosing *not* to notice behaviour that at other times would be regulated or punished. They were "defining deviancy down," according to Moynihan, because, by the older standards, there is more bad behaviour than would be good for society to recognize. Thus, the St. Valentine's Day Massacre of 1929 in which four gangsters killed seven gangsters was a major event, while similar and more deadly events that are now daily occurrences in many cities may not garner any news coverage. According to Moynihan, we are "getting used to" a higher level of disorder. Moynihan also notes, however, that the United States is imprisoning an increasingly higher proportion of its population, and that more and more actions are "on the books" as deviant or criminal (Moynihan 1993). What this must mean, then, is that more and more things are punishable, but that fewer of those who do them are being punished, at least officially.

In 1996, James Hawdon put a new spin on the definition theme by observing that cycles of "actual" deviance (such as the use of cocaine) are *followed* by moral panics over the deviance, only once the behaviour itself is declining (Hawdon 1996:183). Hawdon argues that the variety of behaviour that goes unchallenged in society will increase during times of social change, especially when new groups are being accepted into the mainstream. Thus, during the years of heavy immigration, industrialization, and urbanization in the United States, the use of many kinds of now-illegal drugs increased dramatically. When the period of rapid change was over, this drug use began to decline. Just at this point, however, "moral entrepreneurs" began conducting successful campaigns to "demonize" and criminalize the drug user, creating more fear of this deviance than the numbers, and the direction of the numbers, warranted. This aspect of Chicago School ideas has been picked up and developed by functionalists, (see Chapter 8) and interaction theorists (see Chapter 10).

ECOLOGICAL APPROACHES

The second modern extension of disorganization theory focuses on the ecological side of the Chicago School tradition.

Modern Canadian research, which is often done by urban specialists rather than by sociologists, has tended to support the major contentions of Chicago School theory. Here, as in the United States, "there is evidence that blighted areas contribute disproportionately to a city's problems" (Boyd and Mozersky 1975:405). Not surprisingly certain forms of subsidized or low-rental housing attract drug pushers, prostitutes, and others who take advantage of the absence of effective community controls in order to engage in deviant activities, and these people then provide role models and opportunities for the children of residents. It is also not surprising that such areas attract more of the kind of policing that results in high arrest rates and less of the kind that relies on strong police-community ties.

NETWORK APPROACHES

The third modern version of social disorganization theory, called "network theory," shares with Chicago School theory an emphasis on urban forms, only instead of ecological processes it focuses on networks of relationships. Network theory looks at such issues as the breadth, depth, and strength of local networks, whether in the context of a residential neighbourhood or a particular company or industry (Bursik 1988:536). When networks are extensive and strong, members of the community are able to supervise and regulate each other's behaviour. When a neighbourhood is well integrated, children are more likely to be socialized into nondeviant roles and occupations. Greenberg and her colleagues (1982a, 1982b, 1985) identify the following three primary dimensions of local social control:

1. *Informal surveillance*: neighbours paying attention to what others are doing, while themselves going about their affairs.
2. *Movement-governing rules*: rules that identify certain parts of the city or the neighbourhood to be avoided, largely because they are unsafe.
3. *Direct intervention*: speaking to others, asking them their business, and admonishing adults or children who are engaged in unacceptable behaviour.

When the neighbourhood suffers from a high rate of population turnover, or is characterized by the type of architectural and urban-planning design that tends to distance residents from one another, a greater proportion of community members feel alienated from their neighbours. Such people are often unwilling, or unable, to intervene effectively if they see disruptive deviant behaviour in their neighbourhood (Sampson 1986, 1987; Simcha-Fagan and Schwartz 1986). When offenders are released from prison into these disorganized neighbourhoods, they are more likely to be rearrested (Gottfredson and Taylor 1986).

SUMMARY

The original characteristics of Chicago School theory were rooted in the conditions of the time, which saw massive changes in migration, immigration, urbanization, and industrialization, along with the gradual separation of academic sociology from the more directly practical work being done by social workers and religious/political reformers.

The Chicago School emphasized an ecological metaphor for the study of social order, and developed concepts and research tactics that exposed the natural areas and zones of the city. Whether the setting was Chicago's Gold Coast or Hobohemia, Montreal's Dufferin District, Halifax's Africville, or the deviant service centre of a company town, Chicago theory traced the origins of its deviant populations to community disorganization. Deviance occurred because people were no longer held together by Old World or rural values, and had not yet developed adequate alternatives.

By the 1950s, Chicago School sociology was overshadowed by newer approaches, but it did not die out entirely. Some of its ideas were absorbed into urban subcultural theories (Fisher 1995), while others entered into the work of architects and city planners or provided a basis for social network theories. While concern over the social impacts of immigration and urbanization has lost its former prominence, the integration and regulation of communities persist as important issues in sociological approaches to deviance.

REFERENCES

Addams, Jane. (1990). *The Spirit of Youth and the City Streets*. Urbana, Ill.: University of Illinois Press.

Adler, Jeffrey S. (1994). "The Dynamite, Wreckage and Scum in Our Cities: The Social Construction of Deviance in Industrial America." *Justice Quarterly* 11(1):33-50.

Ames, Herbert Brown. ([1897] 1972). *The City Below the Hill*. Toronto: University of Toronto Press.

Anderson, Nels. ([1923] 1962). *The Hobo: The Sociology of the Homeless Man*. Chicago: University of Chicago Press.

Bantingham, Paul, and Patricia Bantingham. (1984). *Patterns in Crime*. New York: Macmillan.

Ben-Yehuda, Nachman. (1985). *Deviance and Moral Boundaries*. Chicago: University of Chicago Press.

Bogue, Donald J. (1949). *The Structure of the Metropolitan Community*. Ann Arbor, Mich.: Horace H. Rackham School of Graduate Studies, University of Michigan.

Boyd, M., and Kenneth Mozersky. (1975). "Cities: The Issue of Urbanization." In D. Forcese and S. Richer (eds.), *Issues in Canadian Society*. Scarborough, Ont.: Prentice-Hall.

Brace, Charles Loring. (1872). *The Dangerous Classes of New York*. New York: Wynkoop and Hallenbeck.

Bulmer, Martin. (1984). *The Chicago School of Sociology: Institutionalization, Diversity, and the Rise of Sociological Research*. Chicago: University of Chicago Press.

Burgess, Ernest W. (1925). "The Growth of the City." In R.E. Park, E.W. Burgess, and R.D. McKenzie (eds.), *The City*. Chicago: University of Chicago Press.

Burgess, Ernest W., and Charles Newcomb (eds.). (1931). *Census Data of the City of Chicago, 1920*. Chicago: University of Chicago Press.

Bursik, Robert J., Jr. (1988). "Social Disorganization and Theories of Crime and Delinquency: Problems and Prospects." *Criminology* 26(4:)519–55l.

Campbell, Douglas F. (1983). *Beginnings: Essays on the History of Canadian Sociology*. Port Credit, Ont.: The Scribbler's Press.

Christakes, George. (1978). *Albion W. Small*. Boston: Twayne.

Clairmont, Donald, and Dennis Magill. (1974). *Africville: The Life and Death of a Canadian Black Community*. Toronto: McClelland and Stewart.

Cohen, Lawrence E., and Marcus Felson. (1979). "Social Change and Crime Rate Trends: A Routine Activities Approach." *American Sociological Review* 44:588–608.

Deegan, Mary Jo. (1990). *Jane Addams and the Men from the Chicago School 1892–1918*. New Brunswick, N.J.: Transaction.

Downes, David, and Paul Rock. (1981). *Understanding Deviance: A Guide to the Sociology of Crime and Rule-Breaking*. Oxford: Clarendon Press.

Durkheim, Emile. ([1897] 1951). *Suicide: A Study in Sociology*. New York: Free Press.

Erikson, Kai T. (1966). *Wayward Puritans*. New York: John Wiley and Sons.

Esbensen, Finn-Aage, and David Huizinga. (1990). "Research Note: Community Structure and Drug Use: From a Social Disorganization Perspective." *Justice Quarterly* 7(4):691–709.

Fisher, Claude S. (1995). "The Subcultural Theory of Urbanism: A Twentieth Year Assessment." *American Journal of Sociology* 101(3):543–577.

Fitzgerald, Mike, Gregor McLennan, and Jennie Pawson (comps.). (1981). *Crime and Society: Readings in History and Theory*. London: Routledge and Keegan Paul.

Gill, Owen. (1977). *Luke Street: Housing Policy, Conflict and the Creation of the Delinquent Area*. New York: Holmes and Meier.

Goodspeed, Thomas W. (1928). *William Rainey Harper*. Chicago: University of Chicago Press.

Gottfredson, Stephen D., and Ralph B. Taylor. (1986). "Person-Environment Interactions in the Prediction of Recidivism." In James M. Byrne and Robert Sampson (eds.), *The Social Ecology of Crime*. New York: Springer-Verlag.

Greenberg, Stephanie, William M. Rohe, and Jay R. Williams. (1982a). "The Relationship Between Informal Social Control, Neighbourhood Crime, and Fear: A Synthesis and Assessment of Research." Paper presented at the annual meetings of the American Society of Criminology, Toronto.

———. (1982b). *Safe and Secure Neighbourhoods: Physical Characteristics and Informal Territorial Control in High and Low Crime Neighbourhoods*. Washington, D.C.: National Institute of Justice.

———. (1985). *Informal Citizen Action and Crime Prevention at the Neighborhood Level.* Washington, D.C.: National Institute of Justice.

Handelman, Stephen. (1995). *Comrade Criminal: Russia's New Mafiya.* New Haven: Yale University Press.

Harries, Keith D. (1980). *Crime and the Environment.* Springfield, Ill.: Charles C. Thomas.

Harris, Chauncey D., and Edward L. Ullman. (1945). "The Nature of Cities." *Annals of the American Academy of Political and Social Science* 242(November):7–17.

Hawdon, James E. (1996). "Cycles of Deviance: Structural Change, Moral Boundaries, and Drug Use, 1880–1900." *Sociological Spectrum* 16(2):183–207.

Helal, Adel A., and Charise T.M. Coston. (1991). "Low Crime Rates in Bahrain: Islamic Social Control—Testing the Theory of Synnomie." *International Journal of Comparative and Applied Criminal Justice* 15(1):125–144.

Hoyt, H. (1939). The *Structure and Growth of Residential Neighborhoods in American Cities.* Washington, D.C.: Government Printing House.

Hughes, Helen MacGill. (1973). "Maid of All Work or Departmental Sister-in-Law? The Faculty Wife Employed on Campus." *American Journal of Sociology* 78:5–10.

Kennedy, L.W., and D. Ford. (1990). "Routine Activities and Crime: An Analysis of Victimization in Canada." *Criminology* 28:137–152.

Laumann, Edward O., John H. Gagnon, Robert T. Michael, and Stuart Michaels. (1994). *The Social Organization of Sexuality: Sexual Practices in the United States.* Chicago: University of Chicago Press.

Madge, John. (1963). *The Origins of Scientific Sociology.* London: Tavistock.

Matthews, Fred H. (1977). *Quest for an American Sociology: Robert E. Park and the Chicago School.* Montreal and Kingston: McGill–Queens University Press.

Moynihan, Daniel Patrick. (1993). "Defining Deviancy Down." *The American Scholar* 62(1):17–20.

Orcutt, James. (1996). "Teaching in the Social Laboratory and the Mission of SSSP: Some Lessons from the Chicago School." *Social Problems* 43(3):235–245.

Park, Robert E. ([1916] 1967). "The City: Suggestions for the Investigation of Human Behavior in the Urban Environment." In Robert E. Park and Ernest W. Burgess (eds.), *The City.* Chicago: University of Chicago Press.

Pearson, G. (1975). *The Deviant Imagination.* London: Macmillan.

Pfohl, Stephen. (1985). *Images of Deviance and Social Control: A Sociological History.* New York: McGraw-Hill.

Robinson, W.S. (1950). "Ecological Correlation and the Behavior of Individuals." *American Sociological Review* 15:351–357.

Rogers, Susan M., and Charles F. Turner. (1991). "Male–Male Sexual Contact in the USA: Findings from Five Sample Surveys, 1970–1990." *Journal of Sex Research* 28 (November):491–519.

Sampson, Robert J. (1986). "Neighborhood Family Structure and the Risk of Personal Victimization." In James M. Byrne and Robert Sampson (eds.), *The Social Ecology of Crime*. New York: Springer-Verlag.

———. (1987). "Communities and Crime." In Michael Gottfredson and Travis Hirschi (eds.), *Positive Criminology*. Beverly Hills, Cal.: Sage.

Schuerman, Leo A., and Solomon Kobrin. (1983). "Crime and Urban Ecological Processes: Implications for Public Policy." Paper presented at the annual meetings of the American Society of Criminology, Denver.

———. (1986). "Community Careers in Crime." In Albert J. Reiss, Jr. and Michael Tonry (eds.), *Communities and Crime*. Chicago: University of Chicago Press.

Seeley, John R. (1959). "The Slum: Its Nature, Use and Users." *Journal of the American Institute of Planners* 25:7–14.

Shaw, Clifford R. (1930). *The Jack-Roller: A Delinquent Boy's Own Story*. Chicago: University of Chicago Press.

Shaw, Clifford R., and Henry D. McKay. (1931). *Social Factors in Juvenile Delinquency*. Vol. 2 of Report on the Causes of Crime. National Commission on Law Observance and Enforcement, Washington, D.C.: U.S. Government Printing Office.

———. ([1942] 1969). *Juvenile Delinquency and Urban Areas*. Chicago: University of Chicago Press.

Shkilnyk, Anastasia M. (1985). *A Poison Stronger than Love: The Destruction of an Ojibwa Community*. New Haven, Conn.: Yale University Press.

Shore, Marlene. (1987). *The Science of Social Redemption: McGill, the Chicago School, and the Origins of Social Research in Canada*. Toronto: University of Toronto Press.

Simcha-Fagan, Ora, and Joseph E. Schwartz. (1986). "Neighborhood and Delinquency: An Assessment of Contextual Effects." *Criminology* 24:667–704.

Stokes, Charles. (1962). "A Theory of Slums." *Land Economics* 48:187–197.

Suttles, Gerald D. (1972). *The Social Construction of Communities*. Chicago: University of Chicago Press.

Thomas, William Isaac, and Dorothy S. Thomas. (1928). *The Child in America*. New York: Knopf.

Thomas, William Isaac, and Florian Znaniecki. (1920). *The Polish Peasant in Europe and America*. Boston: Gorham Press.

Thrasher, Frederick. (1927] 1963). *The Gang*. Chicago: University of Chicago Press.

Tobias, J.J. (1972). *Nineteenth-Century Crime: Prevention and Punishment*. Newton Abbot, Devon.: David & Charles.

Zorbaugh, Harvey W. (1929). *The Gold Coast and the Slum*. Chicago: University of Chicago Press.

FUNCTIONALIST
AND STRAIN
PERSPECTIVES

By the 1950s, functionalism had become the dominant theory in North American sociology. More theoretical and less descriptive than Chicago School theory, the functionalist approach focuses on the interrelationships of parts of society with each other and with society as a whole, and looks for unsuspected and unintended linkages between the parts. At the core of functionalism is the idea that deviance (both the "real" behaviour of deviants and the image of deviance shared among people) is a natural product of the social order, and may even have positive effects on the system. Any behaviour that persists in the face of strong disapproval must be contributing in some way to the survival of the system; otherwise, the process of cultural evolution would ensure that it would die out. If the purpose of the behaviour is not obvious, the perspective claims, we must simply be more persistent in our search for the social function it is fulfilling.

In the functionalist view, rules and rule enforcement are part of the processes that hold the social system together. While they may vary widely from culture to culture and over time, rules are always related to each other and to the system as a whole. The fact that profit making may be illegal in one society (with a state-controlled market) and highly valued in another (within a capitalist system) is not arbitrary. The rules "fit" with everything else in the social order. Introducing market reform in places that are state controlled and have a black-market economy can precipitate painful changes in many other parts of the system.

STRUCTURAL FUNCTIONALISM

The mainstream functionalist approaches to deviance are emphatically structural; that is, they attempt to show that social conditions are frequently structured in such a way that they unintentionally produce deviance, just as a highway can be engineered with the unintended result that many accidents occur at particular points on it (Mann and Lee 1979). Chicago School theory blamed weak structure for *permitting* deviance to occur. Functionalists went beyond this by claiming that the structure *caused* deviance. According to the functionalist concept of *structural strain,* strain occurs when the person is not just allowed (by weak structures) to commit deviant acts, but is in fact pushed toward deviant acts by the way in which the parts of the system come together.

If, for example, medical schools produce too many doctors who are all socialized to expect to lead lives of affluence in major urban areas, the result will be strain. There will be too much competition for too few legitimate medical needs in these areas. The health system may then suffer from various kinds of medical deviance such as unnecessary surgery, extra billing, and failure to report the misuse of health cards. These problems of medical deviance are related to aspects of the system that are usually regarded as positive: competitive schooling, respect for science and medicine, the value of universal high-quality medical care, and so on. The issue here is that doctors are not just "allowed" to commit deviance by a lack of effective supervision and control in the occupation; they are also pushed toward deviance by the way in which cultural expectations and structural realities come together. The same pattern can be seen with many forms of deviance.

Often associated with functionalism is the idea of *subcultural solutions* to strain. Police officers, for example, are often placed in a situation of strain by the expectation that they will simultaneously serve, protect, and control. Keeping order, enforcing the law, and pleasing the public are not always compatible. For example, arresting someone for using drugs at a rock concert may precipitate life-threatening disorder. Similarly, maintaining order on the city's mean streets may not always be possible within the limits of official guidelines (Lee 1981). At the same time, the police have more freedom than the average person does to use (or misuse) force. The combination of repeated strain and opportunity that police officers all have in common fosters a subculture that supports behaviour some might see as brutality or corruption.

Strain-induced deviance may or may not be supported by a subculture. The medical intern who endures long hours and stressful conditions in the emergency ward experiences strain between the demands of the hospital and the demands of the body. Such strain may be resolved by the readily available solution of drug abuse. The intern, however, is much less likely than the police officer to find others in the environment who will culturally support a decision to obtain and use drugs illegally. Similarly, it has been argued that, in modern times at least, serial killers are ambitious people who have been thwarted in their drive toward acceptance in the class they aspire to join (Leyton 1986), and who perceive their victims to be typical members of the class they feel has rejected them. Although their problem (frustrated ambition) is common enough, they do not have the support of a serial killer subculture.

ORGANIC AND CYBERNETIC MODELS

The early functionalists (Herbert Spencer, Emile Durkheim, Bronislaw Malinowski, and Alfred Reginald Radcliffe-Brown) shared with disorganization theorists a view of society as a kind of superorganism. Like a physical organism, each society acts to maintain itself in its environment. According to the organic model, if change occurs in that environment, the society responds to protect itself, or even to improve its well-being. It may evolve over time through both internal development and adaptation to its surroundings. Like the human body, society has a "head" (management functions) and "circulation" (communication, defence, and delivery functions), and the relationship of each of these parts to every other part in the system is one of interdependence. Most parts perform some specialized function on behalf of the organism; those that no longer serve any purpose become vestigial and die out. In this view deviance is much like germs. We need exposure to germs to maintain our immune systems, but some deviance, like some germs, may be too much.

Later functionalists like Harvard's Talcott Parsons shifted from the organic analogy toward a more mechanistic, cybernetic model of society. In this model, society is a homeostatic, self-regulating system that (as long as it is healthy) maintains a balance (equilibrium) of its internal parts in the face of a changing environment. A thermostat is an example of a homeostatic device. It turns on heating or cooling equipment whenever the temperature rises or falls beyond a preset comfort level. Deviance is a kind of excessive "heat" in the system. It triggers a "cooling off" response (social control). When there is too little deviance, the system adjusts to create more. The relation between deviance and control is seen as an endless feedback loop in a computer-like mechanical system.

STRATEGIC ASSUMPTIONS OF FUNCTIONALISM

Functionalist thinkers use two basic strategies in their approach to deviance. The first begins with assumptions about the functional requirements of system survival. Each social system, if it is to survive, must adapt to its external environment, meet some basic goals, maintain a minimum level of integration, and replace its members over time (Parsons and Smelser 1956). Each society meets these needs in its own way. Deviance may emerge when the approved means are not quite adequate or are poorly integrated. Thus, individuals or groups may use amphetamines or cocaine in an attempt to live up to impossible standards in the workplace, or use marijuana to "get mellow" in a sometimes terribly stressful world. Such drug use may actually serve the short-term needs of a society in a state of change.

Functionalism helps us understand the ambivalence and even inconsistency of social reactions to "deviance." Our attitudes toward some kinds of behaviour change when the needs of society change. Homosexuality, for example, is less tolerated in wartime, when countries need more "cannon fodder" (manpower), and a premium is placed on procreation. In functional terms, society "naturally" responds by regulating dysfunctional deviance.

Functionalism can also explain why "cults" (nontraditional religious organizations such as the Moonies) are seen as deviant by the wider society. The recruitment of "other people's children" is a necessary means of survival for these groups, at least until they have lasted long enough for their own members to have children. This characteristic of cults, that they take young people from their families and turn them against their original faith, makes cults disreputable in the wider society, but is absolutely necessary for their long-term survival (Kanter 1972).

Box 8.1   Functionalism and the Survival of Experimental Social Systems

In comparing nineteenth-century communes that served over time with systems that did not, Kanter (1972) isolated the functional mechanisms that were characteristic only of the successful groups: continuance, cohesion, and control.

Continuance
The long-lasting groups had mechanisms to ensure that new members had a "stake" in the community. These mechanisms usually took the form of nonreturnable investments (time, money, goods), initiation rituals, or personal sacrifices such as a vow of abstinence from alcohol, meat, eggs, personal clothing, or even sex.

Functionalism and the Survival of Experimental Social Systems (cont.)

Cohesion

Belonging was secured by processes that made members renounce personal relationships that might interfere with their full commitment to the group as a whole. Relationships with outsiders, including friends and family, and even sexual intercourse between group members was regarded as a distraction that might reduce loyalty to the group as a whole. Some groups regulated sexuality by physically separating the men from the women at all times (celibacy). Others solved the same problem by introducing a policy of "free love" and punishing those who were selective. The functional equivalence of celibacy and free love might not be obvious, but it is shown by the fact that some groups experimented with both forms over the course of their existence. Cohesion was fostered by imposing a commonality of experience of group members. Systems of job rotation ensured that occupational differences would not interfere in this process. In addition, children were often raised communally, and clothing was strictly regulated to avoid distinctiveness.

Control

Commitment was also fostered by mortifying the group member's old social self and inducing a new transcendent identification with the group. Mortification was often achieved through a process of group criticism or public self-criticism. Transcendant identity was cultivated through communal religious rituals and the development of a charismatic leadership.

The characteristics of successful communal societies are the very characteristics that make most outsiders uncomfortable with "cults." Outsiders see new members giving up everything they own to the group; cutting their ties with family, friends, school, or jobs; living in places that are protected from outside intervention; engaging in unusual sexual arrangements; walking about in a liminal state of identity transformation; and treating their group's leader as a new God-on-earth. The surrounding society is inclined to interpret these characteristics as some kind of exploitative plot, rather than as the survival mechanisms of a new religion. If the new group survives long enough to produce its own children as new members who can be raised "in the faith," many of these mechanisms are no longer needed, and the group can move to a more respectable status in the wider social order.

A second basic strategy of functionalism is to look at deviance that has persisted and try to find out what effects it produces that would explain its contribution to the survival of the system. The notion that anything that persists must have a good purpose is certainly debatable, but many functionalists proceed on this basis. This strategy has radical implications, for it suggests that the deviant is wrongfully punished for behaviour that not only is induced by the system but also serves its purposes. The idea that the deviant is produced by respectable society is an uncomfortable one.

THE CENTRAL CONCEPTS OF FUNCTIONALISM

FUNCTION

The concept of function is central to functionalist theory. A part or process of the social system is functional to the extent to which it contributes to the maintenance of the system. According to Merton ([1949] 1968), "[S]ocial function refers to observable objective consequences, and not to subjective dispositions (aims, motives, purposes)" (24). What is positive for a particular system is any part or process (mechanism) that helps it survive. To say that a particular practice is functional, however, is not to say that it is a "good thing" (the treatment of deviants often helps to sustain political systems with little or no intrinsic value) nor is it even to claim that it is the best way of fulfilling the function. There are often functional alternatives (different ways of achieving the same end). For example, society can discourage deviance either by penalizing it or by rewarding other kinds of behaviour.

MANIFEST AND LATENT FUNCTIONS

In Durkheim's work, readily understood and intended functions were simply called "purposes," while the word "function" was reserved for the less obvious processes that were discoverable through a theoretical analysis of specific cases. In Merton's ([1949] 1968) version of functionalism, *manifest functions* are those with visible and comprehensible consequences, while *latent functions* are those whose consequences are less obvious and often unrecognized. Despite their hidden nature, our understanding of social life cannot progress without an appreciation of the latter type of function.

> The introduction of the concept of latent function in social research leads to conclusions which show that "social life is not as simple as it first seems." For as long as people confine themselves to *certain* conse-

quences (e.g., manifest consequences), it is comparatively simple for them to pass moral judgements upon the practice or belief in question. Moral evaluations, generally based on these manifest consequences, tend to be polarized in terms of black or white. But the perception of further (latent) consequences often complicates the picture. (Merton [1949] 1968:68 [author's italics])

An example of a latent function is provided by Jordan (1969), who notes that, although colonial slave codes were manifestly aimed at the slaves, they actually made little sense except as a means of imposing discipline on slave owners. By establishing guidelines for slave ownership, the slave codes introduced a conformity of practice that helped maintain the economic system. This example also shows the tendency of functionalism to justify behaviour that supports the system without providing an occasion or forum for questioning whether preserving the system is a worthy goal. Another example of latent function is the role of Judas in the final days of Jesus. The manifest consequences of Judas's betrayal are obvious, but it also had latent consequences that help explain the rise of Christianity and its endurance as a major religion.

Sometimes a function that is manifest at the outset of a practice gradually becomes latent. Compulsory schooling, for example, was introduced explicitly as a means of getting "trouble-making" children (whose parents were working in factories) off the streets and under control. Legislation against child labour had made street urchins a recognized social problem, just at a time when industrialists were demanding increasing numbers of workers who could read, do basic math, and be relied upon. Thus, the public education system was deliberately designed to train working-class children in the knowledge, habits, and ethics that would make them good workers within the industrial capitalist order. Over time, this manifest function has been revised: public schools now share many of the educational ideals that originated in upper class educational settings, and their original purpose has become less obvious.

DYSFUNCTION

Early functionalism tended to be Panglossian; that is, it assumed that if anything existed for a long time, there must be a good reason or purpose to it. Recognition that not everything conformed to this assumption came slowly and only partially. Robert Merton attempted to explain anomalies by introducing the concept of *dysfunction*. Dysfunction occurs when a part or process lessens the effective equilibrium of a system and contributes to stress or strain instead of the smooth operation of the whole. Dysfunctional elements, which can be manifest or latent, are analogous to serious bacterial or viral infections in the human body: they might stimulate the body's defence mechanisms and make it stronger, or they might overwhelm the defence mechanisms and weaken it (Cuzzort and King 1989:154).

Consider an example of dysfunction taken from ancient times. When the Romans conquered the Greeks, they adopted many of their cultural habits, among them the use of lead-lined pots for cooking. Food cooked in such vessels became highly lead toxic. The lower classes, who cooked in earthenware pots, were spared, but those who moved up in the system and adopted upper-class ways experienced, along with the privileged, sterility, heavy child mortality, and mental impairment, all of which were caused by the unrecognized process of lead poisoning. This situation may well have contributed to the fall of Rome (Cuzzort and King 1989:154–155).

THE FUNCTIONS OF DEVIANCE

Unlike the pathological approach, which treats deviance as "bad" and needing cure, functionalism challenges us to look for the latent positive consequences that may be an integral part of deviance. In examining prostitution, for instance, we may follow the pathologists and look for what is wrong with prostitutes, or we may consider the impact of their presence on the institutions of society and discover that, along with

---

Box 8.2   Major Positive Consequences of Deviance from the Functionalist Perspective

1. *Clarification of rules.* Deviance may cause an unknown or unclear rule to be specifically and clearly stated. Rules are often only crude indicators or general understandings about the nature of relationships. Consider the recent explosion in sexual-harassment cases. Each case compels members of the group to attempt to specify the exact nature of sexual harassment and the extent to which it should be punished. In this and other cases, conflicting interpretations of social rules and prohibitions are worked out and become precedents for similar disputes in the future, whether they take place in the court of public opinion or in a real court. Criminal prosecutions often reveal problems in the social control system. An example of this was seen in Belgium, where the deaths of children at the hands of a pedophile ring exposed not only police incompetence, but also higher

---

Major Positive Consequences of Deviance from the Functionalist Perspective (cont.)

level police/political protection for the offenders. Public reaction, including protest marches, has forced a clean-up and reorganization of police in Belgium, and also caused other European countries to examine their systems to see how well they are working.

2. *Testing of rules.* While every society needs some rules, it does not follow that all rules are good. Deviants may break rules in order to challenge their validity. The clearest example of this is the test case, in which an individual breaks a law, seeks to be convicted, and then appeals the case to the higher courts. If the law involved is ruled unconstitutional, the government will usually abandon or revise it. The test case is exemplified in Dr. Henry Morgentaler's career as a provider of illegal abortion clinics. It has been said that Morgentaler would probably have been left alone had he not deliberately made his activities as public as possible. But he wanted to change the law, not just evade it. He succeeded in doing so, although at the cost of a prison term during which he suffered a heart attack. The person who tests the rules serves as guinea pig in the determination of which way the issues will be resolved. He or she may win and be vindicated, or else lose and become another "prisoner of conscience."

3. *Alternative means of goal attainment.* Bell (1953) sees organized crime as a ladder out of the ghetto for people with few or no legitimate job opportunities. The offspring of such people will have greater access to respectable positions in the social order. In a similar vein, Merton (1949:73) argues that although the political machines that characterized local American politics were corrupt, they responded to local needs more effectively than the less corrupt, but inaccessible, parts of the political system.

4. *Safety valve.* A certain amount of deviance in each society serves as a kind of safety valve, a "time out" from the demands of full conformity. It may be disparaged or it may even be encouraged (within limits). The violence of a soccer match, the rowdiness of a hockey game, the street disorder of the Mardi Gras, or the alcoholic binge of New Year's Eve give people a break from the strains of responsibility and propriety. Rag days, charivari, and festivals are other licensed outlets for the ventilation of repressed feelings and desires.

Major Positive Consequences of Deviance from the Functionalist Perspective (cont.)

Davis ([1937] 1980) argues that prostitution also performs a safety-valve function in providing a sexual outlet for clients who might otherwise be tempted to abandon their spouses for more sexually rewarding (legitimate) relationships; from this perspective, prostitution protects the stability of the family. In a similar vein, pornography can be seen as a relatively safe alternative to seriously deviant behaviours like rape (Polsky 1969).

5. *Tension release and solidarity.* Dentler and Erikson (1959) suggest that groups characterized by high tension and stress regularly seem to find or produce at least one deviant member. In their study of Quaker work groups, they found that those in which at least one person acted, dressed, and spoke differently (and drew attention as a result) were more integrated and cohesive than those without such as person. They also concluded that the more extreme the deviant, the higher the group solidarity.

   In one air force basic training group studied by Daniels and Daniels (1964), the deviant was a protestant clergyman's son named Axel. This clumsy, bumbling, helpless, soft, off-beat person violated many of the norms of the group. Axel was always on the wrong foot, in the wrong place, or without his equipment. Since the group was treated as a whole, his failures cost the group many privileges. Axel often received cruel teasing and punishment from the group, such as being locked out without his pants, or being given a GI shower (cold water and beating with stiff brushes). But over time, the flight marchers who ran the camp singled Axel out and used him as an object of humour. Axel became linked to the officers and men through a joking relationship. He became a kind of "licensed fool." Seeing Axel do everything wrong made others feel better about the demands being placed on them. Their laughter provided a much needed release of tension. In later years, when the men gathered to talk about their military service, Axel was often remembered.

6. *Boundary maintenance.* Deviance may provoke a response that helps integrate the society (Coser 1956). If the group unites to support the value that has been violated, the value will be reinforced and the integration of the community will be increased. When the deviant can be treated as a monster or outsider, he or she becomes an external enemy around whom the rest of society can unite in opposition. The witchcraft craze, which is

Major Positive Consequences of Deviance from the Functionalist Perspective (cont.)

discussed extensively in Chapter 3, is a good illustration of this process. The persecution of witches shored up the threatened authority of the Church and at the same time gave communities a united focus for action that reinforced their beliefs and values.

7. *Scapegoating.* An almost universal phenomenon in human societies is the search for scapegoats when things go wrong. In preliterate societies, if the rain did not come, it was believed that the gods had been provoked. The offenders were sought out and ceremonially punished in a manner intended to re-establish good relations with the powers of life and death (Sagarin and Montanino 1977:56). In Hitler's Germany, it was the Jews and the "degenerates" who were blamed for social ills. Their destruction was instrumental as well as symbolic. By attacking "deviants," the authorities tried to make it appear that they were solving Germany's problems; at the same time, their actions distracted the population from considering how these problems might otherwise have been handled.

8. *Raising the value of conformity.* When the deviant is punished, the value of conformity is enhanced. By labelling people failures, rule breakers, and unworthy, we simultaneously establish ourselves, relative to them, as successful, law-abiding, and worthy. On the other hand, if deviance is not punished, people may lose much of their motivation to conform. Terrorism, white-collar crime, and political corruption are hard to control, a reality that can have demoralizing effects on the social order.

9. *Early warning system.* Deviance may serve as an early warning system for problems in the social order. For example, an outbreak of racist incidents may indicate the need for better multicultural education or for any number of other changes to the system. A high dropout rate in a particular school may warn of the need for revised classroom policy.

10. *Protection of vested interests.* Many vested interests are represented in our current patterns of establishing and treating deviance. The criminal justice and mental health systems depend for their survival on the existence of deviance. Furthermore, the pattern of finding deviance in society tends to preserve the balance of power in that most deviants are "discovered" among members of the lower class and other marginal groups. Bringing these groups under surveillance and control diverts attention

> ### Major Positive Consequences of Deviance from the Functionalist Perspective (cont.)
>
> from the actions of more powerful people. A company CEO, for example, may demand certain results, but it is the lower-level employees, not the CEO, who must cut corners legally and morally to achieve these results (or else lose their jobs). If the deviance is exposed, the CEO is rarely held responsible. Thus, exposing deviance at the lower level protects the interests of people at the higher levels, thereby helping to maintain the system.

"dysfunctions" (harmful consequences), prostitutes also bring "eufunctions" (beneficial consequences) to the system as a whole (Cohen 1966).

But what about control? Just as functionalism can reveal the positive effects of deviance, it can also reveal the negative effects of social control. Some of the ways in which control can have negative consequences are:

1. Too much regulation may reduce the learning of self-control and may stifle creative responses to new situations.

2. Regulation means giving some people power over others, and this power sometimes can be abused. For example, in 1970, the War Measures Act was used to control the "apprehended insurrection" of Quebec separatists brought about by the small radical FLQ. This legislation was used by police in various parts of the country to go after people who had absolutely nothing to do with the Quebec Crisis, such as drug addicts and teenagers. As a result of these abuses, the War Measures Act was replaced by the much more limited Emergencies Act.

3. Regulation intended to reduce one problem may lead to others. If people were forced to be granted permission before having children, the number of children growing up in "dysfunctional" families might be reduced, but a wide sector of the population, who failed to abide by the rules, would be criminalized.

4. The treatment of deviants (imprisonment, avoidance) may actually reduce their motivation to return to conformity, or even make it impossible. A criminal record is a bar to employment in many areas, and deviant status such as transsexualism or even extreme ugliness might have similar effects.

5. Pushing deviants into a space outside the respectable social world and treating them badly may actually increase their bonds with each other, helping to create deviant subcultures.

Box 8.3   How Deviance Can Contribute to Social Change

Armed with hideous neckwear, Tom Stevenson has defeated a government office dress code requiring male employees to wear ties.

"It's discriminatory," he says. "People are just as good with or without a tie."

Stevenson, 45, and three others were suspended for a day when they arrived for work, lacking neckwear, at the Windsor regional tax office in July, 1989.

Refusing to be tied down, they grieved that suspension and were vindicated last month, when a three-member arbitration board found management unfair in forcing ties on employees.

"There may have been a time, many decades ago, when a tie was a necessary part of a respectable office dress," the board ruled. "That is no longer so."

Moreover, neckwear worn by Stevenson after his suspension was so ugly that no tie at all would look better, the board concluded.

Stevenson, a draftsperson at the tax office, had protested the dress code by wearing admittedly awful ties to work.

He happened to own a collection of more than 300 ugly ties, including fish-faced, dog-depicting, flower-strewn and psychedelic neckwear samples. The collection earned a small measure of notoriety even before Stevenson tied one on for work, having won a "hideous tie" contest sponsored by a local newspaper in 1988.

A selection of horrible ties deemed acceptable by management was presented to the arbitration board as evidence that the rules didn't make sense. And the board agreed.

"We have serious doubts that an employee observed wearing those ties would present a better image to the public than one who wears no tie at all," the panel concluded.

Robert Speroni, manager at the Windsor tax office, had told the board that male employees lacking ties presented a poor and unprofessional image to the public.

According to the office dress code, ties were even to be worn beneath crew-neck sweaters, where they would be virtually invisible.

The board found that employers have the right to require ties, but only where they have evidence that workers' failure to wear ties results in a loss of corporate image.

Management's personal preference alone can't justify restrictions, the panel concluded.

Source: Leslie Papp, "Man's Awful Neckwear Had Office Boss in a Knot," *Toronto Star*, March 27, 1991. Reprinted with permission—The Toronto Star Syndicate.

Gary Marx (1993) lists many situations in which social control contributes to, or generates, rule-breaking behaviour. He argues, for example, that pre-emptive police actions, such as efforts to make a crowd move on, may actually create deviance such as resisting arrest or disorderly behaviour. He notes that police buying money for the purchase of illegal drugs not only serves the manifest function of helping catch drug dealers, but also serves latent dysfunctions in that it means more markets for drugs, more informers, and more homicides due to underworld control of informers.

DEVIANCE AT A DISTANCE: PARSONIAN FUNCTIONALISM

Talcott Parsons's American "ivory tower" version of functionalism is so abstract it often seems apolitical. Davis (1975:66) calls it "deviance at a distance" because of its focus on social patterns many levels above the participating actors. Indeed, Parsonian functionalism gives little consideration to "the disruptive, the deviant, the tension-producing, conflict-generating, and change-inducing forces" of human social life (Friedrichs 1970:145). When it does look at conflict and deviance, it tends to see them as disruptions of the social order, not, as Durkheimian sociology had done, as natural or even beneficial (Coser 1956:21).

Despite the impression it conveys of being above politics, Parsonian functionalism carries a conservative message. It maintains that any behaviour that does not contribute to meeting the needs of the social system will die out over time, as more effective social systems come into being, and implicitly suggests that speeding up this process (i.e., getting rid of deviance) might be a good thing.

Parsons (1947) argues that structural changes in the occupational system of society have affected the family in ways that tend to produce male delinquency. The modern economy takes the father out of the family for much of the day. Boys and girls both tend to be raised by the mother, so that they come to regard being "good" and acting in terms of the expectations of the reasonable adult world as a feminine trait (Parsons 1947:172). When the boys reach manhood, they reject this model, and, in the absence of a male model to guide them, tend to behave in ways that reflect this rejection. Thus, boys are more likely than girls to engage in antisocial and destructive behaviour.

In discussing how aggressive tendencies are produced within systems, Parsons (1947) suggests that some systems suppress overt aggression, creating a large reservoir of aggressive impulses that may pose problems if a "channel" like out-group hostility becomes available to them. Thus, in Parsonian terms, the Holocaust was a

product of a faulty social system that suppressed natural aggression and then channelled it against an out-group. It is the structure, not individual morality, that
explains the behaviour.

ROBERT MERTON, STRAIN THEORY, AND ANOMIE

Robert Merton developed a version of functionalism as a middle-range alternative
to the highly abstract "grand theory" of Talcott Parsons. Merton focused on
specific, delimited forms of social behaviour: deviance (1938, [1949] 1968), political criminals, the social organization of science, propaganda, mass persuasion
(1946), and so forth. He did not try to integrate these separate interests into one
overarching theory of social behaviour.

Merton is best known for his revision of the concept of anomie. To Durkheim's
concept of anomie he added the idea of strain. The result was the American version
of anomie (sometimes called anomia). According to Kornhauser (1978):

> The charm of Merton's strain model consists one-third in its apparent
> simplicity, one-third in its seeming plausibility, and one-third in its
> virtual mandate to range sociologists squarely behind the poor. (143)

On the other hand, Merton's strain theory does not challenge the desirability of
the American Dream (supposedly the source of the strain that produces deviance),
and, above all, it predicts that deviance will occur mainly among the poor. When we
deal with conflict theories in Chapter 12, we will show that there is considerable
evidence that advantaged classes commit their share (or more) of deviant acts, a
reality that is hard to explain using Merton's approach.

Anomia was the state of structural "strain" between the almost universal
cultural goals of the society and the much more restricted institutionalized means
for achieving them. Unlike Durkheim's anomie, Merton's was a condition of stress
or tension, not one of disorganization. In Merton's view, deviance was a form of
adaptation to the strain that existed between "culturally prescribed aspirations and
socially structured avenues for realizing these aspirations" (Merton [1949]
1968:188). If, for example, success is visualized as a two-storey suburban home
with two late-model cars in the driveway, and 2.2 children who will take tennis and
piano lessons and attend university, then many people in society will find themselves
structurally blocked from reaching this goal in legitimate ways. In contrast, others
will be born into families able to give them every opportunity (health, wealth,
education). The structurally advantaged will fail only if they throw the opportunity
away.

Merton's theory locates the primary cause of deviance as the socialization of individuals in all social classes to want what only those in privileged social strata can obtain by nondeviant means. Merton challenged Freud's idea that human needs are innate and incompatible with the social order. According to Merton, needs are socially created (via socialization to cultural norms). As Merton expressed it, "If the Freudian notion is a variety of the 'original sin' doctrine, then the interpretation advanced in this paper is a doctrine of 'socially derived sin'" (quoted in Cullen 1984:76). In Merton's schema, there are five alternative modes of adaptation to the means/end relationship, modes that are largely determined by the availability of means in particular parts of the social structure (see Table 8.1). These five are conformity, innovation, ritualism, retreatism, and rebellion.

Table 8.1 Merton's Theory of Anomia: Modes of Individual Adaptation

Modes	Cultural Goals	Means
1. Conformity	+	+
2. Innovation	+	−
3. Ritualism	−	+
4. Retreatism	−	−
5. Rebellion	+/−	+/−

Source: Adapted from Robert K. Merton, *Social Theory and Social Structure* (New York Free Press, 1968).

Conformity to the rules is the most likely adaptation to the strain between desirable goals and acceptable means, when the means are readily available or closely regulated (i.e., when there is little strain or few alternatives). In this view, upper-middle-class children who have caring parents are less likely to cheat than less advantaged children who have the same goals. Similarly, conformity is the most likely adaptation in a school or institution in which the competitive process is carefully supervised and offenders are given meaningful punishments.

Merton's concept of *innovation* covers behaviour such as cheating, stealing, or creative solutions. This response is to be expected when success is heavily emphasized, but much less attention is given to the means used. Students know what happens when marks are important but no supervision of testing is provided; honour systems do not work if the stakes are high. Their professors may, like Sir Cyril Burt (discussed in Chapter 5), violate the "norms of science" (cheat) when they find themselves unable, otherwise, to reach the research recognition goals they have learned to value (Broad and Wade 1982; Hackett 1994).

Similarly, athletes find themselves in situations in which winning brings fabulous wealth and prestige, losing means loss both of funding and the chance to compete again, and drug controls always lag slightly behind the most current products on the market. The findings of the Dubin Inquiry in the late 1980s, which brought Canadians a daily dose of stories about Ben Johnson, Charlie Francis, Dr. Jamie Astaphan, Angela Issajenko, and others, clearly showed that the problem of cheating in athletics is a serious and systemic one, not just the case of a few "bad apples" (Issajenko 1990; Francis and Coplan 1990). Finally, in many countries with controlled economies, legal markets do not always meet consumer needs, and many citizens "innovate" by participating in black markets. In Canada, the introduction of the GST was enough to provoke some people into joining the illegal "parallel" economy (Muncie and McLaughlin 1996). In some Western nations, this parallel economy constitutes more than one-third of the gross national product.

In Merton's view, any culture that places great emphasis on wealth, power, and prestige, but does not at the same time respect and emphasize the use of legitimate means to attain it, is likely to have many innovators. Some of these will find new and better ways of doing things, but many will simply take a criminal path.

Ritualism occurs when the means are accepted, but in a manner that is disconnected from the purpose that the means are supposed to serve. A professor at a prestigious university in Ontario once bragged at a party that he had all his lectures memorized. He had been teaching the same things in the same way for twenty years, despite the fact that his field has undergone many changes in that time. Such ritualist adaptation is favoured in institutions that pay little more than lip service to the value of what undergraduates are taught. Similarly, bureaucratic red tape is often the product of conditions that produce ritualists; forms are filled in and filed, but little is accomplished.

Retreatism occurs when the standard social goals and institutionalized means are both rejected, but no particular substitutes are developed. Unlike the innovator, the retreatist does not bother to cheat, because the goals do not seem worth the trouble. Unlike the rebel, the retreatist has no alternative agenda. Retreatist adaptation is exemplified by students who drop out of school and take up life on the streets in order to escape from the pressure to succeed academically. (Of course, not all "street kids" are there for such passive reasons) (Webber 1991). Retreatism is often associated with passive drug use and other forms of escapism (reading romance novels, vegetating in front of the TV all day). Merton has linked suicides, psychosis, some artists, and alcoholics to the retreatist mode.

Rebellion occurs when the goals and means established in the society come under attack. Minorities, for example, usually seek the kind of education that will enable them to compete for well-paid responsible jobs. In this respect, they accept the goal and the means to achieve it. At the same time, however, they may want to change what is taught (or the way it is taught), so that it accommodates their culture and their needs. They may also want to see the end of privileged access to schools and jobs. The result can be a rebellious adaptation to the strain.

Although Merton's schema is often misinterpreted as an individualistic, psychological explanation for deviance, it actually is a structural explanation of the conditions under which a significant number of individuals find the adaptations to be the best choice. He does not predict that every person who experiences strain will respond with deviant actions.

ALBERT COHEN AND STATUS FRUSTRATION

In 1955, Albert Cohen expanded on Merton's idea of structural impediments to success (1955). He explained male, lower-class delinquency by showing that there is strain between the middle-class standards of the public school system and the resources and needs that lower-class boys bring into the classroom. Gang delinquency, in Cohen's view, is a group solution to status frustration. Cohen's theory has four basic assumptions:

1. Lower-class youth tend to do poorly in school due to the use of middle-class (universalistic) standards of evaluation. This is not a question of different IQ levels or initial motivation, but a reflection of such factors as the absence of books and quiet study space in the home, and the need to be hard and tough in order to survive on the street.

2. Poor school performance leads to gang formation, as those who have been rejected by the system join forces. As well, given the negative characteristics of the disadvantaged home, lower-class youth tend to rely heavily on the peer group for guidance, and on the street as a meeting place.

3. The function of the gang is to provide an alternative status system in which its members can enjoy acceptance and success.

4. The values of the delinquent gang are triumphantly and flagrantly oppositional to those that are taught in the schools. Overall, they are nonutilitarian (objects that are stolen may be destroyed or discarded, and violence may have no rational purpose); malicious (targeting smaller, "innocent" victims, as well as other people's weak spots); and negativistic (opposed to the values of the dominant classes). They are characterized by "short-run hedonism," and by an emphasis on "autonomy of the gang." (Cohen 1955:24–31)

Figure 8.1   Strain and Subcultural Models

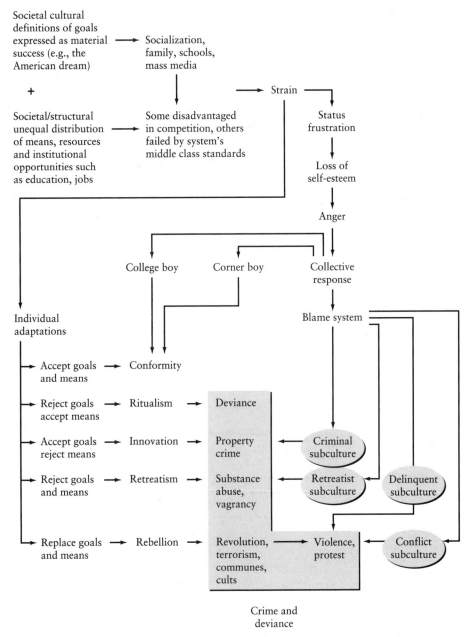

Source: Stuart Henry and Dragon Milovanovic, *Constitutive Criminology: Beyond Postmodernism.* London: Sage, p. 140. Reprinted by permission of Sage Publications.

Thus, according to Cohen, the gang does not just reject middle-class norms, it flouts them. Middle-class values such as long-range planning, preparation for gainful employment, postponement of gratification, acceptance of personal responsibility, cultivation of personableness, control of physical aggression, orientation toward success and achievement in the occupational world, and the virtual worship of possessions are rejected in favour of "free rogue" values (Cohen 1955:104).

Cohen recognizes two other options or "paths" for the lower-class male. Some may be able to overcome their disadvantaged position and compete in the universalistic status system. These youths may become "college boys" instead of delinquents. Others who are not attracted to the aggressive gang may become "corner boys" (i.e., youths who enjoy "hanging around the corner" with their friends). They make the best of their situation, and generally temporize with the middle-class world from which they will eventually seek working-class jobs (Cohen 1955:128–130).

Lending support to Cohen's theory is Elliott and Voss's (1974) investigation of the correlation between school dropouts and arrests for delinquency. In a sample of 2000 students in California, they found that delinquency peaked just before dropout and subsequently declined. (The decline was particularly notable with respect to those who found a job and got married.) This finding supports Cohen's assertion that school experiences might be a factor in delinquency.

COHEN'S THEORY APPLIED TO WOMEN

Cohen shows a fairly typical tendency, found also in later theorists work, to treat women's deviance as trivial, and men's deviance as more worthy of interest and respect. Cohen sees the delinquent boy as an admirable specimen of "rogue male" whose untrammelled masculinity has a certain "aura of glamour and romance" (Cohen 1955:140). When Cohen discusses female delinquent styles, however, he sees a different pattern. According to Cohen, lower-class girls have only one important goal, which is to have successful "relationships" and to marry well. Since these girls are, according to the theory, not bothered by such "masculine" interests as ambition, action, and mastery, they do not experience strain in the same way that boys do. Failure in school does not lead to delinquency, but failure in the dating game may. Cohen argues that the delinquent girl is mainly sexually promiscuous, and she acts this way because, for some reason, she is not able to succeed in personal relationships without "cheating" this way. Cohen provides virtually no data on this point, and actually argues that the different focal concerns of the two sexes are "so obvious" that no further analysis is necessary (Cohen 1955:142).

Box 8.4   Young and Dangerous: Native Gangs Terrorize Winnipeg

For 21 years, Sister Lesley Sarouman has been walking the same one-block stretch in north-central Winnipeg. The daily trek down Ross Avenue from her home to Rossbrook House—a refuge for street kids she helped to establish in 1976—has given the Roman Catholic nun an unfolding view of a neighborhood in social decay. The once-vibrant blue-collar residential area is now scarred by neglected and, in some cases, graffiti-covered homes. Sometimes at night she is startled by sound of gun shots or the ruckus of fights between street gangs. "In the last four years things have really changed rapidly," says the soft-spoken Sarouman. "There's a climate of fear that wasn't there before."

Streets of fear have become common in the Manitoba capital. In recent years, a growing number of street gangs, made up mostly of disillusioned and disadvantaged young natives, have staked out their turf in an escalating struggle to control criminal activity in their territory ...

With an estimated 800 youths involved in the loosely organized gangs, there is nothing subtle about their tactics. Assault, armed robbery, drive-by shootings, prostitution and murder are all part of the gang-related violence that is making parts of north-central Winnipeg seem more like the streets of East Los Angeles ...

"People come [to Winnipeg] thinking they will have a better life in the city, but they end up being trapped," says Dave Chartrand, spokesperson for the Manitoba Métis Federation. "The kids see what happened to their parents and don't see any hope for themselves." Gang activity is the most recent manifestation of that hopelessness. Since its 15-member gang unit was formed in the summer of 1995, Winnipeg police have made 440 gang-related arrests. Last year, among Winnipeg's 29 murders—up from 16 in 1995—the most grisly involved the torture and murder of three men in what police said was gang-related retribution. Ironically, the increase in gang activity comes at a time when the overall crime rate is actually falling in Winnipeg, as it has been across Canada in recent years ...

Although as many as nine gangs are thought to be operating in Winnipeg, the landscape is dominated by the Warriors and the Indian Posse. Smaller gangs, with names like Deuce, East Side Crips, and Nine-O are thought to be linked to the two larger gangs. Like farm teams, they become training grounds for kids, some as young as 10, who aspire to joining the big leagues ...

> ### Young and Dangerous: Native Gangs Terrorize Winnipeg (cont.)
>
> While many involved in gang activities have been sent to prison, gang members themselves say the flow of new recruits more than replenishes their membership. "We grow by the day—it will never stop," one member of the Indian Posse told *Maclean's*. Giving his name as Enemy Wind, he proudly displayed tattoos etched on his hands, including one that reads "Bonded by blood." Then he rolled up his sleeve to show an Indian Posse tattoo on his bicep: a clenched fist holding a pistol. That insignia, he said, is reserved for only the highest members of the Posse. His eyes hidden by sunglasses, he said that gang life is about belonging. "The gang is my family," he declared. "It always will be. I can no more leave the gang than you can leave your family ..."
>
> *Source:* From Dale Eisler, "Young and Dangerous," *Maclean's*, February 3, 1997, 24–25.

RICHARD CLOWARD, LLOYD OHLIN, AND DIFFERENTIAL OPPORTUNITY THEORY

According to Richard Cloward and Lloyd Ohlin, learning environments and opportunities are not equally distributed in the social system. A person's class, gender, race, and neighbourhood can make access to particular kinds of deviance or conformity easier or more difficult. Not only do slum children generally have less access to legitimate careers, but they also experience differential access to illegitimate careers. The neighbourhoods in which they grow up can influence whether they will be exposed to drug-trafficking careers, gangsterism, organized crime, disorganized vandalism, or none of these. Cloward and Ohlin (1960) thus extend Merton's anomia schema by introducing the concept of differential *illegitimate* opportunity.

Cloward and Ohlin's theory is intended to explain only those delinquencies that are "specifically provided and supported by delinquent subcultures" (Cloward and Ohlin 1960:9). In other words, they see delinquents as performing subcultural delinquent roles, not as expressing individual psychopathology or engaging in independent deviance (e.g., shoplifting) without the knowledge of their peers (Cloward and Ohlin 1960:9–10).

Included in Cloward and Ohlin's theory are descriptions of three kinds of delinquent subcultures typically encountered among adolescent males in lower-class
districts of large urban centres. These are the criminal, conflict, and retreatist
subcultures.

A *criminal* pattern of gang behaviour is basically an economic response to
strain. Criminal gangs seek monetary gain through crime. This pattern emerges
when there is visible, successful adult criminal activity in the neighbourhood that
allows boys to see a career path toward criminal success. Moreover, successful adult
pimps, racketeers, bookies, or numbers runners may provide not only role models
but also work opportunities for youths. The juvenile thief gains status by "pulling
off a big score" and having money to spend. The apprentice in organized crime
gains status by proving himself to be a "right guy" who can take the heat from
police and rivals. While the criminal gang breaks the law, it is not usually negativistic or disorderly. Destructive, purposeless behaviour would interfere with group
success, and is reined in, either by the gang itself or by the adult criminals with
whom the gang deals.

When the neighbourhood lacks a stable pattern of adult criminal behaviour, or
when youths do not mix with older criminals, the *conflict* form of gang behaviour
emerges. Violence between gangs becomes a way of asserting control in a disorganized environment and earning a measure of status and success in the process. The
street gang member attempts to achieve a reputation through violence and intimidation of others.

In some neighbourhoods (which may be dominated by either criminal or
conflict gangs), some youths are unable to take successful advantage of either legal
or illegal opportunities. They are "double failures" who have succeeded neither at
school nor in delinquency. These youths may form *retreatist* gangs that are dominated by escapist activities such as drug use (Cloward and Ohlin 1960:25).

Double failures are often rejects from conflict or criminal gangs. Despite this,
they may adhere to a status system that provides a sense of success. "The drug
addict wins deference for his mastery of the resources and knowledge for maintaining or increasing the esoteric experience of his 'kick'" (Cloward and Ohlin
1960:10). The "esoteric experience" that is sought may involve alcohol, marijuana,
hard drugs, sexual experimentation, dance and music, or anything else that provides
"out of this world pleasure" (Cloward and Ohlin 1960:26). Retreatist gang
members may achieve a modicum of success through peddling drugs, acting as
pimps, shoplifting, and small-time hustling.

While they recognized that delinquent subcultures were not confined to lower-
class areas or large cities, Cloward and Ohlin felt that lower-class delinquent subcul-

tures represent the most distinctive and integrated forms of organization, and that they present the most costly and difficult problems with respect to control and prevention. They shared with Albert Cohen a belief that the middle-class offender (whether in a gang or not) is more amenable to individualized forms of control or therapy, which parents or community can provide. In contrast, the lower-class gang offender cannot readily be reached by individualistic solutions. He (or the rare she) needs to be uprooted from the culture in order to be "cured."

Spergel (1964) partially tested Cloward and Ohlin's ideas. In what he called the "Racket neighbourhood," Spergel found that juvenile delinquency was linked to organized crime through such operations as loan-sharking. Youths participated at lower levels and gradually worked their way up into more "responsible" positions within the criminal organization. In this neighbourhood there was little gang conflict and little drug use. In "Slumtown," a disorganized neighbourhood that lacked an organized crime presence, fighting gangs dominated the scene. In "Haulburg," a theft neighbourhood, teens participated in burglary and joy-riding forms of car theft. There was little gang warfare and no organized property crime. Property crime was less organized than in "Slumtown." Spergel did not find a retreatist pattern in these communities.

Cloward and Ohlin's theory provided the basis for a massive antipoverty program in the 1960s, which was launched in New York City. The Mobilization for Youth Project attempted to alleviate strain in lower-class communities by improving education, creating work opportunities, and organizing for local improvements. This program unfortunately had little effect on serious delinquency. Other programs with similarly good intentions have also failed to make a significant dent in the inequalities of opportunity that differentiate the privileged classes from those of lesser status (Adler and Laufer 1995).

STRAIN THEORY REVISED: AGNEW'S GENERAL STRAIN THEORY

Beginning in the mid-1980s, Robert Agnew made popular a revised version of strain theory that includes, but also goes beyond, Merton's original formulation (Agnew 1985, 1989, 1992; Agnew and White 1992). Rather than Merton's single source of strain (the disjuncture between cultural goals and structured means to them), Agnew proposed three forms of strain. Strain occurs not only when we fail to achieve goals, but also when others take away from us something that we value (either property or respect) or when we are confronted with unpleasant circumstances. Thus Agnew's research included questions about peer group, teacher, and parent–adolescent "hassles." Agnew felt that negative circumstances alone did not translate into deviant action. Deviance would occur only when the conditions of strain were coupled with a psychological state of "negative affect" (disappointment, anger). Thus, the individual may attempt to deal with his or her feelings by instrumental, retaliatory, or escapist behaviour. Adolescent theft, violence, and drug use can be outcomes when more positive responses are not available or not chosen (Agnew 1992). At this point, the theory has mainly been tested by Agnew. Other research has modestly supported it, but has also suggested that it should be linked with social control theory, and social learning theory, rather than be developed on its own (Paternoster and Mazerolle 1994:252; Farnworth and Leiber 1989). Agnew has conceded that his theory "shares many, perhaps most, of its independent variables" with social control and learning theories, but argues that his version is superior in a variety of ways (Agnew 1995:373).

SUMMARY

Functionalism and strain theory highlight the consequences of deviance. Functionalism has been particularly fruitful in its insistence that we look beyond the manifest purpose of things by examining their latent consequences. This perspective focuses attention on behaviour that despite its deviant status is almost universal. The full meaning of such behaviour is often unrecognized by the people who condemn it. By emphasizing the conservative implications of their theories, at the expense of more radical possibilities, functionalists and strain theorists contributed to the control of deviance rather than to its liberation. Although functionalist and strain approaches can be traced back to the 1930s, they reached the height of their popularity in the 1950s. In the 1960s (despite the revival that occurred in the 1980s), they were overtaken by interaction theories, which will be discussed in Chapter 10.

REFERENCES

Adler, F., and W.S. Laufer. (1995). *The Legacy of Anomie Theory.* New Brunswick, N.J.: Transaction.

Agnew, Robert. (1985). "A Revised Strain Theory of Delinquency." *Social Forces* 64:151–167.

———. (1989). "A Longitudinal Test of the Revised Strain Theory." *Journal of Quantitative Criminology* 5:373–387.

———. (1992). "A Foundation for a General Strain Theory of Crime and Delinquency." *Criminology* 30:47–87.

———. (1994). "The Contribution of Social-Psychological Strain Theory to the Explanation of Crime and Delinquency." In *Advances in Criminological Theory*. Vol 6. New York: Transaction Books.

———. (1995). "Testing the Leading Crime Theories: An Alternative Strategy Focusing on Motivational Processes." *Journal of Research in Crime and Delinquency* 32(4):363–398.

Agnew, Robert, and Helene Raskin White. (1992). "An Empirical Test of General Strain Theory" *Criminology* 30:475–499.

Bell, Daniel. (1953). "Crime As an American Way of Life." *Antioch Review* June:131–154.

Broad, William, and Nicholas Wade. (1982). *Betrayers of the Truth: Fraud and Deceit in Science*. Oxford: Oxford University Press.

Cloward, Richard A., and Lloyd E. Ohlin. (1960). *Delinquency and Opportunity: A Theory of Delinquent Gangs*. New York: Free Press.

Cohen, Albert K. (1955). *Delinquent Boys: The Culture of the Gang*. Glencoe: Ill.: Free Press.

———. (1966). *Deviance and Control*. Englewood Cliffs, N.J.: Prentice-Hall.

Coser, Lewis A. (1956). *The Functions of Social Conflict*. New York: Free Press.

Cullen, Francis T. (1984). *Rethinking Crime and Deviance Theory: The Emergence of a Structuring Tradition*. Totowa, N.J.: Rowman and Allanheld.

Cuzzort, Raymond Paul, and E.W. King. (1989). *Twentieth-Century Social Thought*. Fort Worth: Holt Rinehart and Winston.

Daniels, Arlene K., and Richard R. Daniels. (1964). "The Social Role of the Career Fool." *Psychiatry* 27(August):219–229.

Davis, Kingsley. ([1937] 1980). "The Sociology of Prostitution." In S.H. Traub and C.B. Little (eds.), *Theories of Deviance*. Itasca, Ill.: F.E. Peacock.

Davis, Nanette J. (1975). *Sociological Constructions of Deviance: Perspectives and Issues in the Field*. Dubuque, Iowa: William C. Brown.

Dentler, Robert A., and Kai T. Erikson. (1959). "The Functions of Deviance in Groups." *Social Problems* 7:98–107.

Elliott, Delbert, and Harwin L. Voss. (1974). *Delinquency and Dropout*. Lexington, Mass.: D.C. Heath.

Farnworth, Margaret, and Michael J. Leiber. (1989). "Strain Theory Revisited. Economic Goals, Educational Means, and Delinquency." *American Sociological Review* 54:263–274.

Francis, Charlie, and Jeff Coplon. (1990). *Speed Trap*. Toronto: Lester and Orpen Dennys.

Friedrichs, Robert W. (1970). *A Sociology of Sociology*. New York: Free Press.

Hackett, Edward J. (1994). "A Social Control Perspective on Scientific Misconduct." *Journal of Higher Education* 65:242–260.

Henry, Stuart, and Dragan Milovanovic. (1996). *Constitutive Criminology: Beyond Postmodernism*. London: Sage.

Issajenko, Angela. (1990). *Running Risks*. Toronto: Macmillan Canada.

Jordan, Winthrop. (1969). *White Over Black*. Chapel Hill: University of North Carolina Press.

Kanter, Rosabeth. (1972). *Commitment and Community: Communes and Utopias in Sociological Perspective*. Cambridge, Mass.: Harvard University Press.

Kornhauser, Ruth. (1978). *The Social Sources of Delinquency: An Appraisal of Analytic Models*. Chicago: University of Chicago Press.

Lee, John Alan. (1981). "Some Structural Aspects of Police Deviance in Relations with Minority Groups." In Clifford D. Shearing (ed.), *Organizational Police Deviance*. Toronto: Butterworths.

Leyton, E. (1986). *Hunting Humans: The Rise of the Modern Multiple Murderer*. Toronto: McClelland and Stewart.

Mann, Edward, and John Alan Lee. (1979). *RCMP vs. The People: Inside Canada's Security Service*. Don Mills, Ont.: General Publishing.

Marx, Gary T. (1993). "Ironies of Social Control: Authorities as Contributors of Deviance through Escalation, Nonenforcement and Covert Facilitation." In Delos H. Kelly (ed.), *Deviant Behavior: A Text Reader in the Sociology of Deviance*. 4th ed. New York: St. Martin's Press.

Merton, Robert K. (1938). "Social Structure and Anomie." *American Sociological Review* 3:672-682.

———. (1946). *Mass Persuasion: The Social Psychology of a War Bond Drive*. New York: Harper and Row.

———. ([1949] 1968). *Social Theory and Social Structure*. New York: Free Press.

———. (1973). *The Sociology of Science: Theoretical and Empirical Investigations*. Chicago: University of Chicago Press.

Muncie, John, and Eugene McLaughlin (eds.). (1996). *The Problem of Crime*. London: Sage and Open University Press, pp. 38–40; 242.

Parsons, Talcott. (1947). "Certain Primary Sources and Patterns of Aggression in the Social Structure of the Western World." *Psychiatry* 10(May):167–181.

Parsons, Talcott, and Neil Smelser. (1956). *Economy and Society*. New York: Free Press.

Paternoster, Raymond. (1994). "General Strain Theory and Delinquency: A Replication and Extension." *Journal of Research in Crime and Delinquency* 31(3):235–263.

Polsky, Ned. (1969). *Hustlers, Beats and Others*. New York: Doubleday.

Rokeach, M. (1974). "Some Reflections About the Place of Values in Canadian Social Science." In T. Guinsberg and G. Reuber (eds.), *Perspectives on the Social Sciences in Canada*. Toronto: University of Toronto Press.

Sagarin, Edward, and Fred Montanino. (1977). *Deviants: Voluntary Actors in a Hostile World*. Glenview, Ill.: Scott Foresman.

Smelser, Neil J., and R. Stephen Warner. (1976). *Sociological Theory: Historical and Formal*. Morristown, N.J.: Silver Burdett.

Spergel, Irving. (1964). *Racketville, Slumtown, and Haulberg.* Chicago: University of Chicago Press.

Tepperman, Lorne. (1977). *Crime Control: The Urge Toward Authority.* Toronto: McGraw-Hill Ryerson.

Webber, Marlene. (1991). *Street Kids: The Tragedy of Canada's Runaways.* Toronto: University of Toronto Press.

SUBCULTURAL AND SOCIAL LEARNING THEORIES OF DEVIANCE

This chapter examines theories that explain deviance as behaviour or ideas that are produced by subcultures and transmitted by learning. Some of these theories focus on the characteristics that make particular subcultures more likely than others to produce deviance. Such theories "blame" deviance on the beliefs and patterns of the subculture, whether it is an ethnic, occupational, leisure, age-group, or class subculture. Other theories within the same paradigm focus on the process of learning, arguing that deviance is learned behaviour (not biological or psychopathic). Most of these theories take their lead from the work of Edwin Sutherland.

SUBCULTURES

Tyler (1871) defines culture as "that complex whole which includes knowledge, belief, art, morals, law, custom and many and any other capabilities and habits acquired by man as a member of society"(10). Essentially, culture is the composite of our learned ways of thinking and behaving. While some cultures are dominant, with enough power to impose their norms and values on the majority of people in a society, others are subcultures, which co-exist with but differ from the mainstream.

Whether they have resulted from a collective resolution of strain, are simply a product of differential history, or are defensive formations, subcultures often involve values and norms (outlined below) that are deviant from the perspective of the wider culture.

1. *Argot.* The subculture is frequently characterized by the use of an insider language. This is particularly true if the subculture is partly ethnic and/or an oppositional subculture such as that described in Alfred Cohen's lower-class delinquency theory (see Chapter 8), but also applies to such mixed groups as the computer subculture, which includes "nerds," "cyberpunks," "hackers," and "hacker-trackers," some of whom are rebels (Sterling 1992). There have been many dictionaries of criminal and drug-user argots (Partridge 1961; Abel 1984; De Sola 1982). The invention of words unique to the group is both a sign of insider status and a way of keeping unfriendly outsiders from knowing the group's business.

2. *Vocabularies of motive.* The subculture may include justifications and excuses for behaviour that serve to neutralize the demands of the dominant culture. The delinquent gang member often sees gang behaviour as brave, heroic, and honourable. The criminal in a white-collar conspiracy may believe that government regulations are ill-advised and not worthy of compliance. The "poacher" uses a vocabulary that justifies the "folk crime" and leaves him (or her) with a sense of being an accepted insider (Forsyth and Marckese 1993).

3. Subcultures are often marked by *distinctive clothing and body language.* The gay community in the 1970s used an elaborate code of signals. Colour-coded handkerchiefs placed in the left or right pocket served, as would an argot, to communicate one's sexual preferences to insiders without attracting the attention of hostile authorities (Miller 1993:260). When these markers are assimilated by the fashion industry (and its heterosexual clientele) new ones take their place.

4. Subcultures may be characterized by *beliefs and norms* that diverge from the mainstream. But, as in the mainstream, there may be considerable variation within a particular subculture. It would be incorrect to see every member of a subculture, even a cult-like one, as a mindless follower of its dictates. Culture is one among many factors that affect how people interpret their worlds and determine how they will behave.

5. Subcultures are developed through repeated contacts and maintained in *mutually supporting networks.* It is difficult to "cure" a deviant whose deviance derives from participation in a subcultural group, since the punishment will most likely make the deviant even more dependent on the group for the satisfaction of physical, material, and psychological needs. The behaviour is not likely to change unless the group changes or the individual leaves it.

BLAMING SUBCULTURES

ETHNIC AND RACIAL SUBCULTURES

Real cultural differences, say, in drinking patterns, may increase the likelihood that particular groups will get into trouble for drunk driving or end up in detoxification centres (Greeley, McCready, and Thiesen 1980; Zeibold and Mongeon 1982). Real differences need to be recognized by authorities, but not allowed to prevent awareness that there are limits to cultural explanations. Thus, while a particular group may have a higher rate of drug abuse than another, it is probable that most members of that group do not use drugs. Policies requiring this one group (but not others) to take urine tests would not only do little to control this kind of deviance, it would also feed public prejudice against the group. Police in particular need to be aware of how subcultural differences will affect police-citizen interaction (Cryderman and O'Toole 1986).

Box 9.1   The Case of Donald Marshall

Racial and ethnic stereotypes have helped to convict innocent persons, and to impede exposure and correction of the injustice. Nowhere is this better illustrated than in the case of Donald Marshall (Harris 1986). Marshall, a 17-year-old Micmac, was accused of the 1971 fatal stabbing of a black youth named Sandy Seale. As a result of grossly improper police procedures (both in mishandling the investigation and in pressuring witnesses), Marshall was convicted of murder and sentenced to life imprisonment.

After he had served more than a decade in prison, Marshall was declared not guilty, and another man, Roy Ebsary, was charged and convicted of manslaughter in the death of Sandy Seale.

A royal commission of inquiry into Marshall's case found that not only had a serious miscarriage of justice taken place with respect to Marshall as an individual, but that racism (the belief that Micmacs were less valuable than whites, and more prone to criminal activity) had tainted the process up to the highest level. The commission concluded that police conduct in the case had been "inadequate, incompetent, and unprofessional," and found fault with the prosecution, the defence, the judge, and the judges of the appeal court for having dealt with Marshall in a manner that was not consonant with his right to equal justice before the law.

The Case of Donald Marshall (Cont.)

While in prison, Marshall had adapted to the brutal inmate code, with its subculture of drugs, alcohol, and intimidation. Upon his release, he had great difficulty returning to "ordinary" life.

Not only are some minorities more likely to be accused of crime, but they are also more likely to be *victims* of crime. This was exemplified in the case of Helen Betty Osborne, a schoolgirl who, in 1971, was raped and killed by a group of whites in northern Manitoba. Not only had the attitudes of whites toward aboriginals led to her selection as a victim, but after her death the same attitudes, which were shared by others in the community, protected the killers for sixteen years. Even then, only one of the participants was convicted. (Priest 1990)

Stereotypes exaggerate cultural differences and treat whole groups as deviant. Over time, various groups in Canada have been targeted in this way for their *assumed* predilections for certain forms of deviance. Among these groups have been the Chinese (targeted for opium use and gambling); the Amish, Hutterites, German-speaking Jews, Japanese, and Italians (as wartime enemy aliens and spies); Italians (organized crime); Portuguese (immigration scams); French Canadians (organized crime and terrorism); the Irish (alcoholism, petty crime, and terrorism); native peoples (alcoholism, family violence, and crime); Sikhs and Armenians (terrorism); and Doukhobors (arson, nudity, and terrorism). More recently, media attention has been given to Asian organized crime. In each case, the stereotypes are poor representations of the real behaviour of most members of the group. Furthermore, such stereotypes divert attention from the wrongdoings of people who are not part of the targeted group, and make it harder for those who have been targeted to obtain a fair hearing.

YOUTH SUBCULTURES

Youth subcultures may arise out of strain or simply out of the gathering together and segregation of large numbers of young people in schools and leisure activities. In Western societies, these subcultures share three common characteristics: (1) they are based on *leisure* rather than on work or family; (2) they are organized around the *peer group* rather than around individual friends, family, or ethnic groups; and (3) they are focused more on *style* than on political or social ideology (Frith 1984). The youth subculture is divided by variations that are based on gender, class, ethnicity, nationality, region, location in the social structure, and opportunity in the environment. Brake (1985:23) divides youth cultures into four groups:

1. *Respectable youth* may dress according to youth fashions, but may avoid involvement in divergent lifestyles. "Straight" (conformist) youth are a negative reference group for those involved in deviant subcultures.

2. *Delinquent youth* have been depicted in the literature as being primarily working class, but recent information shows that the middle class also produces members of this group. Adolescent males are involved in theft, violence, or vandalism, while females tend to be involved in prostitution or runaway behaviour. More recently, the phenomenon of gang graffiti, especially "tagging" and "piecing," has caught the attention of many writers (Krauss 1996; Ferrell 1993; Lachmann 1988). Tagging is the writing of a stylized version of the individual's subcultural nickname or "tag." It may also be the "tag" of the crew to which the individual belongs. Piecing is the painting of large murals on walls (Ferrell 1993:74–77).

3. *Cultural rebels* are members of a largely middle-class group that emulates the older "bohemian" tradition of living on the edge of the artistic community, using soft drugs, and embracing nonmaterialistic values.

4. *Politically militant youth* represent a wide variety of political viewpoints, ranging from the left (Greenpeace) to the far right (neo-Nazism).

Cross-cultural influences strongly affect youth subcultures. A subcultural element that is a solution to a problem in one country or area may be adopted as a fashion statement in another. Consider the differences between English and Canadian "punk" subcultures. In England, punk subculture appears to result from strain in the educational and employment systems. Educational "streaming" channels some young people toward boring, oversupervised, and poorly paid occupations (Brake 1985:62). Not surprisingly, some of these "deselected" youth are alienated from the mainstream. When they come together in the school system, they develop defiant, provoking subcultures that attract other alienated individuals. Punk fashion and behaviour can be seen at least in part as a statement: "You are treating us like garbage, so we will dramatize our status by wearing garbage."

In contrast, punk in Canada serves mainly as a fashion that links young people with similar interests. While it is hardly pro-establishment, it does not make a weighty political statement. Brake (1985:144–162) argues that the less clear-cut social-class delineation of youth status in Canada (when compared with status lines in Britain and income disparities in the United States) has made its youth subcultural forms more a matter of style and shared activities than a collective solution to status problems. It is not clear, though, why youth status deprivation in England produces a punk culture; meanwhile, in the United States, similar "deselection" conditions produce "street elite" fighting gangs (Anderson 1994; Katz 1988). Brake's work does not look ahead to forecast such newer phenomena as "slackers," skateboarders, vamps and riot girls, or computer hackers.

OCCUPATIONAL SUBCULTURES

Deviant occupations such as prostitution, thieving, gambling, and drug trafficking all develop their own subcultures, which are in part a reaction to the dominant culture and in part an expression of common problems and experiences that cannot be shared with "straight" outsiders. Prostitutes, for example, may, within their subculture, see their role as equal or even superior to that of women who marry for money and security. In this subculture, prostitution may be justified as a kind of social or psychotherapeutic service for men who might otherwise resort to rape or leave a string of broken homes in their search for sexual experience. It is more likely, however, that prostitutes see their work simply as a way of making money. From the subcultural perspective, it performs a more honest and valuable function than do many legal occupations. Prostitutes' argot calls customers "johns" and work "turning tricks." This subcultural argot often overlaps with the language of the drug user and the criminal underworld, a fact that reflects the overlapping of "disreputable" worlds.

Even within "respectable" occupations, subcultures may emerge and express points of view that would shock the average outsider. The jokes that doctors, police officers, and lawyers tell each other often reflect a "them/us" dichotomy. The root of the subculture is common experience that cannot be shared with outsiders. The doctor or police officer knows that keeping up-to-date professionally or going by the book is not always possible. Outsiders cannot be trusted with evidence of this, however. Professionals may even protect colleagues whose behaviour is dangerous or unethical because they, too, feel vulnerable to outsiders' misunderstandings.

Nonprofessionals too may develop subcultures in which deviance is excused or justified. In the aftermath of a serious railway accident in Western Canada, an inquiry revealed that employees on the trains had been putting in extraordinarily long hours and had adapted to the stress and fatigue by changing the safety signal system to allow themselves to sleep on the job. The inquiry placed much of the blame for the accident on a railroad culture that supported such risky behaviour.

Mars (1982) provides a British perspective on the deviance of workers. He divides occupations into "hawk," "donkey," "wolfpack," and "vulture" types, each of which has a distinctive ideology, set of attitudes, and view of the world. Hawks are found in occupations that emphasize individuality, corner-cutting autonomy, competition, innovation, and control over others. These types are found among business managers (entrepreneurs), academics, professionals, journalists, owner-taxi drivers, waiters, and fairground barkers. Donkeys are found in jobs characterized by isolation and subordination (e.g., supermarket cashier). Their deviance is likely to take the form of excessive sickness and absenteeism, cheating people (or the company) at the cash register, or sabotage of equipment. Wolves are found mainly in more traditional working-class occupations (e.g., mining), where the work is organized into teams. Teamwork is vital to success and security, and the individual who refuses to participate in group pilfering may not survive in the job. Vultures are found among travelling sales representatives, driver-deliverers (couriers), and others who have considerable freedom and discretion during the workday. An example of a vulture "fiddle" is the practice of "dropping short" (giving less gas to the customer than was ordered) and selling the surplus privately, often to thieves who require the gas to power the equipment they use to cut up stolen cars.

Mars emphasizes that the deviance associated with each work type is not the anarchic behaviour of "bad apple" individuals, but rather behaviour that is enforced by the work groups themselves. A worker who steals too much, thereby endangering his or her colleagues in deviance, will provoke the enmity of the group.

LOWER-CLASS SUBCULTURES

Walter Miller (1958) argues that male juvenile gangs are simply a by-product of the lower class's core culture. Unlike the strain theorists discussed in Chapter 8, Miller does not see the delinquent subculture as an oppositional response to strain. He argues that the lower-class culture is unique in boasting a "distinctive tradition many centuries old with an integrity of its own" (19) and goes on to characterize this distinctive tradition by addressing six focal concerns: trouble, toughness, smartness, excitement, fate, and autonomy.

1. *Trouble.* Individuals in the lower-class milieu are evaluated in terms of their actual and potential involvement in troublemaking activity. The subcultural values surrounding this kind of activity are ambivalent. Being able to handle oneself in a fight or a tight situation lends prestige, but getting caught and having to "pay" is attributed to foolishness and incompetence. Thus, rule-violating behaviour may or may not be respected, and may, therefore, either be sought or avoided. Other aspects of the lower-class culture favour involvement in activities such as fighting, drinking, and sexual risk taking, which may lend themselves to the creation of "trouble."

2. *Toughness.* In Miller's view, the lower class assigns great importance to physical prowess, skill, fearlessness, and daring. The lower-class male wants to be

seen as emphatically masculine. While sentimentality may be given a limited place (as exemplified by the stereotypical heart-shaped tattoo encircling the word "mother"), the culture generally rejects weakness, ineptitude, effeminacy, caution, and overt emotionality. The maintenance of the macho image may involve seemingly irrational violence or intimidation of others (Katz 1988:218). In this culture, women are treated as objects of conquest.

3. *Smartness.* The kind of smartness valued by the lower-class culture is not academic intelligence but rather "street smarts," which includes the ability to control and manipulate others; to gain advantage through instinct, knowledge, and strategy; to avoid being outsmarted or shown up by others; and to achieve wealth without working hard for it. The culture rejects the overly trusting person, as well as the "drudge," who can only make money through uninteresting, demanding work.

4. *Excitement.* The fact that most lower-class work is exhausting, repetitive, and boring places a premium on thrill, risk taking, change, and action. This may result in run-ins with police or high-risk/high-reward projects involving theft.

5. *Fate.* In contrast to the middle-class emphasis on planning for the future, members of the lower-class are more likely to see the future as a matter of fortune or luck—a reflection of their relative lack of socioeconomic opportunity.

6. *Autonomy.* Members of the lower-class subculture express ambivalent feelings toward autonomy. The omnipresent desire to say "take this job and shove it" is counterbalanced by the fact that lower-class males often choose to work in authoritarian environments such as the army. The kind of autonomy that is most respected is a personal one, in which self-discipline is rejected in favour of super-ordinate discipline. Lower-class males associate being externally controlled with being cared for, and frequently test authority in order to see whether it is firm.

When lower-class youths form delinquent gangs, the focal concerns discussed above become part of their subculture. In the gang milieu, however, two additional focal concerns appear. The first of these is *belonging* (concern about maintaining group membership in good standing), and the second is *status* (concern about being respected).

Edward C. Banfield and *The Unheavenly City*

In the early 1970s, Edward C. Banfield (1970) raised a storm of controversy with his book *The Unheavenly City: The Nature and Future of Our Urban Crisis*, which appeared to blame race and lower class culture for crime and other social ills. At seminars and symposia his ideas were hotly debated, he was sometimes prevented from speaking by mobs of protesters, and reviews critical of the book were numerous (Marmor 1972). Even though the book was thoroughly revised in 1974 to meet the criticism of its racism, the new version still appeared to blame crime and squalor on the culture of the lower classes and marginalized racial groups. It expresses considerable pessimism about the possibility of changing that culture by improving opportunities, raising welfare payments, improving schools, or providing more police (Banfield 1974:234–235).

Banfield argues that some people will be chronically unemployed (because they don't want a boring job), will turn new housing into slums (because they have no respect for property), will graduate functionally illiterate students or will result in more dropouts (because they can absorb schooling but not "education"), and will maintain high levels of violent crime and disorder whether police are present or not. According to Banfield,

> The serious problems of the city all exist in two forms—a normal-class and a lower-class form—which are fundamentally different from each other. In its normal-class form, the unemployment problem, for example, consists mainly of young people who are just entering the labour market and who must make a certain number of trials and errors before finding suitable jobs; in its lower-class form, it consists of people who prefer the "action" of the street to any steady job. (235)

At the root of the differences between normal- and lower-class forms is "an outlook and style of life which is radically present-oriented and which therefore attaches no value to work, sacrifice, self-improvement, or service to family, friends or community" (235).

Banfield makes use of the work of sociologists from many different perspectives to create this crime-ridden image of the unreformable, pernicious, lower-class culture. For example, he speaks of the characteristics of the youth subculture described by strain theorists, but denies the strain theory explanation for them. He also quotes Alvin Gouldner (1963:175) to the effect that many lower-class men cannot be lured "away from a life of irresponsibility, sensuality, and free-wheeling aggression," because they do not consider the offer of three square meals a day and respectability to be attractive enough to be worth giving up promiscuous sex, freely expressed aggression, and wild spontaneity. Gouldner, however, does not explain the source of this behaviour, when it occurs, as coming from lower-class culture.

Since Banfield locates many social problems in the lower class, he devotes considerable effort to estimating whether that class is growing or shrinking. He reveals his attitude to this class when he discusses the lower-class woman who cannot or will not plan ahead, who regards pregnancy (and everything else) as something that "happens to" one if one is "unlucky," who is not much troubled at the prospect of having a baby whose life chances will be poor, who may be incapable of following simple directions ("take a blue pill each day until they are all gone and then take the red ones") and who in all likelihood must adapt herself to the demands of a man who, if he has any interest in the matter at all, wants to claim "credit" by getting her pregnant (without, of course, assuming responsibility for her or the child afterward). (Banfield 1974:242)

Thus, in Banfield's view, the dangerous class is reproducing itself at a faster rate than the "normal classes." The policy implications of this inaccurate image of the causes of social problems created an outcry—from the public and from the academics—against Banfield's work.

THE SUBCULTURE OF VIOLENCE

Another variant of the subcultural argument is found in Wolfgang (1958) and Wolfgang and Ferracuti (1967), who argue that rates of violent crime, particularly homicide, will be high in regions where little value is given to human life, and where the subculture sees many kinds of behaviour as requiring a violent response. Wolfgang (1958) uses this interpretation to explain a continuing pattern that shows higher rates of homicide among visible minorities than among whites. Wolfgang and Ferracuti (1967) expand the theory to account for other high-crime (homicide) areas, including Colombia, South America, and Sardinia, Italy. Other observers regard violence not as an inherent subcultural value but rather as a conditioned response: people who have experienced violence (war, oppression) learn to be violent (Silberman 1978).

The subculture of violence approach has also been applied to particular sports. Colburn (1986) suggests that fistfights in hockey, which may sometimes constitute illegal violence, are in fact a part of cultural understandings that are shared by the players. Fights can be social rituals that express a subcultural version of honour, fairness, and respect for the opponent. The fight may be defined as "good" or "dirty" depending on the extent to which it conforms to subcultural norms that bear little relation to either the formal regulations of the game or the Criminal Code of Canada (Smith 1975; Vaz 1972). Similar observations have been made with respect to fan-generated violence at soccer matches, rock concerts, and other emotionally charged events.

CANADIAN CULTURE VERSUS U.S. CULTURE

The United States and Canada differ substantially in their rates of violent crime and other forms of deviance; for example, the average number of adults in prison per 100,000 population for Canada changed from 81.1 to 92.1 between 1980 and 1990; for the United States, the rate for the same period changed from 140.2 to 310.1 (Mihorean and Lipinski 1992). Such differences have been attributed to deeply entrenched cultural disparities that have their roots in both history and economy. Historically, Canada was a counterrevolutionary society. Its traditions have tended to reinforce respect for institutional forms of authority, unlike the United States which came into being as a result of rebellion against such authorities. The U.S. constitution guarantees to each *individual* the inalienable right to life, liberty, and the pursuit of happiness, as well as the right to bear arms. The Canadian constitution, in contrast, promises peace, order, and good government, and qualifies all individual rights with the *collective* adjective "reasonable." Individuals can have all the rights they need, as long as they are reasonable with respect to the rights of the whole.

A good deal of Canada's economic history is the history of enterprises that required heavy capitalization and thus encouraged collective rather than individual endeavours. Major American industries were often initiated by robber barons who bent many rules on their way to fame and fortune (Josephson 1962). While Canada's early settlements had their problems, the Canadian frontier was characterized by far less individual or vigilante violence in the resolution of social conflict than was the American frontier. Canadians have also shown a far greater tolerance of administrative abuses of power in the name of "the greater good" (Friedenberg 1980).

The relationship between the population and the police has been quite different in Canada than in the United States. In Canada, police presence generally preceded rather than followed the path of settlement, whereas the reverse was true of the United States. In the Yukon, for example, American miners dealt out justice through extralegal "miners courts," while Canadians in virtually the same area, and under the same conditions, relied on the North West Mounted Police (Hatch 1991:27). Canada is distinctive in having a police officer (the red-coated "Mountie") as a national symbol.

THE TRANSMISSION OF CULTURE: LEARNING THEORIES

EDWIN SUTHERLAND AND DIFFERENTIAL ASSOCIATION

Edwin Sutherland (1883–1950) began his professional career at the University of Chicago, where he did his doctoral thesis on unemployment, using the mildly reformist approach characteristic of Chicago School work. By 1934, however, a new approach was emerging, which did not reach full expression as the "theory of differential association" until 1947. Sutherland concentrated on violations of criminal and administrative laws. His followers, however, have extended his ideas to wider contexts of rule violation such as drug abuse, homosexuality, prostitution, aggression, suicide, and mental illness.

Sutherland used the concept of *differential association* to explain why some people become criminals while others do not. What is differentially associated, however, is not people but definitions. Definitions are normative meanings that are assigned to behaviour. They define an action or pattern of action as right or wrong (Akers 1985:49). Definitions may be favourable to actions that violate the laws (DFVL) or unfavourable to violation of the law (DUFVL).

Most of us are exposed to both kinds of definitions. We see people praising and practising honesty, fairness, and good work; we also see people justifying all sorts of wrongdoing and behaving dishonestly and unfairly. We see some people pay for their movie tickets and others sneak in. We hear definitions about the appalling physical consequences of drug use (not to mention the legal consequences) and we hear definitions that underline the ecstasy of a drug high and the right to experiment. We see the advantages of getting along with authorities, but we also respect people who stand up for themselves and their chosen way of life.

Sutherland presented his theory of differential association in a series of nine propositions that have strong associations with the behavioural psychology of learning, specifically vis-a-vis operant conditioning (see Chapter 6). Taken at face value, this suggests that people are merely reflections of the messages they receive from their intimate social groups. These nine propositions are:

1. *Criminal behaviour is learned.* While this statement in itself may not be very striking, Sutherland uses it to negate all other explanations, whether biological or psychological. Every Oliver Twist needs his Fagan, which is to say every criminal needs teachers. Without this influence, an individual will not become a criminal.

2. *An individual learns criminality through interaction and communication with others.* Criminality is not learned from reading trashy novels or watching violence on television, *unless* the reading or viewing is backed up by interaction with people who support its messages. A movie about gang violence will not precipitate more gang violence unless there is peer group pressure to follow the model it provides. The communication does not have to be verbal or a matter of conscious teaching. Our parents may not directly condone cheating on income tax, avoiding customs duties, or speeding, but we may get these messages by the way they talk about these subjects. If we grow up in a family in which alcohol use is praised, we are far more likely to think that alcohol is beneficial than if we grow up in one in which it is used only for ceremonial occasions or not at all (Brown, Creamer, and Stetson 1987; Wilson 1988).

Figure 9.1   Differential Association: Ideas that Discourage or Justify Deviance

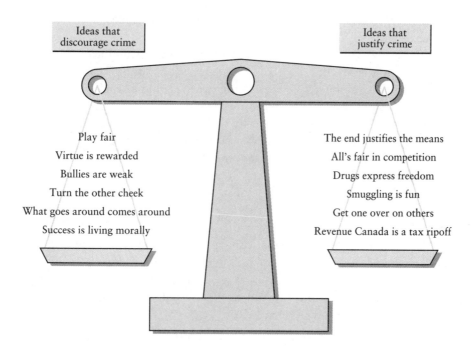

Source: Adapted from E. Sutherland and Donald Cressey, *Criminology,* 10th ed, Lippincott-Ravin Publishers, Philadelphia.

Box 9.2   Learning Theories Tend to Support the Idea of Censorship: Waiting for *Crash*

Ever since it was launched at the Cannes International Film Festival last May, leaving an audience of the world's most jaded filmgoers dazed and confused, David Cronenberg's *Crash* has been on a collision course with controversy. Splitting the jury at Cannes, it came away with an unprecedented prize for "audacity, originality, and daring." *Crash*, a tale of characters who get their sexual kicks from car accidents, went on to become a box-office smash last summer in France. It has also made an impressive dent in Canada, racking up $1.3 million in damage at the box office in just one month. But in the United States, *Crash* appears to have hit a serious roadblock in the form of media mogul Ted Turner.

Cronenberg told *Maclean's* last week that Turner saw the film and was so outraged by it that he halted the American release ... Cronenberg finally talked to a New Line executive who, the director says, privately confirmed that Turner's outraged response to *Crash* was the reason for the delay ... Cronenberg recalls "He said Turner was morally offended and worried about copycat incidents."

The notion that viewers might get behind the wheel and act out *Crash* scenarios on the open road strikes Cronenberg as absurd. "I can't imagine what Turner is thinking," he says. "It he worried that people are going to masturbate in their cars and smash into each other? Or that they are going to take long, lingering car washes with their girlfriends ... or *what*? ...

Crash is not the only Canadian movie that has run into trouble with the American rating system. Last year, the Motion Picture Association of America, the ratings umpire, asked Toronto director Patricia Rozema to make cuts to her lesbian romance, *When Night is Falling*, to avoid the NC-17 brand [rating]. "If it were a heterosexual love story, they wouldn't have thought twice about it," says Rozema ...

The moral context for sexual content carries significant weight in the eyes of the MPAA, according to Rozema. "Even *Basic Instinct* could be tolerated to a greater degree because it was a cautionary tale of vicious killer dykes, whereas the entire context of my film is that these were regular folks and that love is a beautiful thing ..."

Source: From Brian D. Johnson, "Waiting for *Crash*," *Maclean's*, November 11, 1996, 72. Reprinted by permission.

3. *The kind of interaction that matters most takes place within small, intimate groups.* Behaviour that is learned through intimate, face-to-face contact with significant others will be more firmly entrenched than ideas learned via formal contacts with the wider social system. There is no cause-and-effect connection between mass-media communication (e.g., pornography) and crime, unless it is reinforced by like-minded others. For Sutherland, the fact that serial killer Paul Bernardo owned pornographic materials and books such as Bret Easton Ellis's *American Psycho* (which tells of a businessman who, like Bernardo, is blond, and who kidnaps and brutalizes young women) would not by itself explain Bernardo's behaviour. The same analysis would help explain why listening to heavy metal music is not strongly related to deviance (Arnett 1996; Singer et al. 1993; Took and Weiss 1994).

4. *What is learned in intimate interaction includes both the techniques of crime and the motives for crime.* The learning of *techniques of crime* is most obvious with respect to criminal "apprenticeships," in which more experienced criminals take on and train others in such activities as using drugs or weapons, picking a lock, hot-wiring a car, or running a confidence swindle. People also learn, as part of their upbringing, how and when to "get mad" about things (and how and when to "talk themselves down" from anger). The professional killer, for example, may use these skills to get "hot" enough to kill or "cold" enough to carry through a stress-producing plan (Dietz 1983). Finally, the future criminal learns techniques for discovering the criminal potential in a situation. Criminal "hustlers" are dedicated to finding an edge that will allow them to cheat and manipulate others.

   Less obviously, criminals learn *motives for crime.* Subcultural values provide explanations, excuses, justifications, and rationalizations. Unlike the psychological concept of motive, which refers to a person's individual internal needs and desires, Sutherland's concept of motive refers to "vocabularies of motive" that we have *learned* through interaction with others. Most of us have learned through those vocabularies that violence is justified under certain conditions. In a recent court case, a man charged with assaulting his neighbour testified that just prior to the attack he had discovered that the neighbour had been sexually molesting his (the defendant's) 9-year-old daughter. The jury understood the "vocabulary of motive" invoked by the outraged father and acquitted him.

5. *"The specific direction of motives and drives is learned from definitions of the legal codes as favourable or unfavourable"* (Sutherland and Cressey 1978:87). Sutherland combines the idea of differential group organization (some groups have more criminal definitions than others) with differential association to

explain that some subcultures evaluate violence, cheating, or general lawbreaking more positively than do others. Culture conflict occurs when law-abiding people are exposed to others who do not believe in the law, or who strongly believe in rules that diverge from the law of the majority.

6. *The ratio of favourable to unfavourable "definitions" of the law as communicated within the group is a determinant of criminal behaviour.* Criminals become criminal when an excess of definitions favourable to the violation of the law conditions them to engage in illegal activity. If DFVL is greater than DUFVL in the group environment, the group member will be criminal.

7. *Certain variables affect the impact of definitions of the legal code.* These variables are frequency, duration, priority, and intensity. The dimensions of *frequency* and *duration* are self-explanatory. If we associate with a person or group frequently and for long periods of time, we are likely to be influenced by their ideas. *Priority* assumes that associations formed early in life are more fundamental than those formed later in life. *Intensity* has to do with the strength of the association between the individual and the members of the group; we are more likely to be influenced by people we admire or care about. This proposition can be used to explain the failure of antidelinquency programs like Scared Straight! (discussed in Chapter 4). Spending three hours in a prison, where the inmates attempt to show just how awful it is, is simply not enough to undo a lifetime of reinforcement of criminal values and behaviour. The program lacks priority, frequency, and duration. It has a certain intensity, but not in the sense that those in the program have a close relationship with the inmates.

8. *Learning criminal behaviour is just like any other kind of learning.* The only difference is *what* is learned, not *how* it is learned. Criminals are normal people who have learned the wrong lessons. Upper-class people learn criminality at work; lower-class people often learn it on the street. Both learn the same way. A person who is capable of learning criminal behaviour patterns is also capable of learning noncriminal behaviour patterns.

9. *The criminal is not exceptional in what he or she wants.* To say that prostitutes or thieves are "in it for the money" explains nothing because people in legal occupations are also in it for the money. Most of us would prefer to get what we want with less effort and less boredom, just as the criminal does. Criminals are exceptional with respect to their means, not with respect to their goals. For Sutherland, the question about crime should be rephrased from "Why do they do it?" to "Why do they do it in this particular way?" (Sutherland and Cressey 1978:75–77).

DANIEL GLASER: DIFFERENTIAL IDENTIFICATION AND DIFFERENTIAL ASSOCIATION

In Daniel Glaser's (1978) view, individuals pursue criminal behaviour to the extent that they *identify* with the apparent perspective of real or imaginary people for whom such behaviour is desirable or acceptable. This theory redirects the Sutherland model toward the recognition of the processes whereby individuals select role models and reference groups. Books and movies may inspire criminal behaviour if individuals identify with the characters portrayed in them.

Glaser further argues that individuals will try to commit crime whenever they feel that the overall gratification to be derived from the behaviour will exceed any unfavourable consequences. We may regard shoplifting as an activity that holds forth the possibility of getting something for nothing. If we give this consideration more weight than we give to the possibility of being caught, publicly humiliated, and presented with a criminal record, we are likely to try it. The calculation includes the weighing of social bonds, differential learning, and learned perceptions of opportunities and costs.

RONALD AKERS AND SOCIAL LEARNING THEORY

Ronald Akers (1985) has also taken the differential association paradigm in a new direction. With considerably less focus on illegal acts, he argues that social behaviour (which includes deviant behaviour) is acquired through psychological processes of conditioning and through imitation and modelling (Akers 1985:46).

The specific process by which deviant behaviour (as opposed to conforming behaviour) becomes dominant in specific situations is *differential reinforcement.* Whether or not a particular behaviour persists depends on the past and present rewards and punishments attached to it, as well as to conceivable alternative behaviour (Akers 1985:57). The behaviour that has been most successful in securing the most desired payoff becomes dominant. The rewards and punishments can be social (praise, promotion, recognition, attention) or nonsocial (the physiological effects of drugs or food).

Akers thus stresses the principles of operant conditioning and modelling far more than Sutherland did, arguing that the learning is entirely operant, and that the small, intimate groups in which learning takes place are important because people we like, respect, and spend time with control our most important supply of reinforcement.

In addressing the criticism that the differential association model fails to account for spontaneous, senseless, or compulsive criminal behaviour, Akers cites the work of

Frank Hartung to show that even the most spontaneous violence usually has roots in a long period of learning. Violent and aggressive people are often found to have had such behaviour reinforced either by their own experiences or by those of others. According to Hartung (1965:140), when a person "loses it" and attacks another, it will normally be found that he or she (1) has experienced incidents of a similar nature that have been rewarding; (2) is not controlled by strong moral injunctions against violence; and (3) has learned violent patterns of thought and action.

Parents may unwittingly encourage and reward their children's violence by modelling the use of force (spanking or hitting the child), and by exposing the child to environments in which violence is a recommended means of defence or attaining desired goals. The aggressive individual may not be aware of the learning process because it has been more a matter of conditioning than of formal, verbal teaching. One implication of this theory is that violent people can be taught to recognize and alter the thoughts that are provoking their violent behaviour.

GRESHAM SYKES, DAVID MATZA, AND NEUTRALIZATION THEORY

The theory of neutralization focuses on many issues raised by Sutherland's fourth proposition about the learning of deviance, which concerns vocabularies of motive. Sykes and Matza (1957) note that most delinquents are not deviant all the time. They participate along with nondelinquents in many conventional activities (school, religious observance, family life), and they often show respect for role models (outstanding teachers, sports figures, etc.). Delinquents, therefore, "drift" (Matza's word) between conventionality and deviance. How do they free themselves from conventional constraints in order to participate in delinquent activities? Sykes and Matza argue that they learn to use the following five neutralization techniques to justify or excuse their participation in the subterranean norms of the delinquent subculture:

1. *Denial of responsibility.* "I didn't mean to do it." "The alcohol went to my head." "I was sleepwalking."

2. *Denial of injury.* "We were just having fun." "I just borrowed it." "The insurance company will pay."

3. *Denial of or blaming the victim.* "She had it coming." "He was just a phony." "They shouldn't have been there."

4. *Condemnation of the condemners.* "The authorities are hypocrites." "Successful people cheat; they just don't get caught."

5. *Appeal to higher loyalties.* "I was protecting my family." "My friends needed me." "The gang comes first."

Research suggests that neutralization theory is most effective when applied to middle-class, white-collar offenders than to most juvenile delinquents, at least with respect to neutralizations that occur before rather than after the deviant behaviour. Hindelang's (1970) self-report study, for example, found that delinquents may resort to using these explanations in their dealings with authorities (i.e., after the fact), but not with each other. The "stand-up man" or "right guy" in the street or in jail is one who does not use excuses, does not justify the behaviour, and does not respect people who do. On the other hand, evidence shows that white-collar offenders do employ techniques of neutralization to justify criminal acts they are about to commit (i.e., before the act). Cressey (1971), for example, studied embezzlers and came to the

---

Box 9.3   Excuses and Justifications: Learned Vocabulary of Motive

Scully and Marolla (1984) studied imprisoned rapists to find out how they explained or justified their actions. They found a consistent pattern of excuses and justifications. Excuses involved blaming the behaviour on forces beyond the rapists's control (emotional problems, drug or alcohol intoxication), while justifications were attempts to make the behaviour seem acceptable (women as seducers who mean "yes" when they say "no"). Scully and Marolla were most interested in how the rapists used this vocabulary of motive (after the fact) to diminish responsibility and to negotiate a nondeviant identity. What these excuses and justifications share with Sykes and Matza's neutralizations is their status as culturally supported vocabularies of motive. In other words, they were not invented by the men in this study. Rather, they exist in the culture and can be "used," just as tools are used, to repair a "spoiled" identity. Although they have come increasingly under attack in our society, these explanations are still recognized and given credence by some people.

Certain acts lack an acceptable vocabulary of motive in our culture. When we ask people why they committed fatal child abuse, for example, the most likely response is denial, concealment, or misrepresentation. When Margolin (1990) interviewed women who had killed their own babies, she found that there were few excuses or justifications that were shared in the group. (Among the few given were sudden loss of control, accident, and psychosis.) By far the largest number of women in the sample responded with complete bewilderment (no explanation) or barefaced lies about how the child died.

conclusion that they typically rationalized what they were doing as "just borrowing," "something the company deserved," or "a fairly common way of getting an entrepreneurial start." In the absence of such culturally approved (but subterranean) rationalizations, Cressey suggests, they would not have committed the prohibited acts.

SUMMARY

Subcultural theories of deviance may emphasize particular subcultures (ethnic/racial, youth, occupational, class), or they may stress the process of learning (differential association, differential identification and anticipation, social learning, and neutralization). In general, these theories blame deviance on the values and beliefs that people learn in the company of others. From their perspective, deviance is "normal" to the groups in which it occurs, deviants are not fundamentally different from the rest of us, they have just learned different lessons, and, in many of these theories, "we are what we learn" and have little free choice in the matter.

REFERENCES

Abel, Ernest L. (1984). *A Dictionary of Drug Abuse Terms and Terminology.* Westport, Conn.: Greenwood Press.

Akers, Ronald L. (1985). *Deviant Behavior: A Social Learning Approach.* 3rd ed. Belmont, Cal.: Wadsworth.

Anderson, Elijah. (1994). "The Code of the Streets." *The Atlantic Monthly,* May, 81–94.

Arnett, Jeffrey. (1996). *Metalheads: Heavy Metal Music and Adolescent Alienation.* Boulder: Westview Press.

Banfield, Edward C. (1970). *The Unheavenly City: The Nature and Future of Our Urban Crisis.* Toronto: Little, Brown and Company.

———. (1974). *The Unheavenly City Revisited.* Toronto: Little, Brown and Company.

Brake, Michael. (1985). *Comparative Youth Culture: The Sociology of Youth Culture and Youth Subcultures in America, Britain and Canada.* London: Routledge and Keegan Paul.

Brown, Sandra, Vicki Creamer, and Barbara Stetson. (1987). "Adolescent Alcohol Expectancies in Relation to Personal and Parental Drinking Patterns." *Journal of Abnormal Psychology* 96:117–121.

Cayley, David. (1990). "The Informal Economy." CBC Ideas Transcript. Toronto: CBC.

Colburn, Kenneth, Jr. (1986). "Honour, Ritual and Violence in Ice Hockey." In Robert A. Silverman and James J. Teevan (eds.), *Crime in Canadian Society.* 3rd ed. Toronto: Butterworths.

Cressey, Donald R. (1971). *Other People's Money: A Study in the Social Psychology of Embezzlement.* Belmont, Cal.: Wadsworth.

Cryderman, Brian, and Chris N. O'Toole. (1986). *Police, Race and Ethnicity: A Guide for Law Enforcement Officers*. Toronto: Butterworths.

De Sola, Ralph. (1982). *Crime Dictionary*. New York: Facts on File.

Dietz, Mary Lou. (1983). *Killing for Profit: The Social Organization of Felony Homicide*. Chicago: Prentice-Hall.

Ferrell, Jeff. (1993). *Crimes of Style: Urban Graffiti and the Politics of Criminality*. New York: Garland.

Forsyth, Craig, and Thomas A. Marckese. (1993). "Folk Outlaws: Vocabularies of Motives." *International Review of Modern Sociology* 23(Spring)17–31.

Friedenberg, Edgar Z. (1980). *Deference to Authority: The Case of Canada*. Toronto: Random House of Canada.

Frith, S. (1984). *The Sociology of Youth*. Ormskirk, England: Causeway Press.

Glaser, Daniel. (1978). *Crime in Our Changing Society*. New York: Holt, Rinehart and Winston.

Gouldner, Alvin W. (1963). "The Secrets of Organizations." In *The Social Welfare Forum. Proceedings of the National Conference on Social Welfare*. New York: Columbia University Press.

Greeley, Andrew M., William C. McCready, and Gary Theisen. (1980). *Ethnic Drinking Subcultures*. New York: Praeger.

Harris, M. (1986). *Justice Denied: The Law versus Donald Marshall*. Toronto: Macmillan.

Hartung, Frank. (1965). *Crime, Law and Society*. Detroit: Wayne State University Press.

Hatch, Alison J. (1991). "Historical Legacies in Canadian Criminal Law and Justice." In M.A. Jackson and C.T. Griffiths (eds.), *Canadian Criminology: Perspectives on Crime and Criminality*, 19–47.

Hindelang, Michael. (1970). "The Commitment of Delinquents to Their Misdeeds: Do Delinquents Drift?" *Social Problems* 17:509.

Josephson, Matthew. (1962 [1934]). *The Robber Barons*. New York: Harcourt Brace Jovanovich.

Katz, Jack. (1988). *Seductions of Crime: Moral and Sensual Attractions in Doing Evil*. New York: Basic Books.

Krauss, Clifford. (1996). "Evolution of Graffiti Spells Out Gang Crime." *Globe and Mail*, October 7, A9.

Lachmann, Richard. (1988). "Graffiti as Career and Ideology." *American Journal of Sociology* 94:229–250.

Margolin, Leslie. (1990). "When Vocabularies of Motive Fail: The Example of Fatal Child Abuse." *Qualitative Sociology* 4:373–385.

Marmor, T.R. (1972). "Banfield's Heresy." *Commentary* July:86–88.

Mars, Gerald. (1982). *Cheats at Work: An Anthropology of Workplace Crime*. London: Unwin.

Mihorean, Steve, and Stan Lipinski. (1992). "International Incarceration Patterns, 1980–1990." *Juristat Service Bulletin* 12(3):10.

Miller, James. (1993). *The Passion of Michel Foucault*. New York: Simon and Schuster.

Miller, Walter. (1958). "Lower Class Culture as a Generating Milieu of Gang Delinquency." *Journal of Social Issues* 14:5–19.

Partridge, E.A. (1961). *A Dictionary of the Underworld*. New York: Bonanza Books.

Priest, Lisa. (1990). *Conspiracy of Silence*. 2nd ed. Toronto: McClelland and Stewart.

Scully, Diana, and Joseph Marolla. (1984). "Convicted Rapists' Vocabulary of Motive: Excuses and Justifications." *Social Problems* 31(June):530–544.

Silberman, C.E. (1978). *Criminal Violence, Criminal Justice*. New York: Random House.

Singer, Simon I., Murray Levine, and Susyan Jou. (1993). "Heavy Metal Music Preference, Delinquent Friends, Social Control, and Delinquency." *Journal of Research in Crime and Delinquency* 30:317–329.

Smith, Michael. (1975). "The Legitimation of Violence: Hockey Players' Perceptions of Their Reference Groups' Sanctions for Assault." *Canadian Review of Sociology and Anthropology* 1:72-80.

Sterling, Bruce. (1992). *The Hacker Crackdown: Law and Disorder on the Electronic Frontier*. New York: Bantam.

Sutherland, Edwin, and Donald Cressey. (1978). *Criminology*. 10th ed. Philadelphia: Lippincott.

Sykes, Gresham, and David Matza. (1957). "Techniques of Neutralization: A Theory of Delinquency." *American Sociological Review* 22:664–670.

Took, Kevin, and David Weiss. (1994). "The Relationship Between Heavy Metal and Rap Music and Adolescent Turmoil: Real or Artifact?" *Adolescence* 29:613–621.

Tyler, E.B. (1871). *Primitive Culture*. London: John Murray.

Vaz, E.W. (1972). "The Culture of Young Hockey Players: Some Initial Observations." In A.W. Taylor (ed.), *Training: Scientific Basis and Application*. Springfield, Ill.: Charles C. Thomas.

Wilkins, Leslie T. (1964). *Social Deviance*. Englewood Cliffs, N.J.: Prentice-Hall.

Wilson, G. Terence. (1988). "Alcohol Use and Abuse: A Social Learning Analysis." In C.D. Chaudron and D.A. Wilkinson (eds.), *Theories on Alcoholism*. Toronto: Addiction Research Foundation.

Wolfgang, Marvin. (1958). *Patterns in Criminal Homicide*. Philadelphia: University of Philadelphia Press.

Wolfgang, Marvin, and Franco Ferracuti. (1967). *The Subculture of Violence: Toward an Integrated Theory in Criminology*. London: Tavistock.

Ziebold, Thomas O., and John E. Mongeon (eds.). (1982). *Alcoholism and Homosexuality*. New York: The Haworth Press. (Special issue of *The Journal of Homosexuality 7*, no. 4).

INTERACTION

THEORIES*

A four-year-old refuses to dress herself. The reason may be one of the following:

    a.   She is not yet ready to do this for herself.

    b.   She is a brat and needs discipline.

    c.   She is "going through a phase" that will soon pass.

    d.   She is upset about a family member's death and is acting out because of it.

The same act may be interpreted in many ways according to the "rules" of the culture in which it occurs, the setting, and the characteristics of the people in the setting. Interpretation will play a role in how others, and even the child herself, respond to the act or, in this case, the apparent refusal to act. The parental interpretation, or "construction of what the behaviour means," may in turn influence the future course of events, further interpretations, and outcomes. In this view, deviance is a human creation—a reflection of the meaning(s) we assign to others and their behaviour, meanings that evolve from our interaction with others and then become "traditions," ready-made labels to be used again and again.

---

* The use of the term "interaction theory" to describe a theory that interprets social behaviour follows custom. But it is somewhat arbitrary, since these theories do not all emphasize interaction. However, they do all emphasize meaning and interpretation, which ultimately emerge from interaction. "Theories of interpretation" (Wilson 1971) is a more accurate term, but one not commonly in use.

Interaction theories focus on the interpretation (social meaning) that is given to behaviour, and on the way such interpretation helps to construct the social world, the identities of people, and, ultimately, how they behave. For example, deviance labels can engender commitment to deviant behaviour. A person who has been labelled a thief may have difficulty finding acceptance among former friends and thus seek friends who are disreputable. Legitimate work may be hard to find, especially in any responsible career, so that illegitimate work becomes more attractive. Along with the change in occupational status and friendship groups, a change in self-concept will likely occur, and this may lead to deviant thoughts and behaviour. The point is well supported in Edwin Schur's *Crime Without Victims: Deviant Behaviour and Public Policy* (1965), and his more recent *Labelling Women Deviant Gender, Stigma and Social Control.* Many studies, however, have shown that, in some contexts, this "amplification of deviance" does not occur (Mankoff, 1971:201; Rubington and Weinberg).

Interaction theories focus on the communication aspects of interaction, whether verbal or nonverbal. They often give more attention to the observers of behaviour than to the behaviour itself. Interaction theories have seven main characteristics.

1. *All interaction theories are concerned with the way in which meaning is constructed.* The infant does not see meaning in the surrounding environment but eventually learns to "make" meaning as part of his or her socialization. While some interaction theories focus on meaning in the actor's life, others focus on meaning that is attributed to the actor by others.

2. *Most interaction theories pay little attention to norm-violating acts that are not remarked upon by observers or treated by the deviant as a permanent part of his or her identity.* Primary (unnoticed) deviance is seen as transitory and virtually accidental; only as deviance is noticed and reacted to (secondary deviance) do these theories come into play.

3. *Interaction theories focus on organized, systematic deviance that is (or threatens to become) part of the deviant's social identity or role.* This role/identity may be forced on or chosen by the individual (or a combination thereof). In each interaction theory, there are central concepts that concern deviance that is structured or "constructed" into patterns of social expectations. Secondary deviance is an example of such a concept.

4. *All interaction theories are sequential. They deal with the social construction of deviance designations, their application, and their consequences.* These theories tend to use participant-observation or rely on accounts given by the individuals

observed because these techniques allow narrative unfolding of events and permit sequential analysis.

5. *All interaction theories deal implicitly or explicitly with the idea of stigma.* For most, stigma is a central metaphor that likens deviance to a contagious form of pollution, a sign of sickness or evil that right-minded people will avoid. The stigmatized individual has, to use Erving Goffman's term, a "spoiled identity." So-called respectable people are warned by the signs of spoiled identity (stigmata) to maintain "social distance." People who associate with stigmatized individuals are also likely to be avoided in a process Goffman calls "courtesy stigma."

6. *Most theorists in the interaction paradigm engage in "underdog sociology."* They see themselves as giving a voice to those who are isolated from the mainstream. According to theorists like Edwin Lemert, underdog sociology distorts the subject matter of deviance by overemphasizing both the oppressive nature of social control agencies and the passivity and innocence of the exploited, degraded, or victimized deviant (Lemert 1972:16). On the other hand, Gouldner (1968) argues that by expressing the perspective of outsiders, the sociologist is in fact helping the authorities to become even more effective in controlling them. Far from standing up for underdogs and helping them to achieve acceptance, the sociologist may be contributing to their oppression.

7. *Most interaction theorists are tacitly supportive of the deviants they study.* In Becker's (1963) world of dance musicians, there are "musicians" and there are "squares." The latter are ignorant and intolerant. And Wolf (1991), in his study of an outlaw motorcycle club, clearly identifies with the outlaw bikers' contempt for middle-class values and authority figures. He describes his participation in the club as a "reflection of my own dark side ... my own youthful rebellion and resentment" (Wolf 1991:10).

EARLY INTERACTION THEORY

CHARLES HORTON COOLEY (1864–1929)

The notion of the "looking-glass self" was central to Charles Horton Cooley's concept of identity. It consists of three elements: (1) how actors imagine they appear to others; (2) how actors believe others judge their appearance; and (3) how actors develop feelings of shame or pride, feelings that become an inner guide to behaviour (Cooley 1902:184). Cooley saw the social self as the root cause of social behaviour, whether deviant or conforming.

GEORGE HERBERT MEAD (1863–1931)

George Herbert Mead was a social philosopher closely associated with the Chicago School. Although his work did not focus on deviance as such, it provided a framework for understanding how the social self is created in interaction. In Mead's terms (1943), the social self is composed of an active "I" that is independent of particular situations, and a receptive "me" that is situated and responsive. While there is only one "I" (except possibly in the case of people with multiple personality disorder), there can be many "me" parts of the self: "me" as a parent, friend, con artist, or drug dealer.

The shape of the "me" is composed of the messages we receive by using others as mirrors of the self. A student who constantly receives negative messages about his or her academic performance is likely to incorporate these messages into the "me" part of the self (unless, of course, they are contradicted by some other valued source of information). As a result, the "I" part of the self may be less assertive and successful, leading to increasing confirmation of the negative view, which then becomes part of the "me." The individual may accept the situation; attempt to change the messages by presenting a new image to the world; or challenge the reflection by questioning its accuracy (e.g., by considering where (who) the criticism is coming from).

Mead (1918) noted the interactional ritual that produces designations of criminality, and the power of the designation "criminal" to cut people off from the world. In doing so, he foreshadowed some of the deviance theories that saw labelling as the source of confirmed criminal careers.

Box 10.1   The Central Concepts of Social Interaction Theory

1. *The social self*, the image that we present to others in interaction, arises out of our interpretation of other people's reactions. It may be *authentic* in the sense that the self that is presented is the same as the self that is experienced, or it may be *inauthentic* in that the presented self is not reflective of the experienced self.

2. *The looking-glass self* is the part of the social self that individuals compose by using others' reactions as mirrors in which to see themselves.

3. *The "me" and the "I" components of the social self.* The "me" is largely the same as the looking-glass self; it is the repository of the images of the self that have been communicated to the social actor. The "I," in contrast, can be impulsive and free.

> ### The Central Concepts of Social Interaction Theory (cont.)
>
> 4. *Significant others* are those who have particular influence in our lives. They often serve as role models.
> 5. *Generalized others* are those being referred to in the cliché "What will people say?" By taking the note of the generalized other, we are able to participate in shared values and activities with people we do not know very well.

FRANK TANNENBAUM AND THE DRAMATIZATION OF EVIL

Interactive labelling theory originated with the work of the historian Frank Tannenbaum. Drawing on sources such as Frederic M. Thrasher's *The Gang*, Tannenbaum (1938) argued that while most young people engage in misconduct (e.g., cutting school, getting into fights, petty theft, and vandalism), only some are caught, and even fewer are processed by authorities (teachers, police, judges) who regard the behaviour as deviant and criminal. But, once apprehended for some misconduct, they are subjected to a process that defines them as "evil." According to Tannenbaum (1938):

> The making of the criminal ... is a process of tagging, defining, identifying, segregating, describing, emphasizing, making conscious and self-conscious; it becomes a way of stimulating, suggesting, emphasizing and evoking the very traits that are complained of. (19–20)

Those subjected to the dramatization of evil process are treated as criminal and are forced to associate with older and more experienced young criminals in the correctional system. Here they come to see themselves as true delinquents, without any hope for legitimate careers.

Only in the 1960s did interaction theory attract a critical mass of scholars who made the approach a significant one. In this period, many versions of interaction theory competed for attention and primacy. Among these were symbolic, reaction, and labelling theories; dramaturgy; phenomenology; social constructionism; and ethnomethodology, all of which are addressed in the sections that follow.

SYMBOLIC INTERACTION THEORY

Symbolic interaction, the earliest, most general form of interaction theory, stems mainly from the work of George Herbert Mead, building on the earlier work of Charles Horton Cooley. Symbolic interactionism emphasizes how meaning emerges out of social interaction and becomes social fact for its participants, and how traditions developed in this way are passed on. The central postulates of symbolic interactionist theory can be listed as follows:

1. Human beings become social as a result of interaction with other socialized human beings.

2. We experience the world through the symbols we have learned in interaction. The meaning we act on comes from the symbols, not directly from the confusing proliferation of messages from the outside world.

3. Our social self is a reflection of our beliefs about how others (especially significant others) see us.

4. Meaning is constantly being modified by interpretation. Assumptions about other people's moral or social respectability are always subject to revision.

Symbolic interactionism deals primarily with how the social self is produced in socialization and influenced thereafter; how the way we appear affects how others see us; and how we see ourselves mirrored in their treatment of us.

SOCIETAL REACTION THEORY

The societal reaction perspective emphasizes when, under what circumstances, and how social responses are formulated and applied. Why do we sometimes jump to conclusions about people's social identities? Where do the categories we use for our evaluations come from? In Kitsuse's (1987) view, deviance is the process whereby members of society *interpret* a behaviour as deviant, *define* people who engage in it (or seem to) as deviant, and, finally, *treat* them in whatever way they have deemed appropriate to that class of deviant.

An example cited by Kitsuse demonstrates this process: a 20-year-old man in a bar was engaged in conversation with a stranger. When the stranger showed interest in the fact that he was studying psychology at university, the young man suspected that the other fellow was a homosexual. When they got into an argument over psychology and the other fellow chose homosexuality to illustrate his point, the youth got up and left—a move he said he made because "by now I figured the guy was queer, so I got the hell out of there" (1987:16). Kitsuse uses this example to show how assumptions about behaviours that *everyone knows* are indications of deviance are used in the process of interpretation and the assignment of meaning.

Societal reaction theorists also focus on the agencies of social control, and on how factors such as vested interests, resources, alternative claims, and organizational needs may influence the issue of who is treated as a deviant, and under what conditions. While this is entirely consistent with symbolic interactionism, societal reaction theory does not give as much emphasis as that theory does to the self-perception of the person who is treated as deviant.

A central concept of the societal reaction approach is *social distance.* The best-known measure of social distance is the Bogardus scale (Bogardus 1933), which asks respondents whether they would willingly welcome someone with a particular racial, occupational, or behavioural characteristic into their family, workplace, community, and so forth. For some people, particular kinds of deviants are not welcome to share the same planet.

Box 10.2   Trouble with Gangs

Enough was enough. Last week the Assembly of Manitoba Chiefs fired Brian Contois, a gang leader of the Manitoba Warriors who, in a harshly criticized move, was hired in January to oversee an antigang youth program in downtown Winnipeg. Contois' dismissal was precipitated by a police drug raid two weeks ago in which he and almost two dozen gang members were arrested.

When Grand Chief Phil Fontaine hired Contois without consulting the assembly, he did so knowing that the soft-spoken 39-year-old belonged to the Warriors, a gang that police say is linked to drugs and prostitution. Fontaine also knew that Contois was out on bail pending drug charges in another case. Last week, Fontaine, who on behalf of the assembly announced the decision to fire Contois, apologized to the Manitoba chiefs for any embarrassment the affair caused ...

Contois was originally hired to oversee the creation of a youth centre intended to keep young natives from joining street gangs. Calls for his resignation soon followed, amid accusation that the centre under Contois could be used to recruit new gang members rather than dissuade them from joining.

Note: Although convicted, Mr. Contois continued to serve in a "Consultant" capacity.

Source: From "Canada Notes," *Maclean's*, March 3, 1997, 23. Reprinted by permission.

LABELLING THEORY

Labelling theory as a term finds its roots in Becker's (1963:9) statement that "deviance *is not* a quality of the act a person commits, but rather a consequence of the application by others of rules and sanctions to an 'offender.' The deviant is one to whom that label has successfully been applied; deviant behaviour is behaviour that people so label [author's italics]."

The foundation for the labelling perspective was laid by Frank Tannenbaum (1938). The theory was largely undeveloped until the publication of Edwin Lemert's *Social Pathology* in 1951. According to Lemert (1951), early acts of deviance may be unnoticed by others and rationalized by the individuals who engage in them. Lemert calls these acts *primary deviance.* If the deviant acts are repetitive and highly visible, and if they attract a severe social reaction, then the individual may incorporate into the "me" component of his or her social self a deviant self-concept, as well as engage in the activities associated with this concept. When this happens, *secondary deviance* has occurred.

Like most later theorists, Lemert qualifies this view of the processes that give rise to secondary deviance by recognizing that "individuals define themselves as deviant in their own terms and independent of specific societal reactions ... the interaction process seen in full organic reciprocity allows that individuals court, risk, even create conditions of their own deviance" (Lemert 1972:19). Thus, deviants are not empty organisms who simply respond to a label. Rather than a mere victim of society, the deviant is a participant in the sequence of events that leads to a confirmed deviant career. The point is well illustrated by the following excerpt from a *Rolling Stone* magazine interview with rock star Pete Townsend:

When did you start smashing guitars?

It happened by complete accident the first time. We were just kicking around in a club which we played every Tuesday, and I was playing the guitar, and it hit the ceiling. It broke, and it kind of shocked me 'cause I wasn't ready for it to go. I proceeded to make a big thing of breaking the guitar. I pounced all over the stage with it, and I threw the bits on the stage, and I picked up my spare guitar and carried on as though I really meant to do it.

Were you happy about it?

Deep inside I was very unhappy because the thing had got broken. It got around, and the next week the people came up to me, and they said,

"Oh, we heard all about it, man; it's about time someone gave it to a guitar," and all this kind of stuff. It kind of grew from there. (Wenner [1968] 1992:191–192)

What was originally an unintended and unwanted act of destruction on Townsend's part was almost instantly transformed into an act that helped to define a rock group's identity and that ensured even more on-stage destruction. Primary deviance had become secondary deviance.

HOWARD BECKER

The work of Howard Becker (1963, 1964, 1974) made labelling theory a major force in sociology. Becker had studied under Everett Hughes at the University of Chicago in the late 1940s and early 1950s. From Hughes' studies on occupation, he took over the ideas of "career" and "master status" and applied them not just to conventional occupational careers but also to outsider careers.

Becker's theory emphasizes the social process whereby the deviant discovers deviant behaviour and learns to participate in it. This is a process that unfolds over time, in sequential stages. The marijuana user is not escaping from social reality, he is accepting and participating in a subcultural form of that reality, and in so doing he is acquiring a status, just as receiving a job promotion involves gaining a status. Public identity as a deviant is not just a label; it is a process and a status. As a master status that overrides other statuses held by the individual, deviant identity structures the course of social interaction. To be given a deviant status is to become an outsider in mainstream society.

EXAMPLES AND CONSEQUENCES OF LABELLING

Chambliss (1987) describes two groups of youths he encountered in his high-school years. The Saints and the Roughnecks both committed serious acts of juvenile delinquency, but only the Roughnecks were labelled delinquent and treated as such. The Saints were young men of middle-class background who were willing and able to assume a "good boy" demeanour in order to deceive both teachers and police. They were careful to conduct most of their pranks, which included vandalism, drunken driving, and theft, away from their home community, so that their image at home remained untarnished.

The Roughnecks, in contrast, did not assume a mask of civility in their dealings with authority figures. Nor did they restrict their brawls to inconspicuous places, as the Saints did. All but one of the eight Saints finished college and found high-status positions in society. Two of the six Roughnecks made it to college on sports scholarships and ended up as teachers, one became a truck driver, and three confirmed the community opinion of them by becoming criminals. Of the criminals, two were convicted of murder and a third was involved in illegal gambling.

Box 10.3   An Interactive Labelling Model

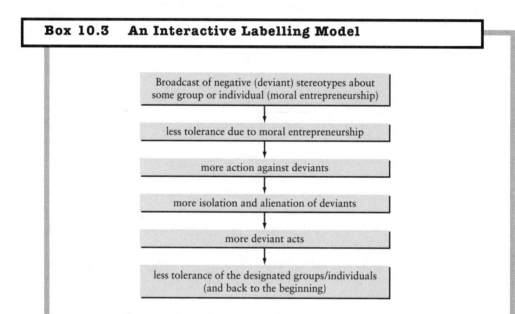

The above model is loosely based on Wilkins's "deviancy amplification feedback loop" idea (1964:90). Jennifer Davis, in describing what she refers to as the "London garotting panic of 1862," uses the deviance amplification theory to explain the events leading up to and following the panic:

> On 17 July 1862 Hugh Pilkington, M.P., was accosted by two men as he walked along Pall Mall on his way from the House of Commons to the Reform Club. He was struck on the head and choked by one malefactor, while another relieved him of his watch. In common parlance, he had been "garotted." Press reaction was immediate and intense. The *Sun*'s comment was characteristic: "The case of Mr. Pilkington is not, in itself, an exceptional case" since "the statistics of garotting in recent years would present a very frightful catalogue of outrages." The sense of alarm over the safety of the metropolis expressed in the press throughout July and the following months was shared by much of London, and, indeed, England ...

An Interactive Labelling Model (cont.)

Study of the Metropolitan Police returns reveals that there were 97 robberies with violence in 1862 (as compared with 33 and 32 in 1861 and 1860 respectively) [but] the startling increase in recorded street violence did not begin until July 1862—after the panic had begun. In fact, from January to June, 1862, there were only 15 robberies with violence ...

In the light of these figures, which overturn simple theories of cause and effect, the garotting panic takes on an increased significance ... In the case of the garotting panic, it is clear that the start of the panic preceded any "crime wave," and that the subsequent bulge in the number of recorded street crimes is attributable more to the panic itself than to an actual increase in robberies with violence. In fact, it was the actions and reactions of the press, public, and various government agencies involved that created the 1862 "crime wave" rather than any significant increase in criminal activity on the streets. Thus, the garotting panic was clearly a "moral panic": one of those episodes in which public anxieties, especially as expressed and orchestrated by the press and by government actions, serve to "amplify deviance" and to promote new measures for its control—in this instance, important changes in nineteenth-century penal policy, which followed in the panic's wake. (Davis 1980:190–191)

Source: From Jennifer Davis "The London Garotting Panic of 1862: A Moral Panic and the Creation of a Criminal Class in Mid-Victorian England," in V.A.C. Gatrell, Bruce Lenman, and Geoffrey Parker (eds.), *Crime and the Law* (London: Europa, 1980).

In another study on labelling, Scott (1969) argues that the disability associated with blindness is a learned social role, one in which the individual learns incapacity. Agencies created to support the blind use their control over services and information to back up their demand that the newly blind person be realistic and not fight the agencies' version of how the blind role should be played. Thus, in Scott's account, people who enter the agency perceiving themselves to have visual impairments of varying degrees come, over the course of their "rehabilitation," to view themselves as blind persons. Consistent with this perception, they adopt attitudes and behaviours that professional blindness workers think blind people should display (Scott 1969:119).

As we have seen, labelling theory emphasizes the way in which being labelled influences how others see us, how we see ourselves, and how we conduct ourselves as a result. Labels on people are just as necessary as labels on cans of soup. They are a convenient way of achieving a fairly high degree of predictability in social life, and thus of facilitating social cooperation. When we interact with others, we make initial assessments of them through the cues given by their appearance, by their background, or by what others have told us. As we interact with other people, we may revise our expectations concerning them. At both points, in our initial assessment and during interaction, we may assign labels to them.

Labels are not just shorthand content summaries. The labels that we employ come from both personal experience and cultural traditions. Often we create or maintain labels that are useful to us, and revise or discard those whose usefulness has been exhausted. Unlike the label on the soup can, the label on a human being is fairly likely to be at least partially wrong.

HARD LABELLING THEORY

While theorists like Lemert use labelling as a sensitizing concept ("soft labelling"), others use it as a full explanation of deviance ("hard labelling"). Thomas Scheff's (1984) theory of mental illness exemplifies hard labelling in its almost deterministic position that the label causes the deviance. According to Scheff, mental illness is a residual category that explains deviance when other explanations fail. He proposes the following nine points as a *complete* explanation of why some people are labelled mentally ill:

1. Residual deviance has many sources.
2. Most residual deviance is unrecorded.
3. Most residual deviance is "normalized" (rationalized or ignored) and transitory.
4. Images of mental disorder are stereotypes learned early in life.
5. Stereotypes of mental disorder are reinforced in everyday interactions.
6. People labelled as mentally disordered are rewarded for accepting the stereotyped role.
7. People labelled as mentally disordered are punished when they attempt to resume conventional roles.
8. Labelling is usually done in a crisis atmosphere, when the residual rule-breaker is confused and may therefore be susceptible to believing the proffered explanation of his or her mental disorder.
9. Labelling is the only important causative factor in careers of residual deviance. (1984:189)

Box 10.4   Central Concepts of Labelling Theory

1. *Career deviance* refers to a sequence of stages through which the actor passes. One sequence might begin with public identification as a deviant, progress to increasing familiarity with others similarly identified, and conclude with acceptance of the identity. Another sequence might involve becoming disabled, receiving secondary gains such as disability payments, and developing physical or psychological problems that cause the disability to continue or get worse.

2. *Moral entrepreneurs* actively participate in forming and enforcing rules, and often profit (socially or financially) by doing so. People who promote the idea that cults are highly dangerous, and who then make a living kidnapping and "deprogramming" cult recruits, are examples of moral entrepreneurs. Although moral entrepeneurship is most often undertaken by groups or organizations, some forceful individuals have performed this role. For example, Harry Anslinger, head of the United States Bureau of Narcotics, launched a propaganda campaign about marijuana in which truth was sacrificed but the Bureau was enlarged.

3. *Moral crusades* are social movements that are aimed at producing changes in the rules or in the ways in which they are enforced. Moral crusades may be led by moral entrepreneurs.

4. *Moral panic* refers to overreaction to some form of deviance. It may be triggered when, say, the drug user or child molester is portrayed in the media as being greater in number and much more powerful than the evidence would suggest. Moral panics may be used by politicians and others to create a common enemy.

5. *Stigma contests* may ensue when the attempt to assign a stigmatizing label to a person or group meets with resistance. A battle or stigma contest is currently being waged between those who impose deviant labels on smokers and those who regard such labels as hypocritical, unconstitutional, or unjust (Troyer and Markle 1983). A stigma contest of longer standing has been fought by abortion activists on both sides of the issue; the charges of murder from pro-life forces have been countered by charges of public nuisance and harassment from pro-choice advocates.

   Sometimes, the people who start a stigma contest find that the tables have been turned on them. For example, Anita Bryant, a well-known actress who spoke out against homosexuals, found herself ostracized within the

---

Central Concepts of Labelling Theory (cont.)

acting community, and lost her job advertising Florida orange juice. Reverend Shay Cullen, a priest in the Philippines, spoke out against child prostitution and drug abuse associated with the United States' military bases there. This effort made him the target of death threats and a deportation drive headed by the local mayor and his city government. His drug rehabilitation centre was picketed and lurid handbills described him as a person who spreads bad things about the Philippines (Johnson 1990).

Thus, in Scheff's terms, most residual deviance, because it is either rationalized or ignored, is transitory. Only when it is attended to, and a label is placed on the person, does such deviance become a "career."

SEEKING STIGMA

Some groups or individuals may seek out and cultivate a stigmatized identity. Wolf (1991), who radically altered his physical appearance in order to gain admission into an outlaw motorcycle club called the Rebels, discovered that his fellow cyclists admired and identified with the "one percenters." One percenters are those accepted into clubs that represent the 1 percent of cyclists who give the activity a bad name. They do not belong to respectable cycle clubs such as the American Motorcycle Association (AMA) or its Canadian counterpart; nor are they "registered societies" with local state or provincial authorities. The term "outlaw clubs" arose following a riot that took place in 1947, in Hollister, California. A group of 500 bikers (about 1 percent of the cyclists present at what was an AMA-sponsored tour and competition) cycled through bars and restaurants, urinated in the streets, and generally engaged in exceptionally rowdy behaviour. Later events have linked outlaw cycle clubs with organized-crime activities, including drug manufacture and distribution, trafficking, prostitution, gunrunning, fencing, and white-collar crime.

Although the biker identity is in part a response to negative social reactions (Wolf recounts being run off the road by "respectable" citizens and hassled by police on the basis of his appearance), bikers clearly see themselves as makers of their own image. They deliberately seek out a lower-class bohemian lifestyle. Other accounts can be found in Yves Lavigne's *Hell's Angels: Taking Care of Business* and Hunter S. Thompson's *Hell's Angels: A Strange and Terrible Saga.*

In another example of stigma-seeking, French author Jean Genet (1910–1986) cultivated an image that was defiantly negative (White 1993). Born an illegitimate child and raised first in an orphanage and then in a rejecting adoptive home, Genet responded by resorting to theft and male prostitution. At the age of 10 he was sent to a reformatory for theft and spent most of the next 30 years in some of the toughest prisons in Europe. In *The Thief's Journal* ([1949] 1964), Genet writes of the effort it took to rid himself of such encumbrances as remorse in order to develop into the most vile, satanic kind of person he could imagine. In so doing, he transformed himself into a nightmare of the respectable middle class that had initially rejected him.

According to Shoham (1970), Genet's relationship with society was characterized by what he calls "the outsider's dilemma." Genet wanted *acceptance* for his critique of the norms, his honesty about himself, and his suffering. Instead, his repeated violations brought him rejection. Having submissively accepted (even welcomed) the labels put on him, and having fulfilled to the best of his ability the expectations of others that he would turn out badly, Genet resented the fact that society did not accord him the respect to which he felt entitled. His quest for acceptance as an outsider was an oxymoron, an attempt to reconcile antithetical goals.

DRAMATURGICAL THEORY

Dramaturgical theory sees social interaction as a kind of improvised drama or stage performance. Its central metaphor is rooted in Mead's characterization of symbolic interactions as being like an improvisational dramatic play or a game (Lemert 1972: 18). Dramaturgical theory makes use of concepts that parallel those of theatrical productions: roles, props, scenes, foreground, background, and so on. People project images of themselves on the social stage in order to be seen (and see themselves) in particular ways and to achieve particular ends. Such performances are achievements, often precarious, and always liable to breaches of "front" that can be embarrassing or discrediting. In this sense, we are all, at least much of the time, imposters who assume social roles that only partly fit us.

The performer may be a person with a "spoiled identity," which can be "managed into" a semblance of respectability by careful self-presentation. He or she might have an embarrassing secret, a criminal record, or a problem that is not evident to others but might become troublesome if it were. The shoplifter, the con artist, the impersonator, and the person who wants to be a lover but does not actually love are all consciously engaged in maintaining the appearance of normalcy; they do this by using their knowledge of how "normal" people behave.

Alternatively, the performer may deliberately stage a performance of toughness, meanness, and inhumanity (alienness) in order to achieve notoriety or inspire awe in others (Katz 1988). Another kind of performer is the student who works at conveying to professors an image of responsibility, intellectual strength, and diligence, while simultaneously presenting a very different social self in the nearest bar or pool hall. We all play contradictory roles to some extent, sometimes as sincere actors and sometimes as deliberate phonies. Without such performances, social order would fail.

Box 10.5   Central Concepts of Dramaturgy

1. *Stigma* is a discrediting stereotype that implies moral pollution or danger and that creates a "spoiled identity." Stigma is roughly the opposite of prestige in that it signals the presence of something shameful. The revelation of the stigmatizing characteristic can reduce the person's status instantly from "whole and usual" to "tainted" (Goffman 1963:2–3). Goffman identifies three stigma types: physical monsters like the Elephant Man, moral monsters (cannibalistic serial killers like Jeffrey Dahmer), and out-groups that are regarded as less than fully human (native peoples and aboriginals during the early settlement periods in North America and Australia).

2. *Stigmatic signs.* Greek stigmatics were individuals with brand marks that identified them as runaway slaves. In the middle ages, a yellow cross signalled a person judged to be a heretic, and a thief might well be branded with a letter T on the forehead or the back of the hand. In Nathaniel Hawthorne's *The Scarlet Letter*, the stigmatic sign is a red letter A that stands for adultery. Physical signs of stigma have been used less in modern times, although the way that the Nazis used the yellow Star of David to stigmatize Jews comes close to it (Shoham 1970:15).

3. *Management of spoiled identity* is undertaken by those who have been or may be stigmatized. Not only is there an incentive for people with secrets to avoid being discovered, but there is also a positive demand that they maintain a particular image of themselves in order to participate in social interaction. Doctors must seem to be competent, even if they are presented with something beyond the scope of their training. The would-be parolee must admit that an offence was committed and express shame and remorse for it. The Christian who is "born again" illustrates one way of leaving a spoiled identity behind.

Central Concepts of Dramaturgy (cont.)

4. *Deviance disavowal* is a repudiation or denial of the stigma that is attached to a condition. Dwarfs, for example, may employ techniques of dress and behaviour that are designed to establish their right to be respected as adults (Truzzi 1975). When they use symbolic signs such as cigars, high-heeled shoes, or canes for this purpose they are using *disidentifiers*.

5. *Symptomatic action* is distinguished by Goffman (1959) from the content of a performance. A person may have good control over the content of a performance but portray it unconvincingly. Conversely, he or she may pull off a convincing performance without actually having a real grasp of the content. The professor who mumbles and shakes in front of the class may be a brilliant scholar, while the person who inspires the trust of others may be a con artist or imposter.

6. *Total institutions,* which include prisons, psychiatric hospitals, monasteries, boarding schools, and military camps, are places in which people live 24 hours a day under a particular authority. The practices in these institutions tend to be directed toward transforming the social self of the "inmate" in such a way that it comes to fit the needs of the institution. Army recruits, for example, lose most of the identifiers that relate the self to civilian life; they are expected to wear a uniform and respond in terms of rank. Institutional practices in turn produce an inmate subculture with elements of resistance.

7. *Moral careers* refers to a sequence of identity transformations that involve entry into—and possible exit from—a state of spoiled identity. The moral career of the mental patient, as outlined by Erving Goffman (1963), moves from a stage in which the individual is presumed sane but eccentric and is accorded respect as a citizen, to a stage in which the individual is considered mentally aberrant and treated as a patient. This may be followed by partial restoration of respectable status as the individual becomes an ex-patient.

Dramaturgy is most closely associated with Canadian-born Erving Goffman (1913–1982), whose many books covered a spectrum from dramaturgical to social constructionist to ethnomethodological approaches (1959, 1961, 1963, 1967, 1979, and others). Goffman coined many of the concepts that dominate this perspective.

THE MANAGEMENT OF STRAINED INTERACTION

Fred Davis (1964) uses a dramaturgical approach to look at the impact of potentially stigmatizing physical handicaps and disfigurements on social interactions. Much of his focus is on the way in which those who are potentially stigmatized manage inter-action so as to achieve normalization of their status, or at least a semblance of this. The person with the disability or disfigurement is faced with a choice between adjusting the presentation of self to fit normal dimensions, or flaunting the condi-tion and demanding that others do the adjusting.

One management technique that can be used with respect to the first option involves taking advantage of the "elastic fictions of normalcy and acceptance" that are part of the cultural equipment of all civilized people. Most of us have been taught to overlook the mistakes and problems of others, usually by looking away while they "repair" their image. The rule of "studied inattention" sometimes conflicts with the equally strong expectation that we look at the people with whom we are talking. One solution to this strain on interaction is to focus attention on a distracting object or topic. People with visual handicaps who have guide dogs often find that others focus on the dog rather than on themselves. This can interfere with the dog's training, but it does facilitate a kind of normalized interaction.

Another strategy, which sometimes has tragic results, involves the attempt to force the body to be "normal." An individual may resort to plastic surgery for cosmetic purposes, or psychosurgery for a neurological condition. Many cures for "deviant" conditions are experimental and risky. In January 1991, a 44-year-old woman died from complications following an operation to remove fat deposits from her hips. The operation, known as liposuction, had been undertaken for cosmetic rather than medical purposes. An estimated 150,000 liposuction operations are performed in North America each year. Other weight-reduction techniques (which are sometimes used for medical as well as for cosmetic purposes) include wiring jaws and stapling stomachs, starvation diets, and taking potentially dangerous and addicting diet pills. As a result of dieting, some people develop life-threatening eating disorders like bulimia and anorexia.

In recent years, people with various stigmatizing conditions have joined forces, not only to give each other support but also to engage in political action designed to educate the rest of society by debunking the myths and stereotypes that surround these conditions.

PHENOMENOLOGY AND SOCIAL CONSTRUCTION THEORIES

Phenomenology focuses on the way in which individuals construct meaning, which then becomes part of their consciousness. According to phenomenologists, our perceptions of the world and our place within it are shaped by our interactions with others. Phenomenology encourages us to look more carefully at the nature and ownership of common-sense constructs of meaning that make society available to consciousness, as well as at the "deep rules" that operate in social situations. A teacher, for example, follows superficial rules by arriving at the right classroom, properly prepared and on time; he or she follows deep rules by constituting the role of teacher in a way that is readily apparent to students, colleagues, and administrators.

For many phenomenologists, the social order is a fragile human accomplishment resting on deep rules that maintain a sense of order and meaning in the face of chaos or meaninglessness. From this perspective, society is a kind of conspiracy that agrees that certain things are real and true and that others are not. Persons who diverge from or challenge this ordering of society do more than just break rules. They threaten us with the possibility that none of it is real. Robert Scott (1972) takes a phenomenological point of view when he argues that "deviance is inevitable because any attempt to impose order on the untidy phenomena of human existence will inevitably result in a certain amount of matter being left out of place." There will always be anomalies, and society must develop mechanisms to protect its symbolic universe. Deviance is a property conferred on behaviour, appearance, or events that transgress the boundaries of the symbolic universe that makes our existence ordered and meaningful.

According to Scott, these boundaries may or may not be clear. The person who experiences a bad LSD "trip" and leaves the symbolic universe is a clear anomaly upon whom we can unambiguously confer the label "deviant." Sometimes, however, when the situation is not clear, deviance becomes a property invoked in order to create and mark boundaries. The witch hunt, for example, served to strengthen the religious worldview by providing clear boundaries. In either case, universe-maintaining mechanisms help to set apart the property of deviance so that it does not threaten the dominant conception of the socially constructed universe (Berger and Luckmann 1967:104–116). Mythology, theology, philosophy, and science have all served as such mechanisms.

Behaviour that violates socially constructed reality may produce a variety of responses that help to maintain a sense of order (Scott 1972). The deviance may be (1) *unnoticed*, as when the teacher fails to observe the cheating student; (2) *denied, debunked, or normalized*, as when we assume that people who claim UFO experiences are hoaxers or else deluded; (3) *excluded,* as when we commit people to a psychiatric hospital or throw them out of our club; (4) subjected to *annihilation,* as when we treat someone as an outsider and therefore of no consequence; or (5) *incorporated,* as when we change the rules to include it.

Jack Katz (1988) engages in a relatively concrete exercise in phenomenological analysis. His theorizing is based on the "foreground" part of crime: the action itself and the actor's experience of it. Indeed, Katz feels that background factors such as class, age, and opportunity are likely to cause the theorist to miss the point entirely. Katz's position is that criminals actively construct their criminal worlds. Instead of simply taking over existing role models or following subcultural norms, they invent and reinvent these as they go about doing whatever it is they want to do.

Much of the crime that is perpetrated by delinquents and killers, in Katz's view, results from the desire of criminals to construct a social identity that is hard, mean, and alien, as well as from their very effective manipulation of their image and environment to support this identity. Crime, Katz asserts, has a sensual, magical, creative, gamelike appeal that is lacking in most conventional law-abiding ways of confirming public identity. Criminality seems to have more creative authenticity than conformity, since it involves actively remaking the world instead of following preset rules. It seems more "righteous" than capitulation to the forces of respectability, in addition to which it uplifts, excites, and "purifies" the self.

Relatively little direct work on deviance has been done from this perspective. In fact, Berger and Luckmann argue that the need to have a theory of deviance at all is merely a by-product of the fact that "official" definitions of reality do not cover what actually happens. They point out that, in a world that institutionalizes military homosexuality and regards it as essential to virility and fighting efficacy, it is the heterosexual soldier who requires explanation and therapy (Berger and Luckmann 1967). Given this view of the radical relativity of deviance, theories of deviance seem contrived and ultimately unimportant.

ETHNOMETHODOLOGY

Leiter (1980) defines ethnomethodology as "the study of the methods people use to generate and maintain their experience of the world as a factual object" (25). Although ethnomethodology is an offshoot of phenomenology, it stresses contexts of interaction (courts, families, and other social settings) rather than the consciousness of individuals. Ethnomethodology does not deny that there may be real causes for things, but it shifts focus from the question "What causes behaviour?" to the question "How do people come to see forces like norms, values, social classes, and institutions as objectively real and as the cause of behaviour?" (Leiter 1980:25).

Ethnomethodology focuses on those everyday things that we think we already know, but that look different when we treat them as problematic instead of as obvious. While other theories may assume that we all share competence with respect to social meanings, and that this does not change much from one context to another, ethnomethodology treats these methods and contexts as matters for investigation. It takes seriously, for example, the question of how members of a social group go about assessing the moral identity of other members. How is a person's past identity reconstructed by others when it is revealed that he has molested young children? What interpretive "work" produces the new identity that the person now owns? While similar to social interactionism, ethnomethodology goes further in examining the processes and contexts associated with the construction of meaning. It does not assume, as social interaction theory does, that the member of the social group is a cultural dupe who simply follows the traditions and expectations of other members.

Box 10.6   Key Concepts of Ethnomethodology

1. *Members* are those who participate in a shared stock of knowledge about the world. Student–teacher interactions are largely problem-free because each party makes correct assumptions about taken-for-granted things. When a student comes from a culture with dramatically different assumptions (e.g., about bribing teachers or treating them as servants), the shared assumptions are violated and "work" has to be done to repair them.

2. *Members' methods* are used by people to minimize their doubts about the reality of the social order in order that they might participate in it. Ethnomethodology looks for recurring members' methods primarily by analyzing transcribed records of everyday conversations.

3. *Recipe knowledge* refers to the presuppositions that are generated in particular settings. The trained social worker, nurse, or teacher has recipe knowledge concerning how the people who come under his or her supervision should be categorized and treated. Actors in the criminal justice system develop recipe knowledge about such things as whether an arrest is a good one or what kind of deals will expedite a case through the system.

4. *Typifications* are constructs that are based on experience and that distil what seems typical or common about routinely encountered people or situations.

Key Concepts of Ethnomethodology (cont.)

5. *Folk typifications* refer to the common stereotypes people use, regardless of their level of education or occupational training. The most studied typifications have been those that emerge in occupational socialization. These tend to reflect not only the distillation of experience and traditions, but also the needs of the organization for efficiency and accountability. For example, Lundman (1980) found that police tend to classify situations into two general categories: those requiring "real" police work and involving substantial threat to persons or property, and those that are "bullshit."

6. *Status degradation ceremony* refers to the interpretive "work" that transforms a person's status and identity to something lower. The model is a court trial, whereby presumption of legitimate status (innocence) is transformed into assumption of guilt and degraded (criminal) status. Similar processes occur in other parts of life. The process whereby we "move" from the status of upright citizen to alleged murderer to murderer is a process of status degradation. Harold Garfinkel outlines this process in the transformation of Senator Joseph McCarthy from an anti-communist hero the American people to a discredited, lying, alcoholic bully, who ended his life in an institution (Garfinkel 1956). Status degradation as a process is similar to Tannenbaum's "dramatization of evil" and Mead's "modern organization of taboo" (Lemert 1972:18).

7. *Retrospective interpretation* refers to the reinterpretation of signs from a person's past as signalling "what they really were, all along." Elements of personal history suddenly take on new meaning as stages on the path to disrepute. Conversely, someone who has been regarded as disreputable may be revealed to be something else. For example, a man who has been labelled a drug addict may turn out to be an undercover police officer, or a thief may become a "born-again" person with very high standards of morality. When this happens, people tend to say that this characteristic was there all along.

8. *Indexicality* refers to the idea that members' meanings are "contextual." That is, they are dependent upon the immediate social context in which the members work out common understanding of the situation. Like the pronouns "I," "you," and "she," the categories of murderer, child molester, forger, or transsexual change with the context. The successful street

---

Key Concepts of Ethnomethodology (cont.)

prostitute learns how to place herself in a context in which her gestures will be correctly interpreted, and customers will find her without the kind of soliciting that can lead to arrest.

9. *Rule using* in ethnomethodology is conceptualized as something the member undertakes in order to accomplish his or her ends. We are essentially rule-using beings, not rule-governed ones. Cognitive rules are used in organizing information to construct social reality. These include the "rule of consistency" and the "rule of economy." Consistency refers to the way in which subsequent conceptions fit earlier ones. For example, if in the past, or in the talked-about experience of friends and family, males who hold hands with males are homosexual, then a man holding hands is homosexual. There is no attempt to test the assumption with other information such as a different culture or special circumstances.

10. *Reflexivity* refers to the role of the observer in creating the phenomenon being observed. Part of the interpretive meaning of a good person or a bad one resides permanently in the categories that exist in the mind of the observer.

HAROLD GARFINKEL

The ethnomethodological approach was pioneered by Harold Garfinkel, who coined the term "ethnomethodology." Garfinkel drew on Talcott Parsons's emphasis on the subjective reality of the actor as a connection between the actor and the social order, and Alfred Schütz's (1970) phenomenological position that there are multiple possible realities that are dependent upon the actor's "work" of interpretation.

However, rather than accept Parsons's assumptions about socialized actors as generally rule-abiding across situations, Garfinkel chose to see the nature of rule use (see Box 10.6, item 9) as problematic and linked to the context of interaction. And rather than repeat Schütz's emphasis on the consciousness of the actor, he focused instead on what the actor does to construct intersubjective meaning. Garfinkel's primary emphasis was on those aspects of social life that are taken for granted and are not questioned. He sought to understand the "members' methods" whereby we minimize our doubts about the reality of the social order in order that we might participate in it.

One way to study members' methods is to disrupt or to not go along with the usual order (Garfinkel 1972). As reported by Garfinkel, students were sometimes assigned the exercise of behaving at home as strangers, as though they were unfamiliar with the common understandings and expectations of daily life. Through this exercise, students came to appreciate the extent to which our use of "members' methods" transforms the reality that we see and to which we respond. It also showed them the considerable extent to which our perception of the world is based on trust in the unspoken, taken-for-granted constitutive rules of social life (not to mention how quickly people who do not use the expected methods are questioned about their sanity or their motives).

The Case of "Agnes": A Double Deception

The case of Agnes became the basis of a chapter and an appendix in Garfinkel's *Studies in Ethnomethodology* (1967), and has continued to provoke comment in the literature (Kessler and McKenna 1985). Agnes first appeared at the department of psychiatry of the University of California as someone seeking to qualify for a sex-change operation. She presented herself as a female who had been saddled with male genitalia. Since she had strongly feminine characteristics, including 38–25–38 measurements, soft skin, and no facial hair, she was able to convince the doctors that hers was a case of "testicular feminization syndrome," and that the surgery she wanted was appropriate.

Agnes had been living as a female for two years and at the time had a boyfriend who knew nothing of her abnormality. In those two years, she had undergone a process of learning the signs by which women demonstrate their gender, and unlearning those signs that had been appropriate for the first seventeen years of her life. She had to learn consciously how to move, how to sit, and how to use social space as most women do. Agnes's painful learning process, as recorded by Garfinkel, brought to the fore many taken-for-granted aspects of gender differences, including the assumption that the whole world is divided into just two legitimate genders.

Agnes received her operation, married, and moved away. Eight years later it was discovered that she had never been a genuinely (i.e., biologically established) intersexed person. She had used hormone pills (beginning at age 12) and skillful manipulation of medical knowledge to convince the doctors and achieve her ends. This discovery added a whole new layer to the issue of how Agnes had manipulated common understandings of the "experts" to achieve a new gender status. She had convinced doctors that she was genuinely intersexed while simultaneously convincing the world that she was a woman. In both roles, she made use of common understandings in order to evoke from others the response she desired.

D.L. WIEDER AND THE CONVICT CODE

The uniqueness of ethnomethodology can be illustrated by its approach to the convict code, an informal (unwritten, unofficial) set of norms that is commonly found in prisons and other total institutions. The convict code specifies the appropriate forms of behaviour for inmates among themselves and in their relationships with staff. The rules outlined in the code (e.g., "Don't snitch on others") are often in conflict with official rules of the institution, as well as with its rehabilitative or educational goals.

A standard sociological interpretation of the code would blame the uncooperative, "tough-guy" behaviour of inmates on the rules that make up the code. The ethnomethodologist would instead look at the interaction of inmates with each other, and with the staff, in those contexts in which the convict code is mentioned. D.L. Wieder (1974) analyzed a California halfway house for paroled prisoners using this approach. He discovered that the code served as an "interpretive scheme" that was selectively used by both staff and inmates, particularly in instances of tension. It was complained about, joked about, and invoked in some circumstances, but not in others. When an inmate referred to the "Don't snitch" part of the code, it was often to explain or justify a failure to report wrongdoing, or to express solidarity with other inmates. When staff members referred to the code, it was often to explain a failure to know what was going on, or to answer inmate complaints. Both inmates and staff used the idea of the code to make sense of and impose order on a particular pattern of events.

While Wieder did not generalize his findings, the use of codes may be found in many other contexts. Teenagers and their parents, for example, may employ mutually recognizable codes when tensions make them useful.

RICHARD V. ERICSON AND MAKING CRIME

A social constructionist application of phenomenology that owes a great deal to ethnomethodology can be found in the work of Richard V. Ericson. Ericson has written several works that focus on the way in which the criminal justice system transforms accused persons into criminals (see, for example, Ericson 1980, 1981; Ericson and Baranek 1982).

In *Making Crime: A Study of Detective Work* (1981), Ericson describes how police detectives, as a result of their training and the contingencies of the work setting, operate in an environment of specialized knowledge, low accountability, and high information control. He shows how the police detective uses the rules set by the Criminal Code and the Police Act as resources with which to make action meaningful and justifiable. In Ericson's view, detectives are constantly faced with the problem of meeting their mandate to discover and prosecute criminals while at the same time "covering their asses" with respect to the bureaucratic rules and the norms of the public.

The result is a system in which police reports are "constructs" that meet organizational goals as much as (or more than) they are accurate descriptions of events. Similarly, the criminal whose file appears in the records is a typified construct that bears some relation to the individual who committed an infraction, but (again) reflects the contingencies of a system designed to produce convictions.

SUMMARY

Symbolic interactionism, societal reaction theory, labelling theory, dramaturgy, phenomenology, social constructionism, and ethnomethodology all treat deviance as a form of meaning that emerges out of social interaction. On the whole, these are sequential theories that emphasize the reactions of the social audience over the nature of the offending behaviour. They tend to see the deviant as an underdog, a relatively innocent victim of oppressive social controls that sustain other people's interests or the social universe. Interaction theories enjoyed strong support in the 1960s, when they helped displace functionalism. By the 1970s, however, they had, in turn, been displaced by conflict and control theories.

REFERENCES

Becker, Howard S. (1963). *Outsiders*. New York: Free Press.

———. (1964). *The Other Side: Perspectives on Deviance*. New York: Free Press.

———. (1974). "Labelling Theory Reconsidered." In Paul Rock and Mary McIntosh (eds.), *Deviance and Social Control*. London: Tavistock.

Berger, Peter L., and Thomas Luckmann. (1967). *The Social Construction of Reality*. Garden City, N.Y.: Doubleday.

Bogardus, E. (1933). "A Social Distance Scale." *Sociology and Social Research* 17:265–271.

Castaneda, Carlos. (1968). *The Teachings of Don Juan: A Yacqui Way of Knowledge*. New York: Simon and Schuster.

———. (1971). *A Separate Reality: Further Conversations with Don Juan*. New York: Simon and Schuster.

———. (1972). *Journey to Ixtlan: The Lessons of Don Juan*. New York: Simon and Schuster.

Chambliss, William. (1987). "The Saints and the Roughnecks." In Earl Rubington and Martin S. Weinberg (eds.), *Deviance: The Interactionist Perspective*. 5th ed. New York: Macmillan.

Cooley, Charles Horton. (1902). *Human Nature and the Social Order.* New York: Scribners.

Cuzzort, Raymond Paul, and E.W. King. (1989). *Twentieth-Century Social Thought.* 4th ed. Fort Worth: Holt, Rinehart and Winston.

Davis, Fred. (1964). "Deviance Disavowal: The Management of Strained Interaction by the Visibly Handicapped." In Howard S. Becker (ed.), *Perspectives on Deviance: The Other Side.* New York: Free Press.

Ericson, Richard V. (1980). *Reproducing Order: A Study of Police Patrol Work.* Toronto: University of Toronto Press.

———. (1981). *Making Crime.* Toronto: Butterworths.

Ericson, Richard V., and Patricia M. Baranek. (1982). *The Ordering of Justice: A Study of Accused Persons as Dependents in the Criminal Process.* Toronto: University of Toronto Press.

Garfinkel, Harold. (1956). "Conditions of Successful Degradation Ceremonies." *American Journal of Sociology* 61(March):420–424.

———. (1967). *Studies in Ethnomethodology.* Englewood Cliffs, N.J.: Prentice-Hall.

———. (1972). "Studies in the Routine Grounds of Everyday Activities." In D. Sudnow (ed.), *Studies in Interaction.* New York: Free Press.

Genet, Jean. ([1949] 1965). *The Thief's Journal.* Translated by Bernard Frechtman. London: Anthony Bland.

Goffman, Erving. (1959*). The Presentation of Self in Everyday Life.* Garden City, N.Y.: Doubleday.

———. (1961). *Asylums.* Garden City, N.Y.: Doubleday.

———. (1963) *Stigma: Notes on the Management of Spoiled Identity.* Englewood Cliffs, N.J.: Prentice-Hall.

———. (1967). *Interaction Ritual: Essays on Face-to-Face Behavior.* Chicago: Aldine.

———. (1979). *Gender Advertisements.* Cambridge, Mass.: Harvard University Press.

Gouldner, Alvin W. (1968). "The Sociologist as Partisan: Sociology and the Welfare State." *The American Sociologist* 3(May):103–116.

Halkowski, T. (1990). "'Role' as an Interactional Device." *Social Problems* 37:546–577.

Johnson, Brian. (1990). "Campaign against Prostitution Puts Priest on Mayor's Hit List." *Globe and Mail,* January 17.

Katz, Jack. (1988). *Seductions of Crime: Moral and Sensual Attractions in Doing Evil.* New York: Basic Books.

Kessler, Suzanne, and Wendy McKenna. (1985). *Gender: An Ethnomethodological Approach.* Chicago: University of Chicago Press.

Kitsuse, John I. (1987). "Societal Reaction to Deviant Behavior: Problems of Theory and Method." In Earl Rubington and Martin S. Weinberg (eds.), *Deviance: The Interactionist Perspective.* New York: Macmillan.

Lavigne, Yves. (1987). *Hell's Angels: Taking Care of Business.* Toronto: Ballantine Books.

Leiter, Kenneth. (1980). *A Primer on Ethnomethodology.* New York: Oxford University Press.

Lemert, Edwin M. (1951). *Social Pathology.* New York: McGraw-Hill.

———. (1972). *Human Deviance, Social Problems and Social Control.* 2nd ed. Englewood Cliffs, N.J.: Prentice-Hall.

Lundman, R.J. (1980). *Police and Policing: An Introduction.* New York: Holt, Rinehart and Winston.

Mankoff, Milton. (1971). "Societal Reaction and Career Deviance." *The Sociological Quarterly* 12(1):204–218.

Maynard, Douglas, and Steven E. Clayman. (1991). "The Diversity of Ethnomethodology." *Annual Review of Sociology* 17:385–415.

Mead, George H. (1918). "The Psychology of Punitive Justice." *American Journal of Sociology* 23:577–602.

———. (1943). *Mind, Self and Society.* Chicago: University of Chicago Press.

Rubington, Earl, and Martin S. Weinberg (eds.). (1987). *Deviance: The Interactionist Perspective.* New York: Macmillan.

Scheff, Thomas. (1984). *Being Mentally Ill.: A Sociological Theory.* New York: Aldine.

Schütz, Alfred. (1970). *Alfred Schütz on Phenomenology and Social Relations: Selected Writings.* Edited by Helmut R. Wagner. Chicago: University of Chicago Press.

Scott, Robert A. (1969). *The Making of Blind Men.* New York: Russell Sage.

———. (1972). "A Proposed Framework for Analyzing Deviance as a Property of Social Order." In R.A. Scott and J. Douglas (eds.), *Theoretical Perspectives in Deviance.* New York: Basic Books.

Shoham, Shlomo. (1970). *The Mark of Cain: The Stigma Theory of Crime and Social Deviation.* New York: Oceana Publications.

Tannenbaum, Frank. (1938). *Crime and Community.* New York: Ginn.

Thompson, Hunter S. (1967). *Hell's Angels: A Strange and Terrible Saga.* New York: Ballantine Books.

Troyer, Ronald J., and Gerald E. Markle. (1983). *Cigarettes: The Battle Over Smoking.* New Brunswick, N.J.: Rutgers University Press.

Truzzi, Marcello. (1975). "Lilliputians in Gulliver's Land: The Social Role of the Dwarf." In Frank Scarpitti and Paul McFarlane (eds.), *Deviance: Action, Reaction and Interaction.* Reading, Mass.: Addison-Wesley.

Wenner, Jann. ([1968] 1992). "Pete Townsend." *Rolling Stone, 1967–1992: The Interviews.* (Twenty-Fifth Anniversary Special *Rolling Stone.*)

White, Edmund. (1993). *Genet: A Biography.* New York: Random House (Vintage).

Wieder, D.L. (1974). *Language and Social Reality: The Case of Telling the Convict Code.* The Hague: Mouton Press.

Wolf, Daniel R. (1991). *The Rebels: A Brotherhood of Outlaw Bikers.* Toronto: University of Toronto Press.

SOCIAL
CONTROL
THEORIES

Why are you not a criminal? When Joseph Rogers asked this question of his students, they were astounded at first, and then produced lists that included such explanations as "My mom would kill me," "I wouldn't want to disappoint the teacher," "I would lose the chance of being successful," and "I would feel ashamed." Rogers sees these explanations as the opposite side of Sykes and Matza's neutralizations. For him, they are *affirmations of connectedness, conscience, and respect for the rules* (Rogers 1970).

Social control theories do not ask why deviants commit deviant acts, at least not directly. They deem it self-evident that many kinds of deviance are alluring, exciting, and relatively easy routes to fun and profit. Further, we are all born deviants. When toddlers wander from the safety of their own backyard, we do not ask why they did it—we ask why fences, training, and supervision did not stop them. The fact that children will wander if allowed to do so is assumed. When social control works, it manufactures conformity; when it fails, it does not manufacture deviance but simply allows the individual to choose the deviant path. This approach is compatible with biological/psychiatric explanations, since these theories assume that people will have drives and needs that must be restrained if civilization is to be maintained (as discussed in Chapter 5), but in control theory the emphasis is on barriers, not motivation.

While control theories have their primary roots in disorganization theory (Durkheim, Chicago School), classical theory (Beccaria, Hobbes), and learning theory (Sykes and Matza) they place greater stress on the immediate social bonds that hold people to conventional paths. They emphasize the relative lack of bonds in the individual deviant's background over the influences of formal agencies of control like the criminal justice system.

With social control theories, we are back in the positivist realm of sociology as an empirical science. A great deal of the work in this field is as much methodology-driven as it is theory-driven. The basic research technique used in control theories has been the statistical analysis of self-report data from large nonrandom samples of high-school or undergraduate students (Kempf 1993:152; Winslow and Gay 1993:17; Nye 1958; Hirschi 1969; Williams and Gold 1972; Johnson 1980). These respondents are asked to fill out relatively simple questionnaires concerning their involvement with family, peers, school, delinquent, and deviant acts. Questions typically range from "Have you ever taken little things worth less than $2 that did not belong to you?" to "Have you ever taken a car belonging to someone you didn't know for a ride without first asking the owner's permission?" (Hindelang, Hirschi, and Weis 1981). This narrows the study of deviance to a limited number of behaviours, and provides very little scope for measuring their seriousness or frequency. An admission of assault, for example, could be in reference to a shoving incident or a fistfight. The full meaning of the encounter is lost in a simple yes or no answer. Similarly, the questionnaire approach tends to make the measurement of social class into a matter of where the respondent lives, family income, or occupational titles. The experience of social class is lost in such partial measures. Thus, while control theory has achieved status as a systematic "scientific" approach, it has sometimes done so at a cost to the depth of its contribution to the understanding of deviance as a whole.

WALTER RECKLESS AND CONTAINMENT THEORY

Containment theory was an early version of the social control perspective. It was developed by Walter Reckless, who was among the first generation of Chicago School graduate students. Reckless and his colleagues focused on the inner and outer factors that "contained" the average person but were absent or weakened in deviants (Reckless, Dinitz, and Murray 1956; Scarpitti et al. 1960; Dinitz, Scarpitti, and Reckless 1962; Reckless 1967, 1973). They were particularly interested in the phenomenon of the "good boy" who lived in a high-delinquency neighbourhood. How was such a person inoculated against criminality?

INNER CONTROLS

According to containment theory, the individual experiences, in varying degrees, feelings of inferiority, hostility, and anger, rebellion, and even organically based urges toward deviant gratifications. If these inner pressures toward deviance are uncontrolled, deviance will occur. Inner controls may be direct or indirect. *Direct* inner

---

Box 11.1   Control Theories Argue that Inner Controls Are Important

Anyone who has ever driven along Ste.-Catherine Street knows that jaywalking is a fine old tradition in Montreal. But city police are not yet ready to concede defeat. After years of ticketing blitzes that failed to deter the wayward, police are trying a new tactic. They are co-operating in a safety-awareness campaign, launched by Quebec's automobile insurance board, which includes bold signs painted on sidewalks at busy intersections, blaring such messages as: "Crossing at any time ... no way!" ... So far, the sidewalk signs seem invisible to some pedestrians who still prefer to jaywalk ... [One police officer expressed] no illusions about the huge task ahead: "Quebecers were brought up crossing anywhere but intersections."

Source: From "Opening Notes," *Maclean's*, November 4, 1996, 15. Reprinted by permission.

---

control is evidenced by the ability to feel guilt and shame (a strong superego, in Freudian terms), while *indirect* inner control is based on the individual's rational interest in maintaining a "stake in conformity" (Toby 1957).

Reckless outlined five self-concept indicators of an effective inner control:

1. A healthy (favourable) self-concept defines the self as conforming and conventional. Deviant activity is inconsistent with such a self-concept.

2. The healthy self-concept is goal directed. Its long-range commitment to legitimate goals serves as insulator against short-range incentives to criminality. The person with a healthy long-term commitment will not risk it for a night of fun, or for peer-group acceptance.

3. The healthy self-concept is characterized by an adherence to realistic, practical goals. Individuals who have such goals are less likely to break down under pressure or resort to short cuts.

4. The healthy self-concept can tolerate frustration and defer gratification. This contrasts with the image of the hedonistic, impulsive delinquent, who is unable to withstand temptations.

5. The healthy self-concept has a long-term commitment to norms and values. The person with effective inner control is not easily convinced that a different set of rules should be substituted for the ones that have always been part of the self. (Reckless and Dinitz 1967)

OUTER CONTROLS

Paralleling his view of the inner life, Reckless felt that the external world provided both pressures toward deviance and "fences" to prevent it. External factors such as poverty, relative deprivation, adversity, insecurity, deviant companions, and deviant opportunities might make deviance more likely unless they are contained by controls.

Like inner controls, outer controls may be direct or indirect. *Direct* outer controls are external to the individual and usually carry with them the threat of sanctions. A security camera in a store is a kind of external control. Direct outer controls are most effective when they are consistent across institutional settings, so that the individual faces a consistent "moral front." *Indirect* outer controls are mainly relational in that the control derives from the need to maintain role relationships. This kind of control is most effective when conforming others hold the power to reward or punish, and when the role networks overlap such that indiscretion in one area will be detected in many, thus multiplying its costs.

Figure 11.1   Elements of the Social Bond Theory

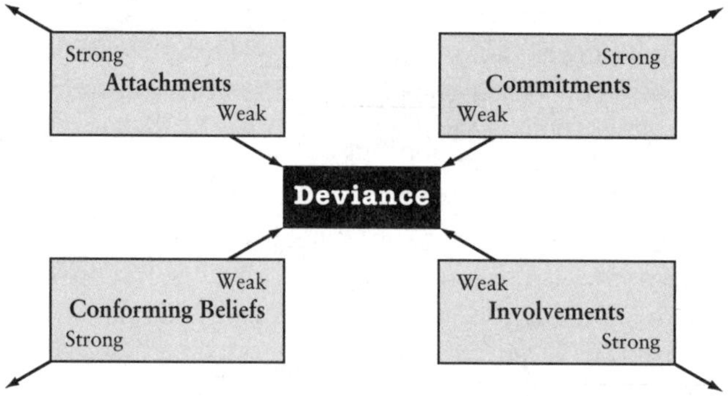

Source: Adapted from Travis Hirschi, *Causes of Delinquency.* Berkly, Calif.: University of California Press, 1969.

TRAVIS HIRSCHI AND SOCIAL BONDING

Travis Hirschi (1969) most clearly stated the basic principles of control theory and made explicit the way in which it differed from earlier theories of deviance. His answer to the question "Why do most of us behave so well?" is that we obey rules because we form a strong bond to conventional society. This bond is composed of four distinct but overlapping elements: attachment, commitment, involvement, and belief. This theory has been gaining popularity over the past twenty-five years (Kempf 1993:143; Vold and Bernard 1986:247): Kempf identified no less than seventy-one empirical tests of this theory in the research literature between 1970 and 1991 (Kempf 1993:148). These studies extended the theory to company executives, rural youth, females, minority youths, and to a variety of kinds of deviance, including drug and alcohol use, adult crime, sexual behaviour, and mental health disorders.

ATTACHMENT

When we are attached to others, we consider their views and opinions, and we expect that our consideration will be reciprocated. Attachment is a combination of caring and supervision. Being attached means having in our lives both significant others and "reference others" (people we use as standards for our own behaviour). If our attachment to our family and school is strong, the authority of those institutions will be strong and their social control will likely be effective.

In Hirschi's work, attachment is measured by the nature of the bond between children and their parents, and by the degree of parental supervision. A typical question about supervision would be "Does your mother (father) know where you are when you are away from home?" while a question about the quality of family relations might be "Do you share your thoughts and feelings with your mother or father?" (Kempf 1993:154). An extreme lack of attachment is characteristic of the psychopath, who neither cares how others feel nor welcomes their attention (supervision). But many people who deviate less extremely experience attachment as confining, and resent the idea that others should have a say in their lives. While not all unattached people become delinquents, lack of family attachment makes some youths available for gang participation. The deviant gang does not attract youths who have strong attachment to conventional (significant or reference) others.

Hirschi argued that any strong attachment, whether to family or peer group, would tend to lead to conformity. He distinguishes between members of conventional peer groups who may have strong attachments and delinquents, whom he regards as socially disabled people who are unable to form close attachments to anyone, and who do not know what real friendship is (Hirschi 1969; Brownfield and Thompson 1991). Indeed, many studies show that delinquent youths have instrumental (utilitarian) rather than affective (emotional) attitudes in interpersonal relationships (Hansell and Wiatrowski 1981; Gordon 1967). On the other hand, there is also strong support for the position that when youths have a stronger attachment to an originally nondelinquent peer group than they have to the family or school, delinquent behaviour is more likely to occur (Erickson and Empey 1965;

Linden and Hackler 1973; Hindelang 1973; Elliott and Voss 1974; Massey and Krohn 1986).

While Hirschi emphasized family attachment over other attachments, some of his followers have given considerable attention to the school as a bonding agent, particularly for youths who have disturbed family backgrounds or who belong to disadvantaged ethnic or racial groups (Wiatrowski and Anderson 1987; Liska and Reed 1985). While Hirschi's original formulation of "school attachment" emphasized the student's GPA, this has not proven useful in later studies (Kempf 1993:158). Boocock (1980:212–236) found that the most important aspect of school attachment as an insulator against deviance is integration into the social system of the school; that is, acceptance by one's peers is more an important bond than academic success.

COMMITMENT

Toby (1957) calls commitment "a stake in conformity." The idea behind commitment is that the more people have to lose by violating norms, the less likely they are to do so. A person in a secure, well-paid, prestigious job risks considerably more by engaging in crime than does someone already familiar to local prosecutors.

Hirschi measured commitment largely in terms of occupational aspirations, judging people who had higher aspirations to be more committed than others. Thus, Hirschi would rank a job requiring university education over a trade profession in terms of its degree of commitment. Later research has shown, however, that commitment toward lower-status positions can be just as intense (Wiatrowski, Griswold, and Roberts 1981; Wiatrowski and Anderson 1987).

INVOLVEMENT

Involvement, when voluntary, is a consequence of commitment. People deeply committed to conventional lines of action are likely to devote much of their time and energy to conventional activities. Students who fall into this category will immerse themselves in productive activities such as homework and organized sports, while youths who lack such involvement are free to engage in nonproductive activities like drug or alcohol use. One study found that the relationship between "involvement" and delinquency was strong, while two others found it to be conditional or unimportant (Kempf 1993:169; see also Macdonald 1989).

BELIEF

Belief is the element of bonding that most closely corresponds to Reckless's inner control. In Hirschi's (1969) theory, belief is the acceptance of the dominant value system of society, and focuses mainly on values such as respect for the police and concern for teacher's opinions. People who are bonded in this way believe in respecting police, obeying the law, and staying out of trouble. They do not share the neutralizing beliefs that police are oppressors, rules are unreasonable, and law evasion is clever. While one would expect participants in established religious groups to be the people most likely to have these beliefs, and therefore the least

---

Box 11.2   Questioning Hirschi: Control Theory's Negative Cases

Giordano (1987) reports her findings from a study of control theory's negative cases. A negative case occurs whenever a person in the research sample provides a pattern of responses that does not fit with the predictions generated from the theory. The most important part of Hirschi's control theory—the bond of attachment—predicts that youths with poor attachment to their families will report more delinquency than youths who are closer to their parents; by the same token, youths with strong family attachments will report less delinquency. Thus, negative cases would be indicated by (1) youths with low attachment who are not delinquent, and (2) youths with high attachment who are delinquent.

In the first part of the study, in 1982, Giordano used graduate students to conduct personal interviews with a sample of 942 youths, aged 12 to 19, who were living in private households in a large metropolitan area. Nearly four years later, 197 youths who had been 14 or 15 at the time of the original survey were reinterviewed. Of the sample of 197 respondents, 150 were classified as consistent with control theory in that they had high attachment and low delinquency, while another 5 were consistent with the theory in that they had low attachment and high delinquency. The remainder were not strictly consistent with the theory.

Some of those interviewed had low attachment to family and low delinquency. In these cases, Giordano found, especially in the case of girls, that delinquency was not a good measure of deviance. Girls were low in delinquency, but reported repeated unwanted pregnancies, or eating disorders such as anorexia nervosa. Among boys, the pattern of low attachment

---

Questioning Hirschi: Control Theory's Negative Cases (cont.)

and low deviance was often mediated by an intense commitment to an activity such as getting a sports scholarship or getting into college or the Air Force.

Others had high attachment and high delinquency. Many of these had high attachment to families that did not oppose delinquency, or even expect it. Some of these young people were involved in violence or hedonistic lifestyles. Giordano noted that for most of these "exceptions" to the theory, a nondeviant self-concept, despite reports of fairly extensive misbehaviour, existed. That is, they defined their deviance as "just having fun."

Thus, despite the apparent contradiction of negative cases, Giordano found that these cases supported the theory as a whole.

Giordano's study does suggest several areas in which the theory needs to be adjusted to accommodate the kind of negative cases she reported. Most important is the need for a clearer conceptualization of the dependent variable. Delinquency may be an important part of what happens when social controls are weak, but it is not the only form of problem behaviour that may emerge. The concept of delinquency used in most social control studies is one that is appropriate to survey self-report methodology. It includes theft, joy riding, underage drinking, assault, drug dealing, and sometimes rape. It does not include psychosomatic illness, sexual promiscuity, or paraphilias (sexual disorders). Second, the theory needs to be revised so that it distinguishes the influence of the peer group and school attachments from the influence of family attachments.

likely to be involved in deviance and crime, the record is far from consistent on this point (Bainbridge 1989:288). According to Hirschi, people from all parts of society share the same basic conventional beliefs and differ only in the extent to which they support or neglect them. Hirschi does not consider, then, that some subcultures are characterized by alternative beliefs.

Hirschi's control theory, still one of the most popular explanations of deviance and crime, will probably generate a great deal more research as areas of ambiguity are worked out. For example, the area of "attachment" has been shown to be far from the simple relationship with a parent or teacher, which Hirschi first postulated: love and supervision are not always linked; schools include more than teachers; and peers may induce conformity or deviance.

HIRSCHI, GOTTFREDSON, AND LOW SELF-CONTROL

In a later work, Gottfredson and Hirschi (1990) depart from Hirschi's original formulation by emphasizing the low self-control of the repeat offender. Gottfredson and Hirschi define the repeat offender according to whether he or she typically uses force or fraud to achieve short-term gains (Hirschi and Gottfredson 1990:959; Grasmick et al. 1993:10). They also extend their theory to include nonfraudulent, nonviolent but risky behaviour such as smoking and alcohol abuse, which are, in this view, "analogous" to crime (Reed and Yeager 1996:360).

Gottfredson and Hirschi begin with several assumptions about risky deviant behaviour. These assumptions apply best to street crimes, not to carefully planned and executed crimes. First, crime is assumed to provide more *immediate* gratification of desires than does noncriminal behaviour. Second, criminal acts provide *easy* or *simple* paths to gratification. Stealing is much easier than earning a paycheque. Fighting is considerably more direct (both faster and easier) than suing. Thus, "diligence, tenacity, or persistence in a course of action" are not required of the criminal (Gottfredson and Hirschi 1990:89).

Third, criminal acts are *exciting, risky,* or *thrilling* when compared with conventional (cautious, cognitive, and verbal) lines of action. The criminal can rely on unreflective speed, agility, or stealth. Fourth, crime (or at least the street crime addressed by Gottfredson and Hirschi) provides *few* or *meagre long-term benefits.* Criminal activities interfere with potentially more profitable long-term commitments to work, family, and friends. Criminals do not have to be stable and reliable. Their low self-control results in unstable marriages, friendships, and employment records.

Fifth, most crimes require *little skill* or *planning.* They do not require extensive cognitive, academic, or even above-average manual skills. Apprenticeship is short and easy or unnecessary. Finally, crimes often result in *pain* or *discomfort for the victim.* Criminals are self-centred individuals who are unable to empathize with the suffering of others. Whatever charm and generosity they display is utilitarian and unrelated to deep feelings.

CHILD REARING AND SELF-CONTROL

According to Gottfredson and Hirschi, the above characteristics are indicative of low self-control. Where does low self-control come from? Gottfredson and Hirschi locate the origins of low self-control in the family, arguing that it is the result of ineffective child rearing. The low self-control personality emerges naturally when there is an absence of discipline, supervision, and affection in the home.

If self-control is to become part of a child's personality, three conditions must be met. First, at least one person must monitor the child's behaviour. Second, the monitor must recognize deviant behaviour when it occurs. Parents who do not recognize the signs that their child is a bully, thief, or drug user will be ineffective in training him or her. Third and last, once aware of the deviant behaviour, the supervising person must "punish" it—not necessarily physically, Gottfredson and Hirschi emphasize, but in a straightforward fashion (e.g., a clear statement of disapproval). Obviously, some families are better able than others to provide these three conditions.

Gottfredson and Hirschi present their theory of low self-control as a "general theory of crime," and their intent is clearly to produce a theory that covers all kinds of crime and most deviance as well. The theory has not faired well, however, with respect to "organizational" or corporate offending that is typical of big business and multinational corporations. Despite the assumptions of this theory, the use of force and fraud are obviously not restricted to undisciplined individuals (Reed and Yeager 1996:357–359).

This theory is still in the testing phase: serious challenges have been made to it that have yet to be resolved. For example, much of the theory seems to be circular: that is, the definitions of low self-control and criminality as personality characteristics seem to overlap, as do criminality and criminal behaviour. Gottfredson and Hirschi have attempted to separate these, but not yet to the satisfaction of their crit-

Figure 11.2   Routine Activities Theory

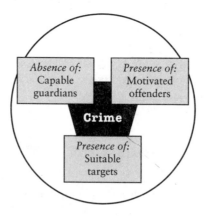

Source: From Lawrence E. Cohen and Marcus Felson, "Social Change and Crime Rate Trend: A Routine Activities Approach," *American Sociological Review* 44, 1978, 588–608. Reprinted by permission.

ics (Gottfredson and Hirschi 1993:52; Reed and Yeager 1996:361). The theory assumes that criminal and deviant opportunities are omnipresent, and does not place any importance on the number or kind of opportunities that the individual meets in the course of a normal day (Sampson and Laub 1993:7; Tittle 1995).

ROUTINE ACTIVITIES: A SITUATIONAL ANALYSIS

In 1979, Cohen and Felson introduced a variant of control theory that evolved from, but went beyond, Hirschi's concept of "involvement" (Osgood et al. 1996:637), and also further developed the ecological thread of the Chicago School approach, which was discussed in more detail in Chapter 7.

Routine activities theory was formulated to explain the ecological patterns of victimization in urban areas. Felson and Cohen argue that the probability of a crime incident increases when there is a convergence in time and space of three distinct elements: motivated offenders, suitable target(s), and the absence of capable guardians. According to routine activities theory, the three-sided convergence depends for its existence less on the particular aspects of the community than on the lifestyle of the potential victims. The person who is unmarried and young, for example, is more likely to be victimized than is an elderly married person, mainly because victimization coincides with activities in which young singles are more likely to engage (e.g., attending sports events, patronizing restaurants or bars, going to work, or simply being away from home). Homes are more likely to be burglarized in areas where both spouses are working, so that the home is empty and undefended during the day. These ideas have been tested in the Canadian context by Kennedy and Forde (1990:137–151), who found that Canadian cities show patterns similar to those found in the United States.

The routine activities formulation can be extended to include other forms of deviant behaviour, simply by substituting "opportunity" for "victim" (Osgood et al. 1996:636). Osgood and his colleagues used this approach to explain the distribution of activities such as heavy alcohol use, illicit drug use, and dangerous driving among young people. Their data support their argument that unstructured socializing activities with peers, in the absence of authority figures is an important aspect of deviant behaviour outcomes. By "unstructured" activities, Osgood and his colleagues mean those that are not structured by rules—for example, those concerning "dating" or participation in sports. They argue that lack of structure allows time for deviance; the presence of peers makes deviant acts easier and more rewarding; and the absence of authorities such as parents reduces the likelihood of negative reactions (Osgood et al. 1996:651).

SOCIAL NETWORK THEORY

While social network theory is not always considered a type of social control theory, it fits nicely with the emphasis of that theory on the relational bonds between people. It can be argued that when our relationships overlap and interconnect, they affect more strongly (i.e., control) our choices vis-à-vis conventional and deviant behaviour. When we compartmentalize our lives into separate worlds, the controls over us are diminished (Krohn 1986:581; Friday and Hage 1976). Thus, if our family, school, church, and sports activities overlap and intersect, we will be more controlled by others than when each of these functions is autonomous, partly because our actions will be visible to people in all parts of the network.

CONCEPTS OF NETWORK THEORY

A social network is composed of persons, groups, or organizations (nodes) that are linked by regularized relationships such as friendship or work interdependencies (Laumann, Caleskiewicz, and Marsden 1978:458; Krohn 1986:582). A personal network is centred on the individual, and is composed of his or her relationships to other people (Laumann 1973, 1976; Krohn 1986:582).

Network multiplexity is a measure of the number of role relations foci (contexts) that are shared by the same people. When a system is multiplex, it has a number of overlapping contexts (Krohn 1986:583–584; Fischer et al. 1977) that increase the probability that a clear and consistent normative system will emerge and be strong enough to impose some constraint on members' behaviour (Wellman 1979:1126–1127). If an individual belongs to several clubs that have nothing to do with each other, the effect of each one on his or her behaviour will be much smaller than if the same clubs were different foci of a single network sharing the same system of beliefs and values.

A person's relationship with family members is likely to be multiplex, especially during adolescence. Many teenagers are caught up in multiplex networks that include family, school, and leisure activities (Friday and Hage 1976). Any unconventional behaviour in one part of the network can produce adverse responses from all other parts. For example, school suspension may lead to being "grounded" at home, removed from sports teams, and gossiped about by co-religionists or fellow club members. In contrast, a nonmultiplex network is one with few overlaps. Youths who hang out in bars instead of going to school may be relatively free of such multiplex networks, or they may be committed to the loose nonconventional networks of the "rounder" (underworld hustler) life, which may foster consistency of deviant rather than conventional behaviour.

The analysis of multiplexity can be extended to work groups, communities, or even societies (Boorman and White 1976; Laumann 1973; White, Boorman, and Brieger 1976). Hutterite society, a close-knit communal form based on Germanic culture and Anabaptist beliefs, is characterized by very high multiplicity (Boldt 1978). Every social role is related to and dependent on every other, and virtually every social interaction in any part of the society is potentially visible to everyone else in the community. Conformity extends even to details such as the patterns in women's scarves and the shape of the buttons on men's clothes. Network theory would predict (correctly) that there would be very low rates of delinquency under such conditions.

In a secularized society like Japan, the intertwining of duty to parents, school, friends, and work, is accompanied by a lower delinquency rate than is found in industrially comparable nations (Clifford 1976). Similar findings are reported by Clinard (1978), who, in comparing Switzerland and Sweden, attributes Switzerland's lower crime rates to such factors as its relatively slow rate of industrial growth (less disorganization), its tradition of political decentralization (more self-control), and its long-standing practice of age integration, by which youths are not cut off from adult values and beliefs. All of these features encourage overlapping networks of relationships from which emerge a natural control that is not dependent on external policing.

Network density is a characteristic of personal networks that is measured as a ratio of the actual direct social ties in a network to the maximum possible number of ties. Expressed in simple terms, a network is dense when nearly everyone in it knows nearly everyone else, and is not dense when people are strangers to one another.

The modern urban environment provides the critical mass of people necessary for the formation of deviant subcultural networks. It also provides many opportunities for people to join deviant subcultural groups without the knowledge or approval of family or religious networks (Kadushin 1983). Granovetter (1973) observes that the stronger the ties among people in a particular group, the weaker the chances the group will form attachments with the wider social system. This means that high-density groups may foster deviance rather than restrict it—whatever deviant values are held within the group will not be constrained by cross-cutting allegiances to other groups.

One implication of network density, which is based on the demonstrable premise that there is a limit to the number of people any one individual can personally know, is that as a community becomes more densely populated, the number of our friends may stay the same, but the number of strangers whose lives may touch ours increases. "Strangers" are not constrained by their relationships to us and to our friends, and are thus more likely to commit acts that might offend or injure us that we will regard as deviant. Craven and Wellman (1973) point out that an important function of ethnic and familial networks in the urban environment is to restrict relations to relatively trustworthy people (also Milgram 1970; Suttles 1972). People who live in multiple family housing or large apartment buildings, for example, may very well know only a small proportion of their neighbours, and this effect can be exacerbated by the high residential mobility typical of many such settings. Thus, the chances that deviance will be contained by the social network rather than left unregulated or regulated only by official agencies of control (the police) are limited (Sampson 1985; Stark et al. 1983).

POWER-CONTROL THEORY

Power-control theory is an offshoot of control theory that emphasizes differences in power among potential deviants. People with power have greater opportunity to avoid surveillance at work and in their neighbourhoods, and more opportunities to commit some kinds of offences without being held responsible for them, either because no one knows, or because they can access the best legal protection available. The presence of power and absence of control create conditions of freedom for unconventional behaviour (Hagan, Gillis, and Simpson 1985:1174).

John Hagan's power-control theory is one of the best known and most controversial of this kind of control theory. Not yet fully formed, it is "an evolving theory with an associated program of research" (Meier 1987:11). As an approach, it aspires to become a structural explanation of crime and deviance; however, it is still in a concept-formation phase, and an appropriate methodology for it is still being developed. Power-control theory work has, to date, focused on how the gendered social class structure is reproduced in the child-rearing practices of families, and how these practices in turn influence the likelihood that girls will be more risk-avoidant and more conforming than boys. This theory is driven by the following six assumptions:

1. The social class system establishes the ranking of individuals in terms of power. At the top of the system are "owners," who are in positions of authority. Below them are "managers," who are subject to authority and who can exercise it over others. At the bottom are *employees,* who are subject to authority and exercise none themselves. In Ralph Dahrendorf's version of conflict theory, which is utilized here, managers and owners occupy the "command class," while lower-status individuals constitute the "obey class."

2. The family exists within a social class system such that the class position of a parent in the occupational sphere is reflected in his or her relative power in the

family (Hagan 1989:145). Because the social class system is patriarchal, the typical family structure is also patriarchal. A significant minority of families can be classified as egalitarian, however, either because both parents work at the same class level, or because neither is employed. Power gains for women are more evident in the upper classes than in the lower ones. In a later study (Hagan, Gillis, and Simpson 1990), the measure of family power had to be revised to account for the fact that some women who do not work outside the home nonetheless have considerable influence within the family, based on other forms of power, such as inherited wealth.

3. The family in which the husband has a command position at work while the wife is restricted to the home and domestic responsibilities (including child rearing) is strongly patriarchal. The mother in the patriarchal family exercises more control over her daughters than over her sons. Girls experience a higher degree of relational controls (working alongside the mother, identifying with the housekeeping role), as well as more informal controls such as curfews. Boys are relatively free of domestic supervision and control.

4. The difference between the supervision of girls and boys has an impact on their propensity for risk-taking. Because their ability to test risk-taking is severely curbed, girls experience a heightened awareness of risk as a negative thing and become relatively risk-averse. Boys are not trained in this way, and continue to appreciate the excitement and fun of risk, which also prepares them for risk-taking positions in the workplace comparable to the ones held by their fathers. Thus, the patriarchal class structure is reproduced in the family.

5. Because boys raised in patriarchal families are both less supervised and less risk-averse than girls, they are more likely to take delinquent risks and therefore come into contact with formal social control systems (child welfare agencies, the school, and police). The dominance of the patriarchal family form, with its pattern of risk and contact, is reflected in the fact that studies on official crime statistics, starting with the pioneering work of Adolphe Quetelet in 1842, have consistently shown that boys have higher rates of official delinquency than girls (Hagan 1989:146).

6. In the egalitarian families referred to earlier, girls are less likely to be encouraged to sacrifice risk-taking in the interests of domesticity. In these families, boys and girls receive more comparable amounts of supervision and control (or lack thereof), and their rates of risk-taking and actual delinquency are much more similar.

> **Box 11.3   A Test of Power-Control Theory: Delinquency in the Great Depression**
>
> The Great Depression of the 1930s had an impact on the organization of many traditional families, as men and women alike became part of the working unemployed. As predicted by power-control theory, this circumstance would produce (1) greater equality between parents, and (2) increased child-rearing responsibilities on the part of fathers, particularly with respect to sons. On the basis of these changes, power-control theory would also predict a greater reduction of male delinquency than female delinquency during the Depression years.
>
> McCarthy and Hagan (1987) used the records of Toronto Family Court to measure male and female delinquency rates during three five-year periods: 1924–28 (before the Depression), 1929–1933 (during the Depression), and 1934–38 (subsequent to the Depression). They found that before and after the Depression, delinquency rates for boys and girls rose and fell together, with the boys' rates consistently above those of the girls. During the Depression years, however, the rates diverged, with male delinquency mainly declining. Girls' rates were less consistent, but the delinquency rate for those aged 13 to 14 increased.
>
> While variables such as referral practices, changes in the law, and changes in social services may have influenced the absolute amount of reported juvenile delinquency, McCarthy and Hagan conclude that only power-control theory can explain changes in the distribution of delinquency by gender during the Depression years.

Hagan's version of power-control theory constitutes an attempt to bridge two major theoretical traditions, namely control theory and conflict theory. The conservative tendencies of control theory and the radical tendencies of neo-Marxian conflict theory and modern feminism (see Chapters 12 and 13) find an uneasy co-existence here. The tensions produced by the attempt to combine different theoretical perspectives appear most notably in power-control theory's conceptualization of "delinquency." As a control theory, power-control gives us an image of delinquency as behaviour that is risk-taking and fun. Delinquency is seen as the result of unsupervised activities and socialization into the risk-taking values of capitalism. As a conflict/feminist theory, however, power-control also sees delinquency as a "construction" of the control apparatus of the patriarchal, industrial-capitalist system, a construction of resistance to it. This inconsistent conceptualization (real behaviour or construct) runs through power-control theory (Hagan and Palloni 1990). Like Hirschi's (1969) control theory, power-control theory emphasizes common forms of delinquency such as theft, joyriding, and vandalism. Hagan and his colleagues have explicitly denied that the theory is formulated to explain serious delinquency or adult crime (Hagan, Gillis, and Simpson 1993:394).

An interesting variation to this emphasis on common delinquency is Hagan's (1989: Ch. 9) study of women's "deviant role-exits." This study sees women, especially those within patriarchally structured families, as being so controlled in their selection of roles that their main paths to freedom, resistance, or expression of repressed inclinations are to leave home (run away), develop a psychosomatic illness or depression, or attempt suicide. Like control theory, and unlike most conflict and feminist theory, power-control theory documents these issues, but does not envisage alternative systems of power-sharing and choice.

Despite these problems of integration, power-control theory has several advantages over earlier approaches to deviance. These include 1) its ability to locate the actual, as opposed to officially recognized, class and gender location of deviance, and 2) its use of alternative methods, such as the use of time-series data. A more detailed explanation of these two advantages follows.

1. *The class and gender location of deviance.* Power-control theory points to the members of the upper classes rather than to the lower classes as people who are free from supervision, and from regulation by others at work and in the neighbourhood, and have greater opportunities to commit deviant acts (Winslow and Gay 1993:17). The upper classes are more free to commit the "low-consensus" deviant acts (drinking, drug use, deviant sexual activity) that are caught in self-report studies (Thio 1988:82–84; Winslow and Gay 1993). High-consensus crimes (ones most of us agree are "bad"), such as strong-arm robbery or murder, may not fit the power-control theory predictions quite as well. Power-control theory argues that official records, which show longer criminal careers for the lower classes, are misleading, since they reflect more policing of the lower classes, rather than more offences in that group (McCarthy and Hagan 1987). Power-control theory stresses the "poverty of a classless criminology" (Hagan 1992).

Power-control theory also locates deviance by gender in a unique way. Most theories of women's crime imply that women are simply less deviant, overall, than men (Jenson 1993). But this is inconsistent with records that show that women's "crime rates" vary (Hagan, Gillis, and Simpson 1993; Steffensmeier and Allan 1996:468). For example, in the first half of the eighteenth century, women constituted up to 40 percent of all defendants in London's Old Bailey Court, but sank to only 10 percent in the twentieth century (Feeley and Little 1991). Similar time-series studies have documented the same changes in other jurisdictions (Hagan, Gillis, and Simpson 1993:387–388). Power-control theory relates these changes across historical settings mainly to the separation of the workplace from the home in the early years of industrialization. In industrialization, women's roles were increasingly restricted to a "cult of domesticity" in the home and family, where their deviance would result in "reintegrative shaming" rather than formal court processes (Braithwaite 1990:93; Hagan, Gillis and Simpson 1993:386). Presumably, the twentieth-century rise in women's criminal convictions from negligible numbers to about 15 percent for serious crimes, and up to 43 percent for minor property crimes, reflects the loosening of this domestic sphere (Steffensmeier and Allan 1996:463).

2. *The use of historical time-series data to test the theory.* The work of Boritch and Hagan (1990) can be used to illustrate how power-control theorists have used historical records innovatively. In this work, Boritch and Hagan examine the records of male and female arrests in Toronto between 1859 and 1955. In particular, they focus on the initial impact on the city of the sudden increase in female labour force participation in the mid-1800s. No longer regulated by family ties, and often living on subsistence-level wages, women's rates of "public order" offences (drunkenness, prostitution, begging) became a recognized social problem, which was heightened by moral panic over its consequences for women's "true calling" as mothers and guardians of virtue and faith. Eventually, panic subsided and newly created institutions like the YWCA residences constrained women within an informal system of social controls. As a result, officially recorded offences by women declined dramatically by the late 1800s. Boritch and Hagan extend this time-series analysis to encompass many of the current interpretations of women's changing gender roles and their involvement in crime including those proposed by Adler (1975) and Smart (1978).

HAGAN'S POWER-CONTROL THEORY AND FEMINIST THEORY

Power-control theory is consistent with the views of theorists who see women's increasing access to opportunities for crime as inherent in the liberalization of women's roles and their participation in the workforce (Simon 1976; Fox and Hartnagel 1979).

O'Brien has extended this theory by asserting that when sex ratios are high (women are scarce relative to men), men use their structural power to control the women, which results in fewer women working outside the home and fewer women being processed as "official" deviants (O'Brien 1991:99; Guttentag and Secord 1983). When there are more women than men, women will become part of the official statistical records of crime and deviance. Power-control theory can also combine with feminist theories that emphasize the strain produced by women's economic marginalization rather than the expansion of their opportunities (Steffensmeier 1980; Giordano 1978; Klein and Kress 1976). According to Steffensmeier (1980), for example, increases in the female crime rate may be due in part to a greater reliance on the formal justice system to deal with women's deviance. Such a view is entirely consistent with power-control theory.

SUMMARY

The dominant assumption of control theory is that deviance is an inherent human tendency, and that it is conformity, rather, that requires explanation. As defined by Walter Reckless, the "good boy" in a high-delinquency area has strong inner controls. Travis Hirschi's early version of control theory focuses on the relative strength of social bonding as a means of keeping people on conforming paths. His later version places greater emphasis on self-control and its sources in child-rearing practices. A recent addition to control perspectives, power-control theory provides a structural view of deviance that attempts theoretical integration of conflict, feminist, and control theories.

REFERENCES

Adler, Freda. (1975). *Sisters in Crime*. New York: McGraw-Hill.

Bainbridge, William Sims. (1989). "The Religious Ecology of Deviance." *American Sociological Review* 54:288–295.

Benson, Michael L. (1985). "Denying the Guilty Mind: Accounting for Involvement in White-Collar Crime." *Criminology* 23:585–607.

Boldt, Edward D. (1978). "Structural Tightness, Autonomy and Observability: An Analysis of Hutterite Conformity and Orderliness." *Canadian Journal of Sociology* 3(3):349–363.

Boocock, S.S. (1980). *Sociology of Education: An Introduction*. Boston: Houghton Mifflin.

Boorman, Scott A., and Harrison C. White. (1976). "Social Structure From Multiple Networks II: Role Structures." *American Journal of Sociology* 81(1):1384–1446.

Boritch, Helen, and John Hagan. (1990). "A Century of Crime in Toronto: Gender, Class, and Patterns of Social Control, 1859–1955." *Criminology* 28(4):567–599.

Braithwaite, John. (1990). *Crime, Shame and Reintegration.* Cambridge, Mass.: Cambridge University Press.

Brownfield, David, and Kevin Thompson. (1991). "Attachment to Peers and Delinquent Behaviour." *Canadian Journal of Criminology* 33(1):45–60.

Clifford, William. (1976). *Crime and Control in Japan.* Lexington, Mass.: Lexington Books.

Clinard, Marshall. (1978). *Cities with Little Crime: The Case of Switzerland.* New York: Cambridge University Press.

Cohen, Lawrence E., and Marcus Felson. (1979). "Social Change and Crime Rate Trends: A Routine Activity Approach." *American Sociological Review* 44:588–608.

Craven, Paul, and Barry Wellman. (1973). "The Network City." *Sociological Inquiry* 43 (1):57–88.

Cressey, Donald R. (1971). *Other People's Money.* 2nd ed. Belmont, Cal.: Wadsworth.

Dahrendorf, Ralph. (1959). *Class and Class Conflict in Industrial Society.* London: Routledge and Keegan Paul.

Daly, Kathleen. (1989). "Gender and Varieties of White-Collar Crime." *Criminology* 27 (November):769–793.

Dinitz, Simon, Frank R. Scarpitti, and Walter C. Reckless. (1962). "Delinquency Vulnerability: A Cross-Group and Longitudinal Analysis." *American Sociological Review* 27(August):515–517.

Elliott, Delbert, and Harwin Voss. (1974). *Delinquency and Dropout.* Lexington, Mass.: Lexington Books.

Erickson, Maynard, and Lamar Empey. (1965). "Class Position, Peers and Delinquency." *Sociology and Social Research* 49:268–282.

Feeley, Malcolm, and Deborah Little. (1991). "The Vanishing Female: The Decline of Women in the Criminal Process, 1687–1912." Paper presented at the Law and Society Association meetings in June in Amsterdam.

Fischer, Claude S., Robert Max Jackson, C. Ann Steuve, Kathleen Gerson, Lynne McCallister Jones, and Mark Baldassare. (1977). *Networks and Places.* New York: Free Press.

Fox, John, and Timothy Hartnagel. (1979). "Changing Social Roles and Female Crime in Canada: A Time Series Analysis." *Canadian Review of Sociology and Anthropology* 16, (1):96–194.

Friday, Paul C., and Jerald Hage. (1976). "Youth Crime and Post-Industrial Societies: An Integrated Perspective." *Criminology* 14:331–346.

Gilligan, Carol. (1982). *In a Different Voice: Psychological Theory and Women's Development.* Cambridge, Mass.: Harvard University Press.

Giordano, Peggy C. (1987). "Confronting Control Theory's Negative Cases." Conference paper in *Theoretical Integration in the Study of Deviance and Crime: Problems and Prospects.* The Albany Conference. Department of Sociology at New York State University, Albany, New York.

Gordon, Robert. (1967). "Social Level, Social Disability, and Gang Interaction." *American Journal of Sociology* 73:420–462.

Gottfredson, Michael, and Travis Hirschi. (1990). *A General Theory of Crime.* Stanford, Cal.: Stanford University Press.

Granovetter, Mark S. (1973). "The Strength of Weak Ties." *American Journal of Sociology* 76:1360–1380.

Grasmick, Harold G., Charles R. Tittle, Robert Bursik, Jr., and Bruce J. Arnekley. (1993). "Testing the Core Empirical Implications of Gottfredson and Hirschi's General Theory of Crime." *Journal of Research in Crime and Delinquency* 30:5–29.

Green, Gary S. (1991). "An Analysis of Embezzlers' Arrest Records." Paper delivered at the annual meeting of the American Society of Criminology, November, San Francisco.

Guttentag, Marcia, and Paul F. Secord. (1983). *Too Many Women?: The Sex Ratio Question.* Beverly Hills, Cal.: Sage.

Hagan, John. (1989). *Structural Criminology.* New Brunswick, N.J.: Rutgers University Press.

——— (1992). "The Poverty of a Classless Criminology—The American Society of Criminology 1991 Presidential Address." *Criminology* 30(1):1–19.

Hagan, John, and Alberto Palloni. (1990). "The Social Reproduction of a Criminal Class in Working-Class London, circa 1950–1980." *American Journal of Sociology* 96 (2):265–299.

Hagan, John, A.R. Gillis, and John Simpson. (1985). "The Class Structure of Gender and Delinquency: Toward a Power-Control Theory of Common Delinquent Behavior." *American Journal of Sociology* 90:1151–1178.

Hagan, John, A. Ron Gillis, and John Simpson. (1990). "Clarifying and Extending Power-Control Theory." *American Journal of Sociology* 95(4):1024–1037.

———. (1993). "The Power of Control in Sociological Theories of Delinquency." In Freda Adler and William S. Adler (eds.), *New Directions in Criminological Theory. Advances in Criminological Theory,* Vol. 4. New Brunswick, N.J.: Transaction, 381–397.

Hansell, Stephen, and Michael Wiatrowski. (1981). "Competing Conceptions of Delinquent Peer Relations." In Gary Jensen (ed.), *Sociology of Delinquency.* Beverly Hills: Sage.

Hindelang, Michael. (1973). "Causes of Delinquency: A Partial Replication and Extension." *Social Problems* 21:471–487.

Hindelang, Michael, Travis Hirschi, and Joseph Weis. (1981). *Measuring Delinquency.* Beverly Hills: Sage.

Hirschi, Travis. (1969). *Causes of Delinquency.* Berkeley, Cal.: University of California Press.

Hirschi, Travis, and Michael R. Gottfredson (eds.). (1993). *The Generality of Deviance.* New Brunswick, N.J.: Transaction.

Jenson, Gary F. (1993). "Power-Control vs. Social Control Theories of Common Delinquency: A Comparative Analysis." In Freda Adler and William S. Adler (eds.), *New Directions in Criminological Theory.* Advances in Criminological Theory, Vol. 4. New Brunswick, N.J.: Transaction, 363–398.

Johnson, R.E. (1980). "Social Class and Delinquent Behavior: A New Test." *Criminology* 18:91.

Kadushin, Charles. (1983). "Mental Health and the Interpersonal Environment: A Reexamination of Some Effects of Social Structure on Mental Health." *American Sociological Review* 48:188–198.

Kempf, Kimberly L. (1993). "The Empirical Status of Hirschi's Control Theory." In Freda Adler and Willaim S. Adler (eds.), *New Directions in Criminological Theory. Advances in Criminological Theory,* Vol. 4. New Brunswick, N.J.: Transaction, 143–185.

Kennedy, L.W., and D.R. Forde. (1990). "Routine Activities and Crime: An Analysis of Victimization in Canada." *Criminology* 28(1):101–115.

Klein, D., and J. Kress. (1976). "Any Woman's Blues: A Critical Overview of Women, Crime and the Criminal Justice System." *Crime and Social Justice* 5(Spring–Summer):34–49.

Krohn, Marvin D. (1986). "The Web of Conformity: A Network Approach to the Explanation of Delinquent Behavior." *Social Problems* 33(6):581–593.

Laumann, Edward O. (1973). *Bonds of Pluralism.* New York: John Wiley.

———. (1976). *Networks of Collective Action: A Perspective on Community Influence.* New York: Academic Press.

Laumann, Edward, Joseph Caleskiewicz, and Peter Marsden. (1978). "Community Structures as Interorganizational Linkages." *Annual Review of Sociology* 4:455–484.

Linden, E., and J. Hackler. (1973). "Affective Ties and Delinquency." *Pacific Sociological Review* 16:27–46.

Liska, Allen E., and Mark D. Reed. (1985). "Ties to Conventional Institutions and Delinquency: Estimating Reciprocal Effects." *American Sociological Review* 50(August):547–560.

Macdonald, Patrick T. (1989). "Competing Theoretical Explanations of Cocaine Use: Differential Association versus Control Theory." *Journal of Contemporary Criminal Justice* 5(2):73–88.

Massey, James, and Marvin Krohn. (1986). "A Longitudinal Examination of an Integrated Social Process Model of Deviant Behavior." *Social Forces* 65:106–134.

McCarthy, Bill, and John Hagan. (1987). "Gender, Delinquency and the Great Depression: A Test for Power-Control Theory." *Canadian Review of Sociology and Anthropology* 24 (2):153–177.

Meier, Robert F. (1987). "Deviance and Differentiation." Conference paper in *Theoretical Integration in the Study of Deviance and Crime: Problems and Prospects.* The Albany Conference. Department of Sociology, New York State University, at Albany, New York.

Milgram, Stanley. (1970). "The Experience of Living in Cities." *Science* 167:1461–1468.

Nettler, Gwynn. (1974). "Embezzlement Without Problems." *British Journal of Criminology* 14:70–77.

———. (1982). *Lying, Cheating, Stealing.* Vol. 3 of *Criminal Careers.* Cincinnati: Anderson.

Nye, F.I. (1958). *Family Relationships and Delinquent Behavior.* New York: John Wiley.

O'Brien, Robert. (1991). "Sex Ratios and Rape Rates: A Power-Control Theory." *Criminology* 29(1):99–114.

Osgood, D. Wayne, Janet K. Wilson, Patrick M. O'Malley, Jerald G. Bachman, and Lloyd D. Johnston. (1996). "Routine Activities and Individual Deviant Behavior." *American Sociological Review* 61(4):635–655.

Reckless, Walter C. (1967). *The Crime Problem*. New York: Appleton-Century-Crofts.

——. (1973). *The Crime Problem*. (5th ed.). New York: Appleton-Century-Crofts.

Reckless, Walter C., and Simon Dinitz. (1967). "Pioneering with Self-Concept as a Vulnerability Factor in Delinquency." *Journal of Criminal Law, Criminology and Police Science* 58:515–523.

Reckless, Walter C., Simon Dinitz, and Ellen Murray. (1996). "Self-Concept as an Insulator against Delinquency." *American Sociological Review* 21 (December):744–746.

Reed, Gary E., and Peter Cleary Yeager. (1996). "Organizational Offending and Neoclassical Criminology. Challenging the Reach of a General Theory of Crime." *Criminology* 34(3):357–382.

Rogers, Joseph. (1970). *Why Are You Not a Criminal?* Englewood Cliffs, N.J.: Prentice-Hall.

Sampson, Robert J. (1985). "Neighborhood and Crime: The Structural Determinants of Personal Victimization." *Journal of Research in Crime and Delinquency* 22:7–40.

Sampson, Robert J., and John H. Laub. (1993). *Crime in the Making: Pathways and Turning Points Through Life*. Cambridge Mass.: Harvard University Press.

Scarpitti, Frank R., Ellen Murray, Simon Dinitz, and Walter C. Reckless. (1960). "The 'Good' Boy in a High-Delinquency Area: Four Years Later." *American Sociological Review* 25(August):555–558.

Simon, Rita J. (1976). "American Women and Crime." *Annals of the American Academy of Political and Social Science* 423:31–46.

Smart, Carol. (1978). *Women, Crime and Criminology*. London: Routledge and Keegan Paul.

Stark, Rodney, William Sims, Robert L. Crutchfield, Daniel P. Doyle, and Roger Finke. (1983). "Crime and Delinquency in the Roaring Twenties." *Journal of Research in Crime and Delinquency* 20:4–23.

Steffensmeier, Darrell J. (1980). "Sex Differences in Patterns of Adult Crime, *1965–1977*: A Review and Assessment." *Social Forces* 58(4):1080–1108.

——. (1981a). "Crime and the Contemporary Woman: An Analysis of Changing Levels of Female Property Crime, 1960–1975." In Lee H. Bowker (ed.), *Women and Crime in America*. New York: Macmillan.

——. (1981b). "Patterns of Female Property Crime, 1960–1978: A Postscript." In Lee H. Bowker (ed.), *Women and Crime in America*. New York: Macmillan.

Steffensmeier, Darrell, and Emilie Allan. (1996). "Gender and Crime: Toward a Gendered Theory of Female Offending." *Annual Review of Sociology* 22:459–487.

Suttles, Gerald. (1972). *The Social Construction of Communities*. Chicago: University of Chicago Press.

Thio, A. (1988). *Deviant Behavior*. New York: Harper and Row.

Tittle, Charles R. (1995). *Control Balance: Toward a General Theory of Deviance*. Boulder, Col.: Westiew Press.

Toby, Jackson. (1957). "Social Disorganization and Stake in Conformity: Complementary Factors in the Predatory Behavior of Young Hoodlums." *Journal of Criminal Law, Criminology and Police Science* 48:12–17.

Vold, George B., and Thomas J. Bernard. (1986). *Theoretical Criminology.* 3rd ed. Oxford: Oxford University Press.

Wellman, Barry. (1979). "The Community Question: The Intimate Networks of East Yorkers." *American Journal of Sociology* 84(5):1201–1231.

Wellman, Barry, and Barry Leighton. (1979). "Networks, Neighborhoods and Communities: Approaches to the Study of the Community Question." *Urban Affairs Quarterly* 14:363–390.

White, Harrison, Scott Boorman, and Ronald Brieger. (1976). "Social Structure From Multiple Networks I: Block Models of Roles and Positions." *American Journal of Sociology* 81:730–780.

Wiatrowski, Michael, and Kristine L. Anderson. (1987). "The Dimensionality of the Social Bond." *Journal of Quantitative Criminology* 3(1):65–79.

Wiatrowski, Michael, David B. Griswold, and Mary K. Roberts. (1981). "Social Control Theory and Delinquency." *American Sociological Review* 46(October):525–541.

Williams, J.R., and M. Gold. (1972). "From Delinquent Behavior to Official Delinquency." *Social Problems* 20:209–229.

Winslow, Robert W., and Phillip T. Gay. (1993). "The Moral Minorities: A Self-Report Study of Low-Consensus Deviance." *International Journal of Offender Therapy and Comparative Criminology* 37(1):17–27.

Zeitz, Dorothy. (1981). *Women Who Embezzle or Defraud.* New York: Praeger.

CONFLICT

THEORIES

A 1986 newspaper story told of three children under the age of 3 who had been left unattended overnight. All of the children had been bitten by rats, including a 5-month-old baby. The children's mother, aged 22, was arrested and, unable to raise bail, kept in jail (Smart 1985).

The theories that we have looked at thus far would most likely locate the cause of the children's suffering as the evil, irresponsible, mentally ill, or undercontrolled mother. Demonic theory would probably call her a witch or say she was possessed. Classical theory might say the law was not severe enough or not well enough enforced. Constitutional theories would look at her inadequate superego, her compulsions for drugs or sex, her need for company, or her depression. The Chicago School would lay some blame on her disrupted family, the kind of neighbourhood she was living in, and the absence of community support for single mothers. The control theories would see her as inadequately socialized and without effective supervision.

Conflict theories, however, would come to different conclusions and would pose different questions. They might ask, for example, how is it possible that a modern, industrial-urban society, which can conduct space exploration and provide huge sports arenas with retractable roofs, has housing that contains rats? How does the economic and political system work so that young mothers with children are assigned such housing? How does it come about that a young woman of 22 is raising three children under the age of three on her own? Was she out making money to help her children live better? Was she being exploited by a pimp or sweatshop employer? Was she hooked on drugs as an escape from hopelessness? Why is the mother criminalized rather than assisted? Why was there no blame attached to the people around her who saw and did nothing, or to the landlord, or to the politicians who set conditions for social welfare? Like interpretive theories, but much more openly, conflict theories tend to "take the side of the underdog."

In *The Red Lily* (1894), novelist Anatole France observed that the law forbids both rich and poor "to sleep under bridges, to beg in the streets and to steal bread." Implicit in this brief statement are several insights relevant to the conflict approach to deviance. First, the rules (whether legal or customary) are made by the powerful and tend to regulate the conduct of the powerless. The law that forbids begging is egalitarian in its formulation (everyone is equally forbidden to beg), but it is not egalitarian in its impact, since it restricts only those people for whom begging is a necessary or preferred source of income.

Second, the rules are part of a system that preserves the preferred way of life for the powerful even when it is harmful for others, or forces them into criminal or deviant roles. A criminal's perceptive perspective on this is summarized in the title of bank robber Micky McArthur's memoirs *I'd Rather Be Wanted Than Had* (1990). McArthur clearly feels that playing the game the way it is set up (obeying the law) is letting others steal from you.

Table 12.1   Comparison of Modern Sociological Theories

	Social Control	**Conflict**
Conception of deviance	Natural	Constructed as excuse for control
Explanation	Failure of internal and external controls	Criminalization serves capitalist interest
Remedies	Strengthen family, civil religion, and other institutions	Modify or overthrow capitalism

Third, people who break the rules do so either out of need or in protest against a system that oppresses them. People may sleep under bridges because they have no other options, or because they resent the controls imposed by missions and agencies for the poor. The auto dealer may engage in price gouging because it is the only way to stay in business given the current structure of the marketplace (Leonard and

Weber 1991). The company engineer who cuts corners on safety may do so because continued employment depends on meeting the unrealistic goals set by upper management (Dowie 1991).

While many conflict theorists take the position that upper-level crime is motivated by boundless greed, most see the upper-level deviant as a participant in a system that rewards cheating and discourages or penalizes honesty whenever it jeopardizes profit margins. Conflict theory's deviants, whether high or low status, are not sick, undercontrolled, or perverse. They are simply individuals who are attempting to make the best of unequal opportunities, either from within the system or outside it.

Other propositions that characterize conflict theory are:

1. *Power is the most important explanatory variable.* The fact that some people have more power than others and use it to maintain or improve their position at the expense of others is the fundamental cause of social problems, including deviance, racism, sexism, war, and environmental degradation.

2. *Groups with clashing interests and values, and with unequal resources, compete with each other, thereby producing winners and losers.* Conflicts do not benefit society as a whole. Rather they benefit some groups at the expense of others, and often at the expense of the whole.

3. *Groups struggle to have their own definitions of right and wrong established as part of the status quo, and even made into law.* The imposition of these definitions and laws serves to constrain their competitors whose customs are made illegal, deviant, or irrelevant.

4. *Definitions of crime and deviance are weapons in the struggle between groups for a share of power in the system.* Successful competitors see their rules enforced and other people's rules marginalized as subcultures. Any law or rule can be understood by posing the question "Who gains?" and by tracing the path back to the interests of those in power.

5. *Deviance is neither normal nor inevitable.* People break rules because something is wrong with the way in which society is structured.

6. *The source of deviance does not reside in the body/mind of the individual, but rather in the unequal relationships between people.* Individualistic explanations of deviance and crime are ideological tools used by those in power to justify the state's use of "therapeutic" intervention (i.e., treating noncomformists with mood-modifying drugs, psychotherapy, psychosurgery, and other mind-altering techniques).

VALUE NEUTRALITY AND PRAXIS

Early pluralist conflict theorists, following the lead of Max Weber and influenced by the scientific bias in society, attempted to separate their roles as theorists/researchers from their role as "concerned citizens." In their quest for value neutrality, they sought to study current realities and future possibilities in strictly empirical terms, and to avoid emotional involvement with the issues of their research. Just as medical researchers would be regarded as having stepped outside their role if they were to give lectures on the perniciousness of a particular disease (instead of studying its origin and how it spreads), so the social researcher given to making political judgments would be seen as having strayed outside professional boundaries.

Later conflict theorists, particularly those following in the path of Karl Marx, have argued that it is not only impossible but immoral to separate the "is" from the "ought to be." From their perspective, the responsibility of the researcher is to engage in either short- or long-term praxis. *Praxis* means combining knowledge and activism to challenge oppressive ideologies or structures. Praxiological research is aimed at the analysis of oppressive social structures and is in itself both academic and political (Harvey 1990:22–23).

According to praxiological thinkers, the social scientist should engage in the critical study of the "real" nature of society in order to expose its structures of domination and undermine the pervasive legitimating ideologies that sustain them. While conflict theorists might, for example, study the law in order to reveal and document its role as an instrument of class oppression, they should not attempt to collect information that could be used to make the oppressive more effective or efficient (Collins 1984:1). Similarly, a conflict approach to social work would attempt to reveal the ways in which social workers are expected to control and contain disadvantaged groups in order to keep the dominant system from being inconvenienced by them. A conflict theorist would try to find ways to transform social workers into agents of change that would empower the disadvantaged.

MARXIST THEORIES

KARL MARX

For Marx (1818–1883), crime and deviance were relatively unimportant by-products of the division of capitalist society into owners of the means of production (the *bourgeoisie),* wage earners (the *proletariat),* and those whose survival depends on crime or welfare (the *lumpenproletariat).* According to Marx, the capitalist system is motivated more by competition than greed. Marxism is a structural theory that emphasizes the system over personal characteristics as the driving force behind social action. Workers are exploited largely because employers who do not exploit them will soon be displaced, through competition, by those who will.

The system of industrial capitalism has produced factories and work places in which workers experience conditions of "alienation," whereby neither the process of work nor the ultimate "product" has meaning for them. The extreme case of this is the assembly line, in which each worker is little more than a cog in a machine that produces machines. Alienation is assumed to lead to many kinds of deviance, such as sabotage, that express human needs for meaningful activity and personal significance.

The needs of successful capitalist enterprise are often at odds with the interests of other groups in society, not just those of employees. The expropriation of lands for commercial purposes, which was a feature of early capitalism, helped create a disenfranchised class composed of "beggars, robbers [and] vagabonds," who were treated by the law as willful criminals, even though much of their behaviour was based on need or protest (Marx [1867] 1987:734).

Marx was ambivalent about the lumpenproletariat of his day, considering a large proportion of them to be social parasites who weakened the ranks of labour (Liska 1987:176; Taylor, Walton, and Young 1973). His colleague, Friedrich Engels, came to the conclusion that crime by the poor was a form of political protest. Many Marxists feel that Marxism cannot be applied to crime and deviance without producing serious distortions (revisionism). As in power-control theory, there is tension between the feeling that crime is *real*, and the theory's revelation that it is *constructed* (Hirst 1972:29; Mugford 1974:595).

WILLEM BONGER

Willem Bonger (1876—1940) was the first criminologist to use the Marxian perspective to explain crime and criminal thought. According to Bonger (1916), capitalism produces crime because it makes everyone in the system greedy. Only by taking the means of production out of the hands of the few, and by distributing resources on the basis of need, would it be possible to avoid the greed-driven (but unrecognized) criminality of the rich and the officially recognized deviance of the poor. Bonger felt that if the structurally induced forms of crime were eliminated, all that would remain would be a small residue of psychopathic forms.

INSTRUMENTAL MARXISM

According to this approach, the state (which includes government, military, and law enforcement institutions) is a tool of the ruling class. Definitions of crime and deviance are made by the state in the interests of the propertied classes. Miliband (1969) provides support for this characterization by documenting the strong ideological and social connections between economic and political elites and the rules that we live by.

Richard Quinney

Richard Quinney has had several theoretical incarnations. In 1977, his approach expressed an instrumental Marxist viewpoint. Quinney (1977) sees crime and deviance as products of the need of the ruling class to control the proletariat. In his view, the criminal law is an instrument of the state and the ruling class in that it is formulated by the state in order to serve the interests of the owners of the means of production.

Quinney attributes the growth of proletariat and "surplus" populations to the crises that afflict capitalism in its later stages. Competition, particularly in periods

Figure 12.1   A Neo-Marxist Model

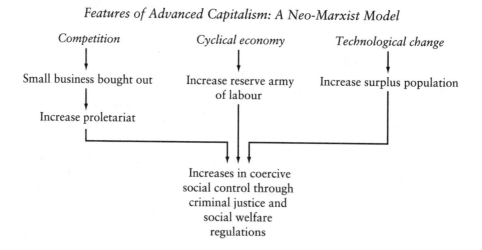

Features of Advanced Capitalism: A Neo-Marxist Model

Source: Adapted from Richard Quencey, *Class, State, and Crime.* New York: McKay, 1977.

of recession, continually depletes the ranks of the owners. By joining the ranks of salaried employees, these displaced capitalists contribute to the growth of the proletariat. At the same time, however, technological advances render an increasing number of wage earners redundant and unemployable, since their type of work no longer exists. Thus, the surplus population also grows. According to Quinney, the control of both populations is performed by two increasingly coercive state institutions, criminal justice and social welfare. Those subjected to these institutional controls are assigned negative labels that justify their loss of autonomy.

STRUCTURAL MARXISM

Structural Marxism argues that it is not the interests of the ruling class alone that are protected by rule making, but those of the capitalist system as a whole. While the interests of the system and its primary beneficiaries normally coincide, in some areas they do not. For example, capitalism requires competition, yet many capitalists do everything in their power to drive competitors out of the market or to create price-fixing arrangements that make competition unnecessary (Sutherland 1949; Goff and Reasons 1978; Snider 1992). If their actions threaten the system, individual capitalists may be criminalized or marginalized.

The structural Marxist approach gives some emphasis to the fact that the owners do not constitute a monolithic class. Indeed, as a group they are characterized by substantial divisions. Marginal members of the class are frequently sacrificed to the legal system in order to convince the public that justice is being served. Smaller marginal companies are much more likely to be successfully prosecuted on pollution and safety charges than are their larger and more "deviant" counterparts (Snider 1992). Similarly, structural Marxism recognizes that the government may on occasion put its own interests (such as getting re-elected) before those of the ruling class (Chambliss and Seidman 1982).

Stephen Spitzer

Much of Spitzer's (1975) theory parallels the ideas of Quinney in its analysis of how surplus population is produced and how invisible controls of the marketplace are replaced by the visible fist of the state. To this he adds the contradictions of capitalism: for example, an education system that produces the necessary workforce but also teaches its members to think, thereby making them potential troublemakers for the capitalist system. For Spitzer, however, definitions of deviance serve to protect the capitalist system as a whole rather than the ruling class per se, as Quinney theorized.

Spitzer identifies groups who threaten the capitalist system as "problem populations" who are most likely to be classified as deviant and targeted for official control.

Included in such populations are those who commit theft, especially if they are poor and steal from the rich (people who commit theft in the form of consumer fraud are exempted from membership in the problem population because they do not threaten the system); workers who organize or strike; and youths who drop out of school. Spitzer argues that criminalization is not the only means of control enforced in capitalist societies. Problem populations may be siphoned into the military or into public works projects; alternatively, they may be co-opted into playing roles within the system (as, for example, when a gang is recruited to help run a recreational centre) or diverted into local political groups that are considered nonthreatening.

CRITICAL THEORIES

THE FRANKFURT SCHOOL

The Frankfurt School was established by Felix Weil in the early 1920s. Among its first generation were Theodor W. Adorno, Max Horkheimer, Herbert Marcuse, Friedrich Pollock, Leo Lowenthal, and Walter Benjamin. Not surprisingly, given its exile to New York during the Nazi period, the school focused much of its research on such issues as the "authoritarian personality" and the inculcation of "false consciousness" that led people to support regimes that oppressed and dominated them. The school disbanded in the late 1960s, just as its traditions were beginning to take hold in North America.

The initial issue addressed by the Frankfurt School was why the socialist revolution prophesied by Marx had not occurred when and where the theory would have predicted. Revolutionary Russia had not been a highly capitalistic country, while capitalistic Western European countries themselves seemed far away from the predicted workers' revolt. In the school's view, Marx had been correct about the increasingly serious internal contradictions of capitalism; however, he had underestimated the extent to which "false consciousness" could be fostered and exploited such that, despite periodic crises, the majority of the people saw the existing system as inevitable, rational, and unchangeable. The domination of society by the state was a combination of external exploitation (which contributed to powerlessness) and ideological indoctrination (which constituted "discipline from the inside" or "surplus repression") (Marcuse 1965:32–34).

The Frankfurt School theorists also challenged the ideas of positivism (including Marxist positivism), which they saw as a technique for producing passivity and fatalism. Instead of studying the status quo as an inevitable condition of life, they treated "social facts" as historical products that can and should be questioned and changed. The critical school theorists generally rejected the scientific method. Their goal was "emancipation and enlightenment" through the revelation of hidden coercion and the discovery of "real" interests (Geuss 1981:55).

ANTONIO GRAMSCI AND HEGEMONY

Neo-Marxists working outside the Frankfurt School have also developed theories that stress the importance of ideas and how they are controlled. Antonio Gramsci (1891–1937), who was imprisoned under Mussolini's fascist regime, argued that Marx's theory needed to be expanded to include not only the economic base but also the repressive and ideological apparatuses of the state (Gramsci 1971).

Gramsci's concept of *hegemony* has been particularly important in the study of deviance. Hegemony refers to a worldview so dominant that people are unable to conceive of alternative possibilities. It is the "common sense" of the society, the fund of definitions and descriptions of social situations and social needs that normally goes without saying. Hegemony emerges out of the combination of dominance that is inherent in hierarchical structures (the opinions of employers are more important than those of employees) and the "manufacture of consent" facilitated by the media, educational institutions, and religion. Thus, hegemony is ideological and cultural authority that represents the perspective of the dominant groups in the society.

Gramsci argued that hegemony was never entirely complete or uncontested, because it competed with the awareness that was produced in the daily experience of people who were oppressed by it. The working class possessed a "dual consciousness" that could be the basis for the development of a revolutionary consciousness. Kinsman (1987) uses the concept of hegemony to raise consciousness with respect to the worldview that supports heterosexuality over every other sexual reality. Similarly, feminists point to the hegemonic characteristics of patriarchy.

PLURALIST CONFLICT THEORIES

Pluralist (liberal) conflict theory traces its roots back to the work of Max Weber (1864–1920). Much of Weber's work can be viewed as an argument with the theories of Karl Marx. Weber felt that the economy was not the only determinant of conflict in the society, or not always the most important one. His successors developed pluralist views of conflict according to which society is characterized by the competition among many different groups, each of which has access to certain power-relevant resources. Groups may variously have many members with education, expertise, wealth, or connections with power-holders.

Conflict between groups results in winners and losers, most of whom remain in the field. Since social change improves the resources of some, and depletes the resources of others, the contest is never entirely over. Pluralist conflict theory allows for groups to improve their position in the whole and to force others to live by their standards, at least in the short term. Deviance definitions are just one weapon powerful groups use to weaken and control competitors who are not strong enough to cast them off. The relevance of pluralist conflict theory for deviance lies in the relationship between "winning" in the conflict between groups and being able to establish rules that give the winner more freedom and the loser more constraints. The people labelled deviant are disproportionately drawn from the losers.

Vold's (1958) theory of group conflict is regarded by many as a classic statement of pluralist conflict theory. In Vold's view, laws and rules are produced by politically organized groups who seek the assistance of government in their efforts to defend their rights and protect their interests. When successful, new rules and laws tend to limit the rights of others and hamper their interests. Thus, crime is a form of political resistance against the rules that are set by other groups; only a very small proportion of it is meaningless or pathological.

Box 12.1   Richard Quinney and The Social Reality of Crime

In *The Social Reality of Crime* (1970), Richard Quinney outlines a pluralistic conflict position in the form of six propositions as follows.

1. *Crime is a definition of behaviour that is made by authorized agents in the political process.* As such, it is not a product of individual psychopathology or immorality. It follows from this that an increase in the number of criminal definitions will be answered by a corresponding increase in the amount of crime.

2. *Criminal definitions reflect the fact that the desires, values, and interests of the most powerful groups (i.e., those with the greatest influence on rule-making) often conflict with the interests of less powerful groups.* These interests may change over time, especially if the composition of the dominant groups changes. More conflict and change in society means more rules being formulated and applied, and hence more crime.

3. *The manner in which the rules are enforced depends on the extent to which authorities see particular infractions as a threat to their interests.* Criminal definitions are applied most vigorously to behaviour that is most conspicuously opposed to the interests of the powerful.

Richard Quinney and The Social Reality of Crime (cont.)

4. *The behaviour of people in less powerful segments of society has a greater likelihood of being defined as criminal, and may be partly structured in response to the criminal definitions that are applied to it.* The pattern that is established by the rule breakers and the rule enforcers may become reciprocally reinforcing, as each group acts in terms of its self-concept and its definition of the other.

5. *The media and other communications institutions play a major role in constructing and disseminating images of crime.* Their influence is such that people in all segments of society tend to agree that particular actions presented in the media are deviant or criminal.

6. *The social reality of crime is constructed by the formulation and application of definitions made by those who have influence over the rule making (political) process, by the development of behavioural patterns in response to these definitions, and by the dissemination of conceptions of crime, by way of social communications media.*

Quinney later dismissed the pluralistic conflict position presented in *The Social Reality of Crime* as a "bourgeois academic exercise," and took up the neo-Marxist instrumental position described earlier in this chapter. He has since become a spokesman for "peacekeeping theory," discussed below.

THE NEW CRIMINOLOGY

An addition to the conflict theoretical approaches was introduced in the 1970s by criminologists who were working in both Britain and Canada. Among the founders of the new criminology were Ian Taylor, Paul Walton, and Jock Young (1973, 1975). Their deviancy theory combined social interactionism, Marxist concepts and categories, and radical attitudes that supported the elimination of capitalist oppression. Although itself short-lived, the new criminology has seen some of its ideas recently revived in human rights theory, which emphasizes using existing human rights codes as the standards by which behaviour should be judged (Galliher 1991; Vaughan and Sjoberg 1986), and left realism, which treats crime and deviance as real problems.

According to the new criminology, systems of control are inherently unjust because their real goals are self-perpetuation and self-aggrandizement. The law is a system that reflects workplace morality as conceived by the upper class as a guide for the lower class, not for itself. Crime is resistance on the part of those who are being "had" by the system. In this view, it is capitalism that is criminally deviant, not only in the sense that it causes crime, but also in the sense that it oppresses, exploits, and degrades human bodies while at the same time distorting and constraining human minds.

New criminology theorists argued that deviance and crime were nothing more than the result of capitalism, and that correctionalism (crime control) was simply a tool of that system. The new deviancy theory strove for a social order in which the "facts of human diversity" would not be "subject to the power to criminalize" (Taylor, Walton, and Young 1973:282). In the idealized society, no one would be a criminal, regardless of their actions. An extension of this is found in "peacemaking theory," which combines elements of Marxian and Gandhian humanism with a religious base to criticize the violence of the criminal justice system and argue for a system expressing compassion, forgiveness, and love (Pepinsky and Quinney 1991: ix). Rock (1979:80) was not alone in seeing this hypothesis as a "drift into other-worldliness" (left idealism), especially when its view of deviants as misunderstood, oppressed freedom seekers was contrasted with the realities of violent crime, brutality, and family violence. Indeed, new criminology theorists tended to focus their attention on issues like soft drug use (Young 1971) and moral panics about hooligans (Cohen 1971), avoiding "left realist" issues like crimes against women, blacks, and the working class (Jary and Jary 1991:330). Left realists argued that however much the ultimate origins of crime were located in the capitalist system, it was necessary to control crime in the interests of all citizens. It is notable that, in the course of studying the empirical reality of crime and crime control, most advocates of this perspective came to adopt less idealistic positions (Goode 1990:80).

Box 12.2   Left Realism: Crime Really Is a Problem

Crime is not an activity of latter-day Robin Hoods—the vast majority of working-class crime is directed within the working class. It is intra-class, not inter-class in nature. Similarly, despite the mass media predilection for focusing on inter-racial crime, it is overwhelmingly intra-racial. Crimes of violence, for example, are by and large one poor person hitting another poor person—and in almost half of these instances it is a man hitting his wife.

Left Realism: Crime Really Is a Problem (cont.)

This is not to deny the impact of crimes of the powerful or indeed of the social problems created by capitalism which are perfectly legal. Rather, left realism notes that the working class is a victim of crime from all directions. It notes that the more vulnerable a person is economically and socially the more likely it is that *both* [author's italics] working-class and white-collar crime will occur against them ...

Realism is not empiricism. Crime and deviance are prime sites of moral anxiety and tension in a society that is fraught with real inequalities and injustices. Criminals can quite easily become folk devils onto which are projected such feelings of unfairness. But there is a rational core to the fear of crime, just as there is a rational core to the anxieties that distort it. Realism argues with popular consciousness in its attempts to separate out reality from fantasy. But it does not deny that crime is a problem.

Source: Jock Young, "The Failure of Criminology," in R. Matthews and J. Young (eds.), *Confronting Crime* (London: Sage, 1986), 23–24. Reprinted by permission.

Box 12.3　The Intellectual Climate of Discourse Theories

Discourse theories have tended to be led by intellectually charismatic figures such as Jacques Derrida, Jean Baudrillard, and Michel Foucault, who are surrounded by acolytes and disciples. While the source of the ideas behind the theories can be traced to the German philosophical tradition, their focus centred on Paris, where the intellectual environment encouraged scholarship that was showy, but often deliberately provocative, opaque, and labyrinthine. It was full of flashy neologisms and startling statements along the lines of the "God is dead" controversy. The successful lecture was one that played a game with the listeners. It produced a good deal of discussion about what the theory really meant in itself and in relation to the ideas of competing savants. Intellectuals played a role not unlike that of celebrity movie stars or sports figures, and had to be "new" all the time to retain the attention and loyalty of their followers. It did not pay to be too easily understood, or too clear about the methods that were used to create stunning, artistic, and deeply philosophical observations. The writings of these intellectuals

The Intellectual Climate of Discourse Theories (cont.)

became bestsellers in the book market, left on coffee tables to show social status. These philosophers were also expected to be at the forefront of various political actions, including campaigns against all kinds of oppression: the student uprisings in Europe in 1968, Algerian immigrants, the Solidarity trade unionists of Poland, and so forth (Miller 1993:15). Given this atmosphere, it is somewhat surprising that this type of thought contributed a great deal to the understanding of deviance and control.

DISCOURSE THEORIES: STRUCTURALISM, POST-STRUCTURALISM, AND POSTMODERNISM

Discourses are modes of making meaning in society. They provide the modes of expression that shape what can be said and thought. Scientific discourse, for example, was not available to people who lived before A.D. 1700, so that other understandings dominated. In many parts of the world, religious discourses still predominate, and may even be gaining strength. In the Western world, the discourses of medicine, psychology, sociology, criminology, and technology tend to dominate the ways in which deviance and crime are understood. Discourse theories attempt to "deconstruct" these discourses, showing how they have been formed, highlighting the ways they channel thoughts so that the dominant powerholders of their time are supported. The channelling may occur through the things that are said, in words, print, or pictures. It may also be through what does *not* appear. Dominant discourses silence or marginalize alternative views. Consider, for example, how the dominant conception of male and female gender roles has, until recently, almost totally suppressed the voices, and even recognition of, alternative sexualities (Burrington 1994).

While discourse theories may take some inspiration from Marxism, and on occasion draw on its concepts, they ultimately reject Marxist ideology and method. Far more than Marx, or even Gramsci, these theories investigate the origins and nature of the dominant modes of expression in society, its accepted truths, and its sacred ideologies. They are critical conflict theories in the sense that they see the dominant discourses of our time (science, medicine, capitalist economics) as forces that produce docile, limited human beings who are disciplined into conformity with the political economy of their time. In a process extending from the fifteenth century beginnings of the Enlightenment, these producing forces have turned out people who see work and discipline as necessary and even good, who are unaware of how they come to be convinced of this, and who lack the emancipatory discourses (ways of thought) through which they could be liberated.

The word "structuralism" as it is used in discourse theories differs from the usual sociological concept of structure as the constellation of roles and the relations between them, which together constitute a social order. The structure sought by the structuralist inheres in the hidden reality that lies behind the production of meanings in the social order, and this is intimately bound up with the nature of language.

Structuralists like Ferdinand de Saussure and Jacques Derrida are distinguished by their conviction that the basis of the social order resides in the structure of language. Poststructuralists (Mikhail Bakhtin, Michel Foucault, Pierre Bourdieu) reject this, arguing that discourses (meaning-constellations) are pragmatically constructed in processes of social communication in particular historical contexts. They are made and remade, and can be challenged by practices that "transgress" their rules—practices that are usually interpreted as deviance *because* they transgress these rules. An example of this can be found in Stanley's (1995) analysis of adolescent joyriding, raving, and hacking as transgressive activities that produce a "wild zone" of unregulated activity that "tactically subverts rationalised space" (91).

The methodology of the structuralist and poststructuralist is generally either hermeneutic (interpretive) or deconstructionist (undoing the social work that has created a social reality). The early study of hermeneutics involved trying to uncover the authentic version of the Bible in a period in which handwritten copies often contained errors. The theory and methodology were later applied to the study of all kinds of texts, and are eventually used to "read" culture as a kind of text.

Box 12.4   Escape From Deviance: Crossing the Post-Modern Divide

Central to the general argument of postmodernism is the thesis that holds that the Englightenment, once it is subjected to a disenchanting critical analysis, will reveal itself as little more than a rhetorical mask for privilege and privileging. Reason, the argument continues, finds its ultimate expression in hierarchies and dichotomies. These in turn become the representational terms for discourses on various collectivities of color, gender, lineage, culture, and praxis. Thus, to take one prominent example, Homi K. Bhabha

Escape From Deviance: Crossing the Post-Modern Divide (cont.)

exposes the purposes behind "colonial discourse": "The objective of colonial discourse is to construe the colonized as a population of degenerate types on the basis of racial origin, in order to justify conquest and to establish systems of administration and instruction." To such post-Englightenment critics, blacks, Asians, women and homosexuals are the major inhabitants of that philosophy's body of warrantable excludables; or in the language of sociology, of ostracized "deviants."

The ultimate source of the marginalization of these victims of the Englightenment is the very idea of *difference* ... Lest one suppose that such hegemonically-driven differences as man/woman and heterosexual/homosexual are to be retained, [Monique] Wittig offers a critique of the totalizing effects of the conceptualizations of what she designates as the "straight mind"—i.e., the representative carrier of the discourse at the root of modern scientific thinking, a discourse that assumes that there is a "core of nature" in modernist cultural discourse ... As Wittig sees the matter:

> I can only underline the oppressive character that the straight mind is clothed in its tendency to immediately universalize its production of concepts into general laws which claim to hold true for all societies, all epochs, all individuals. Thus one speaks of *the* exchange of women, *the* difference between the sexes, *the* symbolic order ... giving absolute meaning to these concepts when they are only categories founded upon heterosexuality or on thought which produces the difference between the sexes as a political and philosophical dogma.

Sources: From Stanford M. Lyman "Without Morals or Mores: Deviance in Postmodern Social Theory," *International Journal of Politics, Culture and Society* 9(2) (1995):212–213 (copyright Human Sciences Press); and Monique Wittig, "The Straight Mind," in Russel Ferguson et al. (eds.), *Out There: Marginalization and Contemporary Culture* (Cambridge, Mass.: MIT Press, [1990]), 51–57. Reprinted by permission.

POSTMODERNISM

The terms "postmodernist" and "poststructuralist" often include the same authors and very similar kinds of work. Modernism refers to the culture of the first half of the twentieth century, expressed, for example, in the highly functional glass and steel towers of buildings such as New York's Seagram Building, completed in 1958 and contemporaneous with a society based on rationality and science. With postmodernism, however, form no longer closely follows function, or any fixed rules. Postmodernism, if it "copies" modernism, does so ironically, comically, with a deliberate avoidance of fixed rules such as functionality or conformity. Postmodern writers give highest value to nonlinear thought (overturning conventions of linguistic order) and to overturning, through deconstruction, the "master narratives" of white-male-Western-middle-class claims to knowledge. Some postmodernists are deeply cynical about all systems of meaning, tending to see the whole world as caught up in the "hyperreal" fantasy-reality of mass-consumerism and media images (Baudrillard 1991).

Many of the issues of great significance to discourse theorists are of little direct concern to deviance theorists. A good deal of discourse theory has centred on disputes over whether the human being is the ultimate basis of reality (the centred subject of traditional theory); or whether text/culture is more real than the individual (the decentred subject of structuralist theory); or whether there is no basis of reality in either individuals or words (the limitlessness of poststructuralist theory).

Unfortunately, it is almost impossible to draw out the implications of these disputes for deviance without at the same time doing some damage to the work as a whole. Efforts to turn the postmodernist/poststructuralist writer Michel Foucault into a sociologist run the risk of distorting and trivializing his contribution. Nevertheless, it is important to recognize the way in which his work on marginalized people and the changing forms of social control has entered into the language of deviance theory.

MICHEL FOUCAULT

Michel Foucault (1926–1984) exerted a powerful influence over academic and cultural life in France and America during the 1980s. A prominent criminologist has written that, to write about punishment and control today without referring to Foucault would be "like talking about the unconscious without Freud" (Cohen 1985:10).

Foucault's concepts enable us to study the way in which both overtly coercive institutions such as prisons, and "helping" institutions such as education, health, and social welfare have a disciplinary function. All of them are increasingly involved in treating their clientele as objects, to be contained and controlled. Foucault analyzed these processes in order to uncover alternative paths, paths that might lead away from objectification and control to "subjectification" and resistance. Subjectification, in Foucault's work, means a procedure whereby one is enabled to constitute one's self as one's own master, reclaiming the subjective, active dimension of the self (Lacombe 1996:350).

Foucault's most important contribution to the understanding of deviance and control lies in his assumption that knowledge cannot be disentangled from power relations. To know something is to delimit it, to place a value on it, and to displace other ways of knowing. An épistème (way of knowing) codifies, classifies, and strait-jackets us by controlling our perceptions and our sense of what is possible and what is not. As Foucault (1979) expresses it, "power and knowledge directly imply one another ... there is no power relation without the correlative constitution of a field of knowledge, nor any knowledge that does not presuppose and constitute at the same time power relations" (272).

The concept of power and knowledge as inextricably bound can be traced as one thread that runs through Foucault's many publications; another thread is his concept of "limit-experiences," which he deliberately sought for himself and which ulti-mately led to his death.

Foucault, Madness, and The Enlightenment

In *Madness and Civilization* (1962), Foucault traces the history of mental illness in European society. In the Middle Ages, up to about 1500, the mentally ill were neglected but free from the constraints of rationality and civilization. After 1500, they were increasingly placed in asylums, where they were "cared for" but also contained and constrained. While the confinement of the mentally ill continued and was seen by the time of the eighteenth century as a humane application of scientific knowledge, from Foucault's perspective, the ideology of rationality that character-ized this period simply represented a different and more insidious form of social control through which people were snatched from the free chaos of insanity and dropped into the "enclosed anguish of responsibility" (Foucault 1962:247, 504). Foucault's view of Enlightenment rationality as a psychological straitjacket is a pervasive theme in the work of anti-psychiatrists like R.D. Laing, David Cooper, and Thomas Szasz.

Foucault believed that traditional conceptions of reality need to be challenged and opposed, and that the technique for doing this is to seek out the *limit-experi-ence.* The madman is thus a hero of sorts, someone who has risked everything to experience alternative worlds, the limit-experience of insanity. Foucault himself often balanced on the edge of what others might call insanity, deliberately pushing his mind and body to the breaking point by alternating between the extremes of asceticism and Dionysian excess. By stretching human experience to its outermost limits, Foucault hoped to arrive at a reality that transcended the conventional dichotomies of consciousness and unconsciousness, life and death, reason and madness, pleasure and pain, and truth and fiction.

However, Foucault was not oblivious to the potential dangers that awaited those who defied the rule of rationality. He saw the Marquis de Sade as a man who, in seeking the innocent freedom of nature, evaded the "Castle of Conscience" and found himself instead in the prison of the "Castle of Murders." De Sade escaped from virtue into the worst sort of vice, just as he escaped from guilt and responsibility into the worst sort of irresponsibility. In Foucault's terms, he was caught up in an endless cycle of transgression, confinement, and "repeated non-existence of gratification" (Foucault 1962:247, 504). In this, as in all his written work, Foucault exposes the "asylums" of our lives without handing us a key.

Foucault and the Straitjackets of Discourse

In Foucault's second major work, *The Order of Things* (1970), he argues that the Enlightenment gave rise to parallel "discourses" (medicine, criminology) that restricted the development of knowledge to those paths that supported increasing control over the individual. While knowledge in the Renaissance could be characterized as an open field in which science and alchemy co-existed, knowledge in the age of reason was defined, enclosed, and "tamed." It was "colonized" by a host of new "disciplines" (ordered ways of thinking), all of which took the form of liberal humanism but were essentially technologies in a political economy of controlled labour (Lemert and Gillan 1982:19). These sciences were, in Foucault's opinion, little more than the parochial fictions of a particular era, ideas that ordered and confined experience.

Foucault and Panoptical Discipline

In *Discipline and Punish* ([1977] 1979), Foucault documents the historical transition from punishment by means of public torture and execution to punishment by means of imprisonment. While the prison was ostensibly a product of rational humanitarianism (more kindness and respect, less pain), Foucault sees it as a form of coercion all the more insidious for its apparent benevolence. The terror of pre-classical coercion was replaced by a mechanism of power that produced "discipline" rather than reform. What it also produced was the criminal, a pathologized individual requiring (so authorities believed) increased surveillance and control (Foucault [1977] 1979:277).

According to Foucault, the prison was only one institution that reflected the dominant coercion of rationality. All major institutions of society exhibited parallel processes of panoptical (as conceived by Bentham) discipline. Authorities in schools, factories, and army barracks established panoptical rules and regulations concerning efficient use of time, attention to tasks, proper deference, dress, cleanliness, and sexual decency. Panoptical discipline produced "docile bodies," obedient people but drained of creative energy (Miller 1993:15, 222).

The Transgressions of Pierre Rivière

I, Pierre Rivière, Having Slaughtered My Mother, My Sister, and My Brother ... is a book Foucault compiled for use in his class. Most of the book consists of Riviere's own account of his life and what his actions meant to him, but it also includes medical testimony, newspaper articles, witness accounts, legal testimony, and judges' opinions. In 1835, Rivière killed his pregnant mother, and his sister and brother in an orgy of violence and mutilation. He then welcomed his own execution as an expiation for his sins and a release from his resentments. The court, however, judged him insane, and commuted his death sentence to life in prison. Five years later he managed to hang himself. Foucault saw this man as a "tragic hero" who faced the abyss between living within the restrictions of normalcy and taking the leap into the terrifying chaos of unregulated use of power. Rivière represented, within Foucault's interpretation, a person whose transgression illuminated the ambiguousness of the line between the permissible and the outlawed, and the connection among repression, transgression, sacrifice, and ordained punishment (Miller 1993:228). *I, Pierre Rivière ...* reproduces the conflicting discourses produced by Rivière, the medical "experts," the legal "experts," the media, and finally, Foucault himself, as each of these discourses attempt to "make sense" of Rivière's actions. For Foucault, Rivière's account does not explain his behaviour, but is in fact part of the crime (Foucault 1975:83).

A History of Sexuality and the Limit Experience

In his unfinished *A History of Sexuality* (1979), Foucault argues that while the discipline associated with social control (the panopticon model) drives pleasure out of our "docile bodies," it cannot prevent it from reappearing "transmogrified" in our fantasies. Pleasure for Foucault takes the form of polymorphous perversions that are sometimes virulent but also sometimes vitalizing in that they release us (temporarily at least) from the burden of rational control and give us a glimpse of the unstructured reality that pre-exists forms of discourse (knowledge). Foucault's personal involvement in sadomasochistic forms of homosexual experience gave this aspect of his work a certain resonance. These "limit experiences" produced in Foucault dissociative states of mind (not unlike those generated by LSD), and thus constituted yet another methodology (Miller 1993:378).

A History of Sexuality also addresses the way in which the regulation of sexuality masks more insidious forms of social control. Foucault points out, for example, how antimasturbation campaigns, while doomed to failure vis-à-vis their ostensible goal (eradicating masturbation), in fact succeeded in achieving their actual goal (increased surveillance of children) (Foucault 1978:42; Harland 1987:159; Smart 1985:95).

Foucault and the Gay Community

Members of the gay community have looked in vain to Foucault's work for support that would link being gay to some kind of essentialist position, or link it with important people of the past who engaged in what are now taken to be gay practices. Foucault believed that biological interpretations of "gay" existence were merely another form of the discourse of positive science, which, by "naming" and "knowing" the homosexual, turns this person into an object of power. For Foucault, sexuality is something that individuals "make" in their everyday experimentation with sex and pleasure. It is not a "reality" to be found in the body or in some physical sign. It can be a means of self-creation and resistance.

Foucault also felt that each historical period was a separate reality, such that Plato, Michelangelo, or Sappho, for example, is not an ancestor of today's gay. Thus while Foucault often participated in activities that helped homosexuals who had become entangled with the law, and did not deny his homosexual activities, he was reluctant to call himself a gay person or to work for gay organizations (this issue is covered at length throughout Miller's 1993 biography, and is also discussed from a slightly different point of view in Gallagher and Wilson [1987]).

POSTMODERNISM AFTER FOUCAULT

The postmodernist critique of society's control apparatuses, and the way in which they "produce" deviants and victims (who are thus, in some sense, not "real" deviants, or "real" victims) continues. Alison Young (1996), for example, provides an extended analysis of the phenomenon of "textual outlaws"(1–26). Her argument is partly based on Durkheim's notion that naming deviants is the way that communities shore up their threatened boundaries (Chapter 7). In Young's version, however, there is no community. Community is an idea or image that has no substance *other than the perception that we are all potential "victims" of deviance.* Conforming "community members" have in common only our fear of the outlaw, who is "sacrificed" to help us maintain the image that we have community. In this analysis, neither the community nor the deviance has any substance, and the only actual harm (if any) is done to the sacrificial deviant.

In another postmodernist account, Charles Acland focuses on the cultural phenomenon of "youth in crisis" (1995). Again, the focus is not on the youth, as such, but on the way in which the understandings of youth are created and used in a "cultural politics" that helps to maintain the very systems that produce youth problems. Acland acknowledges that there is real violence and real victimization in the lives of youths, but that is not the focus of his interest.

CONSTITUTIVE CRIMINOLOGY: BEYOND POSTMODERNISM

Recent work by Stuart Henry and Dragan Milovanovic (1996) ventures beyond Foucault and other postmodernists. Their approach agrees with the postmodernists that modernism (exemplified by positivism and control theory, for example) is compromised by its commitment to the interests and viewpoints of powerholders. It also accepts the postmodernist position that deconstruction can be used to "undo" modernist thought and reveal its contradictions and assumptions. Henry and Milovanovic, however, argue that the knowledge that humans coproduce the world they live in does not have to be an endless regression of sceptical deconstruction. They argue for an affirmative position: if we understand how the reality is created, we can find ways to reduce or eliminate its harmful aspects. In *Constitutive Criminology*, they suggest the development of "replacement discourses" (1996:x–xi), whereby deviance and crime are transformed from violations of the norms (the modernist position) to objectively discernable uses of power in ways that harm, impair, or destroy others. The deviant is the "excessive investor" in the accumulation and expression of power and control, so that others are harmed. In this effort to create a definition of crime and deviance that is not dependent on current notions of citizens and authorities, Henry and Milovanovic move into uncharted waters where the processes of control no longer generate the conditions of deviance.

Henry and Milovanovic, along with other writers, have observed that postmodernism sometimes degenerates into a nihilistic exercise whereby the existence of "reality," even socially constructed reality, is denied. While we will likely never be able to access any aspect of reality without using language (discourse), this does not mean reality does not exist—only that we cannot reach it without linguistic tools. Too many postmodernists assume that reality is made by language, rather than understood through it. Each discourse will distort our perception in some ways, while focusing it in others. Henry and Milovanovic have attempted to create "replacement discourse" that will be less distorting, and less harmful, than the current discourses of deviance and control.

SUMMARY

Conflict theories differ from other theories in stressing the role of differential power in the establishment of the categories of deviance and their application to disadvantaged groups. These theories raise the question of whose interests are served by the existence and use of deviance labels, and their answers often suggest that it is the social order rather than the deviant that needs to be transformed. Some conflict theories are more optimistic than others in assessing the prospects for a nonhierarchical social order—one in which one group does not have its own interests served at the expense of other groups. By extension, conflict theories as a whole are ambivalent about the possibility of either a world without deviance or a world in which deviance is no longer wielded as a weapon of power. No recent theorists have claimed that the solution to this use of power will be as simple as a political revolution led by or on behalf of the "textual outlaw."

Change in the processes of deviantization will require a fundamental transformation of social consciousness. It seems appropriate to observe here that, until the postmodernists begin to write in more accessible language, the average citizen will be unlikely to even be aware of this challenge to common beliefs and understandings. In the meantime, Marilyn Porter's (1995) observation that "unlike Marxism or feminism, postmodernism is *not* rooted in involvement outside the academy and it is manifestly *not* informed by commitment or passion" poses the serious challenge to postmodernists that they should link their critiques to a constructive program (430). Perhaps we should look more to what postmodernists (such as Foucault) do than to what they have written.

REFERENCES

Acland, Charles R. (1995). *Youth, Murder, Spectacle: The Cultural Politics of "Youth in Crisis."* Boulder, Col.: Westview.

Baudrillard, Jean. (1991). "La Guerre du Golfe n'a pas eu lieu" (The Gulf War Never Happened) *Liberation*, March 29.

Bonger, Willem (1916). *Criminality and Economic Conditions.* Boston: Little, Brown.

Burrington, Debra. (1994). "Constructing the Outlaw, Outing the Law, and Throwing Out the Law." *Utah Law Review* 2:255–267.

Chambliss, William, and R. Seidman. (1982). *Law, Order and Power.* 2nd ed. Reading, Mass.: Addison-Wesley.

Cohen, Stanley (ed.). (1971). *Images of Deviance.* Harmondsworth, Middlesex: Penguin.

————. (1985). *Visions of Social Control: Crime, Punishment and Classification*. Cambridge, England: Polity Press.

Collins, Hugh. (1984). *Marxism and Law*. New York: Oxford University Press.

Dowie, Mark. (1991). "Pinto Madness." *Deviant Behavior and Human Rights*. Englewood Cliffs, N.J.: Prentice-Hall.

Foucault, Michel. (1962). *Madness and Civilization*. New York: Pantheon.

————. (1970). *The Order of Things*. London: Tavistock.

————. (1973a) *The Birth of the Clinic: An Archeology of Medical Perception*. London: Tavistock.

———— (ed.). (1975). *I, Pierre Rivière, Having Slaughtered My Mother, My Sister, and My Brother*. Translated by Frank Jellinek. Lincoln: University of Nebraska Press.

————. (1978). *A History of Sexuality: An Introduction*. London: Allen Lane.

————. (1979a). *Discipline and Punish: The Birth of the Prison*. Translated by Alan Sheridan. New York: Random House.

Gallagher, Bob, and Alexander Wilson. (1987). "Sex and the Politics of Identity: An Interview with Michel Foucault." In Mark Thompson (ed.), *Gay Spirit: Myth and Meaning*. New York: St. Martin's Press, Stonewall Inn Editions.

Galliher, John F. (1991). *Deviant Behavior and Human Rights*. Englewood Cliffs, N.J.: Prentice-Hall.

Geuss, Raymond. (1981). *The Idea of A Critical Theory: Habermas and the Frankfurt School*. Cambridge: Cambridge University Press.

Goff, C., and C. Reasons. (1978). *Corporate Crime in Canada: A Critical Analysis of Anti-Combines Legislation*. Toronto: Prentice-Hall.

Goode, Erich. (1990). *Deviant Behavior*, 3rd ed. Englewood Cliffs, N.J.: Prentice-Hall.

Gramsci, Antonio. (1971). *Selections from the Prison Notebooks of Antonio Gramsci*. New York: International Publishers.

Harland, Richard. (1987). *Superstructural: The Philosophy of Structuralism and Poststructuralism*. New York: Methuen.

Harvey, Lee. (1990). *Critical Social Research*. London: Unwin Hyman.

Henry, Stuart, and Dragan Milovanovic. (1996). *Constitutive Criminology: Beyond Postmodernism*. London: Sage Publications.

Hirst, P.Q. (1972). "Marx and Engels on Law, Crime and Morality." *Economy and Society* 1 (February):28–56.

Jary, David, and Julia Jary. (1991). *The HarperCollins Dictionary of Sociology*. New York: HarperCollins.

Kinsman, Gary. (1987). *The Regulation of Desire: Sexuality in Canada*. Montreal: Black Rose.

Lacombe, Dany. (1996). "Reforming Foucault: A Critique of the Social Control Thesis." *The British Journal of Sociology* 47(2):332–352.

Lemert, Charles C., and Garth Gillan. (1982). *Michel Foucault: Social Theory and Transgression.* New York: Columbia University Press.

Leonard, William N., and Marvin Glenn Weber. (1991). "Automakers and Dealers: A Study of Criminogenic Market Forces." *Law and Society Review* 4(February):407–424.

Liska, Allen. (1987). *Perspectives on Deviance.* 2nd ed. Englewood Cliffs, N.J.: Prentice-Hall.

Marcuse, Herbert. (1965). "Repressive Tolerance." In R.P. Wolff et al. (eds.), *A Critique of Pure Tolerance.* Boston: Beacon Press.

Marx, Karl. ([1867] 1987) *Capital: A Critique of Political Economy.* New York: International Publishers.

Miliband, Ralph. (1969). *The State in Capitalist Society.* London: Wiedenfeld and Nicholson.

Miller, James. (1993). *The Passion of Michel Foucault.* New York: Simon and Schuster.

Mugford, S.K. (1974). "Marxism and Criminology: A Comment on the Symposium Review." *Sociological Quarterly* 15(Autumn):591–596.

Pepinsky, Harold, and Richard Quinney (eds.). (1991). *Criminology as Peacemaking.* Bloomington, Ind.: Indiana University Press.

Porter, Marilyn. (1995). "Call Yourself a Sociologist—And You've Never Been Arrested?!" *The Canadian Review of Sociology and Anthropology* 32(4):415–437.

Quinney, Richard. (1970). *The Social Reality of Crime.* Boston: Little, Brown.

———. (1977). *Class, State, and Crime.* New York: McKay.

Rock, Paul E. (1979). "The Sociology of Crime, Symbolic Interactionism and Some Problematic Qualities of Radical Criminology." In D. Downes and P. Rock (eds.), *Deviance and Social Control.* London: Martin Robertson.

Smart, Barry. (1985). *Michel Foucault.* London: Tavistock.

Snider, Lauren. (1992). "Commercial Crime." In Vincent Sacco (ed.), *Deviance: Conformity and Control in Canadian Society.* Scarborough, Ont.: Prentice-Hall.

Spitzer, Stephen. (1975). "Toward a Marxian Theory of Deviance." *Social Problems* 22:638–651.

Stanley, Christopher. (1995). "Teenage Kicks: Urban Narratives of Dissent Not Deviance." *Crime, Law and Social Change* 23(2):91–119.

Sutherland, Edwin H. (1949). *White Collar Crime.* New York: Holt, Rinehart and Winston.

Taylor, Ian, Paul Walton, and Jock Young. (1973). *The New Criminology: For a Social Theory of Deviance.* London: Routledge and Keegan Paul.

———. (1975). *Critical Criminology.* London: Routledge and Keegan Paul.

Vaughan, Ted R., and Gideon Sjoberg. (1986). "Human Rights Theory and the Classical Sociological Tradition." In Mark L. Wardell and Stephen P. Turner (eds.), *Sociological Theory in Transition.* Boston: Allen and Unwin.

Vold, George. (1958). *Theoretical Criminality.* New York: Oxford University Press.

Young, Alison. (1996). *Imaging Crime.* London: Sage.

Young, Jock. (1971). *The Drugtakers: The Social Meaning of Drug Use.* London: MacGibbon and Kee/Paladin.

HIGHLIGHTING AND INTEGRATING THE FEMINIST THREAD IN DEVIANCE THEORY AND RESEARCH

Feminist writers have often complained that the chapters on women, in the few books that have them, tend to be placed at or near the end of them, a placement that suggests their lack of importance (Young 1996:34; Daly 1997). Recently, it has been argued that this complaint is exaggerated (Gelsthorpe and Morris 1990). Throughout this book, the places where women's contributions have been ignored, underestimated, or even plagiarized by men (as in the Chicago School of the 1920s) have been documented, but the main story has been that of the dominant theories and themes about men, by men.

Drawing women's "excluded and devalued" material together at the end of this book is not meant to suggest its lack of importance, but rather to highlight its meaning for the field. By showing the direction that a full inclusion of women might take, we can break free from the masculinist canon's myopic treatment of women's issues and distorted view of humanity as male. A similar process of inclusion needs to be put in motion for the other voices silenced and marginalized by the "canon" of establishment social science.

PRE-FEMINIST THINKING ABOUT DEVIANT WOMEN

Traditionally, women in deviance and criminological studies have been treated mainly in two ways. In the first, it has been assumed that what is true of men is either also true of women or does not matter (e.g. Mark and Lesieur 1992). In the second, females have been discussed in ways that emphasize individual biological or psychological abnormality, and ignore the influence of gendered social conditions (Smith

1995:113–114). In other words, female deviants are either normal women, incapacitated by maternity and hormones, or they are abnormal women, masculinized and doubly deviant. In this material, women's deviance is associated with unsupported assumptions about feminine wiles, sexuality, and intelligence (Konopka 1966). For example, when strain theorists argue that men deviate in order to achieve culturally mandated goals (a nonbiological explanation), they dismiss women as "not subject" to this strain, due to their overriding needs for marriage and procreation. And when interactionist theorists look at women, most fail to recognize that the constructed concept of "femininity" is deviant in relation to the standard, which is a constructed, predominantly male conception of normality.

A variant of this idea is the claim that as women move out of domestic servitude, their crime and deviance will become more like men's. In particular, their rates of serious criminal activity will climb (Adler 1975; Simon 1975). Feminist thinkers, discussed below, are more likely to see the rising "deviance" of women as a product not of their emancipation but of their lack of freedom, along with their economic marginalization, and their increasing public presence where any deviance may be observed.

Box 13.1   Common Characteristics of Feminist Theories

Kathleen Daly and Meda Chesney-Lind (1988) outline common characteristics of feminist theory as follows.

1. *Gender is related to biological sex differences, but it is not simply derived from them.* Rather, gender is as a complex social, historical, and cultural product. Feminists differ in the extent to which they feel that gender is related to essential differences between men and women as opposed to constructed differences.

2. *Gender relations are fundamental to the organization of social life and social institutions.* Any change in gender relations will necessitate change in many other aspects of life. Men will not inevitably "lose out" if women gain, since the changes may improve life for men as well. For example, if women are freed from the need to be "emotional," men may be freed from the need to deny their emotions.

3. *The present organization of gender roles does not reflect a symmetrical division of labour.* Gender relations constitute a hierarchical ordering in which men's roles are dominant and more highly rewarded than women's roles.

> ## Common Characteristics of Feminist Theories (cont.)
>
> 4. *The systems of knowledge we have inherited are those of men who held dominant positions in the social order.* Some theorists look behind this reality to uncover the ways in which inherited knowledge controls men even as it privileges them over women.
> 5. *Women should not be peripheral, invisible, or mere appendages to men in the development of knowledge.* In fact, they should be at the centre of intellectual inquiry. For some feminists, this means that women should no longer be marginalized in the academic world; for others it means that they should be given privileged places within it.

FEMINISM(S) AND CONFLICT THEORIES

Most feminist theories fall into categories that parallel with "masculinist" (patriarchal) versions of conflict or postmodernist theory. Marxist conflict theories have provided the basis for Marxist feminist theories; pluralist conflict theories relate to liberal conflict feminist theories; and social constructionist and poststructuralist discourse theories correspond, at least in part, to radical feminist theories. Queer theory (explanation from the standpoint of gays, lesbians, and sometimes bisexuals and transsexuals) parallels the feminist branches of conflict theory (Seidman 1994; hooks 1994; Namaste 1994; Warner 1992).

MARXIST FEMINIST THEORIES

While they diverge in many ways, Marxists and Marxist feminists have in common a belief that social class (economic position) as a variable is more fundamental than gender (Simpson and Elis 1994; Hartmann 1981; Jaggar 1983; Ferguson 1989:20–26). Gender relations, Marxist feminists feel, will be resolved once the central issue of class relations is resolved. From their perspective, women's position in society is a consequence of the hierarchical power relations of capitalism. These relations objectify women by assigning them social roles that serve men's interests (interests that are themselves created and maintained by the system). Female deviance and crime, and the deviance of youths raised by single mothers, result from women's marginalized economic position within both the legitimate world and the world of crime (Messerschmidt 1986; Klein and Kress 1976). When men are freed from oppressive capitalist relations, women, the doubly oppressed, will also be freed. Marxist feminists use the Marxist paradigm to argue for revolutionary changes in the political economy of nations, and to combat what they view as the "false consciousness" of groups like Real Women that enshrine the traditional female role and support the patriarchal hegemony that sustains the capitalist system.

Box 13.2 Busted in the Pool

Fatima Pereira Henson thinks it is only fair that the law treat the sexes equally. But even after the Ontario Court of Appeal in December overturned the indecency conviction of former Guelph, Ont., student Gwen Jacob for going topless on a hot day in July 1991, Pereira Henson of Cambridge, Ont., says she had "a funny feeling" that men and women would continue to be treated differently. (The court ruled that women are not breaking the law by baring their breasts in public if they have no sexual motivation.) So on Feb. 21, Pereira Henson went swimming in an indoor city pool in just a pair of cycling shorts. "This was not an easy thing to do," says the 34-year-old mother of two daughters about going topless in public. "But this was a matter of principle." Pereira Henson got the response she expected—the lifeguard asked her to put on a top or leave. After she refused, the Cambridge police arrived and issued her a $55 ticket for trespassing. Pereira Henson, who refuses to pay the fine, has hired a lawyer and requested a court date to plead her case. City officials are also talking to a lawyer. "We're working with our solicitor," says Wayne Taylor, Cambridge's commissioner of community services, "and we don't wish to make any comment." The bare facts speak for themselves.

Source: From "Busted in the Pool," *Maclean's*, March 10, 1997, 13. Reprinted by permission.

LIBERAL CONFLICT FEMINIST THEORIES

Liberal conflict feminists see gender as one among many valid, competing categories in society, others of which are class, ethnicity, and race. Containing and balancing these sometimes contradictory interests can and does at times give rise to intense stress within this part of the feminist movement. Such was the case when a women's hostel in Toronto was rocked by a political coup staged by women of colour within the organization. In the resulting media frenzy, the reputations of many people were shredded by charges of racism, lesbianism, emotional instability, greed, and ingratitude; there were no winners. Similar strains have emerged over issues like pornography and prostitution, which have different meanings for women at different levels in the economic system (Bell 1987).

Liberal conflict feminists are further characterized by their support for initiatives designed to improve women's position within the existing structure rather than to overthrow the system. Thus, they advocate "fixes" such as affirmative action (job quotas), provision of day care for working mothers, better education for women, and less "streaming" of women into domesticity or "caring" professions. This form of feminism tends to attract moderates, who target specific injustices and practices for remediation (e.g., laws that punish prostitutes but not their customers and the differential treatment of girls in sports), but who do not challenge the system as a whole, and often reject the label "feminist."

Box 13.3   Coming Out

When Queen Victoria affixed her signature in 1885 to a law prohibiting homosexuality between men, she brooked no suggestion that it be expanded to include females. Women, she said flatly, simply did not do such things.

They did, of course, but laws weren't needed to render them invisible. Sexual and social mores did that, and, to a large extent, still do ...

A lot of young, politicized lesbians wonder where the payback is for their participation in the women's movement. Where are the feminists when gay bookstores are targetted by Canada Customs, raided by police, and lesbian pornography—made by, with, and for women—is ruled obscene.

"Feminists accuse us of copying males in our porn," says Toronto writer Sue Campbell. "But if we don't have our own images, we'll never have our own freedom" ...

Source: From Lynda Hurst, "Coming Out," *Toronto Star,* June 26, 1993, D1. Reprinted with permission—The Toronto Star Syndicate.

RADICAL FEMINIST THEORIES

Non-Marxist radical feminists focus on the importance of language and communication in constructing differences between men and women. These theorists tend to challenge the rules, especially those that define appropriate gender roles. On a small scale, Carolyn Heilbrun challenges the stereotype of the "good girl" through her fiction when she has her heroine engage in a number of "vices" (Heilbrun 1988:122).

Mary Daly has gone much further than this in developing not only a radical feminist philosophy, but a whole new language (with its own dictionary) in which to express it. In her autobiographical book, *Outercourse,* Daly describes her many battles with the omnipresent powers of patriarchal authority.

> As I Re-member my own intellectual voyage as a Radical Feminist Philosopher, I am intensely aware of the struggle to stay on my True Course, despite under mining by demons of distraction that have seemed always to be attempting to pull me off course. These I eventually Dis-covered and Named as agents and institutions of patriarchy, whose intent was to keep me—and indeed all living be-ings—within a stranglehold of the foreground, that is, fatherland. My True Course was and is Outer course moving beyond the imprisoning mental, physical, emotional, spiritual walls of patriarchy, the State of Possession. Insofar as I am focused on Outercoursing, naturally I am surrounded and aided by the benevolent forces of the Background. (Daly 1992:1)

In Daly's vocabulary, "foreground" is a "male-centred and monodimensional arena where fabrication, objectification, and alienation take place; zone of fixed feelings, perceptions, behaviours; the elementary world: FLATLAND." This in turn refers to yet more definitions that express the vision that is not expressible within the language as it exists. Background, on the other hand, refers to "the Realm of Wild Reality: the Homeland of women's Selves and of all other Others; the Time/Space where auras of plants, planets, stars, animals and all Other animate beings interconnect" (Daly 1992:1).

Box 13.4   The Question of Feminism

Woman, the eternal dark continent of Western culture, is the blind spot of criminological [and deviance] theory. The criminological complex seems content to keep women in the place of beggars at the banquet, feasting on crumbs. A women's tradition seems endlessly fragmented, scattered, divided within itself—and always already devalued. And yet: feminists continue to struggle to speak and to be heard, to keep the *question* of the Other alive.

Source: Alison Young, *Imaging Crime: Textual Outlaws and Criminal Conversations.* London: Sage, p. 34. Reprinted by permission of Sage Publications.

POSTMODERNISM AND FEMINISM

Postmodernism, by exposing the "canon" of masculinist modernist approaches and highlighting its exclusions and distortions, has fit well with the feminist agenda of inclusion. Feminists have been quick to seize, for example, on the deconstruction of biological discourse. Postmodernism challenges the long-held assumptions (from Lombroso through to Polk and Freud) that women's biology makes them unfit for full inclusion in the public world. The main problem of postmodernism, though, as shown in the work of Foucault, is that it is very good at "deconstructing" but has (thus far) no mechanism for the production of alternative discourses that would be less damaging or more liberating. We do not yet have an overall conception of an alternative path or paths that would avoid the pitfalls of the past. It is possible that in the praxis of liberating ourselves (men and women, dominant and minority groups) from the distortions we can now recognize, new paths will be discovered.

THE DEPICTION OF WOMEN IN DEVIANCE STUDIES: A SUMMARY AND CRITIQUE

From the misogyny of demonology to the most philosophical of discourse theories, women have been either misrepresented or neglected. We have seen women's ways classified as witchcraft by priests and judges; classical theorists used of the model of "reasonable man" as a measure for establishing rational law, and early constitutional theorists pathologizing female anatomy and intelligence. It is not difficult to refute the earlier work. Modern theories, such as Lawrence Kohlberg's theory of moral development (more fully discussed in Chapter 6), require further consideration. Kohlberg concludes that women generally operate on a lower level of moral development than men. According to Carol Gilligan in *In a Different Voice* (1982), if this were true, women would commit more offences than men, which they clearly do not do. (You may remember the same problem arose with respect to Lombroso's assertion that women were nearer to our atavistic ancestors than men were.) Gilligan proposes that women's moral development is not lower than men's, but that it is different from men's. Using the same test with respect to both is an example of masculinist bias. Gilligan argues that there are (at least) two distinct "moral voices," and that Kohlberg recorded and legitimated only one. The "other" voice, according to Gilligan, is "an ethic of responsibility," a concrete morality centred on relationships. It is a matter of "theme" in addition to gender (Gilligan 1986:327) and emerges for women out of the girl's identification with her mother, which encourages her to learn about connecting and about maintaining relationships. The male moral voice, according to Gilligan, is "an ethic of rights," an abstract morality that invokes concepts of justice and rules. Gilligan sees this arising out of the boy's need to separate himself from the mother. By adulthood, men and women often have developed the capacity to work with *both* kinds of thought, although women tend to begin their analysis from the caring perspective and frame it in the justice mode, while men begin with justice and then move toward understanding and compassion (Gilligan 1986:329–330). In Kohlberg's terms, when women develop the capacity (desire) to think in abstract legal terms, they advance a stage in moral development. When men develop the capacity to think compassionately, they remain at the same level they were before. Gilligan's point is that the measure of moral development is biased. It presents the male perspective as the "human" perspective, and women's differences from this as deviance or inferiority.

Other constitutional theories define the adjusted woman as someone who accommodates the political economy of capitalism by remaining in the background, supporting the working man, and keeping the family intact. The "missing woman" is evident in Kingsley Davis's theory of prostitution (discussed in Chapter 8), in which he explains prostitution exclusively in terms of male or family needs, not those of women.

Interpretive theories have reported that women are often labelled deviant for behaviour or appearance that is accepted—even valued—in men (Schur 1984). They have linked women's susceptibility to such labels to their weaker power position. Thus, women who behave and appear in ways that contravene social expectations are labelled deviant while those who accept these social expectations are regarded as inferior. Either way, the emphasis on appearance renders women objects to both themselves and others.

Power-control theory similarly regards women in the context of family and relational controls. Despite the use of critical theoretical vocabulary ("patriarchy") and some insightful work, the theory itself shows no critical awareness of the realities it documents. Women can either remain in the home and raise risk-averse daughters who will follow in their footsteps and commit themselves to the domestic role; or they can seek jobs with authority and raise risk-taking girls who will be judged delinquent for doing what their brothers do.

Conflict theories have provided an arsenal of concepts that have helped illuminate women's position and potential in society. They have greatly enriched feminist analyses. However, in their treatment of women many of them encompass views that are just as myopic as those in earlier theories. When they do address the subject, it is usually only to express notions about women's "natural" passivity, their lesser corruption due to their nonparticipation in the economy, and their meagre abilities relative to those of men (Bonger 1969:59–64). The new criminology included not a single word about women (Leonard 1982:176). The currently fashionable structuralism of Jacques Lacan posits a phallocentric universe that is immutable, thus providing no basis for women to challenge its hegemony (Fraser 1992; Leland 1991; Mitchell 1982). The poststructuralism of Foucault demonstrates the power of *men* to construct their own reality, but says nothing about women.

In their examination of women, all of these mainstream theories use as their yardsticks standards that were designed for men and naturally represent them best. Standard measures of delinquency, for example, have produced a biased and distinctly anemic image of women. As Millman (1975) expresses it, mainstream theories of deviance

> have come to associate women with the dullest, most oppressive aspects of society, or else to view their deviance in narrowly sex-typed (and unappealing) terms, yet to see in our male deviants the expression of creativity and courage to stand up to society's hypocrisies. (251)

This conceptual imperialism has meant the exclusion of women's views, even from women themselves (Smith 1973; Millman and Kanter 1975:viii).

TOWARD A NEW INCLUSIVE THEORY OF DEVIANCE

The reality of gender might be integrated into a theory of deviance in several ways. The simplest and least satisfactory way is to simply change the pronouns in the theory to include "she" as well as "he." This tactic, while avoiding the trap of arguing that differences between men and women are somehow essential and immutable, ignores the gender differences that do in fact exist in any given historical period.

A slightly better technique is to learn more about women by using them as research subjects (Shaver 1993; Reinharz 1992). Most mainstream theories would require major revision in order to accomplish this without falling into Kohlberg's trap of seeing women as inferior members of the human species—not as good as men when they are good, not as interesting or successful when they are bad.

A third approach is to construct a theory based on the assumption that women's reality is or should be more privileged than men's. In such a theory, women's experiences of menstruation, childbirth, cooperative labour, and so forth could be presented as being morally superior to the more limited competitive/aggressive experiences of men. Dorothy Smith, a Canadian sociologist who is internationally recognized for her work in the sociology of knowledge, has proposed that we should consider what it would mean to construct a sociology that begins from the "standpoint of women" (Smith 1981).

Smith argues that the feminine standpoint is potentially more inclusive than the masculine one in that it encompasses all of those things that men, in order to be men, have repressed. Her discussion of this point parallels Foucault's treatment of the Enlightenment as a period characterized by the repressive expansion of knowledge as power. Smith maintains that the Enlightenment produced the dichotomies of reason/emotion, mind/body, culture/nature, self/others, objectivity/subjectivity, and knowing/being. The first part of each dichotomy was appropriated by men, while the second part became the domain of women. Even within "women's" categories such as virgin/whore, the acceptable side is within the patriarchal structure and the unacceptable side is defined as resistance to the patriarchal structure (Martinez 1994). There is no ground free for self-definition. Men have repressed their understanding and awareness of what could be expressed as women's concerns. Women, according to Smith, have remained in a position from which they can (if they choose) transcend these damaging dualities.

If we agree with MacKinnon (1982:636) that there is no such thing as a nonsituated, genderless, universal standpoint, and that what we currently see as reality is in fact knowledge from a male standpoint, then what might happen if we could change that standpoint? What would the study of deviance be like from a female standpoint?

One path toward the creation of the new theory is through "praxis" in which we look at the effects of the actions of women (and men) who have sought to break free of the established understandings of the way that the world is. We can look at the impact of women's increasing involvement in the public sphere and the changes that are already occurring as a result of it. The changes involve not only how deviance is explained in terms of its causes, but, far more importantly, how it is defined. The change from "rape" laws to "sexual assault laws" is more than a simple matter of semantics. The emergence of wife battery, child abuse, and elder bashing out of the family closet and into the public eye reflects a change in the sources of legitimized knowledge (Adelberg and Currie 1987). Another change can be found in the increasing attention given to victims (whether of crime, deviance, or legitimized but harmful practices). It is partly because of the women's standpoint that victims are no longer readily blamed for their victimization, while perpetrators can no longer call upon legitimated dogmas such as Scully and Marolla's "excuses and justifications" to exculpate themselves for their actions. In a similar vein, it is no longer entirely acceptable to treat variations in sexual expression as signs of individual pathology.

It would be unjustifiably idealistic, however, to assume that a woman's standpoint (even if it could be easily formulated and brought into being) would necessarily lead to a nonoppressive form of knowledge and practice. As Hrdy (1981) notes, if there are in fact

> no important differences between males and females in intelligence,
> initiative, or administrative and political capacities ... [then] the feminist

ideal of a sex less egotistical, less competitive by nature, less interested in dominance, a sex that will lead us back to "the golden age of queendoms, when peace and justice prevailed on earth," is a dream that may not be well-founded. (190)

Ultimately, we need understanding(s) of behaviour that are not just versions of patriarchy or any other system of dominance. This may take the form of a new "replacement discourse" based on a universalistic notion of "justice," based on the "person" apart from such details as gender, race, and culture (Lyman 1995:225), or it may find some other basis that cannot be deconstructed as a biased form of power manipulation.

In a system based on this understanding, deviance labels would be more closely connected with physical harm to persons or the environment than with maintaining particular forms of social order. Most behaviour now called deviant or criminal would be understood as conflict between individuals, conflict that can evoke repair, resolution, and new understandings so that shame, ostracism, and punishment would be unnecessary (Christie 1993). Arriving at a society that does not regularly produce and punish deviants' self-defeating cycles of fear and punishment, however, will not be easy.

SUMMARY

Deviance studies have, in the main, excluded or devalued the perspectives of women. Attempts to rectify this situation have helped to broaden the scope of the field, but have not yet produced a solution that will break up the old rigidities without simply replacing them with new ones.

Biological determinist explanations of deviance dominated much longer and more fully with respect to women than with respect to men. Attempts to move beyond the unwarranted emphasis on women's biology, appearance, and dependent roles toward a fully sociological or political picture of women's deviance have not yet drowned out the discourse of pathology. Most of the newer work in the field of women's deviance is being done by men and women who take one of the many versions of the "feminist" perspective. Some are liberals who seek to reform society so that women's roles will no longer handicap them. Some are Marxists who seek to change the economic system so that neither men nor women are oppressed and exploited. Some are radicals who seek a much deeper structural and ideological overhaul of the discourses that guide us, so that women are no longer trapped in categories that they have not made for themselves.

Postmodernist thought has provided an example and a methodology for deconstructing the images and theories that have imprisoned women's bodies and minds in multitudes of deviant attributions and categories. Postmodernism has shown the possibility of a different kind of freedom in a society without fixed standpoints and rigid truths. While much of this material is utopian, and some of it merely replaces male dominance with female dominance, it has helped us to move beyond the restrictive dominance of positivist expertise, just as an earlier period moved beyond the ignorance of demonic superstition and fear.

REFERENCES

Adelberg, Ellen, and Claudia Currie (eds.). (1987). *Too Few to Count: Canadian Women in Conflict with the Law.* Vancouver: Press Gang Publishers.

Adler, F. (1975). *Sisters in Crime.* New York: McGraw-Hill.

Bell, Laurie (ed.). (1987). *Good Girls/Bad Girls: Sex Trade Workers and Feminists Face to Face.* Toronto: The Women's Press. Made up of papers presented at a conference, Challenging Our Images: The Politics of Prostitution and Pornography.

Bonger, Willem. (1969). *Criminality and Economic Conditions.* Bloomington, Ind.: Indiana University Press.

Christie, Nils. (1993). *Crime Control as Industry.* New York: Routledge.

Daly, Kathleen. (1997). "Different Ways of Conceptualizing Sex/Gender in Feminist Theory and their Implications for Criminology." *Theoretical Criminology* 1(1):25–52.

Daly, Kathleen, and Meda Chesney-Lind. (1988). "Feminism and Criminology." *Justice Quarterly* 5:497–538.

Daly, Mary. (1992). *Outercourse: The Be-Dazzling Voyage.* San Francisco, Cal.: Harper.

Ferguson, Ann. (1989). *Blood at the Root: Motherhood, Sexuality and Male Dominance.* London: Pandora.

Fraser, Nancy. (1992). "The Uses and Abuses of French Discourse Theories for Feminist Politics." In Mike Featherstone (ed.), *Cultural Theory and Cultural Change.* London: Sage.

Gelsthorpe, L., and A. Morris (eds.). (1990). *Feminist Perspectives in Criminology.* Buckingham, England: Open University Press.

Gilligan, C. (1982). *In a Different Voice.* Cambridge, Mass.: Harvard University Press.

———. (1986). "Reply by Carol Gilligan." *Signs* 11(2)324–333.

Hartmann, Heidi. (1981). "The Unhappy Marriage of Marxism and Feminism: Towards a More Progressive Union." In Lydia Sargent (ed.). *Women and Revolution.* Boston: South End Press.

Heilbrun, Carolyn. (1988). *Writing a Woman's Life.* New York: Ballantine.

hooks, bell. (1994). *Teaching to Transgress: Education as the Practice of Freedom.* New York: Routledge.

Hrdy, Sarah Blaffer. (1981). *The Woman That Never Evolved*. Cambridge, Mass.: Harvard University Press.

Jaggar, Alison. (1983). *Feminist Politics and Human Nature*. Totowa, N.J.: Rowman and Allanheld.

Klein, Dorie, and June Kress. (1976) "Any Woman's Blues: A Critical Overview of Women, Crime and the Criminal Justice System." *Crime and Social Justice* 5(Spring-Summer):34–49.

Konopka, G. (1966). *The Adolescent Girl in Conflict*. Englewood Cliffs, N.J.: Prentice-Hall.

Leland, Dorothy. (1991). "Lacanian Psychoanalysis and French Feminism: Toward an Adequate Political Psychology." In Nancy Fraser and Sandra Bartky (eds.), *Revaluing French Feminism: Critical Essays on Difference, Agency and Culture*. Bloomington: Indiana University Press.

Leonard, Eileen B. (1982). *Women, Crime and Society: A Critique of Criminological Theory*. New York: Longman.

Lyman, Stanford M. (1995). "Without Morals or Mores: Deviance in Postmodern Social Theory." *International Journal of Politics, Culture and Society* 9(2):197–236.

MacKinnon, Catherine. (1982). "Feminism, Marxism, Method and the State: An Agenda for Theory." In N. Keohane, M. Rosaldo, and Barbara Gelpi (eds.), *Feminist Theory: A Critique of Ideology*. Chicago: University of Chicago Press.

Mark, Marie, and Henry R. Lesieur. (1992). "Commentary: A Feminist Critique of Problem Gambling Research." *British Journal of Addiction* 87:549–565.

Martinez, Theresa. (1994). "Embracing the Outlaws: Deviance at the Intersection of Race, Class and Gender." *Utah Law Review* 1:193–207.

Messerschmidt, James. (1986). *Capitalism, Patriarchy and Crime: Toward a Socialist Feminist Criminology*. Totawa, N.Y.: Rowman and Littlefield.

Millman, Marcia. (1975). "'She Did It All For Love': A Feminist View of the Sociology of Deviance." In Marcia Millman and Rosabeth Kanter (eds.), *Another Voice: Feminist Perspectives on Social Life and Social Science*. New York: Doubleday.

Millman, Marcia, and Rosabeth Moss Kanter (eds.). (1975). *Another Voice: Feminist Perspectives on Social Life and Social Science*. New York: Doubleday.

Mitchell, Juliet. (1982). "Introduction—I." In J. Mitchell and J. Rose (eds.), *Feminine Sexuality: Jacques Lacan and the Ecole Freudian*. New York: Pantheon.

Namaste, Ki. (1994). "The Politics of Inside/Out: Queer Theory, Poststructuralism, and a Sociological Approach to Sexuality." *Social Theory* 12(2):220–231.

Reinharz, S. (1992). *Feminist Methods in Social Research*. New York: Oxford University Press.

Schur, Edwin M. (1984). *Labelling Women Deviant: Gender, Stigma, and Social Control*. Philadelphia: Temple University Press.

Seidman, Steven. (1994). "Queer Theory/Sociology: A Dialogue." *Sociological Theory* 12(2):166–177.

Shaver, Frances. (1993). Unpublished paper. "Prostitution: A Female Crime?" In Ellen Adelberg and Claudia Currie (eds.). Vancouver.

Simon, R.J. (1975). *Women and Crime*. Toronto: Lexington.

Simpson, Sally S., and Lori Elis. (1994). "Is Gender Subordinate to Class? An Empirical Assessment of Colvin and Pauly's Structural Marxist Theory of Delinquency." *The Journal of Criminal Law and Criminology* 85(2):453–480.

Smith, David. (1995). *Criminology for Social Work*. Houndsmills, England: Macmillan.

Smith, Dorothy. (1973). "Women's Perspective as a Radical Critique of Sociology." *Sociological Inquiry* 44(1):7–13.

———. (1981). "The Experienced World as Problematic: A Feminist Method." *Sorokin Lecture Number 12*. Saskatoon: University of Saskatchewan.

Warner, Michael. (ed.). (1992). *Fear of a Queer Planet: Queer Politics and Social Theory*. Minneapolis: University of Minneapolis Press.

Young, Alison. (1996). *Imaging Crime: Textual Outlaws and Criminal Conversations*. London: Sage.

INDEX

To the owner of this book

We hope that you have enjoyed *Deviance & Social Control,* and we would like to know as much about your experiences with this text as you would care to offer. Only through your comments and those of others can we learn how to make this a better text for future readers.

School _____ Your instructor's name _____

Course _____ Was the text required? _____ Recommended? _____

1. What did you like the most about *Deviance & Social Control?*

_____

_____

_____

2. How useful was this text for your course?

_____

_____

_____

3. Do you have any recommendations for ways to improve the next edition of this text?

_____

_____

_____

4. In the space below or in a separate letter, please write any other comments you have about the book. (For example, please feel free to comment on reading level, writing style, terminology, design features, and learning aids.)

_____

_____

_____

Optional

Your name _____ Date _____

May ITP Nelson quote you, either in promotion for *Deviance & Social Control* or in future publishing ventures?

Yes _____ No _____

Thanks!

You can also send your comments to us via e-mail at
college_arts_hum@nelson.com

PLEASE TAPE SHUT. DO NOT STAPLE.

TAPE SHUT

TAPE SHUT

FOLD HERE

TAPE SHUT

TAPE SHUT

Nelson

MAIL ➤ **POSTE**
Canada Post Corporation
Société canadienne des postes
Postage paid   Port payé
if mailed in Canada   si posté au Canada
Business Reply   Réponse d'affaires
0066102399   01

0066102399-M1K5G4-BR01

ITP NELSON
MARKET AND PRODUCT DEVELOPMENT
PO BOX 60225 STN BRM B
TORONTO ON M7Y 2H1